Foxy Ned Hanlon

Foxy Ned Hanlon

*The Baseball Life
of a Hall of Fame Manager*

TOM DELISE AND JAY SEABORG

McFarland & Company, Inc., Publishers
Jefferson, North Carolina

ISBN (print) 978-1-4766-9396-5
ISBN (ebook) 978-1-4766-5140-8

LIBRARY OF CONGRESS AND BRITISH LIBRARY
CATALOGUING DATA ARE AVAILABLE

Library of Congress Control Number 2024007835

© 2024 Tom Delise and Jay Seaborg. All rights reserved

No part of this book may be reproduced or transmitted in any form or by any means, electronic or mechanical, including photocopying or recording, or by any information storage and retrieval system, without permission in writing from the publisher.

Front cover: Manager Ned Hanlon (National Baseball Hall of Fame Library, Cooperstown, New York)

Printed in the United States of America

*McFarland & Company, Inc., Publishers
Box 611, Jefferson, North Carolina 28640
www.mcfarlandpub.com*

Dedicated to my wife Christine Sarames Delise,
the love of my life.
—Tom Delise

To Maria and Erin for their encouragement and support.
—Jay Seaborg

Table of Contents

Acknowledgments	ix
Introduction: Out of the Shadows	1
1. From the Mills to the Majors (1857–1888)	3
2. Around the World and the Brotherhood (1888–1891)	19
3. A New Sheriff in Town (1892)	32
4. Building a Champion (1893)	48
5. The Oriole Way (Spring, 1894)	61
6. The Pride of Baltimore (1894)	75
7. Band of Brothers (1895)	91
8. Dirty Jack Comes to Town (1896)	106
9. Chasing History (1897)	119
10. Summer of Discontent (1898)	133
11. Hanlon's Superbas (1899–1900)	146
12. All They Thought of Was Pay Day (1901–1905)	162
13. Porkopolis Purgatory (1906–1907)	175
14. Baseball in the Blood (1908–1937)	184
Epilogue	198
Appendix 1. Timeline of Hanlon's Life	205
Appendix 2. Ned Hanlon Player and Manager Statistics	207
Appendix 3. Ned Hanlon Coaching Tree	210
Appendix 4. Major Baseball Rule Changes from Hanlon's Birth Through His Career	211
Chapter Notes	213
Bibliography	227
Index	231

Acknowledgments

As we became interested in the old Orioles of the 1890s, it seemed remarkable that no biography of Ned Hanlon had ever been written. This book is an attempt to bring to life a man who is long overdue for a deeper examination of his contributions to baseball. We would like to thank the following people who gave us invaluable help in telling his story.

All the kind people at McFarland & Company. Editor Gary Mitchem was always willing to quickly and kindly address any questions that we had. Thanks also to Lori Tedder and Lisa Camp for their assistance.

Cassidy Lent and John Horne at the A. Bartlett Giamatti Research Center at the National Baseball Hall of Fame in Cooperstown, New York, for all their work in assembling files and photographs.

Mike Gibbons and Shawn Herne at the Babe Ruth Birthplace & Museum for allowing us access to their excellent materials.

Burt Solomon for his guidance and his interesting insight regarding Ned Hanlon's Orioles and his support of our endeavors. His wonderful book, *Where They Ain't: The Fabled Life and Untimely Death of the Original Baltimore Orioles, The Team That Gave Birth to Modern Baseball*, is a must-read for any baseball fan. His book was the spark that inspired us to write Hanlon's biography.

Rob Schoeberlein, Baltimore City Archivist, and Charles Duff for locating photos of Ned Hanlon's 1401 Mt. Royal Avenue House.

Cassie Epes at the Otis Library in Norwich, Connecticut, for her help in researching Ned Hanlon's family.

The staff of the Enoch Pratt Library in Baltimore, Maryland.

Dr. Edward Papenfuss for his help in locating property records.

David Grinnell, Coordinator of Archives and Manuscripts at the Archives at the University of Pittsburgh Library System, for his help in researching sportswriter Ella Black.

Edwina Reeve, granddaughter of Ned Hanlon; Michael Reeve, great-grandson of Ned Hanlon, and Robert Saunders, great-grandson of Ned Hanlon, for their time in discussing their famous relative and providing us insight into his life and times and his relationship with John McGraw.

Howie Blank, who served as proofreader extraordinaire. He made many useful recommendations and caught many embarrassing errors.

Christine Delise for proofreading, her overall support of the book, and her willingness to put up with a husband who was sequestered away in research and pecking away for countless hours at a computer.

Acknowledgments

Kristin and Jamie DeVan and Kris Seaborg for proofreading several chapters and offering suggestions.

Tim Durkin and Bruce Damasio, long time friends and fellow Oriole fans, who endured endless conversations regarding this book.

Maria Petrucci for her support and encouragement throughout the project, for asking questions that helped focus the writing, and for her willingness to allow her husband the freedom to put aside other tasks to focus on bringing Hanlon's story to life.

Any errors in the book are the sole responsibility of the authors.

Introduction: Out of the Shadows

As Ned Hanlon lay dying in his daughter's house in Baltimore in the early days of April 1937, there was much for a man of his introspection to contemplate. Being a man of devout piety, he would have felt assured that he would soon be reunited with his beloved wife, Ellen, and his brave son, Joseph, who had been lost on a brutal field in France in 1918. He may have looked forward to seeing once again his old comrades from the glorious playing fields who had preceded him in death: Dan Brouthers, Wilbert Robinson, Wee Willie Keeler, Hughie Jennings, Steve Brodie, and of course, John McGraw.

Moreover, Ned Hanlon had to realize that he had led a remarkable life. His parents had immigrated from Ireland in 1854, just three years before he was born in Montville, Connecticut, and his large family then settled in the nearby mill village of Taftville. Ned, like most of his family, worked in the textile mill from a young age. He had left that world far behind to become a star baseball player on a World Championship team and was part of an All-Star team that traveled and played in Australia, Asia, and Europe. While a player, he became a staunch advocate for players' rights and a key leader in the Brotherhood of Players that fought against the hated reserve clause and led to the creation of the Players' League in 1890.

When his playing career ended, he became the manager of one of the most famous and colorful teams in baseball history, the Baltimore Orioles of the 1890s. During this time, he proved himself to be an astute judge of talent and was credited with either inventing or refining tactics to new levels of precision that astounded and frustrated his opponents. With the Orioles and later the Brooklyn Superbas, he won five pennants and ultimately was elected to the National Baseball Hall of Fame in 1996. His managerial tree includes Hall of Fame managers John McGraw, Connie Mack, Wilbert Robinson, Casey Stengel and Miller Huggins, just to name a few. Its more modern branches include Leo Durocher, Billy Martin, Earl Weaver, Tony LaRussa, Bobby Cox, Buck Showalter, and many more.

When his managerial career ended, he attempted to bring baseball back to Baltimore, the city that had become his home, after both the National and American Leagues had abandoned it. He bought the Eastern League Orioles team with an eye to having it eventually join the major leagues, and when that did not materialize, he became a key player in the formation of the Federal League Baltimore Terrapins in an attempt to create a third major league. And finally, when he left baseball altogether, he spent the remaining years of his life as an unofficial statesman for the game, frequently asked by reporters for his comments about the changing times of the sport he loved so well.

He rubbed shoulders with some of the most important players and baseball men in the history of the game: Henry Chadwick, Harry Wright, Albert Spalding, Cy Young, Connie Mack, Charles Ebbets, John Montgomery Ward, Honus Wagner, Clark Griffith, Cap Anson, Amos Rusie, Kid Nichols, Charles Comiskey, and countless others whose names are well-known today. Many of these men called him friend, and virtually all respected and admired him for his contributions to the game and as a man.

Ned Hanlon witnessed the game grow from the very beginning of the National League until it was radically transformed by Babe Ruth's prodigious accomplishments. He began his career during a time when baseball was a very different game from its modern counterpart. Fans were called "cranks," only one umpire officiated in a game, home teams could decide whether to bat at the top or bottom of the first inning, players did not wear gloves, and foul balls did not count as strikes. During his long career as a dominant voice on the National League's rule committee, his keen insight had an indelible influence in transforming the game from a sport in its infancy into what became a widely popular national pastime.

Yet despite all his remarkable achievements, Ned Hanlon is largely unrecognized except by historians of nineteenth-century baseball or devoted fanatics of the game. When he is mentioned, it is generally as an ancillary figure in the history of the old Orioles teams, and even then, his contributions to the amazing accomplishments of that team are often minimalized or appropriated by others. He is also normally depicted as a stern, taciturn man without a sense of humor, and that is not a fair portrayal of a man who had a keen wit and who developed strong and familial bonds with the men who played for him that lasted until their deaths.

When Steve Wulf was writing an article on Hanlon in 2015, he traveled to his hometown in Montville. He saw no evidence of Hanlon in the town, no street, no statue, no Little League parks named after him. No one he spoke to knew who Ned Hanlon was. When Wulf visited the Montville Historical Society to inquire into their native Hall of Fame son, there was no sign of Hanlon. When the director of the institution was asked about Hanlon, he admitted that he had never heard of him.[1]

In the very last years of Hanlon's life, the famous sportswriter Fred Lieb, who would later be awarded the Baseball Writers Association of America Career Excellence Award by the National Baseball Hall of Fame, wrote a letter to Hanlon, seeking information from him. At the end of the letter, he wrote, "With all credit to Robbie, McGraw, and Keeler, the gallant departed Orioles, both Mr. Heydler [recently retired National League President] and I feel that the modern baseball fan knows little of the man that put that great team together and made it click."[2]

Lieb's comment is even more salient today. Despite being referred to as the "Father of Modern Baseball" by *Sporting News* at the time of his death, Ned Hanlon has become a figure whose baseball accomplishments are obscured by the shadows of time.

The purpose of this book is to give those accomplishments the attention that they deserve.

1

From the Mills to the Majors (1857–1888)

The beginning of Ned Hanlon's baseball career and the birth of the National League arrived at almost the same time. As a young boy, Hanlon loved the game, and by the age of ten he wanted to be a ball player.[1] When he was 12 years old and working in the Ponemah Mills in his home town of Montville, Connecticut, the Cincinnati Red Stockings went on their celebrated tour in 1869, taking on all comers throughout the country. A baseball lover like young Ned had to be filled with excitement when he heard that the famous Red Stockings, led by Harry and George Wright, had traveled to Springfield, Massachusetts, just 65 miles from Montville, and beat the Mutuals by an astounding 80–5 score.[2]

The Red Stockings made history that year when they were undefeated in the 57 official games they played, and their tour proved to be a pivotal moment in the history of baseball. The ensuing publicity helped propel the sport from an amateur pastime into a professional business and was a key inspiration in the formation in 1871 of the National Association of Professional Baseball Players—the first attempt to create a professional league.

At 15 years old, Ned was highly regarded enough as a ball player to play for the best local teams, which consisted of seasoned players far above his age. He began as a pitcher, and at this time, all pitchers were required to throw underhanded. Hanlon was renowned for throwing with a swiftness that made him unhittable to local clubs, and it was said that while he was pitching in an exhibition game against the Boston Red Stockings, he attracted the attention of their pitcher, Albert Goodwill Spalding. This encounter allegedly led to Hanlon becoming a professional.[3] This may be an apocryphal tale, but by 1876, the year the National League came into existence, Hanlon had left home and a prospective life in the mills to join a team in Providence, Rhode Island.

Noted sportswriter Sam Crane related a story about when Hanlon first joined the Providence club. Hanlon's teammate, pitcher Morrie Critchley, told Hanlon to go out and buy himself a rubber coat, rubber boots, rubber gloves, and a rubber cap because no matter how hard it rained, professional games had to be played. The young Hanlon did as he was told and appeared on the field in the new regalia. His teammates kept him out in the pouring rain for more than an hour, fielding batted balls before he was let in on the joke.

Hanlon then laughed "that little giggling splutter of his," and said, "Waal, by gosh, I can go fishing for bullheads up in Taftville with the rubber uniform, all right, be jee."

Crane said, "Mention rubber uniform to Eddie today and he will explode with laughter and say, 'Well, I got even with Big Critch for that joke, for I made three home runs off him the next year in one game.'[4]

Tim Murnane, who had a brief career in the major leagues and later became a sportswriter for the *Boston Globe*, recalled that he saw Hanlon play in his first game. That day, Hanlon played third base, and his Providence team beat Falls River, 6–0.[5] He played with Falls River in the New England League in 1877, with Rochester in the International Association in 1878, and finally with Albany in the National Association in 1879. Shortly after, Hanlon left Albany to play for the Cleveland Blues in the National League.[6]

* * *

When Ned Hanlon began his major league career in 1880, the rules and practices of the game were very different from today. Fielders caught the ball barehanded, and it took seven balls to earn a walk. There was no pitching mound, and the pitcher had to throw the ball from within a six-by-four box, the front end of which was 45 feet from home plate. The pitcher had to release the ball from at or below the waist, and the batter had the privilege of requesting that the pitcher throw either a high or a low ball. A ball that bounced in foul territory that was caught on one bounce was an out, and home plate was a square made of stone or iron and angled so that one point of it faced the pitcher.

Moreover, the year before Hanlon joined Cleveland, the National League had decreed that to help limit players' salaries, up to five players on each team could be reserved for the upcoming season.[7] The reserve clause, as it became known, bound a player to the team that reserved him for as long as it wanted him. Players came to hate the reserve clause because it removed virtually all leverage that they would have in negotiating contracts and establishing working conditions. As the owners became more draconian in dealing with the players, it would lead to the formation of the Brotherhood of Players and the Players' League, organizations established to protect the rights of players. Ned Hanlon would be a key figure in both.

* * *

Ned Hanlon played in his first major league game when the Cleveland Blues opened the season at home on May 1, 1880, against the Buffalo Bisons. Playing left field and batting fifth in the order, he came to bat four times and rapped out a single, drew a walk, and scored two runs in a 7–4 Cleveland loss. Hanlon had three putouts and was credited with an error for "slow-handling of a ball,"[8] but he also made one of the spectacular plays for which he would become famous when he "made a splendid foul-bound catch that struck the ground fully thirty feet from the foul line."[9]

On June 12, 1880, Hanlon became a part of baseball history when the Blues visited the Worcester Ruby Legs. In front of a meager crowd of about 700 fans, Worcester's Lee Richmond beat the Blues, 1–0, and in the process, pitched the first perfect game in major league history. Hanlon, batting ninth that day, had the distinction of being the final out when he grounded out to shortstop.[10]

The Blues finished the season in third place with a 47–37 record, 20 games back of the powerhouse Chicago White Stockings of Cap Anson. In his inaugural season in the major leagues, Hanlon had performed well, if not spectacularly, and hit .246 in a season where the league average was .245. Cleveland, however, was not sufficiently impressed

1. From the Mills to the Majors (1857–1888)

to sign Hanlon as one of their reserved players for the following season, so he was free to look for a new baseball home.

* * *

At the end of the 1880 season, the Cincinnati Reds were expelled from the National League for violating rules regarding the bans on Sunday baseball and selling alcohol at games. Cincinnati's loss was Detroit's gain, and their eager application to join the National League was accepted. The Detroit Wolverines were born.

Frank Bancroft, who had managed the Worcester Ruby Legs in 1880, was hired as the first manager of the new team, and he signed a number of players not reserved by his old Worcester club, including catcher Charlie Bennett. He convinced Ned Hanlon to sign as the center fielder, and Hanlon and Bennett would be mainstays of the Wolverines during the entire eight-year history of the club.[11]

Ned Hanlon was listed in the 1870 census as a 13-year-old working in the local cotton mill. By the 1880 census, he was listed as a professional baseball player (Babe Ruth Birthplace & Museum).

Detroit got off to a rough start as the team lost eight of their first nine games, but they then rebounded to win 12 of their next 16. In a game at Detroit's Recreation Park in May against Worcester, Bancroft benched Hanlon because he claimed that he would have difficulty hitting Lee Richmond's left-handed curves. The *Detroit Free Press* disagreed with the move and declared that Hanlon could have hit better against Richmond than any other Detroit player.[12] This platooning, however, was a strategy that Ned Hanlon would later embrace and utilize in his managing career.

During his first season with Detroit, Hanlon gained a reputation as a superior defensive player. His teammates and fans were amazed at his ability to take his eye off of fly balls and then anticipate where they would land.[13] People also remarked on his speed, excellent base running, and hard-nosed style of play. An incident that illustrates the aggressiveness of the young Hanlon occurred when infielder Bob Ferguson tried to block his way as he ran to second base: "Hanlon went against him like a battering-ram, and Bob landed about six feet northeast by west of where he got in Hanlon's road."[14]

The Wolverines performed reasonably well for a new franchise, finishing in fourth place in the eight-team league with a 41–43 record. Bancroft was sufficiently impressed with Hanlon to reserve him for the following season, and Detroit remained his baseball home for the next seven years.

* * *

The 1882 season was notable for the strange uniform requirements that the League instituted. All players were required to wear silk jerseys that were color-coded to their positions. For example, orange and black vertical striped jerseys were worn by second basemen, catchers wore scarlet ones, pitchers light blue ones, and so on. All players were required to wear white pants, white belts, and white ties. Only stocking colors were different in order to distinguish between teams. The silk was extremely hot, and the players hated the uniforms and claimed they made them look like jockeys or clowns. They were also unpopular among fans, who were confused by the whole idea. Thankfully for all concerned, these outlandish uniforms were abandoned during the season.[15]

From the very beginning of his career, Hanlon's intelligence and gravitas, even at a young age, made him a favorite of sportswriters. He was regularly sought out by them to comment on topics related to his teams and on virtually all aspects of the game. When he was interviewed in January, he said he believed the club would be better in 1882 and that it would be a mistake to ask pitcher George Derby to both manage and captain the club. Although he felt Derby would be a good manager, he believed a pitcher should be allowed to rest between innings and not give instructions to his players at bat. When asked his opinion of the new rule requiring "gentlemanly behavior" on the part of all players, Hanlon strongly supported it.[16]

The Wolverines got off to a good start, and after a victory against Buffalo on July 21, they were 28–20 and just one-and-a-half games behind the league-leading White Stockings. Then they stumbled and went 14–21 for the remainder of the season, falling to fifth place while the White Stockings surged ahead to edge the Providence Grays to win their third straight pennant.

When Frank Bancroft resigned after the season to manage the Cleveland Blues, Detroit hired Jack Chapman to replace him. Chapman was a grizzled baseball veteran who had played on the Brooklyn Atlantics team that ended the 81-game winning streak of the Cincinnati Red Stockings in 1870. He had also previously managed National League teams in Louisville and Worcester, and he was one of two nineteenth-century players who had been given the wonderful nickname "Death to Flying Things" because of his skill in running down fly balls. He had an excellent reputation as a man of few words who was able to control ball players and get the best out of them.[17]

Under Bancroft, the Detroit Wolverines had compiled a decent 83–84 record, but the hiring of the well-respected Chapman and the fact that the team had shown signs of being competitive in its first two years raised hopes that they were ready to take the next step towards a championship.

* * *

Before the 1883 season began, Chapman held a meeting with the players to make his expectations clear. He gave each of them a code of conduct document that prohibited arguing with umpires, drinking or carousing, card-playing, and smoking while in uniform. He set an 11 p.m. curfew, warned players to avoid gamblers, and instructed them to be gentlemen at all times. He told them they were responsible for repairing and cleaning their own uniforms. He also announced that fines would be imposed for infractions, and he warned the men that the board of directors had assured him he would be fully supported.[18]

Whether the Wolverines' off-field conduct adhered to Chapman's expectations is uncertain, but the team's play on the field certainly did not do so. Although the team had a decent start and was 15–9 on June 5, they would steadily maintain a losing pace for the remainder of the year. Pitching was a problem the entire season, and by the end of July there was conjecture that some players were purposely playing poorly so that they would be released and could then sign for more money with other teams. Chapman, no stranger to these tactics, declared that he had no intention of releasing anyone and informed the players that if they did not perform well, he would suspend them.[19] The Wolverines finished 40–58 and in seventh place, 23 games behind pennant-winning Boston.

Despite the Wolverines' poor showing, the club rehired Chapman as manager. In their public statement, they justified the action by stating that he used excellent judgment in handling the team, was popular among the players, and was well-known as an honest manager.[20] When the season was over, Detroit announced it would reserve ten players, one of whom was Hanlon. Chapman expressed optimism for a better year in 1884 and announced that he would take his team south in the spring to better prepare them for the start of the season.[21]

* * *

After a week of practice in Richmond in April 1884, the team played a series of exhibition games and opened the season on May 1 in Philadelphia. The home team scored six runs in the first inning and four more in the second, while the Wolverines added an embarrassing 14 errors in a 13–2 loss.[22] This sloppy performance was an ominous sign that a dreadful season for the Wolverines was at hand. Indeed, the team lost its first 11 games on their way to a 4–20 start.

In the middle of this horrendous streak, a highly critical article about Jack Chapman was published in the *Detroit Free Press*. The reporter claimed he had a letter from a team member that stated Chapman was a severe and unjust man who threatened the players with fines, suspension without pay, and even expulsion if they made errors. The players were said to be afraid when a ball was hit at them for fear of making an error and receiving a tongue-lashing from the manager. The unnamed player alleged that "The men have no heart to play and never will have so long as he manages the team. He blows up every day before we go into the field and raises h—l when the game is over."[23]

However, a different story emerged when the Detroit players stood behind their manager in a letter they sent to *Sporting Life*. They claimed that no player on the team wrote the letter referred to in the *Free Press*, and they insisted that the article did Chapman an injustice. It further stated that the players were satisfied with Chapman and that he was doing everything in his power to make the team successful. They attributed the team's poor play to injuries, bad luck, and bad weather, and they protested that their relationship with Chapman was excellent.[24] Ten players signed the letter, and Hanlon's name was the first one listed.

Regardless of what the situation with Chapman may have been, the Wolverines had an abysmal season. They finished solidly in last place with a 28–84 record, a whopping 56 games behind the pennant-winning Providence Grays.

While Hanlon was hitting leadoff and roaming center field for the Detroit Wolverines in the 1880s, Billy the Kid was shot and killed, the Gunfight at the OK Corral occurred, and Clara Barton incorporated the American Red Cross (collection of Tom Delise).

After a loss to New York that ended the season, the *Detroit Free Press* was relieved: "At last the long agony is over; the base ball season of 1884 is closed, and the Detroit club stands in the league where a fool stands in his class." The finger of blame was pointed directly at the players, who were accused of spending their evenings drinking and even showing up to games drunk. The paper urged the board to make sure that all players who did not abide by the rules would be punished severely.[25]

When he was asked for the cause of the dismal season, a furious Wolverines President William Thompson also blamed the players. He argued that they were receiving salaries larger than most professional men, and he claimed that every team had players who were consorting with gamblers and throwing games. He said most of them were not honorable enough to adhere to their contracts, and when he confronted them about their poor play, they would insolently tell him that if he didn't like the way they played, he could give them their release and they would make more money elsewhere. Thompson summed up his diatribe by saying, "As a class, always excepting those who are worthy and honest, I believe them to be in the most ungrateful set of men I have ever met, and I am done with them."[26]

Disgusted with the state of the club, Thompson stepped down as president, and all the other directors resigned as well. The shareholders elected a new board, and foremost among them was Frederick Kimball Stearns, who would assume control of a club in total disarray and soon remake it into the champion of professional baseball.[27] Under his leadership, the club immediately began to make a concerted effort to find better players.

After the season, Jack Chapman resigned, and later in the following year he became the manager of the Buffalo Bisons. He was replaced by player-manager Charlie Morton, who had managed the American Association Toledo Blue Stockings. Morton announced that he would take the team south for spring training, and he believed the prospects for the Wolverines were "growing brighter every day."[28]

The team would begin to make improvement, but Charlie Morton would not be around to see much of it.

* * *

After sweeping Buffalo in three games to open the 1885 season, Detroit lost 13 in a row and was 7–31 on June 24. The *Detroit Free Press* was highly critical of the efforts of the players and said, "They have not come upon the diamond this week and showed by their actions that they intended to win. On the contrary, their actions would convey an impression that they had come out to perform the duty of being beaten again….There has been no vim or snap in their movements, and very little in their play."[29]

In June, the Western Association folded, and Bill Watkins, who managed the Indianapolis Hoosiers in that league, was hired by Detroit to replace Morton as manager. Key players from the Hoosiers joined Watkins in Detroit, including future Hall of Fame outfielder Sam Thompson, catcher and first baseman James "Deacon" McGuire, and third baseman Jimmy Donnelly. Beginning on June 25 when Watkins took over, Detroit won 14 of 19 games.[30]

Later in the season, Detroit seized upon a chance to add talented players to their roster when they swooped in and bought the financially struggling National League Buffalo Bisons. They immediately signed four excellent Bisons players, Dan Brouthers, Hardy Richardson, Deacon White, and Jack Rowe, who became known as the Big Four. The deal outraged other owners because of the high salaries that were given to the players, and because they did not have the opportunity to sign them themselves.[31] National League president Nick Young claimed the deal was in violation of league tampering rules, but Buffalo directors argued that it was a legitimate purchase of the majority of the team stock.[32] After much discussion, it was decided that the deal would be upheld, but the Big Four would not be allowed to play for Detroit until 1886. At the end of the season, the Buffalo team was dissolved.

Hanlon, who was a close friend of Brouthers, was instrumental in making the Buffalo deal happen. Over 20 years later, Brouthers asserted that although Watkins generally received the credit for making the deal, it was Hanlon who suggested to the Detroit owners that they buy the Buffalo franchise, sign the players they wanted from it, and then sell the team to some other city.[33]

As the Wolverines prepared for the 1886 season, only Hanlon and Charlie Bennett remained from the franchise's first year. Hanlon, in particular, was regarded as a bastion of stability for the team: "Ned Hanlon continues to play ball. Rum does not muddle his head, which consequently keeps level."[34] In addition to his sterling defensive reputation, Hanlon also continued to receive accolades for his skill as a base runner, and *Sporting Life* commented, "It is a striking illustration of Ned Hanlon's daring and speed that for two years Buck Ewing has never once succeeded in throwing him out at second on a steal. And Buck is one of the surest throwers in the League."[35] In 1885, Hanlon had the best offensive year of his career as he hit .302, just one point behind the team's batting leader, Sam Thompson.

* * *

Prior to spring training in 1886, it was reported that Hanlon and Bennett were refusing to sign because they were upset with the November release of outfielder George Wood. Hanlon denied this, saying, "No, that rumor is off the track. If I refused to sign every time a player was released from the Detroit Club, what an animated base ball existence I would lead." He declared that the real reason for the holdout was a salary disagreement that he thought would be worked out in the near future. He said he regretted the departure of Woods but admitted that some sacrifice was needed to provide for salaries of the Big Four.[36] Hanlon's holdout ultimately ended in March, when he met with management in New York during the League meeting.[37]

Hanlon, who had been named captain of the team the previous year, also went public to refute criticism that he had not made better base runners of his charges. He claimed that he did not have the proper material to coach, and said, "You can't make something out of nothing....It requires a peculiar combination of alertness, good judgment and daring to make a base-runner. If after a certain amount of coaching a man doesn't learn when to run himself, his case is nearly hopeless."[38] "In response to calls that he should be replaced as captain, he argued that since he had worked hard in the position under difficult circumstances, he was entitled to remain captain now that Detroit was becoming a good club."[39]

The Big Four's much-anticipated debut on Opening Day saw the visiting Wolverines soundly beat St. Louis, 9–2, behind Charles "Lady" Baldwin, who would have a breakout year and lead the majors with 42 wins. They moved into a tie with Chicago for first place on May 11 and would not relinquish the lead until August 26. During that time, Chicago stubbornly stayed right on their tail, never falling more than four-and-a-half games off the lead.

There was an incident in July that would be a precursor of discontent during the next few seasons. In a tie game in the 11th inning, pitcher Pretzels Getzien fell apart and surrendered ten runs that resulted in a 12–2 loss. To make matters worse, the Wolverines committed 12 errors in the game, and five of those were by Getzien. An angry

Watkins fined Getzien $10 for each of the ten runs, and he also fined Hanlon $25 "for poor play."[40] Hanlon went 2–5 in the game, scored a run, and did not commit an error, so it is not entirely clear how he drew the wrath of Watkins. It is likely that as captain he was blamed for the team's poor play.

In early August, Detroit signed slugging second baseman Fred Dunlap, who had hit .412 for St. Louis of the Union Association in 1884. However, Dunlap had only been with the team a short time before there was a rumor that he would replace Hanlon as captain because he would be firmer in dealing with recalcitrant players. When Hanlon approached Dunlap about the rumor, Dunlap assured him that he had no intention of replacing him. However, he admitted that he was told that the captaincy would be given to him if he wanted the position. An angry Hanlon confronted Watkins, who reassured him that he wanted him to remain captain. Hanlon was not mollified and said that because he was not appreciated, he would not remain in the position unless he was paid extra for the duty. Watkins agreed to pay him an extra $200.[41]

In August Detroit slumped, primarily due to the poor pitching of Getzien and Baldwin, who were suffering from sore arms. After a sloppy loss to Philadelphia in late August, the team fell out of first place, and the players were called into the directors' box, where "the riot act was read to them in seven different languages." Various directors gave long speeches during which the players were reminded that they were being paid large salaries and were expected always to give their best efforts on the field. They were also told that taking naps on the bench would no longer be tolerated. By the time the chastised players reached the dressing room, things got worse. Hanlon took Getzien to task for his poor play, and he responded by telling Hanlon to go to Hell. Hanlon informed him that the remark would cost him $25, which caused the enraged pitcher to unleash a string of further curses. Hanlon assessed him $25 per oath, and by the time Getzien ran out of breath, he had accumulated $200 in fines.[42] Getzien would appeal to the Detroit directors to have the fines dropped, but they backed Hanlon and refused to do so.[43]

On September 22, Detroit found itself six-and-a-half games back, but they rallied to win nine of their next 10 games to close the gap to just one game on the last day of the season. Alas, the pennant hopes of the Wolverines and their fans fell short as they dropped a doubleheader to Philadelphia while the White Stockings beat Boston to win the pennant.

* * *

Hanlon spent the off-season involved in business matters, and along with other members of the team, lent his name to the advertising of Claflin's baseball shoes of Philadelphia. He spent a great deal of time at a thriving hat store he had opened in New York City as well, and it was said that he could not stop talking about the business.[44]

He was brimming with optimism for the coming season and said, "The size of my hat is still seven-and-a-quarter, and I don't expect to increase the size even after the Detroits have won the league pennant and knocked out the Browns for the world's championship."[45] A *Sporting Life* correspondent noticed that Hanlon's business interests must have agreed with him as he had "grown exceedingly stout" and was estimated at 200 pounds, no small increase for a man of Hanlon's frame.[46]

With Watkins' vote of confidence as captain and a raise in his salary to $2,250,[47]

Hanlon turned his attention eagerly to the coming season. Early in spring training, he shed the excess weight he had put on, and he got in the habit of getting up early every morning to study the new rules. He made sure that a copy of *Spalding's Guide* had been placed in the hands of each member of the team, and he instructed them to study it carefully. In one lively discussion regarding the new rule that awarded a walk as a hit, Hanlon insisted that it would be a good change because it would encourage players to work for a walk. He claimed that a player who was a "waiter" (one who took pitches) was just as valuable to a club as a free hitter.[48] Long before Bill James and *Moneyball*, Hanlon was advocating the connection between on-base percentage and runs scored, and he believed that a wise combination of hitters and waiters was the satisfactory way to build a team.

* * *

The 1887 season opened with a 4–3 Detroit victory at Indianapolis on April 28, and from the time when the Wolverines moved into first place on May 4, they never relinquished the lead. There was a humorous incident during the early part of the season that illustrates the type of tactics used in the 1880s. With the Wolverines were at bat and Dan Brouthers on third base, there was a lull in play during which no time out had been called by the umpire. Hanlon, who was coaching third, asked the opposing pitcher to have a catch with him while they waited. When the pitcher obliged and tossed the ball to Hanlon, he made no attempt to catch it, but instead stepped out of its way and yelled for Brouthers to run home. To the chagrin of them both, the umpire disallowed the run and sent Brouthers back to third.[49]

Even though the team was playing well, throughout the season some players and members of management expressed their dissatisfaction with Waitkins. In June, when some directors criticized him for retaining Hanlon as captain because he had benched Getzien, Watkins' patience reached its limit. He testily retorted that he must have full control of the team, and if they insisted on interfering with him, he would resign. The directors, not wanting to lose Watkins, backed off.[50]

The resentment of some players for Watkins' style of management was stirred up once again when, after three straight losses to Philadelphia in July, he suspended Lady Baldwin without pay for "indifferent play." Catcher Fatty Briody and pitcher Stump Weidman were also suspended, and Briody was also fined for drinking. These moves, and others like them, helped to propagate the belief that Watkins played favorites, because it was noted that he did not hesitate to discipline the "lesser lights" on the team, but he would never fine or discipline the members of the Big Four.[51] Watkins was also under fire for the way in which he distributed playing time and what were termed by the press his "asinine experiments."[52]

Despite all the turmoil during the season, the Wolverines won the pennant by three-and-a half games over Philadelphia. They then prepared to play the American Association pennant-winning St. Louis Browns in a "World's Series," which was a forerunner of the modern World Series between the American and National League which began in 1903. The American Association had begun operation as a major league in 1882, and since 1884 the pennant winners for these two leagues had played a championship series.

The 1887 series was unique because it was the longest championship series in the history of baseball. It was a best of 15 series, and of these games, three were played in

Sportsman's Park in St. Louis, two in Detroit, and the rest in a number of neutral cities including Pittsburgh, Brooklyn, New York, Philadelphia, Boston, Washington, Baltimore, and Chicago.

The formidable Browns had won three straight American Association pennants and were led by player-manager Charles Comiskey, an excellent pitching staff headed by Bob Caruthers and Dave Foutz, and outfielder Tip O'Neill who hit .435 that season.

The series opened in St. Louis, and the Browns won, 6–1, behind a four-hit performance by Caruthers. While in Washington for Game 10, the Wolverines held a commanding 7–2 lead in the series, but the game that day at the Swampdoodle Grounds was rained out. It was decided that the next day, a morning game would be played in Washington, and then the teams would travel to Baltimore by train to play an afternoon game at Oriole Park, home of the American Association Orioles.

After an 11–4 victory for the Browns in the morning game on October 21, the two teams immediately boarded a train to Baltimore for a game that was billed by the *Baltimore Sun* as "The Greatest of All Games."[53] On that cold, raw day, the Wolverines would win their eighth game of the series to clinch the championship with a 13–3 victory. Even though Detroit won the series that day, the two teams continued to play the remainder of the scheduled games, which would be little more than exhibitions. The series mercifully ended on October 26 with a meaningless Browns win in St. Louis. In all, Detroit won 10 of the games in the series.

With their victory, the Detroit Wolverines were awarded the first Dauvray Cup, a silver trophy awarded to baseball's champion. The cup was donated by Helen Dauvray, a well-known New York actress and fan of the New York Giants. Within a few months she would also be the wife of Giants star John Montgomery Ward. Gold medals were also issued to each player on the winning team. The Dauvray Cup is considered by some to be the first World Series trophy.

* * *

In 1885, star player John Montgomery Ward of the New York Giants formed the Brotherhood of Professional Baseball Players to address what players felt were deteriorating working conditions. In 1887, Ward tried to force the National League to recognize the union and to negotiate with them concerning the reserve clause. The National League refused to recognize the union, and this started rumors that the players would organize to form a new league. As the Brotherhood gained strength, Detroit fans worried about the effect the union might have on re-signing their players. When asked if he believed that Detroit players would jump to a Brotherhood league if it was formed, Director Stearns said that he did not think so because the players on the team had been treated so well. He alluded to the fact that some players had withdrawn from the Brotherhood, and he confidently declared that the Detroit players, except for Hanlon and one or two others who were well known as dedicated members of the Brotherhood, would not be "led by the nose by Johnny Ward or anybody else."[54]

The Brotherhood proved to be less of a factor in re-signing players than concerns about the manager and salaries were. It was reported that eight players on the team had formed a combine and pledged not to sign with Detroit if Watkins remained the manager. When asked about it at his hat store in New York, Hanlon confirmed the report and added, "Mr. Stearns has heard this, too, and I think that he is taking some action in the matter."[55]

Indeed, Hanlon had written a letter to Stearns in which he harshly criticized Watkins,[56] and *Sporting Life* reported that Hanlon was "saying some ugly things about Watkins" and warned that it might not be wise for him to say things that would make his manager vindictive against him.[57]

Fred Dunlap had been sold to Pittsburgh in the off-season, and he made it clear that he was happy to leave Detroit because he could not tolerate what he felt was unjust criticism from Watkins. He described him as the hardest manager he had ever played under, and when he was asked if Watkins was responsible for Detroit's championship, he was quick to deny it: "No, he is not, despite stories to the contrary. Hanlon is the man." He claimed Hanlon showed Detroit management how to assemble a winning team, and said, "I give him credit for it. Why, when Chicago crawled up close on us last season, Watkins was badly rattled and wanted to resign, but Hanlon ridiculed him out of it. Hanlon is a great fielder and will strengthen any club."[58]

Director Stearns made it clear that management would not be forced into firing the manager, and he announced that Watkins would return. When he was reminded that players had said they would not sign if Watkins was retained, he said, "That would be their privilege, and we should endeavor to get along without them."[59]

* * *

During Hanlon's holdout, he made an offer to buy his release from Detroit, but Stearns refused.[60] When Detroit's president returned from the spring League meeting, he was asked why Hanlon hadn't signed. He said that Hanlon wanted more money and that management would not give him any more than the $2,500 they offered him to play and captain the team.[61] Other members of the team finally gave up and signed when it became obvious that Watkins would manage the team in 1888. Hanlon, however, refused to yield.

Publicly, the Detroit management took the stance that they did not care whether Hanlon signed or not, but Hanlon's teammates certainly did. Throughout the spring, they muttered in discontent because he was not with them. They knew the value of his defensive abilities, particularly the pitchers, who knew that when opposing sluggers began to knock the ball deep to the outfield, he would be sorely missed. Just as importantly, his teammates recognized his abilities as a leader and knew that the championship of 1887 would not have been won without him. To play without Hanlon in the coming season would shake their confidence in their ability to win another championship.[62]

Hanlon was a holdout through virtually all of spring training until finally, at the team hotel in Louisville on April 9, Watkins read a telegram to his players that announced that Hanlon was ending his holdout and would join the team in Cincinnati the next day. The news was greeted joyfully and immediately created a "cheerful effect" among the players.[63] Hanlon's new contract called for a salary of $2,800 and the captaincy of the team.[64]

Watkins met with his team for an hour in an effort to create harmony and restore some sense of morale. He told his team that he expected them to conduct themselves honorably and cautioned them to take good care of themselves so they would be able to play to the best of their abilities. He concluded by expressing his personal confidence that the team would once again be champions.[65]

But it was not to be. After losing five of their first six games, Watkins was disgusted and said he could not imagine how a team consisting of the same players who performed so well last year could now play so poorly. He returned to the practices that had made him so unpopular with his players. He laid off Baldwin without pay for allowing 12 stolen bases in a 16–7 loss to Indianapolis, and he also fined Hanlon $10 for failing to slide on a stolen base attempt.[66]

Despite the discontent brewing within the team, Hanlon continued to display the type of leadership that made him so respected by his peers. During a game in May against Pittsburgh, the Wolverines were playing uninspired ball, and although they scored a run in the first inning, they failed to get a hit in the next three innings. In the meantime, Pittsburgh scored six runs. When the Wolverines came to bat in the fifth inning, Hanlon took control, yelling out, "Now here, everybody brace up. We must do them right here." The players, inspired by Hanlon's bravado, scored three runs. The next time they came to bat, Hanlon rallied them once again, screaming, "Now get after them again!" The Wolverines responded to Hanlon's exhortations, scoring four times to take an 8–6 lead. However, Pittsburgh rallied and scored five times to take a three-run lead going into the final inning. But Hanlon refused to allow defeat that day, and he shouted out, "What are we here for?" and continued to energize his players yet again. The Wolverines scored eight runs in the ninth, and Hanlon cranked out a key hit in the middle of the rally. Pittsburgh was held scoreless in the ninth, and Detroit came away with a victory that thrilled their fans.[67]

In early June during a four-game sweep of Washington, the defending champs were honored with an invitation to go to the White House, and they received congratulations from President Grover Cleveland for their 1887 championship.[68] Soon after this visit, dissension fermented yet again, and injuries began to take their toll. The team received a key blow when they lost Lady Baldwin to a sore arm. Baldwin had won 42 games in 1886, but arm troubles limited him to just 13 wins in 1887. Finally, he could go no more, and his promising career was essentially over.

On July 28, Detroit started the day one game ahead of the Giants for the league lead, but with their game that day they began a disastrous 16-game losing streak that would see them fall into third place, 12 games behind the Giants when it ended on August 22. During the streak, the fans grew increasingly disgusted and stopped coming to games. The players continued to complain about Watkins, and Watkins was angry at both the players and the Detroit management that he felt did not allow him complete control of the team. Hanlon had been spiked in Indianapolis[69] near the beginning of the streak, and he had remained laid off until after it was over. His loss likely was a key factor in the collapse, as his leadership could have provided ballast that could lift the team over the acid-tongued criticism of Watkins.

By the time the losing streak finally ended, any hope of a second consecutive pennant was dashed. A few days later, the patience of Bill Watkins ran out, and he resigned. After Watkins was gone, he was an easy target at which to direct blame. He was accused of blaming too many losses on hard luck, of being inconsistent in administering discipline, and of keeping his players in such a state of nervous excitement that they could not perform well. It was also said that he was not a creative and inspirational leader.

Hanlon related a story to illustrate Watkins' poor management when he told of a time when a fly ball floated in between himself and Sam Thompson. Neither was able to reach the ball, and when the players returned to the bench after the inning, Watkins was

Hanlon, like all players when his career began, did not use a glove in the field (National Baseball Hall of Fame at Cooperstown, New York)

livid with rage and fined both players. Hanlon angrily retorted that it was unfair to fine players who were trying their best. Watkins snapped back that the fine would stand. As the game continued, Hanlon and Thompson played well, making valuable contributions that led Detroit to victory. After the game, Watkins "crawled around to Hanlon, apologized effusively and rescinded the fine."[70]

After Watkins resigned, club secretary Robert Leadley assumed managerial duties, and when he was asked about his plans for the team, he did not exactly inspire the organization with confidence: "I hardly know," he said. "The outlook is not very brilliant, but I shall take hold and do the best I can and trust the rest to fortune."[71] Under Leadley, the Wolverines treaded water, going 19–19 for the remainder of the season, and the team finished fifth in the league, 16 games behind the pennant-winning Giants.

The 1888 season ended with a whimper, and the rough and wild ride that was the Detroit Wolverines franchise would come to an end with the season. The franchise had its brief shining moment when it became the undisputed champions of the baseball world, and then just as quickly, it was all over, and the franchise is all but forgotten to most baseball fans today.

* * *

Ned Hanlon has usually been referred to as a below-average hitter, but his career numbers, which can be found in full in the Appendix, tell a different story. He was clearly not an excellent hitter, but considering how many times he was above the league average in several offensive categories, it does demonstrate that he was a solid major league hitter.

Furthermore, Hanlon was a speedy and excellent base runner. Records for stolen bases were not kept for the first six years of his career, but after they were in 1886, Hanlon stole 329 bases, an average of 55 per season. Baseball pioneer Ted Sullivan cited "Johnny Ward, Hanlon, and a handful of others as players who mastered the evasive slide in the 1880s."[72]

Sam Crane, a former player and sportswriter, wrote of Hanlon, "I have seen 'Eddie' slide into three bases in one inning, tearing along the ground like a battering ram, when his legs were like raw beef from ankle to hip—yes, and come out the next day and do it again."[73]

Above all, it was Hanlon's defensive ability that made him an acclaimed player in his time. He had great range and led all National League outfielders in putouts in 1882 and 1884. Sportswriter Fred Lieb recalled hearing his old sports editor, Jim Price, claim that "In some respects, Hanlon was better than [Tris] Speaker, because he played during the greater part of his career without a glove. How he could snatch long drives out of the air with his bare hands was uncanny."[74]

In 1912, Irwin Howe, the official statistician of the American League, was asked to compare Hanlon to Ty Cobb. He responded by saying that Hanlon had been "a fleet outfielder, who led a team of world champions for Detroit when the present day 'Peach' was a mere blossom. Had any fan at that time suggested however mildly that any mere fielder in the future take the place of Captain Hanlon in the affections of Detroit, he would instantly have become an object of interest to the doctors."[75]

After the Wolverines disbanded, John Ward said, "Much of the success of the Detroit team has been due to the untiring zeal of their captain, Ned Hanlon. Others have generally managed to appropriate the credit, but to him it has really belonged."

Ward maintained that although the Detroit team consisted of many great players, "without a spirit like Hanlon's, to stir them up and keep them at work, they would never have won the proud title of world's champions."[76]

During his time in Detroit, Hanlon served under managers with different styles and abilities, and from them he absorbed valuable lessons about what worked and what didn't. Ned Hanlon was a born leader, and his inherent leadership skills had been severely tested in the crucible of the tumultuous Wolverines teams. What emerged was a man who would change baseball.

2

Around the World and the Brotherhood (1888–1891)

Gilded Age America was a bustling, energetic time and place with an increasingly confrontational attitude beginning to form between management and labor, a result of the explosive growth of industry. New inventions were coming into the marketplace, and cities were expanding rapidly as immigrants came to the United States seeking better lives. It was a time when change was in the air, and that sense of changing times was reflected in the social, political, and economic fabric of the country.

The 1880s had seen movement on the labor front that reflected some of the concerns of workers, specifically the fact that their labor was being exploited for the financial well-being of the capitalists who owned and operated the businesses. The reality that many of these laborers were also immigrants added to the tension between the two groups. In 1886, the Haymarket Riot took place in Chicago, resulting in the arrest and execution of five men. In 1892, the Homestead Strike occurred just outside of Pittsburgh, where Pinkerton detectives engaged in a gunfight with striking workers at Andrew Carnegie's steel mill. In short, it was a time when labor and management were often at odds over just what the American workplace should look like.

In 1886, one of the most important events in the history of the labor movement took place when the American Federation of Labor was born. The Brotherhood of Professional Base Ball Players was formed even earlier by John Montgomery Ward, a star of the New York Giants. Ward, who would later become a lawyer, was just as interested in protecting the rights of baseball players as other union leaders of the time were committed to protecting the rights of their workers.

The Brotherhood was formed due to players' concerns about capping salaries at a time when the popularity of baseball was growing, bringing with it growing revenues for the owners. Another major concern of the players was the increasing use of the reserve clause. If a player was reserved, he was bound for life to the team with which he originally signed. At first, owners could reserve only five players, but by 1883 it had become 11, and it would eventually bind all the players of a team. As a result of the reserve clause, a player could either sign for what the team proposed, or he would be out of the National League.

As baseball owners worked together to lower costs and thereby raise their own profits, they were essentially acting as a trust. Club owners argued that they were simply bringing player salaries more in line with other workers of that time period, and they argued that they were actually being generous to players who may not have had any other marketable skills. However, the players regarded themselves as artisans rather than line workers in a factory, and they maintained that because their athletic careers were short, they needed to maximize their earnings. Management and labor in baseball were on a collision course.

* * *

In 1888, former star player, sporting goods entrepreneur, and Chicago White Stockings President Albert Goodwill Spalding arranged for a World Tour to promote baseball around the globe. Spalding saw himself as an ambassador of the sport, but it was not merely his love of the game that prompted the tour. He realized the benefits that the expansion of baseball could have for his sporting goods business.

Spalding signed most of the members of his team, led by his player-manager, Cap Anson, to go on the tour. He also signed a team of All-Stars from other National League teams which would oppose his White Stockings in exhibition games, including John Ward as captain and Ned Hanlon as the team's center fielder and leadoff hitter. Spalding was particularly attracted to Hanlon for his renowned leadership skills and considered Hanlon to be a man of character.[1]

The tour began on October 20 with a game at West Side Park in Chicago, and then played its way westward across the country until reaching San Francisco, their overseas port of departure. During a game in Denver, on a long fly ball hit to deep center, Hanlon made another of the spectacular catches for which he had become famous:

> Almost out of sight into the blue air sailed the ball, and away across the field sped Hanlon at a rate that a professional sprinter would have been proud of ... just once Hanlon turned to look above, and then ran on again faster, if possible, than before. Suddenly, however, he stopped, turned his face to the crowd, ran backward for fifteen or twenty feet, then threw his hands above his head; at the same instant his heel struck a hillock of sand and pitched him headlong through the air upon his back. As he fell, however, his right hand was held above him, and as he sprung to his feet the crowd saw that he held the ball. For probably five seconds that big assemblage held its breath, and then, as the famous outfielder started in for the diamond and the balance of the All-America players turned toward their bench, such a cheer went up as one rarely hears on the ball field.... .It was, indeed, a scene for an artist, and Hanlon was cheered and cheered until he paused to raise his cap in front of the grand stand.[2]

The first overseas stop was in Hawaii, where they did not have time to play a game, but they were celebrated with a lavish luau arranged by King Kalakau. The next stop was New Zealand, where they played one game before moving on to Australia. There they played 11 games in four cities during a stay that lasted three weeks. From there they played one game in Sri Lanka (Ceylon) and proceeded to Egypt, where they played on the Giza plateau which stretched in front of the Pyramids. While there, the players were photographed as they unceremoniously perched on the Sphinx.

While in Cairo, the players saw the first American newspapers since they left the United States three months earlier, and they were incensed to learn of the "Brush Classification Plan" that was proposed by Indianapolis Hoosiers owner John T. Brush.[3] According to the plan, all players would be placed into one of five levels based on their on-field play and off-field behavior. Each class had a corresponding salary cap—Class A players could earn $2,500 annually, and with each level the maximum decreased $250 until it was set at $1,500 for Class E players.

The players muttered that they thought that Spalding had arranged the trip as a way to get Ward, Hanlon, and other key members of the Brotherhood out of the way while the Brush Plan was instituted. Ward felt personally betrayed by the news because one motive he had for going on the tour was that he believed it afforded him the opportunity to discuss players' concerns with Spalding, who was considered to be one of the more reasonable owners in the league. The fact that Spalding had once been a player also made him more likely to be sympathetic to the concerns of the Brotherhood. Spalding immediately met with a disgruntled Ward and assured him that the Brush Plan was "not only impracticable but positively dangerous," and he tried to convince Ward that everything would be satisfactorily settled when they returned to the United States. Ward, however, would not be placated, and the Brush Plan would ultimately be one of the key factors leading to the creation of the Players' League in 1890.[4]

Amid rumors that Ward would be leaving the tour, they traveled to Italy, and in Brindisi the mail caught up with them. Hanlon was kidded by his comrades when he received a letter written in a "neat feminine hand." Hanlon only smiled in response to the jests of his comrades, and he refused to reveal the identity of his correspondent.[5] The letter's author was certainly Ellen Kelley, a teacher who was his hometown sweetheart. Hanlon and Ellen would marry barely a year later, on February 6, 1890, in a ceremony conducted in the church just a few blocks from the homes of their families.[6]

After playing games in Florence, Rome, and Naples, and visiting famous sites such as Pompeii, the group traveled to Paris, where they had some interesting adventures. One night at their hotel, journalist Harry Palmer, Ward, Hanlon, and a few others gathered to plan a "programme of wickedness." The first stop of the evening was at the Comedie Francaise, and after enjoying some light entertainment there, they made their way to the Latin Quarter and the Jardin Bullier. There they found themselves in the middle of a wild party. "What a crush, what wild hilarity, what exaggerated costumes, and what shockingly short skirts!" wrote Palmer. One of the dancers knocked Hanlon's silk hat clear up onto a chandelier. He retrieved it and, "taken aback by the sexy dance," he encouraged his fellow partiers to move on to their next destination.

But the night soon became even more risqué. From the Bullier they proceeded to the Eden Theatre just in time for the midnight show. The men were seated in the dress circle, and when the orchestra began to play, the stage doors opened to reveal "a hundred dancing girls dressed in extremely revealing costumes." The dancers moved out into the orchestra, where they drew audience members into their dance, and Hanlon and most of the tour's bachelors quickly found themselves enthusiastically dancing with the irresistible women of Paris "who spoke just enough English to make them all the more interesting." After the events at the theatre concluded, the men headed out to explore the other nightspots of the city, and they did not return to their hotel until after dawn.[7]

After playing a game at the Parc Aerostatique in Paris on March 8, the tour members endured a miserable, storm-wracked trip across the English Channel before landing in London. They played 10 games in 11 days in six cities in England, and the Prince of Wales, the future Edward VII, and Prince Albert attended a game in London played at the Kennington Oval. The next morning, they were given a private tour of the Houses of Parliament during which they witnessed "a lively debate in the House of Commons concerning Irish home rule and the treatment of Irish political prisoners." This was certainly a profound moment for the many Irish players in the group.[8]

That afternoon, they played at the Lord's Cricket Ground, and the highlight of the game was another wonderful diving catch by Hanlon that the players thought was almost an exact replay of his catch in Denver.[9] The next morning, John Ward left the team due to his concerns with the Brush Plan. His rapidly increasing marital difficulties also were a factor in his departure. Hanlon replaced Ward as captain of the All-Stars, and in that position he showed the leadership and strategic abilities that would later earn him fame as one of baseball's greatest managers.[10]

Of his time in England, Hanlon said, "England is a fine country but it will never do for baseball. The Englishmen like cricket, because they can drop off to sleep during a game and wake up in a half hour and find they have missed nothing."[11]

The final European stops were in Glasgow, Dublin, and Belfast. While they were in Ireland, a number of the men were able to reunite with family left behind, and they were struck by how their lives were so drastically removed from their origins. As Mark Lamster, the author of a definitive work about Spalding's World Tour, poignantly noted, "While their relatives appeared to be rooted firmly in a rural existence that evolved at a generational pace—if even that quickly—the travelers seemed to be hurtling toward the twentieth century, with all of its wonders, technological and otherwise."[12]

Finally, the tour made its way home across the Atlantic and arrived on April 6 in New York. Two days later, the players were honored for their achievements with a dinner at Delmonico's restaurant. Past National League President Abraham Mills served as master of ceremonies, and 300 guests, including Mark Twain and Theodore Roosevelt, attended.[13] In the speech Twain gave that night, he famously said, "Baseball is the very symbol, the outward and visible expression of the drive and push and rush and struggle of the raging, tearing, booming nineteenth century." A major point emphasized during the evening was that baseball was purely an American game and did not evolve from rounders or any other British game. Stimulated by this idea, in 1905 Spalding formed a commission with Mills at its head to determine baseball's origin. The "Mills Commission" would use dubious evidence to determine erroneously that the game was invented by Abner Doubleday in Cooperstown, New York, in 1839.

After leaving New York, the Tour moved up and down the East Coast, playing in Boston, Philadelphia, and Washington. While in Washington, they were invited to the White House, where they all shook the hand of President Benjamin Harrison. When Spalding invited the President to a game scheduled for later in the day, Harrison said he was too busy to attend, and he stunned the players by saying that it would also be unseemly for the President to be seen at a ball game.[14]

The tour finally concluded with a game on April 20 in Chicago, where it began exactly six months earlier. Then the players scattered to join their teams for the upcoming season, which began on April 24. Hanlon's Detroit contract had been picked up by Pittsburgh, so he traveled there to join his new team.

During the tour, Hanlon and his comrades had played 68 games on five continents and visited some of the most exotic places in the world. A son of Irish immigrants who had once been a child laborer in a textile mill was now a man who had rubbed shoulders with kings, princes, and a president. Ned Hanlon could now claim to be a man of the world.

* * *

Hanlon's first year as a player with the Alleghenys would be an important one for the advancement of his baseball career. By August, the team's inconsistent play placed increasing pressure on manager Horace B. Phillips, and he began acting oddly. Club owner

William Nimick questioned team captain Hanlon and players Fred Dunlap and Billy Sunday about the mental state of their manager. Hanlon reported that Phillips would "say one thing today, and he'll tell you something entirely different tomorrow. And he'll go up in the air and ask why something was done without consulting him, when it was Horace who ordered it."[15] Phillips was given a two-week leave of absence to try to recover his senses, but his condition did not improve, and he was institutionalized for mental illness. After Phillips' departure, Ned Hanlon was appointed the manager of the Alleghenys.

The move was greeted with enthusiasm in Pittsburgh. A local paper proclaimed that he would have much to learn while in his new job, but "he is intelligent and apt… a more energetic and trustworthy manager could not be secured than Hanlon. He is a practical man and his experience is long and varied."[16] In addition to being promised a free hand in running the team, his salary was increased to $3,100.[17]

When Hanlon assumed his managerial duties, Pittsburgh was in seventh place with a bleak 35–53 record, 20½ games behind the league-leading Boston Beaneaters. Under Hanlon's leadership, the team responded with a much-improved 26–18 mark and ended the season at 61–71, good for fifth place. A major contributor to the turnaround was pitcher Pud Galvin. The aging future Hall of Famer was only one year removed from his final season in the major leagues, and he was showing signs that the end of his career was imminent. Under Phillips, Galvin was 11–13, but when Hanlon became manager, he became rejuvenated and won 12 of 15 games. It was the first indication of Hanlon's ability not only to make significant improvement to an underachieving team, but also to find a way to squeeze out one last flourish of high production from a seemingly washed-up player.

At season's end, fans of the Alleghenys were optimistic that with a few changes in personnel coupled with Hanlon's skillful managerial ability, the team might make significant improvement in the coming year.

They would be greatly disappointed.

* * *

Throughout the 1889 season, a cloud of uncertainty hovered over the National League and the American Association as it became evident that a new league was being formed. This league would be run by financial investors in partnership with the players, and it would come to be called the Players' League. This caused Pittsburgh fans to be concerned about the prospects for their team. President Nimick reassured them, claiming that they would have a club in the coming season and that Ned Hanlon would manage it.[18] Nimick had already had in-depth discussions with Hanlon about such issues as where to hold spring training and what moves to make to improve the team.

Hanlon, however, would not commit to the Alleghenys, and he said, "Mr. Nimick knows as well as I do what our understanding was. I will be able to make a statement after Monday's Brotherhood meeting." When Nimick asked Hanlon if he would return as manager in 1890, Hanlon said he would not take the job for less than $4,000. Nimick immediately agreed to that salary, but Hanlon evasively replied that he might not even play ball in the coming season, so it was too soon to come to a financial agreement.[19]

The Players' League was born of the discontent that had been simmering among players for years regarding the reserve clause and the salary cap. When the Brush Classification Plan was revealed while key union leadership was on Spalding's World Tour, it provided the spark that caused the frustrated rank and file of the Brotherhood to become more strongly unified. On July 14, 1889, representatives from each Brotherhood chapter met to actively plan a new league that would be more financially equitable for all.

It became official on November 4, when the Brotherhood met in New York. When John Ward rose to address the membership and declared that "a new regime is now consummated," the room erupted in applause.[20] Ward appointed a committee consisting of Hanlon and four others to draft a statement that would announce the creation of the Players' League to the press.

The Players League was constructed to provide an equal split of profits between players and investors. This would ensure higher salaries for the players, and they were also encouraged to become investors in the league. To encourage competition throughout the season, a bonus pool was established which would be distributed to each club based on where they finished in the standings. This money would be divided among the players. Overall, it was an imaginative model.

The Players' League also intended to implement some new rules designed to improve the game, and at the same time distance themselves from the other leagues. These included increasing the number of umpires to two, moving the pitching box to 51 feet, using a livelier ball, and outlawing the use of caps to catch fly balls. There would be no sale of alcohol at the ballparks, no Sunday games, ticket prices were set at 50 cents, and efforts were made to eliminate professional gambling from the sport.[21]

Despite their declared intent to create a unique environment which could reflect the rising concerns of the American working class, the hypocrisy of the Players' League cannot be ignored. The higher ticket prices they established and the prohibition of Sunday games were a conscious effort to exclude working-class spectators from attending. In addition, although Ward had announced the League's solidarity with working-class men, it would receive harsh criticism for using non-union labor in the construction of some of their ballparks.

Most damning of all, despite their efforts to distance themselves from some of the policies and procedures of the existing leagues, there was one unfortunate way in which the Players' League remained in lockstep with their adversaries. Black men would not be allowed to play in their league.

* * *

Although John Ward was the driving force behind the creation of the Brotherhood and the Players' League, Ned Hanlon was his right-hand man virtually from the beginning. Hanlon had known Ward since they first met while Hanlon was playing for Rochester in 1878. Ward was heavily recruited by Rochester, but he also had received an offer from Providence. Hanlon, tasked with trying to convince Ward to sign with Rochester, was approached by a conflicted Ward, who pleaded with him: "Mr. Hanlon, put yourself in my place and tell me what to do, advise me just as if you were speaking to a brother."

Hanlon looked awkwardly at the floor, then turned to Ward and said, "Go to Providence." Ward became a star there, and a warm, life-long friendship with Hanlon began that day "because of the sacrifice of Hanlon, who wanted me at Rochester."[22]

Hanlon played a crucial role for the Players' League in attracting investors, and Cleveland streetcar magnate Al Johnson claimed that Ned Hanlon was the first person to bring up the subject of the new league to him.[23] Johnson recalled how during the 1889 season, Hanlon told him that he and Ward were fed up with the National League because its leadership had broken their word so often to them. According to Johnson, when Ward and Hanlon were on Spalding's Tour, they decided on a plan to raise capital in selected cities and build ball parks in them for the new league.[24] Hanlon convinced Johnson to support the efforts of the Brotherhood, and he not only became one of the League's chief financial backers, he became the owner of the Cleveland Infants in the new League as well.

In addition to recruiting Johnson, Hanlon had been working diligently in Pittsburgh to attract men with financial means and connections to support a Players' League club in the city.

He and Johnson had been able to recruit W. W. Kerr, who was the manager of Exposition Park, a plot of land which was just a short walk from downtown Pittsburgh via a bridge across the Allegheny River.[25] Ultimately, this would be the location of Exposition Park, the home of the Pittsburgh Burghers of the Players' League. Kerr and Hanlon also targeted Pittsburgh Mayor William McCallin, who had the political influence to smooth the way for construction of the new park. McCallin expressed enthusiasm and became a stockholder. Hanlon continued to work to recruit other investors, and he said, "Depend upon it, the affair is a great go."[26] Despite his optimism, Hanlon struggled to line up the necessary investors to raise the $20,000 in stock.[27] *Sporting Life* dryly commented:

> If Pittsburgh had to raise money for a World's Fair, that important event would be held [in] about 2092. No doubt Ned Hanlon and Al Johnson believe this to-day. Not knowing this town's coldness to schemes of public education and ventures not clearly sure things, they have been hustling to sell an article known as baseball in this money tight burg for nearly a week.[28]

In a league meeting in November, Hanlon reported to the players and backers that he was having difficulty securing Pittsburgh investors. New York capitalists at the meeting pledged that if he couldn't get the money in Pittsburgh, he would get it in New York, and they assured him Pittsburgh would have a club.[29] After the meeting, Hanlon, Ward, and Johnson went to Pittsburgh to meet with prospective investors, and they were able to meet the goal of selling $20,000 in capital stock by the end of November.[30] Hanlon himself invested $2,000 in the club.[31]

As late as November, Nimick staunchly stuck to the notion that Hanlon would not throw in with an upstart league: "I still refuse to believe that Hanlon has deserted us, and I won't believe it until he has notified us…but I still have faith in Hanlon."[32] He would soon see that he was mistaken when Hanlon raided the Alleghenys' roster and signed Fred Dunlap, Jake Beckley, Al Maul, Pud Galvin, and six others to his own Pittsburgh Burghers team of the Players' League. Hanlon himself would serve as the player-manager. Bereft of its best players, the National League Pittsburgh franchise would fall from the 61–71 record of 1889 to a truly horrid 23–113 mark in 1890.

* * *

The Players' League attracted many of the established stars of the day, including future Hall of Famers John Ward, Buck Ewing, Dan Brouthers, Ed Delahanty, Charles Comiskey, King Kelly, Old Hoss Radbourne, and Roger Connor, among others. In total, the Players' League signed 56 players from the National League and was able to rise in stature above the American Association to provide a serious challenge to the National League.[33]

This was made clear from the opening day of the season as Players' League teams in all cities that had two teams significantly outdrew National League clubs. The Boston Reds of the Players' League drew between 8,000 and 10,000 fans, while Boston's National League Beaneaters drew only 3,800 at the South End Grounds. In Pittsburgh, the Burghers drew 8,500 to Exposition Park, while the Alleghenys drew only a paltry 1,697 at Recreation Park.[34]

The Players' League continued to outdraw the National League throughout the season. For the year, the Players' League total attendance stood at 980,887 as opposed to 776,042 for the National League and 803,200 for the American Association. These figures support the oft-cited players' argument that fans attended games to see the players, especially star players, and not managers or owners. The American Association numbers can be attributed to the fact that most of their teams were unchallenged in their cities by any other professional league.[35]

Throughout the season, the National League worked hard to lure as many players as it could to rejoin them, but they had little success. For the most part, the newspapers weighed in to support the players of the new league. An editorial stated that "Every Players' League man who is approached by National League emissaries is offered a direct insult, because in singling him out as the object of temptation the magnates show that they consider him one who is either weak or venal. They never would personally approach men like Ward, Hanlon…and others of like unflinching loyalty."[36]

Despite the successful launch of the league, by mid-summer Hanlon was not only trying to win more games, but he was also actively fighting rumors that the Players' League was on shaky financial footing and would fold at the end of the year. In an attempt to squelch these rumors, Hanlon declared that he would buy back the stock of anyone who wanted to bail out of the Burghers. Alluding to the plight of the helpless Alleghenys, he added, "I know this is a good town and feel sure we will have it all to ourselves next year; in fact, we have it that way now."[37]

Throughout the season, Hanlon's club struggled on the field. The team hovered around .500 for the first month and reached their high-water mark for the season when they were 32–30 on July 12. The Burghers ended with a 60–68 record, good for sixth place, well behind the pennant-winning Boston Reds, who finished at 81–48. As a player, Hanlon had a good season for the Burghers, with a batting average of .272 and an on-base percentage of .383. He finished fourth in the league in stolen bases with 65 and first in outfield putouts with 297.

The day after the season ended, it was reported that some of the Burghers had made a habit of overindulging during the season. Hanlon, obviously aware of this, made a flurry of roster moves, and the *Pittsburgh Press* applauded his actions, declaring that it was necessary to weed out the "dead wood" to protect the interests of his majority stockholders.[38]

The moves were certain to cause outrage among some players, but they clearly demonstrate that Ned Hanlon knew exactly what type of ball player he wanted on a team that he would manage. He had his mind set on remaking the Burghers into a team whose minds were more on baseball and less on John Barleycorn.

* * *

On January 16, 1891, the Players' League folded. Ultimately, the League was betrayed by financial backers who had determined that the League did not have the financial resources to continue competing with the National League.[39] Ed Koszarek, in

The Players League: History, Clubs, Ballplayers, and Statistics, identifies another key reason for the demise of the upstart league: "The Players League was led by men with baseball knowledge but little financial knowledge; the National League was led by men with some baseball knowledge and greater financial acumen. In the end, the Players League leadership could not match the National League's financial management."[40] Despite its superior attendance totals, the Players' League lost a total of $125,000, with Boston the only team to make a minuscule profit. Pittsburgh was one of the biggest losers at $20,000.[41]

In the end, four Players' League franchises, New York, Brooklyn, Pittsburgh, and Chicago, accepted offers to consolidate with the National League. Bad feelings, however, particularly on the part of National League magnates, would linger. One unnamed National League official considered the leaders of the Brotherhood to be men who had "knifed us in the back."[42] The war with the Players' League would also spell the eventual doom of the American Association. Unable to recover from the strain of a three-league war, the American Association merged with the National League after the 1891 season.

What was the true legacy of the Players' League? The League reflected the growing chasm between labor and management that was developing as the nineteenth century drew to a close. The Players' League anticipated the sort of profit-sharing that would be the cornerstone of the National Football League in the mid-twentieth century. It provided players with the potential to grow financially secure, encouraging them to invest in the league as well as play in it. In this way, once a ballplayer was no longer able to perform on the field, he might still benefit from the game by being an investor. Nevertheless, the Players' League may simply have failed because of its "impractical, utopian structure."[43]

After the league's demise, Al Johnson expressed his admiration for what Hanlon had done to help create the Players' League:

> You can talk of the loyalty of a Ward, a Ewing, a Keefe and so on, but give me Ned Hanlon above everybody else. He stands to-day as the hero of the Players' League. He is the only ball player in that League who has held to the contract he signed. Not a penny has he received for his work this season, although he has played better ball than ever before.[44]

Sporting Life reporter Ella Black, the country's first nationally circulated female baseball writer, said she was glad to hear of Al Johnson's complimentary words about Hanlon, and she agreed that Hanlon deserved "all the good that can be said of him." Pittsburgh treasurer W. W. Kerr, however, disputed part of Johnson's claims, and he indignantly declared that Hanlon had been paid all the money he was due and that the club was careful to set aside money so that all the players were paid in full.[45]

After his outburst, however, Kerr was quick to compliment Hanlon, saying that no one connected with the league had "worked harder for its success, made more sacrifices for it, and remained more loyal than Ned Hanlon, and this is fully appreciated by everybody connected with the Players League whether capitalist or player."[46]

The two primary leaders of the erstwhile league were bitterly disappointed by its demise. John Ward disgustedly attributed its failure to "stupidity, avarice, and treachery."[47] Ned Hanlon seemed even more disillusioned. Ren Mulford of *Sporting Life* wrote that Hanlon deserved to have a monument erected to him for the faithfulness that he had displayed to the Players' League. He painted a picture of the forlorn Hanlon: "I never saw such a change in a man in my life. The Ned Hanlon I had met after the journey around the world was a rosy-cheeked, jolly fellow. This Ned Hanlon sat at the table dreaming idly, tapping the plate with his knife. He is the martyr of another cause, which, if not lost, has certainly not succeeded."[48]

For Hanlon, the failure of the Players' League radically altered how he regarded the business of baseball. When he became a manager and part of ownership, he adopted the tactics that he had fought against in the unrealistic dream that was the Players' League.

* * *

As the battle between the three leagues came to an end, Ella Black correctly predicted that Hanlon would be named the player-manager of the Pittsburgh Alleghenys for the upcoming season. Black warned, however, that hard feelings toward Hanlon still existed among National League officials because of the work he did for the Players' League. She declared that Hanlon likely had been named manager merely to appease Players' League people for a time, and he would be replaced at the first opportunity by someone who had showed more loyalty to the National League. Black added that she hoped that would not occur, because she believed Pittsburgh would regret it if they lost such a capable manager and conscientious player.[49]

With the demise of the Players' League, there was a scramble to sign available players. A number of teams were interested in Lou Bierbauer, a highly regarded second baseman. Hanlon, attempting to get the jump on his rivals, went in the depth of winter to the Presque Isle Peninsula, just outside Erie, Pennsylvania, to find Bierbauer. He crossed the harbor in a bitter storm to reach him, and he was successful in getting Bierbauer to sign a contract. The American Association Philadelphia Athletics claimed that Hanlon had violated the complicated agreement the leagues had made regarding the signing of players after the consolidation, and an official of that club huffily protested that "The action of the Pittsburgh club in signing Bierbauer was piratical." Henceforth, the Pittsburgh club would be called the Pirates.[50]

Hanlon continued his rebuild of the Pirates when he signed catcher Connie Mack and brought back players who had played with him on either the Alleghenys, the Burghers, or both. These players were Jake Beckley, Pud Galvin, Fred Carroll, and Al Maul. Regarding Hanlon's pursuit of good players for his club, *Sporting Life* commented that "If Pittsburg does get them, it will be simply in recognition of Ned Hanlon's personal services and sacrifices for the Players League, and not for anything that his club has done."[51]

While he was looking for pitchers, Hanlon jokingly declared, "I used to be a pitcher once upon a time, and I still think I could hold Johnny Ward level. If I thought it would add any to the interest of the game, I might be persuaded to go into the box for two innings."[52]

For Hanlon and the Pirates, however, the season would leave little room for humor, as it was filled with turmoil. After getting off to a decent start that saw them in second place at 15–12 on May 26, they lost 19 of their next 24 games to fall to seventh in the league. The *Pittsburgh Dispatch* laid the blame for the Pirates' poor play on injuries and players who were rebelling against Hanlon. There were reports that players were out carousing deep into the night, reporting late to games, and missing trains. One of the main violators, pitcher Mark Baldwin, "blackguarded and abused Manager Hanlon in the most shameful way," and he had boasted that club President J. Palmer O'Neil had excused the fines Hanlon had laid upon him for violating team rules.[53]

Hanlon was facing criticism because he upset some of the players who claimed that he had "but one mode of treatment, and that he applied it to all." Although he was considered a conscientious manager, "he has not the knack of making himself agreeable. He is continually finding fault, not in a bold, courageous manner, but by side glances and growls that fall hard on the players and knocks all the liveliness out of them. His treatment makes them feel tired."[54]

There is no question that the team was divided and that a conspiracy to displace Hanlon as manager existed among some of the players. Hanlon's defenders claimed that his only fault was that he tried to make the malcontents on the team obey his rules, and for that club officials should be thankful.[55] It was the opinion of the *Pittsburgh Daily Post* that as a captain, Hanlon was doing a good job, but as a manager he was struggling:

While Hanlon played in Pittsburgh from 1889 through 1892, Carnegie Steel and the Heinz Ketchup Company were founded in that city. The first telephone line was opened between Pittsburgh and New York City (Babe Ruth Birthplace & Museum).

> As a leader on the field Honest Ed's long and honorable career is recognized by all, his experience gives weight to his command and forces respect. The dual position of manager and captain is one very, very few men are capable of filling.... His soul is set on giving Pittsburgh a winning club.... So wrapped up is Ned in his mission that he thinks of nothing else. During a close game on the home grounds the spectators have seen him walking nervously to and fro—never still for a moment. He is overjoyed when the team wins, and just the opposite when it loses. It is too much to expect a man of his temperament to keep constant watch over a lot of ball players. He is likely to view things too rigidly and use harsh words when kind words are more to the point.

The *Daily Post* described the attributes of a good manager, claiming that he should always be cool under fire, know when to distribute praise and when to criticize, and use judgment in deciding which approach to use based on how it suited the different natures of his players. Then the reporter revealed his true agenda and proposed that the man who possessed all the "qualities of a first-class manager" was none other than team president J. Palmer O'Neil.[56]

It is clear that it was O'Neil, and not Hanlon, who was at the heart of the problems with the Pittsburgh team. O'Neil fancied himself a baseball coach and manager, and he actively interfered with Hanlon's attempts to instill discipline by providing players with a sympathetic ear. He was constantly talking with the players and sending them telegrams in an attempt to coach them. While the team was in Philadelphia, he wired Jake Beckley with the following astute coaching tip: "Jake, swing your good right arm boldly. We must win to-day." To Pete Browning, he offered this sage advice: "Pete, line 'em out strong and often. We must win to-day."[57]

By the end of June, realizing that the other directors would not allow him to manage the team, O'Neil went about trying to replace Hanlon with William McGunnigle, who had won pennants with Brooklyn teams in both the American Association and the National League. The *Pittsburgh Dispatch* reported, "It now looks certain that Hanlon is to be ingloriously and unfairly pushed to the one side to suit the whims of one or two people who know nothing about baseball. No matter what is done it is safe to say that Hanlon will have the sympathies of all fair-minded baseball patrons. He has not had a fair trial, and if Mr. McGunnigle is to be put in charge, it is to be hoped that he will not be humbugged and bothered as much as Hanlon has been."[58]

Things became embarrassing for everyone concerned when after a win against Cincinnati on June 22, O'Neil ordered Hanlon not to accompany the team on a road trip to Cleveland the next day. Hanlon was astounded, and he refused to obey O'Neil's order, insisting that he was the manager and that O'Neil did not have the authority to stop him. O'Neil tried to justify his action by claiming that a player on the team had stated that he would not play for Hanlon under any circumstances. Hanlon immediately questioned that player, who strongly denied that he had ever made such a statement. A third party testified that instead of saying that he would not play for Hanlon, the player in question had actually said he "liked to play under Hanlon as much as he had like to play under any manager he had ever known."[59]

Hanlon returned to O'Neil and confronted him with the player's report, and in turn, O'Neil became "wrathy" with Hanlon, claiming that the player in question had spoken with him in confidence. After the squabbling was over, Hanlon disobeyed O'Neil and went with the team to Cleveland. The *Pittsburgh Dispatch* moaned that "Probably never a baseball team left Pittsburgh in a more broken up condition than the local team left yesterday morning."[60]

The *Dispatch* sided with Hanlon, and while acknowledging that he may have shortcomings, it reminded readers that just weeks earlier, O'Neil had publicly announced that he would put down any conspiracy against Hanlon. O'Neil was accused of making Hanlon a scapegoat and "humiliating a very brave and honest fellow." The *Dispatch* called upon the directors to either fully empower Hanlon to be the manager with the ability to discipline unruly players or remove him from the position. It concluded by saying, "It is a farce and an insult to Hanlon to call him manager if Mr. O'Neil is to have leading strings on him."[61]

The entire fiasco became almost comical in late July when McGunnigle and Hanlon both showed up at Exposition Park, claiming the right to manage the club. O'Neil was out of town, so McGunnigle withdrew from the confusing scene and said he would wait until the directors met to decide the issue. The directors, annoyed with the antics of O'Neil, decided to give Hanlon full control of the team and sent letters to the players instructing them to report only to him. When the directors notified O'Neil of this, he quickly returned to town and signed McGunnigle to manage the team in defiance of the rest of the board. The *Pittsburgh Dispatch* was disgusted by the entire situation, and it attributed the deplorable state of the club solely to the "imperious" actions of O'Neil.[62]

It was reported that the majority of players wished for Hanlon to be retained, and two directors sent a telegram to him while the team was in Cleveland that read: "McGunnigle bounced, O'Neil dethroned, and you are boss. Hustle the boys up and win games." When the telegram was read to the players, they were reported to have "held a jubilation" at the news.[63]

When the team returned from their road trip, however, they were stunned to find that somehow O'Neil had been able to convince a majority of the directors to sign McGunnigle because it would be best for the team if the manager was not a player. In a move heavy with irony, McGunnigle was given full control of the team on and off the field, and as a condition for the board's capitulation, O'Neil agreed to have his powers reduced.

Could it have been that Ella Black's prediction regarding hard feelings on the part of National League magnates had played into the firing of Hanlon? Or could it be that J. Palmer O'Neil was simply a prototype of the meddling administrator that could later be seen in such baseball men as George Steinbrenner?

Upon assuming control, McGunnigle played it close to the vest when he was asked about the changes he would make, but he did announce that Hanlon would remain as captain. He expressed confidence that the team was a good one and said he would wager a hat that they would finish in the first division.[64] It would not be so, as Hanlon flatly refused the captaincy and Pittsburgh finished tied for last in the league, 30½ games behind the pennant-winning Boston Beaneaters.

According to the *Pittsburgh Dispatch*, the whole mess was "a disgrace to the entire organization and made them a laughingstock of the entire country," and it predicted that any franchise that could not keep the directors' hands off the wheel was destined to failure.[65]

The entire situation was a valuable lesson for Ned Hanlon as he later pursued his managerial career. He never allowed himself to be put in such a situation again. When Baltimore later came to him with an offer to manage, Hanlon had an iron-clad set of conditions that had to be met before he signed with the team. He insisted on no interference from owners or directors. He would be the boss and would run the team his own way. His success or failure would be the result of his own abilities.

3

A New Sheriff in Town (1892)

Within just a few years after it was founded in 1876, there was increasing animosity building against the National League in a number of important American cities. After its first season, the National League had expelled the Philadelphia and New York franchises because they did not make their final western road trips. After the 1880 season, the League expelled the Cincinnati franchise because they refused to adhere to its rules prohibiting Sunday baseball and alcohol sales at games. Other cities were frustrated that their requests for admission into the league were rejected. As a result, some interested parties who wanted to have a major league team decided to start their own league. In November 1881, these parties met, and the American Association was born.

The new league brought changes that were bound to please most baseball fans. First, ticket prices for the new league would be only 25 cents, as opposed to the 50 cents charged by the National League. In addition, teams would play games on Sundays, if local laws did not prohibit it. Finally, clubs would be allowed to sell alcohol at their games. The new circuit quickly became nicknamed "The Beer and Whiskey League," not only because of its alcohol sales, but also because several owners made their living as brewery operators.

Before the league even began play, their Brooklyn club dropped out at the last minute, and there was a scramble to replace it. Baltimore, although it did not even apply for a franchise in the league, was selected by American Association president Denny McKnight because of its large population and because there was no competing National League team in the city. McKnight, who also owned the Pittsburgh club in the new league, selected Henry Myers, a player on his roster, to be the new manager of the Baltimore franchise.[1]

The first Orioles team left much to be desired as they compiled a 19–54–1 record, had a league-worst team batting average of .208, and committed a league-high 490 errors in just 74 games. Granted, due to primitive equipment and notably uneven playing surfaces of the time, many more errors were made in the nineteenth century than today, but 490 is still an astounding total.

By the next year, William "Bald Billy" Barnie and Alfred T. Houck assumed ownership of the Orioles. Barnie had played briefly in both the National Association and the National League, a catcher whose career was cut short by a crippling injury to his hand. Barnie became the manager of the club, and within a few years he bought out Houck to become the sole owner.[2]

Once he assumed total control of the team, Barnie quickly realized that he would need financial help to keep the struggling franchise alive, and he found that help in Henry "Harry" Von der Horst. Harry was the elder son of John H. Von der Horst, and together they were the owners of J. H. Von der Horst & Son Brewery, also known as the Eagle Brewery. In 1884, much to the chagrin of his father, Harry bought a 50 percent stake in the Orioles from Barnie.[3] Until John Von der Horst's death in 1894, there would be considerable friction between the father and son concerning how much money was being spent on the ball club,[4] and this hampered Barnie's ability to spend what he needed to put a winning team on the field.

Along with his love of the game, Harry Von der Horst also loved being a baseball owner for the opportunity it afforded him to rub shoulders with important people in Baltimore and to be in the public spotlight. He also realized the potential that the team would have for selling the products of his brewery at the games. Baltimore in the 1880s was rapidly becoming a rival to Milwaukee as a brewing center, and at one point there were 33 breweries supplying the bars and beer gardens of the city.[5] Owning a ballpark would help the Eagle Brewery get an advantage over its competitors.[6]

After the 1889 season ended, the Orioles were in financial trouble. Moreover, when the Players' League began operations in 1890, there were three leagues in open war bidding for players, and a number of key Orioles jumped to the Players' League. In November, Billy Barnie, seeking the stability that being in the strong National League would provide, applied for admission into the League but was rejected. Later that month, Barnie and Von der Horst decided to drop out of the American Association and join the minor league Atlantic Association in an attempt to avoid the league wars and get their financial house in order.[7]

The Orioles performed well in this lesser league, and they were solidly in first place on August 25 with an impressive record of 73–24. By that time, however, the American Association was in a bind when the Brooklyn Gladiators ran out of money and the team was dissolved. The Association came to Barnie with cap in hand to see if the Orioles would like to rejoin the League. The Orioles accepted the offer and finished out the Gladiators' schedule.[8]

The following year, after the Players' League folded, the Orioles finished a surprising third, but the tumultuous league wars had taken a financial toll on the American Association, which was now on its last legs. After the season, an agreement was reached between the two remaining leagues that resulted in the dissolution of the foundering Association. As part of the deal, the National League agreed to expand, adding four Association teams: the Louisville Colonels, St. Louis Browns, Washington Senators, and Baltimore Orioles.

* * *

Harry Von der Horst was happy to be in the more prestigious National League, but he had also become increasingly dissatisfied with a team that performed poorly on the field during almost the entirety of their 10 years in the American Association. The team finished in last place four times, never finished higher than third, and compiled a dismal 10-year record of 489–602.

Although Barnie had struggled to find and keep good players, it wasn't until late in the 1890 season that he made the first of two moves that would propel the team's rise to prominence in the National League in the coming years. The first was when he signed pitcher John "Sadie" McMahon and catcher Wilbert Robinson, who were known as the

"Dumpling Battery" for their stocky physiques, when the Philadelphia Athletics of the American Association went bankrupt.[9]

According to some reports, McMahon had murdered a man in Wilmington, Delaware, four years earlier, but he was ultimately acquitted. He was a rowdy, hard-drinking man, but he was graceful and had excellent command of a variety of pitches, including a fastball, curve, change-up, and overhand drop pitch. Many years later, he claimed he was never knocked out of the box or delivered an intentional walk.[10]

Wilbert Robinson, called affectionately "Uncle Robbie" by his teammates, was a good-natured, hard-nosed catcher who was a loyal family man and lovingly referred to his devoted wife, Mary, as "Ma." His minor league manager, William Prince, described Robinson as a great catcher whose best quality was his personality. Prince said, "His good nature was a sure remedy to drive away all the blues. No cliques could last while Robbie was around. He taught us to look at all such things as a joke, and drew us together as a sociable, harmonious club."[11]

Prince's description was an excellent appraisal of the type of man Robinson proved to be throughout his life. His character and temperament would be the ballast that helped steady, as much as was humanly possible, the contentious and fiery personalities that constituted the 1890s Baltimore Orioles.

Although Robinson's nature made him one of the most beloved characters in baseball, he was a spirit of pure flame while competing on the diamond, and throughout his career as a catcher and manager, he became known as an expert in improving and handling pitchers.[12] He also was skilled at disputing umpire calls quietly and usually attempted to avoid showing them up in front of the crowd.[13]

On August 24, 1891, Barnie's other major contribution to the soon-to-be famous Orioles arrived in Baltimore in the person of an 18-year-old, ferocious man-child and enfant terrible named John Joseph McGraw.

Born in Truxton, New York, John McGraw had a challenging childhood. He left home when he was only 12 years old after his mother and four siblings died of diphtheria and his grief-stricken father turned to drink and became abusive.[14] He developed an intense love for baseball and decided at an early age that he was going to be a professional ball player. While playing for the Cedar Rapids Canaries, an old American Association player and friend of Bill Barnie recommended McGraw to him. Barnie sent for him, and many years later, McGraw recounted their first meeting:

> I walked into Barnie's office and announced myself as ready to do a lot of business. For a whole minute he stared at me.
>
> "You don't mean to say that this is the ball player I've been writing about. Why, you're just a kid—can you even play ball?"
>
> "If you don't think so," I retorted, "just get me out there and watch my smoke. I'm a bigger fellow than I look." I weighed 121 pounds.
>
> I got my chance right away at short. I was so nervous, though, that when the first grounder came to me I kicked it all over the lot.
>
> Then came my great chance in my first big league game. The bases were full when I came to bat and—I struck out.
>
> "Kid," Barnie said to me, "what was it you said about smoke?"[15]

Despite McGraw's inauspicious beginning, Barnie signed him to a contract for $200 a month for the remainder of the 1891 season,[16] and in 33 games, McGraw hit .270, had an on-base percentage of .359, and made 17 errors in 90 chances.

Sadie McMahon was a solid major league pitcher who compiled an 85–57 record in his first three years in the American Association (Babe Ruth Birthplace & Museum).

Wilbert Robinson in his rudimentary catching gear. Note his right-hand pinky, which was partially amputated due to injury in the 1896 season (Babe Ruth Birthplace & Museum).

One incident that occurred early in his rookie year made his intense and fierce nature abundantly clear to his teammates. While he was sitting at the end of the bench, a teammate playfully shifted his weight so that McGraw was unceremoniously dumped on the ground. As the players howled in laughter at the prank, they were flabbergasted when the youngster attacked the jokester, and as McGraw was reaching for a bat to inflict further damage, he was restrained by teammates who ultimately calmed him down. The word, however, was out: mess with John McGraw at your own peril.[17]

As a player for the Orioles and later as a Hall of Fame manager for 31 years with the New York Giants, McGraw would prove to be a force of nature who "could drive his teammates to another level of play. So he was to serve as the soul of a team that was about to be born."[18]

During McGraw's first two years with the Orioles, however,

The lean and hungry John McGraw was 18 years old and eager for baseball fame from the moment he joined the Orioles in 1891 (Babe Ruth Birthplace & Museum).

the club was in constant financial struggles and attendance was decreasing. Von der Horst was also becoming concerned about the reputation that the team was garnering among the fans and the press. Not only were the Orioles ostracized because of their "kicking" (a term then widely used for umpire harassment) and rowdy conduct with fans and opposing players, but they were also ridiculed for their exceptionally poor play. In a game on April 30, 1892, that the Orioles lost, 13–1, in Pittsburgh, a report of that game was indicative of what fans around the League were saying about the Orioles:

> Probably the local club would be bankrupt before the season ended, because no one would go to see the class of ball that has been put up by the Baltimore misfits during their stay here. They managed to disgust 3,500 people yesterday afternoon by the rankest kind of playing that has been seen here for many years. If they cannot put up a 100 per cent better article of ball, the sooner they retire from the league the better.[19]

Concerned about the effect a rowdy club might have on ticket sales, Von der Horst expressed his personal outrage and assured the people of Baltimore that he was determined that his players act as gentlemen and that they abstain from kicking and rowdyism.[20] At the end of the 1891 season, Von der Horst's concerns about his club caused him to resort to a time-honored sports stratagem to correct the team's problems: he fired the manager. So "Bald Billy" Barnie, who for nine years had served the team and the American Association well and faithfully in many ways, was gone. Throughout his career, Barnie demonstrated himself to be a knowledgeable baseball man and able executive who was credited with discovering a number of famous ballplayers, including Hall of Famer Mike "King" Kelly. After Barnie's death in 1900, *Sporting Life* carried his lengthy obituary, calling him "one of the best-known base-ball men in the country."[21]

When Harry Von der Horst fired his manager, it was a step he undertook in order to improve the situation of his ball club as it entered the more prestigious and competitive National League.

But it was about to get worse — a lot worse — before it would get better.

* * *

To replace Billy Barnie, Von der Horst promoted his star outfielder, George Van Haltren, to player-manager for the 1892 season. Any hopes for a quick improvement were dealt an ominous blow when on a windy and cold Opening Day, the 5,000 fans who showed up saw the Orioles soundly trounced, 13–3, by the Brooklyn Bridegrooms. The Orioles lost 10 of their first 11 games, and grumbling began to percolate that Van Haltren was incompetent. It didn't help his case when on April 19, the Orioles were forced to forfeit a game they were winning against the Giants in the sixth inning because Van Haltren neglected to notify the umpire before the game that they had a time deadline to catch a train to Boston. It quickly became clear to Von der Horst that Van Haltren was not going to be the manager he envisioned, so he stripped Van Haltren of his managerial duties and appointed his club vice-president and lead beer salesman, John Waltz, as a temporary manager while he searched for a full-time one.[22]

Waltz's first game as Orioles manager took place in Pittsburgh on April 29. The Orioles lost that day in a 12–3 blowout, and they were also beaten the next day in the game where their "rankest kind of playing" was described above. When he was

THE VONDERHORST BREWING COMPANY

–:Brewers of the:–

Purest Extra Pale Standard

BEERS.

OFFICES : { 10 Belair Avenue. Room 2 American Building.

Telephone 779.

Before hiring Hanlon, Baltimore Orioles owner and brewery operator Harry Von der Horst was desperate to find a manager for the team, and until he could, he had his lead beer salesman John Waltz fill in (Babe Ruth Birthplace & Museum).

not watching the Orioles being trounced by the Pirates, Waltz became intrigued with Ned Hanlon as a prospective manager. Hanlon did not play in either game due to a knee injury, but Waltz knew that Hanlon had not only previously managed the Pirates, he also had been a much-heralded player and captain of a championship team. Waltz immediately sent Von der Horst a telegram urging him to make an offer to Hanlon to manage and play for the Orioles.[23]

On May 5, the *Baltimore Sun* reported that the Pittsburgh directors had given Von der Horst permission to negotiate with Hanlon, and by the next day it was reported that he had signed as manager and captain of the Orioles and would begin his duties in Cincinnati the following day. Hanlon's appearance as a player would not take place for several weeks due to his injured leg, but he announced that he would wear a uniform and coach from the lines and from the bench.[24]

After the deal was completed, Hanlon met with reporters and tried to temper their optimism about the immediate future success of the team, saying, "a club that is demoralized by losses cannot be reorganized in a day or a week, but it can be steadily improved until the players are doing all that is possible for them to do."[25]

On the morning of May 9, Von der Horst called a meeting to introduce the players to their new manager. He made it clear to the players that Hanlon now had complete control of the team and that they were expected to obey all orders from him. He warned them that no protests of Hanlon's decisions would be heard.

Hanlon then addressed the team. He said that they were a talented group of individual players, but if they were willing to sacrifice individual accomplishments and work as a unit, they would be victorious as a team. He told them to have courage, never give up until the last man was out, and strive to constantly improve themselves. He explained that to be good ball players, they must not only use their hands and feet, they should also use their heads. He informed them that they were partners with the officers of the club because the better the team did, the more renumeration they would receive. He appointed Van Haltren as the captain and concluded his remarks by saying, "United we stand, and divided we fall."

The *Baltimore Sun* reporter who was present for Hanlon's speech wrote that his remarks were well-received by the players, "all of whom are enthusiastic at the prospect of winning games under his skillful and intelligent leadership."[26]

Despite Hanlon's inspirational opening speech and the alleged positive reception of it by the players, Hanlon likely did not realize the extent of the dysfunctional mess he had just inherited. Of course, Von der Horst knew, and that was exactly why he hired Hanlon in the first place and why he acceded full control to his new manager. He was tired of dealing with the players' attitudes and demands and wanted to wash his hands of all that. Nevertheless, considering the events that would unfold during the remainder of the season, Harry Von der Horst deserves more credit than history has given him for making the Orioles into the champions they would become. During the trial by fire that Hanlon was about to undergo, Von der Horst kept his word and did not interfere with any decision Hanlon made, and he allowed him a totally free hand in what proved to be an almost total reconstruction of the team.

Once Hanlon assumed control, the season was filled with a dizzying number of transactions, signings, and releases that took place as he began the process of building the team he had imagined. He had to find the right players and create an environment where they could bond and thrive. It would take a bit longer than Hanlon and the

Baltimore fan base would have liked, and he would have to make some enemies in the process, but "Ned Hanlon was about to put together one of the most colorful and successful outfits in the game's history."[27]

* * *

Shortly after taking over the club, Hanlon announced that he had formulated a system of playing that he intended to drill into his men in their morning practices. The local press was impressed with him and observed that he made a constant study of the game and had "well-designed ideas upon such points as sacrifice hitting, base running, and fielding stratagems. He is continually talking to his men about their duties, and has aroused their ambition and enthusiasm."[28]

The 1,319 fans who showed up when the Orioles beat the Philadelphia Phillies on May 24 at Union Park thoroughly enjoyed the game and applauded the improvements they saw in the team. The *Sun* was also impressed and reported that Hanlon's morning batting practices had resulted in "marked progress in intelligent batting," and that "the sacrifice hitting was timely and skillful."[29] These developments provided some hope that better days for the team were near.

Along with improving the tactics of the team, Hanlon was also evaluating his players, so he turned his attention to the cocky youngster, John McGraw. The general consensus had been that McGraw was "a marginal player on a sorry club,"[30] and for that reason both Barnie and Van Haltren had kept him on the bench for the most part. But McGraw's brash and fiery attitude appealed to Hanlon, who would demonstrate an affinity toward players of that mold in the coming years. Nevertheless, in the way he handled McGraw early in his tenure, it seems he was not totally convinced that McGraw would develop into anything more than a utility player. To save money on team expenses, he had even left McGraw behind on some road trips. Hanlon tried to find the best fit for him and experimented by using him at every position except pitcher, catcher, and first base.[31]

Finally, after watching McGraw for a while, Hanlon decided it would be best to send him to a minor league team in Mobile, Alabama, for some seasoning. Baseball historian and sportswriter Fred Lieb related the story of when Hanlon approached McGraw about the idea:

> "John, I think I'll send you to Mobile for a little experience. You can play there every day. It will be good for you."
>
> "Good nothing!" yelled back McGraw. "I know all about Mobile, and how it gets 130 in the sun on their diamond in July and August. It's a hell-hole, that's what it is. I'm trying to put on a little weight, and I'd just melt away down there.
>
> I'd quit playing ball before I would go to Mobile. Besides, what's the matter with the way I've been playing around here?"
>
> Young Mac argued so loudly and intensely that Hanlon said, "All right, I won't send you there. We can always use you as a utility player."[32]

Hanlon's opinion of young McGraw's potential was evident when he was approached by Chicago Colts manager Cap Anson, who offered Hanlon a deal which would send Jimmy Ryan to the Orioles for McGraw. Ryan was in the middle of an 18-year career during which he batted .308 and collected 2,513 hits. But Ryan had a reputation as a serious drinker, and that was likely a contributing factor in Hanlon's refusal to accept the offer. He told Anson, "Thanks, Cap, but I think I'll keep my little fighting rooster."³³ Thirty years later, McGraw fondly remembered this deal that never was, saying, "Hanlon refused [the trade], much to my delight. That was an important moment in my life. If I had gone to Chicago, I would have missed those happy days on the Orioles—might have missed my chance to progress."³⁴

June began badly for the Orioles as they lost six of their first seven games that month. Hanlon was not pleased, and he said, "I have not the proper material to work with. As soon as we collect a team of intelligent and ambitious players, I expect it to win many games."³⁵ Hanlon's use of the word "ambitious" was the first sign that not all of the problems with the Orioles were simply due to a lack of talent and that some of the players needed an attitude adjustment. Maybe he was sending a signal to Von der Horst to loosen the purse strings, but as the month progressed, financial problems arose that made it questionable whether the Orioles would have the financial wherewithal to obtain players of quality.

By agreement of all National League clubs, rosters were cut back to 13 in a league-wide, cost-cutting move.³⁶ Moreover, the Orioles themselves were also feeling the strain caused by poor attendance, and Von der Horst was forced to meet with the players to let them know there would be a reduction in their salaries beginning in July. Hanlon's salary was also reduced, but he did agree with Von der Horst that all the cuts were necessary. Von der Horst promised all concerned that their salaries would be increased if the club can could rise in the standings and if attendance increased.³⁷

At least one uplifting and historic moment occurred for the Orioles when Wilbert Robinson made history on June 10 as he rapped out seven hits in seven at-bats as the Orioles spanked the Browns, 25–4, in the first game of a doubleheader they swept at Union Park.³⁸ That record of most consecutive hits in a nine-inning game stood alone until September 16, 1975, when it was tied by Pirate Rennie Stennett.

In the meantime, Hanlon was attempting to help the Orioles by playing in the field himself. On June 22, he played left field in both games of a doubleheader in Philadelphia. He had a single in the first game and added a single and double in the second.³⁹ On June 28, in a game that the Orioles lost to the Giants, 7–5, McGraw was complimented for his fine fielding at shortstop, and Hanlon was praised for his work in center field and for throwing a runner out at second base trying to stretch a single into a double. He also drove home a run with a hit and had a sacrifice hit.⁴⁰ Unfortunately, Hanlon's play in the 1892 season would not provide much help to the team. He played in only 11 games and compiled a .163 batting average. These would be the last games he played in the major leagues.

By late June, however, problems with the players' behavior that were festering finally reached the point where Hanlon felt the need to impose some basic rules on the team. He took a page out of his old manager Jack Chapman's book, had rules printed on individual cards, and handed one to each player at a meeting. Hanlon's signature was printed at the bottom of the cards. The rules stated:

- Players must report at the grounds not later than 9:45 a.m. and 2:45 p.m.
- None but the players are allowed in the dressing room.
- During the progress of the game players in uniform, when not actively engaged, must remain seated on the bench.
- When at home or abroad players must retire not later than 11:30 p.m. and arise not later than 8:30 a.m.

- At all times, whether at home or abroad, players must dress neatly and behave like gentlemen.
- A penalty will be attached for any violation of the above rules.[41]

These rules certainly cannot be considered severe, and Hanlon's decision to publish them clearly indicates that some of the Orioles were not adhering to the very basics of reasonable behavior that he, or any other competent manager, would expect from professional ball players. It can be surmised that because Hanlon thought these expectations were so obvious, he had not declared them immediately upon becoming manager. Unfortunately for some of the more recalcitrant players, more drastic methods than rule cards would be needed in order to establish the winning culture that Hanlon demanded.

First, in mid–July, Hanlon released the Orioles' talented center fielder, Curt Welch, whose uncontrollable love of the bottle had previously caused him to wear out his welcome with both the Browns and the Athletics. The problem continued in Baltimore, and Hanlon let him go because, as one reporter colorfully put it, Welch "was addicted to the worship of Bacchus."[42]

In early August, left fielder Jocko Halligan, whom Hanlon signed in late May, sucker-punched second baseman Cub Stricker in the team's Boston hotel, breaking his cheekbone. Stricker was unable to play for more than a week, and although Halligan was immediately remorseful, Hanlon suspended him without pay for the remainder of the season and sent him home.[43]

Another serious frustration for Hanlon, and for Orioles fans as well, was the increasingly uninspired play of ex-manager George Van Haltren. Likely upset at being relieved as manager, one of the best players in the game was dropping easy fly balls, on purpose it seemed to many, and running the bases with what appeared to be complete indifference. It became so bad that a *Baltimore Sun* article was titled "Wake Up, Van Haltren" and stated that the previous day, Van Haltren was loudly jeered by fans when he "gave an exhibition on how not to run the bases" and that his "peculiar actions" on the base paths were largely responsible for the Orioles' loss to Philadelphia.[44]

About three weeks later, Van Haltren's lazy base running habits had not seemed to abate, as indicated by the publication of a scathing poem:

Van Won't Slide

They all went out to see the game
  The people love so well;
'Twas feared the contest would be fierce,
  The birds all looked so well.
The crowds were much excited when
  The ball flew far and wide;
Out went the side, by thunder, 'cause
  Van Haltren wouldn't slide.
They nagged him up on richer feed
  And humored him in style;
They begged him and entreated him
  And offered him a pile.
They threatened him and "lawed" him
  And they said he was a "snide"—
It was no use, the club got licked,
  Van Haltren wouldn't slide.

> They took him to the wooly West
>   To give him change of air,
> Likewise to lose a few more games
>   To free their minds from care.
> Then they got mad and sent him home
>   His head in shame to hide,
> So now he plays no ball at all,
>   Because he wouldn't slide.
>   TAILENDER[45]

As is evidenced repeatedly in the press coverage of the time, George Van Haltren had clearly demonstrated for quite some time that he had absolutely no interest in playing for the Orioles. Everyone in the stands could see it, the newspaper reporters could see it, and of course, Hanlon could see it. Finally, Hanlon forced the moment to its crisis when Van Haltren "acted like a dead man" in a game, and the umpire had to chastise him for holding up the game because he was moving so slowly to get into position. Hanlon confronted Van Haltren after the game and told him that he was sending him home. Van Haltren replied, "That suits me."[46]

Yet Van Haltren wasn't the only problem for Hanlon. On the same day that the *Sun* reported his suspension, it also reported that some of the players sympathized with Van Haltren. But through it all, and through all that was to come, Von der Horst publicly stated his commitment to Hanlon and refused to listen to appeals by players who came to him with complaints about their manager. For their part, the local press firmly declared their approval for the firmness Hanlon and Von der Horst were showing in their discipline of unruly players.[47]

The plight of the Orioles was quickly descending into farce, and the fans were getting increasingly disenchanted. This can be illustrated by an incident when a small boy went to the *Baltimore Sun* office and handed in a sheet of note paper which recounted a description of a cracker-eating contest among his friends which he hoped to have the paper publish. The *Sun* sarcastically suggested that this was the type of contest that the Orioles should consider entering, since "they cannot play ball" and it would be "a pastime in which they would be peerless."[48]

When the Orioles returned from the western road trip, Hanlon was surprised to find George Van Haltren waiting for him in uniform in the Union Park clubhouse. Van Haltren expressed his desire to return to the team, and he promised Hanlon that he would play better ball. Hanlon took the high road, whether he privately believed Van Haltren or not, and told him that he was glad to hear him say so. Hanlon promised that if he did play well, all that happened in the past would be forgotten, but he warned Van Haltren that he expected him to set a good example for the team. He cautioned him that if he failed to live up to his word, he would be suspended without pay.[49]

Considering Hanlon's practical and realistic nature, it is doubtful that he believed that Van Haltren would be a new man and play up to his capabilities. He had to realize that this was just a temporary fix and that as long as Van Haltren was on the team, he was be a disease that would infect the club. Hanlon, ever mindful of the big picture, allowed Van Haltren to return, no doubt with the hope that he could stay on the team long enough for Hanlon to trade him.

During an early September series in Pittsburgh, while rumors swirled that Hanlon was about to make a deal to send Van Haltren to the Pirates, a number of other unpleasant incidents occurred. First, Sadie McMahon became enraged when he found that two days' pay had been deducted from his paycheck for games he had missed without getting permission from Hanlon. He threatened to "punch Ned's head," but instead angrily stormed out of the room. Hanlon also notified pitcher George Cobb that he was being given his ten-day release. Cobb's wife, who was present at the game, rushed into the office, where she told Hanlon in no uncertain terms what she thought of him personally. Finally, Sadie McMahon and pitcher Tom Vickery, both drunk, spoke with some Pirates players and gave "a bright red account" of their treatment by Hanlon.

It is interesting to note that the Pirates players were not sympathetic to the complaints, and after the drunk Baltimore pitchers left, one of the Pittsburgh players said, "I don't think Hanlon is as much to blame as these fellows assert, and there is certainly an effort being made by some of the players of the Baltimore team to cause him as much trouble as possible. It was rather significant when Van Haltren talked last night of leaving the team."[50]

When word of the drunken players' statements to the Pirates reached Hanlon, he described the McMahon situation in a statement to the press:

> McMahon absented himself from the club recently when he was expected to pitch against St. Louis, and on the following day when he reported for duty, he was not in proper condition to work. At that time, I fined McMahon two days pay. McMahon caused a scene by calling at baseball headquarters, where he was forthwith suspended. Pitcher Vickery absented himself on another occasion. He came to the clubhouse, but Captain [Harry] Stovey soon disposed of him….I was engaged to get a winning team for Baltimore and I mean to do it if possible. The first requisite for such an organization is discipline and concerted work. Some of the players seem to think that base-ball is only an amusement. They do not seem to realize the great amount of money invested in the game, and they think they can do as they please. Baseball is as much a business as any mercantile pursuit. The players are paid very well for the little expected of them in return. They are supposed to be in condition for about six months in the year, and McMahon seldom pitched more than two games a week. If any clerk in a banking or business establishment acted in the way that McMahon has done he would be dealt with more summarily than was the pitcher.[51]

Hanlon's description of McMahon as not being in condition to work was a euphemism for being drunk, and the press reported more directly that McMahon and Vickery were released because "they were indulging too freely in the flowing bowl."[52] Player drinking was a problem that Hanlon had tried unsuccessfully to eliminate in his Pittsburgh managerial tenure, but this time he had ownership's support, and he was committed to curtailing it in Baltimore. However, it was not just drunkenness that McMahon was guilty of, it was flagrant insubordination as well. So Hanlon dropped the hammer on McMahon, and he suspended him for the final 22 games of the season.

It was a tough stand to take with a star player who had been a workhorse for the team since the day he arrived in Baltimore. Just the year before, McMahon had a spectacular year for a winning Orioles team when he led the league in games pitched (60), games started (57), innings pitched (509), and wins (36). In 1892 the team, and McMahon's results, declined. McMahon was described that year as a good pitcher but also as someone who soon was disgusted by poor defense behind him.[53] Indeed, the 1892 Orioles led the league in errors with 584 in 152 games.

The team's poor play, and its inevitable effect on McMahon's pitching, may very well at least partially explain the frustrations that led to his confrontation with Hanlon. A fierce competitor like McMahon had to be greatly peeved to watch his team boot balls all over the field while he was throwing his arm out on the mound. His record of 19–25 in 1892 was more indicative of a bad team than a bad pitcher. It would be enough to drive any pitcher to drink, although McMahon never needed encouragement in that area even in the best of times.

Later events would clearly demonstrate that Hanlon knew McMahon's value and wanted to keep him, but things had reached the point where Hanlon had to take firm action. This move sent a very clear signal to the rest of the Orioles that Hanlon was serious about seeing that his expectations were met.

Once McMahon was suspended, a shortage of pitchers made Hanlon retract George Cobb's release and also reinstate Tom Vickery, but the two would provide little help to the floundering team. After the disastrous weekend in Pittsburgh, Cobb went 0–7 in his remaining starts, and his record for 1892 was an awful 10–37. It was his only year in the big leagues. Tom Vickery finished at 8–10 and was released at the end of the season.

It seems that not only McMahon and Vickery were regularly overindulging in drink. Just a few days after they were suspended, it was reported that the Orioles "seem[s] to have had more trouble with its players getting drunk than any other club in the league this season."[54]

Throughout the country, the press reported that some Orioles players were demoralized and complaining bitterly of Hanlon's treatment of them and that Hanlon had been hissed by the home crowd when he appeared in the coaching box.[55] Finally, in late September both Hanlon and Van Haltren would get what they both desperately wanted: to be rid of each other. Hanlon traded Van Haltren to Pittsburgh for the virtually unknown outfielder Joe Kelley and

"Handsome" Joe Kelley patrolled left field for the Orioles and was one of their most popular players. He was called the "Kingpin" of the Orioles.

$2,000. In doing so, Hanlon made the first of the many crafty, one-sided trades that he orchestrated over the years that earned him the nickname "Foxy Ned." In succeeding years, Hanlon would make many transactions that haunted his trade partners and made them afraid to deal with him. As one baseball historian wrote, "In judging men, and swapping ball players, Hanlon had moments akin to clairvoyance."[56]

When the trade was announced, Hanlon publicly complimented Van Haltren as being a great player, but he also did not pull any punches when he said that his poor baserunning and his propensity for dropping easy fly balls had cost the Orioles a number of close games. Hanlon said that he saw potential in Kelley, and he predicted that he would be popular with the fans. He summed up the situation by saying, "It's better to have a good ballplayer than a great one who, for some reason, doesn't play as well as he should."[57]

Baseball fans in Baltimore were shocked by the trade of Van Haltren. In spite of his recent unmotivated play, he was widely regarded throughout the league as a star. The thought of trading him for an unknown and inexperienced player made some people think that Hanlon did not know what he was doing. However, Hanlon saw that Kelley was fast, was aggressive at the bat and on the base paths, and displayed power. He saw a ballplayer who needed instruction in the fundamentals, but he also recognized that Kelly had an indominable spirit and a burning desire to win.[58]

In 1912, Hanlon looked back on that trade and said, "Some of the Baltimore fans did not like the trade very much, but I kept quiet. Of course, everyone knows how Van Haltren went downhill and Kelley became one of the greatest outfielders in the country."[59] Hanlon's contention that Van Haltren went downhill after leaving the Orioles is not accurate. In 1893, Van Haltren hit .338 for the Pirates. He went on to play 10 years with the Giants, where he had eight straight seasons with an average of .300 or higher. In a 17-year career, he collected 2,544 hits with a .316 batting average. Nevertheless, Hanlon can be forgiven for his pride in the deal for Kelley, someone who became known as the "Kingpin" of the Orioles and ended up in the Hall of Fame.

At first, it looked like the trade might fall through. Kelley refused to report to Baltimore because he had heard rumors that the team was about to drop out of the league due to financial problems. Hanlon made a special trip to Kelley's home, and when he convinced him that Baltimore was remaining in the league, he agreed to report.[60]

The Orioles struggled on, and they ended the season with a 46–105–5 record. At the end of the year, Hanlon realized that a near-total make-over of the team would be necessary, and more money would be needed to sign players of quality. For Von der Horst, however, money was a problem. His spending ability was still being impeded by his father, and the Orioles only managed to draw 93,589 fans for the entire season, the lowest total in the league.

Hanlon was ready to provide a solution to the problem. During his time as a player and manager, he had been careful with his money, and he had a knack for successfully investing in real estate and other business enterprises. He had amassed quite a sum of money for an athlete of that period, and as a result, he was in a financial position to invest personally in the Orioles.

At a meeting of the club's board of directors on March 14, 1893, Harry Von der Horst stepped down as president, stating that the job was interfering with his responsibilities at the brewery. Hanlon was elected the new president, and he made a deal with Von der Horst in which he loaned the club $7,000. Von der Horst gave Hanlon a quarter of the stock in the club as collatoral.[61] Hanlon had not only taken full control of the club as president and manager, but he also became a significant financial investor in the club and infused the organization with much-needed cash.

* * *

With all the changes that were occurring at a break-neck pace both on and off the field, the Baltimore writers and players besieged Von der Horst with questions, but he had had enough of the day-to-day responsibilities of running the ball club and responded, "I'm tired of the players coming to me with their complaints. Let them take their beef to the new boss, Hanlon. Anyway, he knows more about baseball, and I know more about beer."[62] Moreover, Von der Horst wore a button that he had specially made that said, "Ask Hanlon," and he pointed to it whenever confronted with questions or complaints about the ball club.[63]

Through his indominable force of will and his singular and steady purpose, Ned Hanlon had survived the tumultuous 1892 season. He had had to deal with some players who were not of major league quality, and some players who were unprofessional, undisciplined, and insubordinate. He had to control a poisonous team attitude that festered in a back-stabbing clubhouse, unfavorable and ridiculing coverage in the press, and even the harangue of an angry player's wife.

But he had survived.

And finally, things were about to get better.

4

Building a Champion (1893)

As he prepared for the 1893 season, Ned Hanlon was busy at work trying to find players to fill out his roster. He knew that Robinson would be his catcher, Kelley would be in the outfield, and McGraw could play somewhere, but he wasn't sure where. He wanted Billy Shindle to play third base and Sadie McMahon to pitch, but there was no certainty that either would sign. And if Hanlon ultimately took McMahon back from his suspension, the pitcher would have to assure Hanlon that he would toe the line.

Hanlon had to find five of his eight starting position players, a back-up catcher for Robinson, bench players, and a pitching staff. At this time in baseball history, there were no scouting departments; instead, managers relied on word-of-mouth recommendations from knowledgeable baseball contacts to help them spot potential players to sign. Danny Long, an old friend of Hanlon's, saw catcher Bill "Boileryard" Clarke and second baseman Henry "Heinie" Reitz play in California, and he recommended both players to him.[1] Hanlon signed them, and they would prove to be valuable acquisitions. Boileryard Clarke, as his nickname suggests, was a perfect fit for the tough, unrelenting style for which the team became famous, and it was said that he was "not one of those catchers who thinks he has done wonders if he

Although he looks cocky in this photograph, Heinie Reitz was a quiet man who was a good, if not spectacular second baseman. A teammate said that he only said three things in a season, but they were all funny (Babe Ruth Birthplace & Museum).

catches two games in one day once in a while."² Reitz turned out to be a solid contributor to the Orioles for five years, but in a sad twist of fate, the unfortunate Reitz would be the first major league player to be killed in an automobile accident when he was hit by a car in Sacramento, California, in 1914.³

Hanlon also re-signed some of the players from the 1892 team. Harry Stovey, an outfielder who was captain of the Orioles in 1892, had written to Hanlon in February, saying, "I feel like a fish out of water when I am not in base-ball, and so I want to be with you."⁴ Stovey, who was 36 years old in 1893, was nearing the end of a good 14-year career during which he accumulated 1,175 hits and had a career .288 batting average. Hanlon signed him and again named him captain.

In addition to Stovey, Hanlon also re-signed outfielder Tim O'Rourke and pitcher Crazy Schmit, then signed a number of new players including outfielders George Treadway and Jim Long and pitchers Kirtley Baker, Jack Wadsworth, and Edward McNabb.

Some of the players Hanlon signed would play very few games for the team that year; in fact, 25 players would take the field in an Orioles uniform in 1893, but 11 of them played fewer than 25 games before either being released or traded. Ned Hanlon found, although he likely already knew it, that to find players who were princes in baseball, you have to kiss a great many frogs.

Hanlon's team was slowly coming together, and people in the baseball world started to take notice and applaud the steps he was taking to improve the club. *Sporting Life* declared that having young players on the team boded well for future success because young players "use all their power to make a favorable impression, whereas the older players are far too prone to swelled heads and indifference."⁵ Although most observers did not go so far as to predict the Orioles to be pennant winners, many regarded them as a team which would acquit themselves much better than in the past.

The steely steadfastness that Hanlon had displayed in dealing with the group of disgruntled and unprofessional players in the past season also impressed many. Harry Von der Horst was also roundly applauded for taking the "wise and bold stroke" to make Hanlon President of the club as well as manager:

> The boys will all know that what Hanlon says "goes," and go it will...in fact it always did, but while there was a superior over him there was a constant temptation to appeal to him and a perpetual hope that he might in some way be downed. Hence cliques and contentions and bickerings and backbitings and a general chewing up with a perpetual fracas and a world-without-end-everlasting fight. No more of that business now. It is play ball or quit altogether....Hanlon pulls the stroke oar, and all will have to keep time and catch no crabs.⁶

In a published analysis of each of the prospective players for the upcoming season, it is worth noting the comments made about John McGraw, if for no other reason than to imagine just how it must have piqued the very paragon of "Little Man Syndrome" when he first read it:

> We know that little cherub, McGraw, can play second base and be quick and active about it. We know he can sneak in his little hit and garner his little self on the initial base quite semi-occasionally, and, no doubt, he will do it this year much better than he did last season, for you must know he is quite an infant yet. He can't vote yet and he can't buy any beer in the good places where they stick up signs that they won't sell to minors. So Two-Bag-Mack will have to drink milk and play ball for all his little anatomy is worth.⁷

* * *

As spring training approached, there were still two players holding out. The first was third baseman Billy Shindle, who had briefly been a teammate of Hanlon's with the Detroit Wolverines and who had a solid year with the Orioles in 1892. The issue was that Shindle had successful business interests in Philadelphia, and throughout the off-season he repeatedly said that he would prefer to attend to those businesses rather than re-sign for the salary reduction that had been previously imposed on all the Orioles. Regardless of the fact that Shindle was playing hard-to-get, Hanlon wanted him badly enough that he went to Philadelphia after the season opened and convinced him to sign.[8] No terms were disclosed, and Shindle was back in the lineup for the Orioles in the sixth game of the season.

Sadie McMahon, on the other hand, was holding out for reasons that likely centered around issues of pride more than salary. No doubt McMahon was still stewing over his suspension, and when he realized that Hanlon's authority was not to be challenged, it is conceivable that he was debating whether he wanted to play for him.

There is no question that Hanlon wanted McMahon on his team, but he wanted him on his own terms. Hanlon had a clear vision of the type of team he was trying to build, and he must have seen that besides his undisputed talent, McMahon had other intrinsic traits that would help transform the Orioles into winners. Nevertheless, Hanlon could not show weakness in trying to bring McMahon back into the fold—he certainly couldn't travel to McMahon's home and try to convince him to sign as he did with Shindle. Because of the reserve clause, Hanlon had leverage. McMahon would either play for the Orioles or he would be unable to play for any other major league team. To complicate McMahon's bargaining position, he did not have a successful business to fall back on to make a living as Shindle did, and there was also no question that the fans and the press universally denounced McMahon's behavior in 1892 as reprehensible.

Throughout the off-season, Hanlon's public stance with McMahon had not wavered, but by mid–February, he had not shut the door completely on McMahon when he declared, "If McMahon expresses a desire to come to terms and do his best for us in the box, he will be added to the list of pitchers."[9] Finally, on March 17, right before the Orioles left for spring training in Charleston, McMahon made his peace with Hanlon and signed a contract with the team.[10]

When the situation between Hanlon and McMahon is considered, it can be argued that it reveals something important about the character of both men. Hanlon showed no compunction in dealing strictly, if not ruthlessly, with discipline problems, yet the fact that he took back McMahon and did not simply trade him away as he did with Van Haltren cannot be solely attributed to the fact that McMahon was a star pitcher. As he had with so many players in his career, the feisty John McGraw being a notable example, Hanlon seemed to be able to see not only the physical talent a player had, but also the redeeming character traits that he possessed. He had to see something in McMahon that made him feel that his previous behavior did not reflect the man he truly was. To at least a small degree, Hanlon swallowed his pride and took back a player who had challenged his authority in the most egregious fashion, and to do this demonstrates a willingness to put aside whatever personal feelings he may have had for the good of the team. This sense of self-sacrifice became something that would define Hanlon as a manager and something he would instill in his players. Most importantly of all, it demonstrates that Hanlon possessed a self-assurance and confidence that are the marks of a strong leader.

On the other hand, the situation also reveals something crucial about Sadie

4. Building a Champion (1893)

McMahon. It had to be no easy task for a man of McMahon's temperament to overcome his wounded pride after a very public suspension and the myriad attacks on him in the press. He was certainly not a stupid or unconscionable man, so he had to have realized that his behavior had been unacceptable, and he was able to summon up the fortitude to at least tacitly admit it by coming to an understanding with Hanlon.

How the two men ultimately resolved their differences is unknown. Perhaps Wilbert Robinson, a friend and teammate of McMahon since their Philadelphia Athletics days, had a hand in the reconciliation. Robinson may have been acting as a go-between between Hanlon and McMahon when he had telegraphed McMahon and encouraged him to join the team in spring training.[11] Regardless of how it happened, both Hanlon and McMahon showed the ability to forgive and forget, and there was no evident blot on their relationship in the future other than the normal squabbling about salary that most Orioles would have with the tight-fisted Hanlon. They were both big enough men that for the rest of their relationship, they honored whatever agreement was made behind closed doors. That is a credit to them both.

* * *

Hanlon found time before he left for spring training to attend a reunion in New York with many of the travelers who went on Albert Goodwill Spalding's World Tour. They dined together and went afterward to see William Gillette's play, *Ninety Days*, which was inspired in part by their tour. The play concerns a young heiress who takes a long sea voyage to Burma, and the players had a mass cameo appearance as traveling ballplayers who come to the rescue of the young woman. A good time was reportedly had by all.[12]

Before Hanlon arrived in Baltimore, the Orioles had not taken any spring training jaunts to the South for financial reasons but instead had worked out in Union Park, weather permitting, and indoors at Johns Hopkins University when it didn't. Hanlon, however, insisted on taking the team to South Carolina for spring training in 1893.[13]

The Orioles' spring training trip garnered attention in the national press, and it was hailed as a way to get the team into condition and stir up interest in the Baltimore community for the upcoming season. *Sporting Life* was effusive in praising Hanlon for the job he was doing with a club that performed woefully and disgracefully in the past year and for the nerve and wisdom he used in handling the issues with Van Haltren and McMahon. It expressed admiration for how Hanlon had "convinced the players that they have no ordinary man to deal with, and that, there must necessarily be a rigid discipline. The season of 1892 was then a preparatory school for that of 1893 ... and that all must play ball. The manager will press the button and the players will do the rest."[14]

The Orioles arrived in Charleston on March 19, and there Hanlon began to whip his players into peak physical condition. In morning and afternoon sessions, he began to drill his charges in the tactics ultimately known as Scientific Baseball, or Inside Baseball. Hanlon continued with daily practices for a week, and these were followed by three practice games in Charleston. Hanlon was happy with the work of his players, and he specifically mentioned that he was impressed with second baseman Heinie Reitz's ability to throw from any position and with the amount of ground that he could cover.[15] As the team wound its way back north for the start of the season, they played practice games in Savannah, Macon, Atlanta, Chattanooga, Nashville, Louisville, and Cincinnati.[16]

By April 19, the Orioles were back at Union Park for their first practice on their home grounds. Four hundred enthusiastic fans watched as the players practiced for 30 minutes in the manner customary before a game. After that, Hanlon and Captain Stovey worked on various plays to improve teamwork and base running.[17] They continued to practice and play exhibition games until the season opener at Washington.

After he returned to Baltimore, Hanlon was enthusiastic about the upcoming season, and he confidently predicted that the Orioles would be stronger than any team Baltimore ever had. He would not predict that they would win the pennant, but he felt his youngsters would perform well and surprise the other clubs in the league. He also announced that the players had come out of their Southern training in good shape and without sore arms because he had instructed them to be careful not to overexert themselves. Hanlon concluded by waxing nostalgic: "The players remind me of the old-time champion Detroit club. They are like one big, happy family. They play together, and if one happens to make a misplay the others pull together and try their utmost to regain the lost chance and help out their comrade."[18]

The work that began in spring training did not end when the players arrived back in Baltimore, and Hanlon continued to work with the team collectively and provided individual instruction. Because he was obtained so late in the season, Joe Kelley had only played 10 games for the Orioles in 1892. Hanlon would make him his personal project in 1893. Every morning, Hanlon took Kelley to Union Park to work on his outfield play and to instruct him in "the finer points of hitting and bunting."[19] Hanlon's work with Kelley would pay off. Beginning in 1893, he hit over .300 for 11 consecutive seasons, with a high of .393 in 1894. Kelley played 11 years for Hanlon in Baltimore, Brooklyn, and Cincinnati in a career that would lead to the National Baseball Hall of Fame.

Not only was he a great ball player, but Joseph James Kelley was also quite a character. He had an engaging personality and he was a handsome, well-built young man with dirty blonde hair parted stylishly down the middle. It was said that he kept a mirror in his pocket when he was stationed in the outfield so he could constantly check to make sure his hair was perfectly arranged with a bang displayed below the front of his cap. Hanlon proved correct in his assertion that Baltimore would love Kelley—he certainly was a hit with Baltimore ladies, and they "loved him almost as much as he loved himself."[20]

* * *

The Orioles certainly seemed ready and eager, and then, unfortunately, the season began. In the opener on April 27 against the Washington Senators at Boundary Field, McMahon was on the losing end of a 7–5 score, and the next day, the Senators beat newcomer Jack Wadsworth, 12–6. Wadsworth went 0–3 for the Orioles while being hit hard, and Hanlon quickly released him.

After the games in Washington, the team played its home opener on April 29 and won their first game of the season when they outlasted the Senators, 8–6, behind Crazy Schmit. Then they lost three straight, rebounded to win four straight, and generally continued this streaky pattern of slightly subpar mediocrity for the rest of the season. They did flirt with a winning record for about a month and a half, and on June 16, they were 22–20, their high-water mark for the season.

Despite the uneven play that characterized the team's season, the Orioles showed significant improvement, and there were a number of reasons for Orioles fans to be optimistic. There was nearly universal agreement that Joe Kelley was destined to have a bright future. Fans were impressed with his exceptional ball-catching skills, his strong throwing arm, and his adroit ability to handle the bat. Heinie Reitz was lauded for his excellent defensive abilities, and Boileryard Clarke earned kudos for his strong throwing arm.[21]

John McGraw was also getting attention, but not all of it was complimentary. Although he was generally regarded as a good player, he was beginning to exhibit the rowdy behavior for which he would become famous. He was taken to task for spouting profane language which was offensive to the women in the grandstand, and his antics were said to reflect poorly on his club, Hanlon, and his captain.[22]

In April, St. Louis Browns owner Chris Von der Ahe offered pitcher Bill Hawke, with whom he had a strained relationship, to Hanlon for $500. Hanlon refused the offer, but when Von der Ahe released Hawke in May, Hanlon scooped him up, and around the same time, he released the ineffective Crazy Schmit. Hawke proved to be steady, but not overly impressive, as he compiled an 11–16 record in 29 games. The headstrong Hawke butted heads with Robinson over pitch calls, and the *Baltimore Sun* firmly sided with Robbie on the issue: "If Hawke would follow Robinson's instructions as to what kind of balls to pitch he would be fifty percent more effective than he is."[23]

Whether or not he was paying attention to Robinson's pitch calls on August 16, Hawke made history when he was the first pitcher to throw a no-hitter from the new pitching distance of 60 feet, six inches, when he blanked Washington, 5–0.[24]

In May it was reported that captain Harry Stovey wanted to be released because he was not getting enough playing time. Hanlon's response was to say that the club was playing well, and he didn't see why he should make a change in his outfield configuration.[25] Just a few days later, Stovey got his wish and was released after playing just eight games, during which he hit .158. After the Orioles released him, he was picked up by Brooklyn, and it would be his last year in the major leagues.

By late May, the Orioles were attracting attention for their energetic and enthusiastic play:

> The Orioles do not know how to quit. Errors? Lots of 'em. Weak hitting sometimes? plenty of it; but the gall and cheek of those youngsters are such that they really do not realize when they are beaten, and so keep at the game with unflagging interest, and occasionally win it in the last inning by sheer persistence that they are not so badly licked as appearances would indicate. They can all say what they like, but that is a thrilling little team....It makes no difference in the result whether this is due to the force of character of Mr. Hanlon or whether it is a cheerful acquiescence by the men; the fact remains that there is intelligent direction and a corresponding effect.[26]

In early June, Hanlon made another brilliant move when he persuaded Louisville Colonels manager Billy Barnie to trade shortstop Hugh "Hughie" Ambrose Jennings and first baseman Harry Taylor to the Orioles for outfielder Tim O'Rourke. At the time of the trade, Jennings was hitting a dismal .136 in 23 games for Louisville. Fred Lieb rather fancifully recreates the conversation between Hanlon and Barnie that resulted in the Jennings trade:

> Hanlon arranged to have a few beers with Barnie after the game. Making conversation, Ned said, "That noisy freckle-face you have playing shortstop isn't hitting a lick, is he?"
>
> Barnie agreed heartily. "He couldn't hit a barn with a paddle," he griped.
>
> "Maybe I could teach him something about hitting," continued Ned. "Want to fix up some kind of deal?"

Barnie, little suspecting that he was to play the role of a kindly Santa Claus, was all ears. "I'm listening, Ned," he said. "What've you got to offer?"

"I might let you have Tim O'Rourke and Bill Brown if you'd let us have Jennings and ... [first baseman] Harry Taylor."

Barnie grabbed Hanlon's hand before Ned had a chance to change his mind.

"It's a deal," he said happily.[27]

O'Rourke, known as "Voiceless Tim" for his quiet nature, was hitting .363 at the time of the trade. He was popular among Baltimore fans, and earlier in the season, when there were rumors that Hanlon was looking to trade him, Hanlon received many letters requesting that O'Rourke remain with the Orioles. O'Rourke did not wish to leave Baltimore, but he finally agreed once he was offered $100 more in pay.[28]

Some Baltimore fans seriously questioned the trade; however, by 1895 both O'Rourke and Brown would be out of the League, and Hanlon's Orioles would have the shortstop of their championship years in place. As was often his habit with younger players, Hanlon took his time inserting Jennings into the lineup with any regularity. He liked to take his time in evaluating young players. He wanted not only to give them time to develop the skills he expected of an Oriole, but also to see how the player interacted with his teammates.[29] This was one of the strategies that would help Hanlon create a sense of cohesive teamwork within the club. Although Jennings only hit .255 in 16 games with the Orioles, the fans quickly changed their minds about the deal by mid–July, when it was reported that "Jennings is one of the most popular of all of the Orioles now."[30]

When he was not playing, Jennings assumed the role of third base coach.[31] He displayed an energetic and animated style while in the box, continually encouraging his teammates and "smoothing down the fretful player, and at the same time, apologizing to the stands for the superb idiotic 'rottenness' of the umpire."[32] Jennings was admired for his excellent judgment regarding when to send or hold runners, and for his ability to keep baserunners alert.[33]

Throughout the month of June, Hanlon continued his wheeling and dealing ways. On June 4, in anticipation of the trade for Jennings and Taylor, Hanlon released first baseman Jocko Milligan, which cleared the way for Taylor to take over that position. Rumors had circulated in the press that Milligan was leading McMahon astray, and that most certainly could explain why Hanlon decided to nip the problem in the bud. He was not about to go down the 1892 road again if he could help it.[34]

On June 16, the Orioles traded second baseman/outfielder Piggy Ward and $1,500 to Cincinnati for pitcher Tony Mullane. Mullane, nicknamed "The Count" and the "Apollo of the Box," had a reputation for being popular with the ladies. He was the first ambidextrous pitcher in the history of major league baseball and had played briefly in his first year in the majors with Hanlon in Detroit. From 1882 through 1884 and in 1886 and 1887, he won over 30 games each year. In 1892, he won 21 games for the Reds, but by the next year, it was reported that Mullane "has outlived his usefulness in this city, and, no matter what ability he may possess, he is of little use if he does not show a desire to do the best for his club."[35]

Mullane was 34 years old when he was traded to the Orioles, and with him Ned Hanlon was rolling the dice. Despite Mullane's excellence as a pitcher,[36] he had been fined and suspended from baseball for a year in 1885 for repeated contract jumping; he was a regular holdout regarding salary issues; and most seriously of all, he was implicated, although later cleared, in a scheme to throw games. Mullane seemed to be precisely the type of player that Hanlon had been trying to rid himself of in the past year. There was concern in the press that Mullane might disrupt the harmonious team Hanlon had put together. Nevertheless, most observers remained confident that Hanlon knew what he was doing, and in his ability to handle players.[37]

Hanlon, however, was desperate for pitching because as the season progressed, Sadie McMahon and, to a limited degree, Bill Hawke, were the only two pitchers that he could count on. As it turned out, Hanlon's gamble paid off as Mullane was an innings-eater that year, throwing 244⅔ in 34 games. He put together a 12–16 record for the Orioles while keeping them in most games that he pitched, and equally important, he had behaved himself in 1893.

While these transactions were taking place, the Orioles were playing much better ball, but after reaching their high-water mark on June 22, they began a disastrous 21-game road trip that began in Philadelphia. On the trip, the Orioles only managed to win five games, and they had fallen nine wins under .500 by the time it was over.

While struggling on the road trip, Hanlon felt the need to give the team a pep talk in a meeting in his hotel room on June 29 in Louisville, possibly to mitigate uneasiness that may have been taking place because of the rapid-fire player moves he had been making all season. He gave them "a useful lecture of a half hour's duration," and in his remarks to the team he complimented McGraw's excellent work and told the players that he did not anticipate making any further changes to the lineup. He expected that they would play better for the rest of the year and that next year they would be in position to compete for the pennant.[38]

It was also obvious that the atmosphere around the team had changed drastically from 1892. Even though the team struggled at times and players were making some frustrating mistakes, especially in base running, team spirit was high. Instead of the back-biting and the bitter and demoralizing cliques, the players openly encouraged one another and exhibited all the signs of a harmonious group. The team was filled with lively characters such as Kelley, Jennings, and McGraw, and even some of the more restrained individuals, such as Heinie Reitz, fit in well. It was later said of Reitz that "he'd say maybe three sentences a season, but all of them funny."[39]

Some credit for the new Orioles harmony certainly has to go to the veteran leadership of Robinson, who knew how disruptive self-serving behavior could be, and who helped build a sense of team in a group of ambitious young players who were trying to prove themselves. But the lion's share of the credit for building a good team chemistry went to Hanlon. He had to identify players who not only had talent, but also had winning and unselfish attitudes. Moreover, he had to find talented players who may have had checkered pasts, but whom he felt he could redeem. Finally, he had to provide the steady hand to allow his players some rein, yet pull on those reins when it was necessary. He had to create an environment where strong-willed individuals like McGraw and McMahon could thrive within a cohesive group. The turnaround of the Orioles did not go unnoticed in the baseball world:

> Ned is a great field marshal....Nothing succeeds like success, they say...but how about the manager who succeeds without success? Ned Hanlon does that...[he] picked up a team of young unknowns on his own judgment entirely, and in the first part of their first season has them playing the prettiest ball on the diamond to-day and all pulling for the club in perfect harmony, with only a small average of success in winning games. Is not that great generalship? There would be no particular merit in winning a pennant with a team composed

of all the stars in the base ball firmament, but there is considerable in keeping a team of light youngsters hanging on like grim life to the tail of the first division....Baltimoreans appreciate such things as this and are proud of their crisp little team and its brilliant manager.[40]

After Harry Stovey left the team, Wilbert Robinson became the captain, and the contributions he made to the future success of the Orioles cannot be underestimated. He hated to lose, and although he would not hesitate to point out the mistakes of his teammates, he would always direct the severest criticism at himself. He would not allow for self-serving excuses, and when some players began to blame base running miscues on the coachers, Robinson shut down that down quickly: "A runner ought to coach himself....The blaming of bad base-running on the coacher is overdone. The base-runner is supposed to have a head of his own, and should blame himself for stupid plays and not others."[41]

* * *

Hanlon had to feel he was coming closer and closer to the excellence that he demanded, but just when it seemed to come within reach, it darted away. McGraw wore his competitiveness as a flaming brand on his sleeve, but Hanlon's competitive fire burned deep within an outwardly reticent demeanor. In an interview after the team returned home, it is informative to hear Hanlon struggle to control his frustration at aspects of his team's performance, while at the same time accepting responsibility, complimenting his players, and expressing optimism for the future of the club:

> Of course, it is a disappointment to me and to the players. But for stupid base running we would have won about ten more games than we did...had not certain Orioles fallen into a trance as soon as they got on base....The Orioles are a good team. They field well enough and bat fairly well, but what is the use of getting on base if he falls asleep there and is caught napping so that he never scores? However, we will have to teach the players how to run the bases. When a manager gets together a club composed almost entirely of youngsters, it is a difficult matter to pick out a team excelling in everything. Most of the Orioles never played in the big leagues before this year, and despite the defeats of the Western trip I still have confidence in them. I believe before the season ends, they will be doing great work.[42]

After returning home, the team was warmly greeted by an enthusiastic crowd of over 2,500 fans who applauded each batter as he came to the plate. It was remarked that "it is very seldom, indeed, that a losing club is treated so handsomely, and it all illustrates the fact that home patrons believe in and admire them."[43] The team's relief at being back in a friendly and encouraging environment seemed to inspire them as they convincingly swept the Brooklyn Bridegrooms in the three-game home stand. During the series, their bats came to life and they scored nine, 10, and 12 runs while McMahon, Mullane, and Hawke picked up victories.

The brief home stand provided the team with only a short respite, and back on the road, they lost nine of 13 games. During a particularly tough stretch on the trip when the Orioles lost seven straight games, Hanlon was trying to put a different public face to the events and was said to be looking on the recent defeats "philosophically," while he optimistically predicted that the team would take over sixth or seventh place. He said, "With their hands they play as well as any club in the country, and next year I think they will play all around in a manner which will show they have learned something from experience."[44]

Hanlon was not alone in his optimism. Bill Watkins, Ned's old Detroit manager

4. Building a Champion (1893)   57

and now manager of the St. Louis Browns, said he would not be surprised if the Orioles finished high in the first division.[45] Pud Galvin, Hanlon's recently retired old teammate, said, "Those Orioles are a likely lot of hustlers, but it takes a couple of years to make pennant winners of a club composed almost entirely of youngsters as they are."[46] These men were well-acquainted with Hanlon's mettle and ability, so they had faith in him to put together a winning team.

Late in August, Hanlon made another of his "Foxy Ned" moves when he bought centerfielder Walter Scott "Steve" Brodie from the St. Louis Browns. Brodie had been given the nickname "Steve" in honor of a Bowery bartender named Steve Brodie who earned his 15 minutes of fame for surviving a jump from the Brooklyn Bridge.[47] Brodie was quite willing to come to Baltimore as he and Browns owner Chris Von der Ahe were not getting along. Brodie had fallen out of favor with Von der Ahe because he heard that Brodie was fostering discontent in the team. But that view was discounted by others who regarded Brodie "to be an inoffensive, decent little fellow, working for the interest of his club."[48]

Brodie was an excellent defensive center fielder who cut a hole in the center of his tiny glove because he preferred to catch the ball with his bare palm.[49] He was also known for having an innate ability to take off at the crack of the bat, turn his back to the infield, and end up in the exact spot where the ball would land.[50] This was a skill for which Hanlon was renowned in

Steve Brodie was the most eccentric of the Orioles, and among his many antics was the time during a game when he grabbed a ladder and climbed over the wall of the outfield to get at a heckler (Babe Ruth Birthplace & Museum).

his own playing days, so it is likely that Hanlon saw something in Brodie that reminded him of himself.

But as a personality, Brodie was nothing like Hanlon—he was a constant chatterbox who would sing, recite Shakespeare in the outfield, and banter with the fans, other players, and himself. It was reported that the only time he fell silent was when he made an error, and "as further punishment, he refused to speak to himself for the rest of the game."[51]

Many years later when he was manager of the New York Giants, McGraw described Brodie as "unconsciously funny. He didn't mean to be funny, and actually took baseball quite seriously. It was his efforts to be serious and to take everything in its full literal sense that made him so amusing to the rest of us on the ball club."[52] McGraw included him in his list of the most "picturesque characters of the game," along with such notables as Rube Waddell, Bugs Raymond, and Babe Ruth.[53]

Indeed, when obituaries of Steve Brodie were published throughout the country at the time of his death in 1935, they invariably referred to him as a famous player and a clown. An extremely durable player, he would set a nineteenth-century record by playing in 727 consecutive games. He also led all outfielders in fielding percentage three times, and he participated in more double plays than any other outfielder of the 1890s.[54]

As the season progressed, Hanlon received numerous requests from fans to see Jennings play, and he finally accommodated them by moving McGraw to left field and starting Jennings at shortstop on August 19 against Louisville. The Orioles won the game, 7–3, behind Bill Hawke, and although Jennings fielded flawlessly, he had an uneventful day at the plate, going hitless in three at-bats.

The Orioles ended the season in eighth place in the 12-team league with a record of 60–70, 20½ games behind the pennant-winning Beaneaters. It was a significant improvement over the 1892 record of 46–101–5 that left them in last place, 54½ games behind the league leader. Moreover, the Orioles seemed to finally solve their early problems on the road when they ended the season by winning nine of 15 road games, another precursor of good things to come.

Hanlon was often asked during and after the season to explain the team's poor play on the road, and he attributed it primarily to the inexperience of his young players. He felt that when they learned to play, they would be able to handle the pressures of the road and not be demoralized by an unfavorable call of an umpire or the derisive and hostile howling of the fans in their opponents' ball parks.[55] He also felt that the large number of losses on road trips might be the result of overeating because of all the delicacies at good hotels. He said that "when players ate more frugally at home and were just glad to get corn beef and cabbage, better ball playing would be the result."[56]

Overall, the Orioles made improvement in every statistical area, and the decline in errors was especially significant.

Year	Wins	BA	OBP	OPS	E	FLD %
1892	46	.254	.325	.668	584	.910
1893	60	.275	.359	.724	384	.929

A number of Orioles had outstanding individual seasons and were establishing reputations as stars. In 95 games, Wilbert Robinson hit .334, which was 63 points higher than he had ever hit in his previous nine years in the majors. He was described as having "a pleasant earnestness that is contagious...and [creates] a happy effect on the team." Throughout the season, he served as a role model for his hustling play, and he was all over the diamond, backing up first and third base and anywhere else it was needed. "Robbie is certainly worth a dozen games to the Orioles that they would not otherwise win."[57]

John McGraw hit .321 with an impressive .454 OBP and was admired throughout the league for his pluck, his lion-like heart, and his ability to rise to any occasion. He was constantly improving and, at just 20 years old, he was already considered one of the most reliable players in the game.[58]

Steve Brodie hit .361 and immediately became a fan favorite. "Handsome" Joe Kelley hit .305 and showed some power with a team-leading nine home runs, and had 22 assists. Sadie McMahon, the prodigal son, started 40 games, pitched 346⅓ innings, and recorded 23 wins against 18 losses—all for an inexperienced team that struggled mightily at times.

Yet even more important than all the individual and on-field improvements was the fact that Hanlon had dealt very successfully with the biggest obstacle the Orioles had to overcome: the disciplinary issues that had plagued the team in 1892.

Sporting Life also noticed the drastic change and said, "the Orioles are the best-behaved club Baltimore ever had. There were no ugly stories about town to detract from their merits ... and it is believed they merit all the good opinions that can be showered on them."[59] Sadie McMahon was even singled out for "trying his best, having a good heart, and being constantly encouraging and good-natured with his teammates."[60]

At the end of the season, Hanlon gave his state-of-the-team address to the press:

> The season as a whole, financially, has been a success for the Baltimore Club....As far as the playing of the team is concerned, I have no fault to find....During the last month the men played 100 per cent better ball than in the earlier months of the season because they are beginning to develop team work, which always requires time. Next year they will do a great deal better....At present it is too far in advance to talk definitely about next year, but I shall do all in my power to have Baltimore represented by a base ball club [of] which the local admirers of the game do not feel ashamed.[61]

* * *

Hanlon quickly went to work to find the players who could improve his club for the next season. He was noted for being a very low-key recruiter who did not make grandiose statements to the press and announce his pursuit of star players, as many other managers did. Instead, he quietly surveyed the field and closed deals suddenly. In many cases, no one was even aware of his interest in a particular player until the deal was done. This led to an additional name for Hanlon: "Silent Ned." The fans and the press were sometimes frustrated with Hanlon's close-to-the vest methods, but no one could argue with his results, so complaints were generally few.[62]

One of Hanlon's key off-season objectives was the improvement of the pitching staff. His philosophy was to put together a large group of good pitchers because he realized that they could suddenly become ineffective or end up with arm injuries. Gossip spread throughout the baseball press that Hanlon was in the market for three or four pitchers, including at least one left-hander.[63] He would indeed add a number of pitchers who would make major contributions to the 1894 campaign; however, most of them joined the team after the season was underway.

Billy Shindle's uneven play had caused tongues to wag that Hanlon was in the market for a new third baseman,[64] and there was also talk that Hanlon would leave McGraw at shortstop. In December, there were trade rumors that Hanlon was going to trade Jennings for Eastern League first baseman Jake Drauby to replace Harry Taylor, who left baseball to practice law. That trade would not materialize, and instead, Hanlon drafted shortstop Frank Bonner from the minor league Wilkes-Barre team.[65]

At the end of the year, there was much praise for the entire Orioles franchise and even the city of Baltimore. The young players were highly regarded for their never-say-die attitude and their scrappy and improved play. Harry Von der Horst was lauded for having the foresight to hire a man of Ned Hanlon's quality and for having the intestinal fortitude to stick by him through the dark times. The city of Baltimore, described as being "in the throes of a rapid transit craze," also received kudos for the increased electric and cable lines they constructed that transported fans to the ball park more quickly and comfortably. But the flattering press that Ned Hanlon received dwarfed it all.

Hanlon was widely credited with inspiring the Orioles with a remarkable "esprit de corps" and building a harmonious environment where the players were willing to make any sacrifice for the good of the club. He was acclaimed for possessing the skill and mettle necessary to take a group of men of disparate skills, temperaments, and personal interests and blend them into a cohesive unit with common objectives. Considering the state of the Orioles when Hanlon took over, observers found the results to be admirable, if not astounding.[66]

As the New Year loomed, Hanlon made another blockbuster trade that cemented his "Foxy Ned" reputation forever. He sent third baseman Billy Shindle and outfielder George Treadway to Brooklyn for his old Wolverines teammate, the famous slugger Dan Brouthers, and a scrawny five-foot-four-inch, left-handed third baseman named William Henry "Wee Willie" Keeler. Brouthers had played sparingly but effectively in 1893 with Brooklyn, and he was nearing the end of a 19-year career. Keeler had only played 41 major league games in two years with Brooklyn and the Giants.

In stating his motivations for the trade, Hanlon said, "I have come to the conclusion that batting is necessary to win games, and I propose to make next year's Baltimore Club second to none in that respect, even if some of the others excel in fielding. The old Detroit Club, which won the championship of the world, relied wholly upon stick-work. Most of its members were poor fielders." He further explained that Shindle's business interests could have resulted in his departure from baseball anyway, and that Treadway wished to play somewhere other than Baltimore.[67]

The deal provided two crucial players for the team that would win the 1894 pennant. In the words of John McGraw, "Manager Hanlon had given us the needed cog to our machine—the key to the combination that made the Orioles the most famous of ball clubs....It was certainly the greatest [trade] ever made by Hanlon—and he made many."[68]

Ned Hanlon and his wife, Ellen, were now the proud parents of two sons. Edward Kelley Hanlon was born in 1891, and Joseph Thomas Hanlon had just been born in March. In a short time, the Hanlon family had come to love Baltimore and to consider it their home.

Everything looked as if it was coming together for Ned Hanlon.

Indeed, because of the excellent group of like-minded players that he had assembled, and because of the innovative style of play which he would implement, Ned Hanlon was now poised to lead the Baltimore Orioles to baseball glory and eternal fame.

5

The Oriole Way
(Spring, 1894)

The addition of first baseman Dennis "Big Dan" Brouthers may not have seemed to make sense at first when compared to the type of player that Hanlon was signing during the past year. At 6'2" and over 200 pounds, he was a big man for that time, and Hanlon had spent the past year putting together a team of speedy and more agile men. Brouthers was renowned as a slugger with prodigious power and not adept at perfecting the small ball style of play that Hanlon would emphasize with his team. Nevertheless, Brouthers was an accomplished hitter who in his previous 13 years had hit over .300 every year, led the league in batting average five times and in slugging percentage seven times. Hanlon had placed an emphasis on youth, and Big Dan was 36 years old and the very definition of a grizzled old veteran.

Big Dan Brouthers was popular with both his teammates and the fans and was regarded as a man of integrity. Although he had performed well for Brooklyn in 1893, injuries had limited Brouthers to just 79 games, and there were concerns about his defensive mobility. Another potential problem with Brouthers was his alleged affinity for the bottle, and one press account felt that he could help the Orioles if he would hit the ball as well as he hit the bottle.[1]

Yet Hanlon's personal connection to Brouthers and the fact that he had proved that he could get the most out of his players generated hope that if anyone could revitalize Dan Brouthers' defensive play and keep him from overindulging, Hanlon could.[2]

William Henry "Wee Willie" Keeler was the wild card in the deal. In 21 games with the Giants, he hit .320, and after the Giants sold him to Brooklyn, he hit .313 in 20 games with them. However, at 5'4" and 140 pounds, it seems that both teams felt his small stature did not bode well for him. Both teams played the left-hander at third base the majority of the time, and he was error-prone and uncomfortable there. To add to his discomfort at that position, opposing batters took advantage of him by bunting often.

Brouthers was excited for the opportunity to reunite with his old teammate, and in a letter to Hanlon, he assured him that he was in excellent condition, was glad to have the opportunity to play in Baltimore, and spoke very highly of Keeler as a player.[3]

* * *

In late January, Hanlon made a surprising move when he offered heavyweight champion Jim Corbett a contract for $10,000 to join the Orioles. Corbett, however, said he had to turn down the offer because of plans he had made to take his parents to Europe. Hanlon made another offer of $1,000 a week for the months of July and August.

Hanlon insisted that Corbett was known to be an excellent ball player, and he said, "I hope he is in earnest about becoming an Oriole. My offer is still open to him and will remain so."[4]

Hanlon's fellow magnates and the press were outraged at the idea. Boston owner Arthur Soden declared that the league would not allow Corbett to play against any of its clubs, and said it was "a lowering of the standard of baseball when we have to descend to such methods to attract spectators or advertise the game." St. Louis Browns President Chris Von der Ahe called it "detrimental to the welfare and best interests" of baseball.[5] The venerable sportswriter and baseball historian Henry Chadwick agreed with the magnates: "It is simply bringing the professional club arena down to the level of the lowest variety show business."[6]

When he was informed that members of the league were contemplating action to stop the deal, Hanlon called it "all bosh" and obstinately declared that he could sign anyone he wanted for any price, and the League could not prevent it. Hanlon argued that he did not intend to play Corbett in the field, but simply planned for him to hit fly balls before the game to give fans a chance to see the heavyweight champion of the world.[7]

Others took a more facetious attitude toward the

In 1894 with the Orioles, the 36-year-old Big Dan Brouthers hit .347, had 128 RBI, 23 triples, and nine home runs, and he only struck out nine times in 615 plate appearances. He had a .342 career batting average, tied for eighth all-time with Babe Ruth and Harry Heilmann (Babe Ruth Birthplace & Museum).

situation. Hanlon's old friend, Giants player-manager John Ward, sent a telegraph to Giants Treasurer Edward Talcott which said: "In order to be up with the times, I would advise the New York Club to sign the Harlem Coffee Cooler (i.e. Frank Craig, a black middleweight boxer) to play in the outfield." Hanlon's old Detroit manager, Frank Bancroft, now a Reds executive, also took a light view of the matter, commenting gleefully: "If Ned Hanlon gets Corbett, the Reds will make a big hustle to secure Queen Lil (i.e., Queen Lili'uokalani of Hawaii) to sell score cards at the main gate."[8] By mid–February, it proved to be much ado about nothing as Hanlon yielded to public outcry regarding the Corbett offer and declared that the deal was off.[9]

* * *

As the team's planned departure for spring training grew ever closer, Hanlon was involved in negotiations with Joe Kelley, Steve Brodie, and John McGraw, all of whom were holding out. McGraw had sent a letter to Hanlon requesting a $600 pay raise. The contract Hanlon had previously sent McGraw included a $300 raise, and Hanlon turned down his request because he felt it was "too much for McGraw to expect, considering the size of salaries being paid by other League clubs to other first-class players."[10] Of course, McGraw bristled, "grumbled about cheap owners," and threatened to stay at St. Bonaventure University, where he was coaching the college team and taking classes.[11]

On March 20, Hanlon was walking down Charles Street in Baltimore when he heard a voice cheerily hail him, "Hello, Mr. Manager!" It was McGraw. At this point, he had still not agreed to terms, but he and Hanlon walked together to the Orioles' offices, and the conversation they had there was evidently fruitful as McGraw signed a contract that evening.[12] Shortly after, both Kelley and Brodie also agreed to terms.

As a result of the plethora of player moves Hanlon made in the last year and a half, by the time the team broke for spring training in 1894, only three players Hanlon had inherited when he took control of the club were still on the roster: John McGraw, Wilbert Robinson, and Sadie McMahon.[13]

Baltimore was the only National League team to travel to the South for spring training in 1894, and it was universally thought that this would give the Orioles a significant advantage in the upcoming season.[14] The excitement level in Baltimore was high as the Orioles who lived out of town gathered in the city for their imminent departure to their new spring training site in Macon, Georgia. When the team left Baltimore on March 17, Hanlon and the players were given a rousing send-off by a crowd of friends and well-wishers at Camden Station. All of the players made their way to the camp except pitcher Bill Hawke, who was still sulking and refused to sign at Hanlon's terms.[15]

* * *

The previous year, as Ned Hanlon prepared for his first full season as the manager of the Orioles, the National League magnates met in March of 1893 at the Fifth Avenue Hotel in New York City to discuss annual concerns. One of the most important items on the agenda was how to address the fact that hard-throwing pitchers such as Amos Rusie and Cy Young were dominating the game. Offense had been stifled to the point where the league batting average steadily declined from .266 in 1889 to .245 in 1892. To correct the imbalance, the owners decided to move the pitching distance back to 60 feet, six inches, and to replace the pitching box with a rubber slab against which the pitcher had to place his foot to deliver the pitch.[16]

These changes would have a profound impact on the game: batters now had a split-second longer to see the ball and swing, base runners now had a split-second better jump, and pitchers now had a longer distance to travel in fielding a bunt. Across the league, the rule changes would have their desired effect as offense increased dramatically. In 1893, the league batting average rose to .280, and even though the NL decreased the number of games from 154 to 132, almost 1,000 more runs were scored.

Scientific innovations in all areas of life were coming fast and furious in the late, nineteenth century, and Ned Hanlon approached the game of baseball as a science. He said,

> The game, like all things, has progressed, and it is today more scientific. It is in some respects like checkers or chess, and must be played upon systematic plans. Modern baseball, as played by the Baltimores, is based upon the idea to keep opposing teams guessing. It is a case of dealing out uncertainties at all times. Against some teams the Baltimores adopt one style of play—against others they shift. They study the weak points of all teams and try to take advantage of those points accordingly.[17]

Hanlon recounted how he would wake up in the middle of the night to jot down plays that could be used scientifically to take advantage of the rule changes.[18] This was the

Wee Willie Keeler's philosophy of "Keep a clear eye and hit 'em where they ain't" epitomized Hanlon's Scientific Baseball approach to the game (Babe Ruth Birthplace & Museum).

beginning of a style of baseball that became known as "Scientific Baseball," or as it was also called, "Inside Baseball."

"Scientific Baseball," as it was developed by Hanlon and his Orioles, was a comprehensive set of strategies that skillfully incorporated different offensive and defensive tactics that would give them an edge against their opponents. At the heart of these strategies was the hit-and-run attack, which the Orioles worked on endlessly in practice, honed and polished to a brilliant precision that frustrated and demoralized their opponents. The Orioles' hit-and-run was so fascinating to fans that Hanlon would demonstrate it for them in pregame practice.[19] John B. Sheridan, who was a sportswriter since the 1880s, wrote that "while the Orioles may not have invented the hit-and-run, he'd never heard of it before 1894."[20] But others disputed that Hanlon and the Orioles invented it. Jack Doyle claimed that when he was playing for the Giants prior to joining the Orioles, he and George Davis used the hit-and-run.[21] Charles Comiskey claimed to have used it before the Orioles did.

But it is always important, as baseball historian Lee Allen said, to keep in mind that "first" is a very dangerous word when used in writing about baseball history,[22] and "the first practitioner of a tactic may not have perfected or really appreciated it."[23] It is also worthy of note that the term "scientific" as it applies to baseball can be traced back as early as 1870, when Dickey Pearce was complimented by the *Chicago Tribune* for having "demonstrated the difference between wild hits to the field and scientific batting."[24] In those early days, the term essentially implied that a batter did not merely try to hit the ball as hard as he could, but tried to place the ball where he wanted it to go—as Wee Willie Keeler would say about 20 years later, to "hit 'em where they ain't."

Along with the hit-and-run, there has been much debate concerning which tactics the Orioles invented and which they merely refined or reconstituted; nevertheless, it cannot be denied that whenever these strategies may have originated, Hanlon saw to it that they were executed by the Orioles with a high degree of teamwork and precision that had not been seen in the game before; as a result, they "shook the complacency of nineteenth century baseball, and they were the forerunners of the game of today."[25]

During the years, the following tactics at one time or another have been declared the inventions of Hanlon's Orioles:

1. The "Baltimore Chop." This was executed by hitting the ball down at a sharp angle near home plate, which caused it to bounce high enough into the air to allow players to use their speed to reach first base before a fielder could throw them out.

2. The cut-off play to thwart a double steal attempt with runners on first and third. The catcher would throw to second, and one of the middle infielders could cut off the throw and throw home if the runner on third tried to score. Another option was that the catcher could fake the throw to second and then nip the runner at third if he fell for the fake throw and started home.[26]

3. According to Orioles backup catcher Bill Clarke, the Orioles were the inventors of the squeeze bunt.[27]

4. They were the first to have the pitcher back up third base on throws intended to go there from the outfield.[28]

5. They were the first to have the pitcher cover first base when the ball was hit wide of the first base bag.

6. Lee Allen, while serving as historian for the National Baseball Hall of Fame, awarded Hanlon "sole credit for the idea of using a left-handed batter against a right-handed pitcher, and vice versa."[29]

It is interesting to note that although the bunt has usually been mentioned as a key component of the strategies associated with the Scientific Baseball of the Orioles, it was a tactic that Ned Hanlon did not particularly care for unless it was to get a base hit. In 1954, when Jack Doyle, the first baseman of the Orioles, was an old man reflecting on his years with the team, he said, "I'll bet you never heard this one in baseball before. Ned Hanlon never used the sacrifice unless it meant winning the game and walking directly to the clubhouse. He called it the coward play and never was in favor of it being used."[30]

Hanlon had publicly declared that he felt that the bunt should be banned when men were on base. He felt the sacrifice bunt was used so often that it took spontaneity from the game and took away the excitement of a hit, a double play, or a spectacular catch that might result from a batter swinging away.[31] Hanlon knew that most people did not want to see a bunt; they wanted to see the players swing away. Other big names of the time such as Cap Anson and John Ward agreed with Hanlon.

Pittsburgh Pirates owner William Kerr also agreed and said, "It is not what the people want to see, this bunting; they want batting….There is an indescribable charm attached to the merry plunk of the bat burying itself in a ball, and it is music to the hearts of the cranks."[32]

* * *

In spring training in 1894, Hanlon was now ready to instruct his players fully in the tactics and strategies that he had been developing and refining since his days as a Detroit Wolverine. A meticulous and routine-oriented man, he ran a strictly structured training camp where not a moment of practice time was wasted.[33] The players were required to be up by seven o'clock every morning, and after a light breakfast they were on the field by 9:30. Morning practice consisted of three hours of running and drills. Then the entire team would run back to the hotel for lunch and a brief rest in bed. They returned to the field for another practice session or an afternoon game. All this was followed by running a mile or two at a nearby horse track, followed by a bath and a rubdown, and bed by 10 p.m.[34]

During Hanlon's practices, hitting drills included working on perfecting the hit-and-run, bunting for a hit, the Baltimore chop, purposely fouling off pitches,[35] and hitting to the opposite field. Defensively, they worked on backing up throws, cutoff plays from the outfield, and cutoffs to defend against the double steal. The pitchers practiced picking off runners, backing up throws, and covering first base on ground balls.[36] Hanlon instructed his players to read the arms and the body position of outfielders so they knew when to attempt to take an extra base.[37] As a prolific base stealer in his day, he instructed the players in nuances of that skill as well.

"Work, work, work, work, all the time," Hughie Jennings said when he was asked years later about what Hanlon's practices were like.[38] Dan Brouthers moaned to Wilbert Robinson while they were running on the track, "This is a devil of an occupation for a man worth $30,000."[39]

Hanlon was relentless, and he steadily drilled the players until he had them playing the game exactly as he wanted it played. Whatever the drill, he kept his men at it until they did it the way he wanted it done—not their way, but his way.[40] Jack Doyle, the slugging first baseman who joined the team in 1896, added that Hanlon didn't train his team as they do today: "He would work for two hours just on play situations."[41]

Joe Kelley was training so hard that spring that he dreamed about baseball. On one occasion, his roommates, McGraw and Brodie, were awakened by Kelley shouting out in his sleep, "Why, he never touched me! He never touched me! You're a pretty good umpire—I don't think! You gave us the worst of it in Baltimore, and you're doing it again here!" When asked about his restless sleep, Kelley said that he dreamed an umpire had called him out on a slide at second base.[42]

But not all the work was physical—there were important cognitive and psychological elements that Hanlon instilled in his players. In the evenings or on days when it rained, Hanlon held mandatory meetings where he would teach them "baseball as she is played," one of his favorite phrases.[43] He wanted players who could think on their feet and take pride in out-thinking their opponents, and he continually quizzed them on plays and strategy. Hanlon and his players "studied the rule book as some lawyers read the law—for loopholes."[44] Years later, Joe Kelley admitted, "When there were holes in the rules, we were quick to take advantage of it."[45] Hanlon also devised a complicated system of hand signals for batters, fielders, and runners that was said "would put the Princeton football eleven to shame."[46]

One of the key tenets of Hanlon's Scientific Baseball was described by Wilbert Robinson when he said, "It was Hanlon who taught us how to do the unexpected. That was his great motto."[47] In 1904, Hanlon bragged about some of the innovative ways in which his team did the unexpected: bunting with a man on third base and two outs, hitting away when a player had a three-ball, no-strike count with men on base, and how once in St. Louis they had laid down five bunts in a row to win a game. Hanlon was also quick to give credit to his players for making this style of play effective: "those lads that I had then could do those things. They'd take advantage of a situation of their own or the other side's creating, and they weren't afraid of losing a bingle if they could win."[48]

Hanlon was the teacher, and his players embraced what he had to offer, but his players were also eager students who had ideas of their own, and the 21-year-old McGraw was not a shrinking violet during these discussions. As will be seen, in his young and rebellious days when the Orioles machine reached greater and greater heights of success, McGraw would grow increasingly jealous of the lavish praise the press heaped upon Hanlon. Consequently, McGraw claimed that it was the Orioles players, and mainly McGraw himself, who had actually developed most of the techniques that made them famous. A McGraw biographer said, "The more successful the Orioles were, the more insolent and overbearing McGraw would become in relations with his manager."[49] However, as will also be seen, McGraw harbored a deep admiration for Hanlon that his pride would not allow him to acknowledge until later in his life.

Once the season began, Hanlon would take his stand behind the catcher during morning practices, directing and criticizing, but during regular season games, he made only occasional comments, preferring to allow his captain to run the team on the field.[50] In this, Hanlon clearly demonstrated the mark of a superior teacher—train your students how to do something, step aside, and let them take ownership of their knowledge and augment it from their own experience. This allowed a man like McGraw to later commandeer at least some of the teachings of Hanlon and claim them as his own.

Nevertheless, Hanlon infused in his players the invigorating idea that they were a tactically superior team to any in the League, and that they could beat anyone. This created a swagger and never-say-die attitude that would be a key aspect of the team's collective personality. McGraw later described the enthusiasm of the young Orioles:

> We talked, lived, and dreamed baseball. That was the secret of our success. Woe betide the player who failed us! His life on the bench was not a pleasant one. He never forgot the roasting. We knew that we had a great ball club and for that very reason I think we won a lot of ball games. We fought each other, of course, but such rows were the result of some player making a mistake. We fought for the welfare of the team. Each player regarded himself as the manager of the other. Hanlon had little to do other than to encourage us to keep on. He had built well.[51]

Hanlon's spring training camps left an indelible mark on McGraw, Robinson, and Jennings—men who later became successful managers in their own right, and they used Hanlon's spring training camps as models for their own.[52]

Above all, one of Hanlon's guiding principles as a manager was to treat his players with respect, and he created an environment which allowed the players to feel they had an ownership in their team. Willie Keeler was impressed with the way Hanlon handled his players, and said, "He is eminently a just man, and a newcomer feels that he will get a good chance to show his ability if he has any. He does not rebuke a man in the hearing of spectators, and thereby take the heart out of a man when he makes a misplay, but points out the mistake next morning in the practice hour and makes a suggestion or two."[53] Indeed, Hanlon's quiet, behind-the-scenes way of correcting players was a trait his players would compliment him for when they reminisced about their Orioles careers.

* * *

Hanlon's Scientific Baseball strategies would not only take advantage of the reduced impact pitchers had on the game, but he was also going to take a different approach when it came to the construction of his roster. When Ned Hanlon was a player, and during the beginning of his managing career, baseball managers were attracted to having large, powerful men on their teams who would try to hit the ball as hard and far as they possibly could in every at-bat. Hanlon would come to reject that approach, and for his Orioles he wanted players with speed and agility, and this enabled him to see the value in smaller and faster men like Wee Willie Keeler, John McGraw, and Heinie Reitz who could hit the ball to all fields and run the bases aggressively and intelligently.[54] These were players like Hanlon himself was during his career. These would be the perfect players not only to execute the tactics that defined the offensive component of Scientific Baseball, but their agility, quickness, and speed also led to much better base running and defensive play.

Hanlon was no longer going to rely on older players who were on the downside of their careers and who brought their personal baggage with them to the Orioles. Hanlon primarily focused on obtaining players who were young and unproven, and players in whom he saw abilities that others could not see. He wanted hungry players with innate competitive fires who were desperate to prove they could thrive in the cutthroat world of 1890s major league baseball and who burned with the desire to win. He wanted players he could mold and fashion into the style of ball he wanted his team to play: fast and aggressive. He wanted to build a true team—one where everyone worked together for the good of the team, one where individual accomplishment was secondary to team accomplishment. As John McGraw would later say, "Teamwork was our middle name; everything had to give way to that."⁵⁵

At spring training that year, the players quickly saw that under the tutelage of Ned Hanlon, there was going to be a baseball brave new world. John McGraw realized it right away:

> I had much to learn when we reported...the next spring...[and] I got an inkling of what Ned Hanlon was trying to do in the way of building up a ball club. It was very clear to me that he was seeking youth and spirit. Up to that time—and that is often true today—baseball people hesitated to try anything new. Veterans can be counted on to do the right thing—at any rate, the usual thing—and there is a tendency to let them go along. But managers, in this sense of security, go too far. They do not realize old-timers are slipping; do not see the necessity of young blood soon enough. In other words, it is a human failing to follow the line of least resistance. The work of building is tedious and nerve-racking. To avoid it is human.⁵⁶

Ned Hanlon would not avoid change—he would embrace it. What he went through in 1892, and to a much lesser degree in 1893, proved that he had the mettle to take on the stressful work of building a team essentially from scratch. John McGraw and the other men who played for the remarkable Orioles teams of the mid–1890s would reap the benefits of his wisdom, creativity, and personal strength of character.

Hanlon overlooked no detail that could aid his team in implementing the tenets of Scientific Baseball, and he worked with Union Park groundskeeper Tom Murphy to tailor the field to their strategies. The grass was kept high along the third base and first base lines, and the lines were slightly sloped to allow bunt hits to stay fair. The home plate area was packed tightly and kept unwatered to aid in the success of the Baltimore Chop. The base paths were also kept dry and hard-packed to enable the Orioles to use their overall superior team speed to advantage. Murphy mixed soap flakes into the earth on the mound so that opposing pitchers could not get a good grip on the ball. Orioles pitchers, aware of this, always kept fresh dirt in their pockets.⁵⁷

It has also been speculated that Hanlon worked alongside groundskeeper Murphy to become a trailblazer in the development and utilization of the pitching mound. It is believed that the mound originated in the late 1880s or early 1890s, and it is unclear who first came up with the idea of elevating the pitching area. Baseball historians John Thorn and John Holway have attributed its creation to John Montgomery Ward, but that has been disputed by others. It seems more likely that mounds originated to provide a pitcher with firmer footing and supply drainage on wet fields, but it is also clear that once overhand pitching was allowed, the more astute players and managers realized that the downward slope allowed for greater pitch speed.⁵⁸

Hanlon certainly recognized the advantage the pitching mound would offer, and like others who did, he may have kept it quiet so it would provide his team with an edge. The existence of a mound at Union Park was noted by Hugh Fullerton of the *Chicago Tribune* when he commented that the pitcher's box was a foot higher than the plate.⁵⁹ In 1899, when Hanlon moved on to manage the Brooklyn Superbas, Buck Ewing of the Giants said, "Brooklyn will have the best of it this season, as Hanlon raised his pitcher's box one foot, making it difficult for the visiting players....Hanlon has no more right to raise his pitcher's box a foot than New York has a right to dig a trench one foot deep from the home plate to the pitcher's box at the Polo Grounds."⁶⁰

Another way that Tom Murphy used creative landscaping was when he allegedly

Groundskeeper Tom Murphy contributed to the success of Scientific Baseball and tailored the playing field to Hanlon's specifications. From left to right: Willie Keeler, Hughie Jennings, Tom Murphy, Joe Kelley, and John McGraw (collection of Tom Delise).

kept the grass high in the outfield to allow for the planting of extra balls that could be thrown in instead of the ball that was hit, if it could be an advantage to the Orioles.

An eyewitness to this "strategy" was Jim Rice, a Baltimore sportswriter of the 1890s, and he told his protégé, Fred Lieb, about a game he had covered at Union Park:

> The St. Louis Browns were playing at Baltimore, and with Joe Quinn on first, Tommy Dowd hit a sharp drive to left center. Kelley cut across the path of the ball, apparently scooped it up, and threw to McGraw to catch Quinn at third base. Just as the single umpire was about to call Quinn out, Brodie, who had been chasing the real ball to the fence, threw it in from deep

center, and gave away another of Baltimore's famous inside plays. After an argument, the umpire forfeited the game to St. Louis.[61]

Rice was not the only one to claim that he witnessed that Orioles trick. The future Hall of Famer Johnny Evers also claimed that he had witnessed it used in Boston when Fred Tenney hit a ball between Keeler and Brodie. According to Evers, they collided while chasing the ball, and as they arose from the ground, each threw a ball into the infield.[62]

The story of the hidden ball trick received many amusing retellings over the years, and it is hard to substantiate whether it is simply a baseball "urban legend" or a trick that the Orioles actually used in games.

Murphy's work on the field would be a great offensive weapon for Ned Hanlon's brand of baseball, and Steve Brodie later told a story that indicates just how seriously Murphy took his work when he described a hard-hit ground ball that made its way to Brodie in center field:

> The ball struck a stone or a bit of uneven earth and, of course, it got away from me. We were playing a game with Cleveland and any game with Cleveland was bound to be close. The batter got an extra base because I had to chase the grounder, and I was hot all over.
>
> On the way to the bench at the end of that half of the inning I spotted Murphy, who prided himself on being a good ground-keeper. By that time, I was good and hot under the collar, so I yelled at him, "Say, Murphy, why don't you send the goat out there to eat a few of those tin cans in centrefield?"
>
> When I reached the bench, the crowd gave me the laugh and Hanlon always has remembered the incident. But Murphy was so sore over the remark that he didn't speak to me for a week.[63]

* * *

As can be seen with the hidden ball trick, some of the "tactics" the Orioles employed over the years were clearly against the rules, or at the very least, certainly outside the realm of the expected ethics of the game. Indeed, the Orioles' philosophy seemed to embody an "If you're not cheating, you're not trying" attitude in the way they played the game. They did virtually anything they could, fair or foul, to win a game, and in the process, became vilified by opposing teams and their fans as a group of hoodlums who were dirty players and cheaters.

Although the Orioles were held up as the poster boys for disreputable tactics, virtually all players in the early years of baseball took advantage of the fact that most games were officiated by a single umpire. It can easily be imagined how enterprising, or perhaps unscrupulous, players attempted to exploit the fact that the umpire did not have eyes in the back of his head, and the Orioles were very well known around the League for cutting corners inside the bases, never touching them, to save ground as they made their way around the base paths. While the umpire wasn't looking, they were also infamous for impeding opposing base runners by sticking out their hips, pulling at them as they ran by, and trying to trip them.

Honus Wagner describes a vivid memory of a game he played against the Orioles when he was with Louisville:

> I hit what should have been an inside-the-park home run. As I rounded first base Jack Doyle gave me the hip. Heinie Reitz almost bowled me over as I passed second. Hughie Jennings tripped me at shortstop, and when I reached third base, John McGraw was waiting for me. I

was lucky to get a triple. After the game, [manager Fred] Clarke gave me the devil for allowing the Orioles to run all over me. The next day I hit a ball down to McGraw at third. I figured it would be a close play at first base. I banged into Doyle with my shoulder and knocked him cold. The ball sailed into right field and I scored. When I reached the bench Clarke was grinning. "That's the way to play the game, you Dutchman," he said. "Make 'em respect you."[64]

Reportedly, John McGraw was noted for grabbing onto a runner's belt just as he was trying to tag up from third on a fly ball. In a famous story told in many versions, Pete Browning of the Louisville Colonels was aware of McGraw's tendency to use this trick, so while he was standing on third getting ready to tag up, he loosened his belt so that when he took off and scored, all McGraw was left holding was the belt.[65]

Over 50 years later, teammate Sadie McMahon recalled another tactic that McGraw used at third base to hinder base runners: "McGraw wouldn't give the bag to the base runner like they do today. He'd stand on the inside corner and make the runner go around. He could touch the base all right, but he couldn't use it to pivot on in turning home. McGraw figured if he had to turn on the outside, he'd have to run wide, and that would slow him down—maybe enough to be thrown out at home."[66]

The Orioles engaged in other unscrupulous tactics to gain an edge or intimidate their opponents. Long before Ty Cobb supposedly did it, the Orioles were known for sitting out in front of their clubhouse, in plain sight of their opponents, sharpening their spikes to a razor's edge. They would pinch themselves until they left a bruise in the hopes of convincing an umpire that they had been hit by a pitch, a technique that Ned Hanlon taught his players to do and claimed that he had done himself in his playing days. Hughie Jennings still holds the major league record for being hit by a pitch, real or faked. He was hit 287 times in his career, and of that total, a startling 202 came in his five full seasons with the Orioles. Wilbert Robinson used to drop pebbles into the shoes of unsuspecting batters while they were at the plate to hamper their base running,[67] and while coaching at third base, backup catcher Boileryard Clarke would use the "phantom runner" trick by breaking for home during the windup to distract the pitcher, or to trick a fielder into throwing home.[68]

Many baseball writers of the time were outraged at the tactics of the Orioles. Tim Murnane, once a major league player himself and later a highly respected Boston baseball writer, accused Hanlon's team of "playing the dirtiest ball ever seen in this country." He accused them of running into the first baseman long after he had caught the ball, throwing masks in front of runners at home plate, grabbing the uniforms of players as they ran the bases, and other dirty tricks.[69]

Although he was regarded as an excellent player, John McGraw was referred to as "that toughest of the toughs and abomination of the diamond…he has the vilest tongue of any ball player…he uses every low and contemptible method that his erratic brain can conceive to win a play by a dirty trick."[70]

The Orioles were also infamous for their boorish behavior towards umpires. Umpire George Burnham said that the Orioles were "the hardest crowd of kickers I ever went against … that Joe Kelley is one of the worst in the business. I am glad I am no longer an umpire. It is the hardest job in the world. People in the stands have no idea of the bombardment of slurs and exasperating remarks the players make at the expense of the umpire. If they knew all that was going on down on the field they would not have so much to say against that much-abused official."[71]

Arlie Latham, a former player and National League umpire, described the

Robinson-McGraw routine with umpires as a kind of precursor to what we today would call the "Good Cop, Bad Cop" strategy:

> Robby sleeps in a salve factory and McGraw eats gunpowder for breakfast and washes it down with warm blood. When a poor inoffensive and well-meaning umpire appears in Baltimore, Robinson meets him at the plate, shakes hands with him and remarks, "I'm glad you came over. They tell me you are doing good work out west. The boys say you are the best in the business, and between us, I'm glad you're here. These are pretty tough games, old man, and that other fellow we had here was a little to the bad.... You want to watch this pitcher we're trying today. Great lad. Keep your eye on that outside corner. We get lots of them on the edge and the other fellow missed a lot of them." And all this time, McGraw is barking and snapping around the umpire's heels and threatening to hit him, and if one system doesn't work the other usually does.[72]

The Orioles did not deny or seem at all embarrassed by these tactics; in fact, they reveled in them and freely adopted them as a badge of honor. Years later, the players of that time (and not just Orioles) would laugh and swap stories in saloons, clubhouses, and in the press about the torments they caused the umpires, but John Heydler, who was a young umpire in the 1890s and later became president of the National League, did not remember those times in the same fond and amusing way:

> We hear much of the glories...of the old Orioles, but the truth about this team seldom has been told. They were mean, vicious, ready at any time to maim a rival player or an umpire, if it helped their cause. The things they would say to an umpire were unbelievably vile, and they broke the spirits of some fine men. I've seen umpires bathe their feet by the hour after McGraw and others spiked them through their shoes. The club never was a constructive force in the game. The worst of it was they got by with much of their brow beating and hooliganism. Other clubs patterned after them. I feel the lot of the umpire never was worse than in the years that the Orioles were flying high.[73]

Although the Orioles of the 1890s were disdained for their propensity to bend and break the rules at every opportunity and for being the toughest, rowdiest, dirtiest, and most foul-mouthed team in history, they were certainly not the first to engage in these unscrupulous tactics. Stories of other teams and other players using the same tactics are legion, and examples of dirty play and hooliganism can be found in virtually every issue of *Sporting Life* and *The Sporting News* throughout this period.

The St. Louis Browns of the American Association, run by player-manager Charlie Comiskey, were also quite well known for the outrageous behavior they regularly exhibited on the ball field. In 1886, John Rogers, the co-owner of the National League Philadelphia Quakers, accused Cap Anson's Chicago White Stockings of doing "anything to win and using questionable tactics and dishonest points of play which the rules seem powerless to prevent."[74]

Baseball historian and statistician Bill James described what he believed to be the difference between the rowdy ball of the 1880s and 1890s: "The tactics of the eighties were aggressive; the tactics of the nineties were violent. The game of the eighties was crude; the game of the nineties was criminal. The baseball of the eighties had ugly elements; the game of the nineties was just ugly."[75]

None of this is mentioned in order to excuse the Orioles. Some of them certainly resorted to unscrupulous, dirty, and at times, indefensibly violent means. In 1895, annoyed at hearing his team criticized for years as being the rowdiest team in baseball, Hanlon struck back by saying that Cleveland was actually the birthplace of rowdy ball. He claimed that the Orioles did not start their kicking tactics until they saw how the Spiders were kicking and getting away with it, so the Orioles began to follow "a bad example that proved contagious."[76]

In the end, it depended upon which newspaper you were reading. In Baltimore, the Cleveland Spiders were the Evil Empire; in Cleveland, the Orioles held that designation. Disgraceful brawling and rowdy behavior typified many of the games between the Orioles and Spiders during this time, and those games are recounted as the stuff of legend. These two teams were certainly cut from the same cloth, and both teams would willingly, if not joyfully, go well beyond the limits of decorum to win a game.

Ned Hanlon made occasional pledges over the years to restrain his team but ultimately was unable to do so. And it is unclear whether he really wanted to. To players like McGraw, that style of play was essential to winning, and in an interview, Hanlon attempted some spin control: "Had the Orioles had less of that aggressiveness, we would never have won any pennants," Hanlon said. "Players are only human, and when they are compelled to suppress all noise and excitement, their hearts will go down in their boots, they will become indifferent, the game will go glimmering and the public will leave in disgust."[77]

* * *

Regardless of their reputation then and now, the Orioles of Ned Hanlon were not merely a group of boorish brutes. They were a group of extremely skilled players, and their success undoubtedly led to increased resentment against them.

Ned Hanlon was a master of psychology, and he was able to take a team filled with colorful characters, diverse idiosyncrasies, and strong personalities and create an environment where teamwork, camaraderie, and confidence became hallmarks of what, decades later, would become known as the Oriole Way. First, he inspired them with his wise, firm, and unwavering leadership through the trying early years, and then he infused them with the intricacies of the scientific workings of the game. When the players saw that Scientific Baseball actually worked and helped them become winners, it gave them unbridled confidence. Finally, he made the players believe that the team was theirs—that they all had a voice in it. Whatever Ned Hanlon devised or refined, whatever strategy he used, he empowered his players to carry out the battle plan. As John McGraw would say many years later, "The great thing about that team was that every one of us, individually, felt that it belonged to him."[78]

When all is said and done, it cannot be denied that Hanlon, no matter what his tactical contributions to the game may be, put together a set of strategies and procedures and molded a group of men into a team that long after the cheering for them stopped, would transform the game of baseball.

6

The Pride of Baltimore (1894)

During spring training, Hanlon was generally happy with the improvement his team showed in individual fielding and hitting, but he was not pleased with the teamwork they displayed, so he gave that more emphasis in practices and through lectures.[1] He also had an occasional discipline issue to deal with. When pitcher Bert Inks overslept one day and arrived when an exhibition game was underway, it was reported that he "had an interesting interview with Mr. Hanlon and purchased an alarm clock."[2]

One important issue for Hanlon was where to play Willie Keeler. In a syndicated column he wrote after he retired, Hughie Jennings related how that was determined:

> When Keeler arrived in the training camp of the Orioles in the spring of 1894, Ned Hanlon did not know exactly what to do with him. Hanlon was never enthusiastic over left-handed third basemen and he had McGraw for third base, so Keeler did not fit in at that position from any angle as far as Hanlon was concerned. One evening soon after Keeler's arrival, Hanlon took him aside and said, "I'm going to make an outfielder out of you. Right field is the spot for you. Start there tomorrow."
>
> Keeler was not enthusiastic about it, but when a manager tells you to play a certain position, there is nothing to do but play it. The next morning when practice started, Keeler went to right field. Walter Brodie was in center and Joe Kelley was in left. Hanlon, sitting on the bench, was watching Keeler closely to see how he would go after fly balls. Hanlon didn't find out, at least not then. Keeler never started after a fly ball. Brodie was catching everything hit into center as well as everything intended for Keeler, and instead of going after the ball, Keeler kept stepping away from it and edging toward the foul line. After about ten minutes of this performance, Keeler came in, walked to the bench, threw away his glove and sat down.
>
> "What's the matter?" Hanlon demanded.
>
> "I'm not going to play the outfield," Willie snapped.
>
> "Why not? What's the matter with the outfield?"
>
> "Oh, the outfield's all right, but it's that guy Brodie out there," Willie replied. "He's got it in for me."
>
> "What's Brodie got it in for you for?" asked Hanlon.
>
> "I don't know, but he keeps on yelling, 'I'll get *you*, you dirty dog! I'll get *you* you dirty dog!'"
>
> The other players on the bench roared with laughter. That was what Brodie screamed at every ball that came his way. He intended the remark for the ball and no human being or animal, for that matter. This was all explained to Keeler and he and Brodie became close friends.[3]

Sadie McMahon had an impressive spring, and he exhibited perfect control and speed that made Wilbert Robinson's eyes bulge out with surprise.[4] Tony Mullane was also pitching well, newcomer Heinie Reitz was exhibiting excellent defense at second base, and Kelley, Brodie, and Keeler showed all the signs of making an excellent outfield. Hanlon was gloating over Wee Willie Keeler's ability to hit to all fields, his speed, and defensive skill in the outfield. After watching Brouthers and Keeler in practice, he commented to a reporter, "I will make those Brooklyn people think they have lost a $10,000 beauty."[5]

In the past year, McGraw had improved both offensively and defensively, but Hanlon was concerned with his lack of range at shortstop. "He experimented with him at third base, and pleased at what he saw, he declared that McGraw was a natural third baseman."[6] By opening day, Jennings had won the shortstop job, and the newly acquired Frank Bonner served as the team's utility man. With Reitz at second and Brouthers at first, Hanlon's infield was now set.

Hanlon also decided that because McGraw could stand at the plate and skillfully foul off balls indefinitely until he either earned a walk or got the pitch he wanted to hit, he would be the team's leadoff hitter. Keeler hit second, and with his excellent bat control, he and McGraw were able to execute the hit-and-run play expertly.[7]

The players embraced the concepts that Hanlon was teaching, and as they became more and more proficient in executing the tactics, their confidence grew. Brouthers, whose opinion Hanlon undoubtedly valued, told him he had never seen a more enthusiastic group of players.[8] As Hanlon put his players through their workouts, he became increasingly aware that "something about the Orioles was starting to become more than the sum of the pieces."[9]

During the spring, Hanlon and Brouthers talked endlessly about the "old Detroit days," and Brouthers would begin many stories with the lead-in, "When Ned and I were in Detroit..." These tales were told so often that the players, tired of hearing them repeated, would good-naturedly cut off their stories.[10] When not trying to ignore Brouthers' stories of the good old days, the players would pass away the time singing with each other, and the players regarded Jennings, Kelley, Mullane, and Clarke as an excellent quartet.[11]

In the spring of 1894, the Orioles began to develop a strong collective identity, and this continued for many of them long after their playing days were over. They became a close-knit group that regularly socialized together, and on the field, they constantly encouraged one another. Orioles avoided taking a teammate to task in public; instead, they brought complaints either directly to Hanlon or privately to the offending teammate. As they prepared for the upcoming season, they became united around one overwhelming purpose: to win baseball games.

Moreover, for some of the Orioles, particularly John McGraw, the team became an extended family unit. Years after his death, McGraw's second wife, Blanche, recalled how he would call upon her before they were married and sit quietly, watching her family relax and interact in the comfort of their home. Blanche described how a desire for this type of family life was "a sort of gnawing hunger" in her future husband.[12]

The Orioles, with all their familial support and squabbling, would be the family that McGraw never had and that he yearned for. In Ned Hanlon, he would find firm guidance and a patient understanding of his turbulent nature that would normally be provided by a father.

Hanlon, buoyed by his club's improvement and confidence, brashly predicted a first division finish for his team. For "Silent Ned," who was given that nickname because he was not "given to oracular pyrotechnics,"[13] this was a bold statement, and it was met with derision by sportswriters in the Northeast such as Tim Murnane, Jake Morse, and Joe Vila.

Baltimore journalists and others outside the New York and Boston orbits, however, noticed the new culture Hanlon had created and commented that the Orioles were no longer engaged in "loafing, drinking, and carousing."[14] Hanlon now had a team of eager, hustling men who had a fierce desire to win.

Although it was acknowledged that he had the team completely under his control, Hanlon was lauded not only for being open to suggestions and advice, but also for having the strength to reject such counsel, if needed. He was complimented for his innovations to the game, his handling of players, his ability to pull off remarkable trades, and his ability to recognize talent in players that other baseball men failed to see.[15]

In Baltimore, the stands at Union Park had been refitted and repaired, and Tom Murphy had kept his promise to Hanlon to have the diamond perfectly smooth and level. Fans were brimming with optimism, and the team received hundreds of requests for reserved seats for the April 19 opener.[16]

The beginning of a remarkable season was at hand.

* * *

The Orioles arrived back in Baltimore on April 15, ready to take on the Giants, a team that had permeated their thoughts throughout spring training. They had been playing the upcoming games with the Giants over and over in their minds, and in their imaginations, they won every time. Win or lose, the Orioles were confident that "the Giants will know they have attended a ball game."[17]

The night before the opening game, the Giants arrived in Baltimore, and Hanlon met his old friend John Ward, who was their manager and second baseman. Both expressed good-natured optimism about their teams in the upcoming games, but when Ward met later with reporters, he confidently told them that he expected to win two games of the series. Privately, he predicted a sweep.[18]

Union Park on Huntington Avenue (now 25th Street) was the home of the 1890s Orioles and the site of their glory years. The building to the left still stands (Babe Ruth Birthplace & Museum).

A special train that had been chartered for a large crowd of Giants fans left New York at 8 a.m., and when they arrived in Baltimore, they were met by Harry Von der Horst, who welcomed them to the city. They immediately saw that Baltimore was at fever pitch, and an estimated 5,000 people were gathered around the Eutaw House Hotel, waiting for the beginning of a parade that would take the two teams to Union Park.

At 1 p.m. the parade started as Sauerwald's Band led the way and played some of the most popular tunes of the day, including "Daddy Wouldn't Buy Me a Bow-Wow" and "Daisy Bell." Behind the band were a carriage filled with newspaper men and a barouche containing Ned Hanlon and John Ward. Then came a series of carriages, each containing an Oriole and a Giant, finally followed by others carrying all manner of politicians and influential businessmen.

The parade made its way through the city, passing the wharves and fish markets of the harbor, the Post Office, City Hall, hotels, saloons, and businesses of all types. Everywhere along the route, the sidewalks were packed with people, and from upper windows, they cheered and waved hats and handkerchiefs. The players were astounded to see the number of people who turned out to see them.

When they finally arrived at Union Park, the area was swarming with fans, electric streetcars, horse-drawn rigs, and bicycles. Over 15,000 tickets were sold, a Baltimore record at that time, and Harry Von der Horst had also distributed over 1,000 complimentary tickets to the mayor, governor, and other important Baltimore politicians and citizens. Hundreds of people who could not obtain tickets filled the rooftops of nearby houses and businesses so they could watch the game.

The ballpark was gaily decorated with American flags and orange and black bunting, and the overflow crowd spilled out along the farthest reaches of the outfield, where management had to set up ropes to keep them back. As the players marched in to great applause, they had trouble staying in line, and one reporter commented that he hoped the teams could play better than they marched. In the bleachers, vendors were hawking their wares: sausage sandwiches, pepsin drops, deviled crab, peanuts, and lemonade.[19]

The rule of the day was that the home team could choose whether to bat in the top or bottom of the first inning. Because only one ball was usually used for an entire game, the Orioles chose to bat first to get a chance to hit a new, clean ball that would grow increasingly dark and soft as the game progressed. As McGraw stepped to the plate to lead off, the crowd roared, and he slammed a ball into left field for a hit. Keeler followed with a hard grounder which the shortstop could not handle, and it looked like the Orioles were off to a promising start. But pitcher Amos Rusie retired Brodie, Brouthers, and Kelley to end the inning.

The game remained scoreless until the top of the third, when McGraw drew a lead-off walk and immediately stole second as catcher Duke Farrell's throw ended up in center field. McGraw was unable to proceed to third on the error because Ward blocked him. Keeler struck out, but the pitch eluded Farrell, and Keeler took off for first. Farrell, having a rough day behind the plate, threw wildly, and McGraw advanced to third on the play. When Brodie's grounder forced Keeler at second, McGraw scored the first run of the game. By the end of the fifth inning, the Orioles led, 5–1, and that was all they needed for an 8–3 victory behind Sadie McMahon. After the game, a mass of enthusiastic fans jumped out of the stands to congratulate the players as they made their way to the clubhouse.[20]

The next day, the Orioles beat the Giants, 12–6, behind Tony Mullane, and Bert

Inks led them to a sweep in a 4–3 victory in the final game of the series. The Orioles had just sent a signal to the baseball world that they were a legitimate pennant contender.

One person who was not thrilled was John Ward, who was annoyed that the Orioles had executed the hit-and-run play repeatedly in the series. He grumbled, "That's trick stuff by a lot of kids. Maybe they are better trained than we are, but we'll show them up in our next series. They'll blow up long before the season is over." Ward made a ridiculous statement when he added, "Besides, I'm not sure what they're doing is legal. As soon as we get to Washington, I'll ask Nick Young, the League president, about it."[21]

In the meantime, New York newspaper man Joe Vila was outraged by the conduct of John McGraw. He wrote that his good play was spoiled by his foul language and rowdy behavior. He warned that if Hanlon did not get McGraw under control, serious trouble would result, and he said players like McGraw should be banished from the League.[22]

Hanlon did not respond to Ward's and Vila's comments. Instead, he could not resist an opportunity to gloat about the trade he made for Keeler and Brouthers: "if the Brooklyn Club has any more 'has-beens' like Dan Brouthers they should send them down to Baltimore, and we will make use of them."[23]

To John McGraw, the series was the inspirational turning point for the team, and as he looked back on it years later, he said, "That one series made the Orioles. Seeing that our stuff had worked, we were full of confidence and cockiness." McGraw, Jennings, Keeler, Brodie, Brouthers, McMahon, and some other Orioles lived that season at the Oxford House Hotel just a few blocks from Union Park. According to McGraw, they were consumed by all things baseball and would meet in the evenings and develop new "stunts" that they could use against their opponents.[24] Their residence at the Oxford House also enabled them to strengthen the personal bonds between them, and when they were not talking baseball, they gathered together to share meals, sing, and read the newspapers on the back porch.[25]

The opening series was the beginning of an excellent start for the Orioles, who won 35 of their first 48 games. The pitching corps was also bolstered when Bill Hawke ended his holdout and joined the team after Hanlon gave him a raise. He pitched his first game on May 17 and threw a three-hitter to beat Washington, 10–2.[26]

* * *

By June, the success of the Orioles had made Baltimore baseball crazy. It was said that if you wanted to do business in the town before 3 p.m. you would have to deal with the incessant chatter about baseball by the clerks and proprietors. After 3 p.m. when the team was home, it would be hard to do any business at all because everyone had gone to Union Park. If the team was on the road, fans would flock to Ford's Opera House, where details of the game were telegraphed and played out on the stage.[27] Throughout the season, you could find all manner of Orioles-related goods for sale: Hanlon bats, Robinson cigars, McGraw mugs, and Kelley oysters, as well as other products.[28] The town had especially embraced Wee Willie Keeler, and it was said "he owns Druid Hill Park, the Shot Tower, the Battle Monument, and all the base ball cranks in the Monumental City."[29]

Hanlon was acclaimed for teaching his men patience at the plate and precise execution of the hit-and-run and the bunt. Moreover, the players were impressing people with their speed, defensive prowess, hustle, and enthusiasm, and even the slow-of-foot Brouthers shocked fans when he slid into first base trying to beat out an infield hit. The old veteran was very impressed with his new team: "I think it is the strongest club that was ever put together....They have a different system from other clubs, better than St. Louis or Boston ever had. It will be two or three years before the other clubs get onto their methods."[30]

Albert Mott, the Baltimore-based reporter for *Sporting Life*, raved about Hanlon, calling him a "great handler of men," and claimed he could get the most out of his players in a short time. To Mott, Hanlon's greatest accomplishment was instilling confidence

Pictured clockwise from the upper left, Willie Keeler, John McGraw, Hughie Jennings, and Joe Kelley became known as the "Big Four" of the championship Orioles (collection of Tom Delise).

into his players and making them realize that their true value lay not in their personal statistics, but in how they contributed to the overall success of the club.[31]

Not everyone shared these flattering views of the Orioles. Outside Baltimore, they were gaining the reputation of an uncouth bunch of ruffians who would not be able to maintain the level of play that they had demonstrated to that point in the season. It was claimed that fans in other cities regarded them as freaks and went to see them play merely out of a sense of curiosity.[32]

By June 17, the Orioles were 28–10 and in first place; however, the outstanding offense was disguising a problem that had the potential to destroy their pennant hopes. In the first game of a doubleheader on June 18 at the old Congress Grounds in Boston,[33] Tony Mullane gave up 16 runs in the first inning, but Hanlon, for some reason, refused to take him out until the sixth inning, by which time Mullane had allowed five additional runs. Wilbert Robinson was so thoroughly disgusted with Mullane's effort, which resulted in 20 men coming to the plate in the first inning, that he angrily called for Boileryard Clarke to replace him, saying that he had no intention of staying behind the plate for a week.[34] The Orioles lost the game by an embarrassing 24–7 score.

Mullane rebounded in his next start for a 9–5 victory against Philadelphia, but then he had two straight poor performances. On June 25, he gave up 17 hits and eight walks in a 15–8 loss to Chicago, and it could have been much worse as quite a few hard-hit balls were converted into outs because of excellent plays by Orioles fielders.[35]

In his next turn on June 28 at Cleveland, Mullane was knocked out of the box after issuing five walks and nine hits that yielded 11 runs in just three innings. Bert Inks, who replaced Mullane, was also ineffective, and the Orioles fell by an 18–11 score. The *Baltimore Sun* remarked that Mullane's work made "a laughingstock of the team" and "would have disgraced an amateur."[36]

Hanlon had seen enough and gave Mullane notification of his 10-day release. He said he had considered making the move for some time, but he was hoping to arrange a trade.[37] In a surprising turn of events, Mullane showed up at Exposition Park, where the Orioles were scheduled to play against the Pirates on July 10, and begged Hanlon to give him another chance. Hanlon allowed Mullane to throw a practice session during which he performed well enough for Hanlon to relent and start him in the game that day.[38]

Hanlon's decision was regrettable. Mullane was once again hit hard and demonstrated poor control. The Orioles gave him a 6–1 lead, but in the fourth inning the Pirates tied the game, and Hanlon replaced him with McMahon, who did not fare much better as the Pirates won, 19–9. "It was rare for the local press to blame Hanlon for anything, but this time they held him responsible for the team's loss because he had allowed Mullane to pitch."[39]

From Mullane's shellacking on June 18 through July 30, the team struggled, and their pitchers gave up 10 runs or more 16 times in 36 games. If it hadn't been for Sadie McMahon, who was 9–3 during that stretch, the Orioles might well have been doomed.

Hanlon knew that he needed to reinforce the pitching staff to have any hope of winning the pennant. His first move was to purchase pitcher Bill "Kid" Gleason from the St. Louis Browns. Gleason, who would later manage the infamous Chicago "Black Sox" who were accused of throwing the 1919 World Series, had won 20 games in each of his past four seasons, including a personal high of 38 in 1890.

Wilbert Robinson enthusiastically declared that if Gleason was on the pitching staff, the Orioles would win the pennant. He reached out to Gleason and encouraged him to sign, saying, "He cannot find a better or pleasanter manager than Mr. Hanlon."[40] Gleason met with Hanlon at Union Park on July 10, signed a contract, and beat Brooklyn in his debut for the Orioles a week later. He was a rough and ready man who was a perfect fit for the Orioles' mentality and style of play, and he provided a big boost to the team as he won 15 of 20 decisions and batted .349.

On July 13, Hanlon made another attempt to strengthen the pitching staff when he traded Tony Mullane to the Cleveland Spiders for future Hall of Famer John Clarkson. Clarkson refused to report to the Orioles unless Cleveland paid him a cash bonus,[41] and when that did not happen, Clarkson retired from baseball. Mullane pitched in just four games for the Spiders that season, and then he too was out of major league baseball.

Before the end of the month, Hanlon made two other deals for pitchers when he acquired Duke Esper from the Washington Senators and traded Bert Inks to the Louisville Colonels along with $2,000 for George Hemming. Esper was 5–10 for the Senators with a 7.75 ERA, and Hemming was 12–19 with the Colonels; however, both men performed brilliantly for the Orioles as Esper went 10–2 and Hemming added a 4–0 record. This additional pitching depth proved to be vital when Sadie McMahon came up with a sore arm and was unable to pitch again after his August 28 start. McMahon had had an outstanding season and was 25–8 when he was injured.

With the pitching staff improved, the Orioles ended the season with a hot streak. Starting with a win against the Browns on August 24, they won 27 of their final 30 games, and Joe Kelley led the team with a .541 batting average in that period.[42] During that time, Orioles pitchers surrendered 10 runs or more only once and kept their opponents to three runs or less 16 times. Hanlon's ability to make shrewd deals to obtain pitching help turned out to be a deciding factor in

Kid Gleason was an excellent pitcher and second baseball before his heart was broken when he managed the infamous Chicago Black Sox, who threw the 1919 World Series (Babe Ruth Birthplace & Museum).

the pennant race because, in spite of their torrid pace, the Giants nipped at their heels until the very end, finishing in second place only three games behind.

On September 25, four days before the end of the season, the Orioles beat Cy Young and the Cleveland Spiders to clinch the pennant. Earlier in the season, Hanlon had pledged to wear the same straw hat until the Orioles won the pennant, and now he threw

The 1894 Orioles, National League Champions. The team went 89–39 and finished three games ahead of the New York Giants, but were swept by them in the first post-season Temple Cup Series (collection of Tom Delise).

it high into the air as his players celebrated wildly on the field.⁴³ The play-by-play of this game was simulated in Ford's Grand Opera House in Baltimore on Compton's Electric Game Impersonator. This device featured a huge diagram with movable pieces to show the positions of players on the field.⁴⁴ When it was over, Harry Von der Horst ran across the stage with an orange and black silk flag reading "Champions, 1894" as the audience rose and gave a standing ovation. As the news spread, the celebration went on all night as the streets filled with fans, and bonfires were lit throughout the city.⁴⁵

After clinching the pennant, the Orioles played their last game in Chicago, and on September 30, they boarded a train for their triumphant return to Baltimore. As they rode home, they were surprised to see that they were wildly celebrated at virtually every station along their route. When the team made a stop in the coal mining town of Grafton, West Virginia, they were greeted by a large and excited crowd who called out for Jennings, a former coal miner himself. Hughie stuck his head out the window and waved as more cheers erupted from the fans on the platform.⁴⁶ As they wound their way home, crowds gathered at even the smaller stations, and the team was so appreciative of the receptions that some were actually moved to tears. One Oriole remarked, "If these folks so far from Baltimore treat us this way, what will the folks at home do when they get hold of us?"

They were about to see, but before then, the team stopped for breakfast at Cumberland, Maryland, where a large banner over the front of the Queen City Hotel, which also served as the train station, welcomed the champions. When the players emerged, they were greeted by a roar from the huge crowd, and they were immediately surrounded by fans trying to shake their hands as a band played "Maryland, My Maryland."

While the team was eating, Hanlon was presented with a large glass baseball bat that was filled with 15-year-old rye whiskey. After breakfast, as the team made its way to the train, they were once again surrounded by eager fans as the band struck up "The Conquering Heroes Come." When Hanlon appeared at the door, the cheers overwhelmed the music, and fans clamored for Hanlon to give a speech. He was pushed forward by the players, and he bowed and smiled at the crowd until they quieted. He said, "Ladies and gentlemen, of Cumberland—in behalf of the Baltimore Base Ball Club I thank you most heartily for this unexpected reception. When we shall have defeated the Giants in the Temple Cup, I am sure that the boys will want to come up here and play an exhibition game in Cumberland."

The crowd cheered, the band played, and then the team boarded the train, which proceeded to Martinsburg, where another large crowd awaited them. During the brief, five-minute stay, the mayor of the town presented Hanlon with flowers and a black and orange silk pennant enclosed in a glass frame made by the ladies of the town.

When the Orioles finally arrived at Camden Station in Baltimore, they were amazed to find 50,000 people waiting to welcome them home. The *Sun* estimated that 200,000 people took part in the celebrations, either at Camden Station or lining the parade route that meandered through the city and ultimately ended at the Fifth Regiment Armory. Over 200 groups took part in the parade, many of which had pigs on their wagons "to represent the rooting interests." Banners and the colors of the team flew everywhere, and the sidewalks were filled with cheering people. Hanlon and Wilbert Robinson rode side-by-side in one of the lead carriages, and they were greeted by signs that promoted Hanlon for governor and Robinson for mayor.

As the players entered the great hall of the Armory, a huge banner hung across the front of the hall that said, "Champion Base Ball Club of the United States: Baltimore, 1894." There the team met Mayor Ferdinand Latrobe, who gave a brief speech and proclaimed that Baltimore "has the best of everything—the best people, the prettiest women, and now the best ball team in the country.... I tell you base ball has done more to advertise this city than anything else, and we are grateful to each of you for it." Latrobe called Hanlon forth to congratulate him.

The Orioles finally left the armory and were conducted to their final destination of the evening: a formal banquet attended by 3,000 fans at the Rennert Hotel.

As the banquet began, Wilbert Robinson stood and called out, "Players of the Baltimore Club!" When the room quieted, Robbie raised his glass and said, "Glasses Up!" When his teammates eagerly obliged, Robbie said, "And now glasses down," and he turned his champagne glass face-down. Robbie's temperance declaration was followed by all the players, although some were reported to have looked longingly at the waiters' trays filled with glasses of bubbly as they passed by during the evening.

All throughout the banquet, calls of "Get at 'em," Robbie's favorite cry during games, rang out. Cheers for Hanlon, and Robbie, and Von der Horst rang out continually. Hanlon's face was "wreathed in smiles," and Harry Von der Horst was "as happy as a boy with a new pair of skates in winter." A huge sphere of ice carved to represent a baseball with an oriole on top and a miniature pennant in its beak was placed on the players' table, and many speeches honoring the accomplishments of the Orioles were given throughout the evening.

Finally, Hanlon was called upon to say a few words. When he stood, he was greeted with a tremendous ovation, and it visibly moved him to the point where it took a few moments to compose himself. Hanlon finally spoke and told the audience how touched he was by the demonstration of affection his team was given, and he said this was the proudest moment of his career. He called the Orioles the hardest-working team in the history of the game, and he described the strain that they had undergone in the last few weeks to ensure that the pennant was won for Baltimore. He concluded by saying:

> It has been fairly and squarely won by sheer merit, and no envious, snarling critic can belittle it. The glory of this achievement I bespeak first for the faithful men who have worn the Oriole uniform on so many hot fields. I am glad of this opportunity to speak my opinion of them. Never has it been my good fortune to be associated with such a body of intelligent, willing men. Their whole soul has been in the fight from start to finish, and all the glory is theirs. That I have been permitted to act as their leader and manager I esteem an honor and privilege. I consider the present Baltimore team the finest body of base ball players ever gotten together....To bring such a body of men together has been no easy task, and right here I wish to say that its accomplishment has been made possible by the good sense and liberality of the gentleman to whom Baltimore is more largely indebted than to any other for its present proud position in the base ball world—a gentleman who has steadily supported the national game through thick and thin, in times of prosperity and adversity. His name I know is on every man's lips. I mean Harry Von der Horst. And now allow me to thank you again, and in closing let me hazard a prophecy that the champions of '94 will be the champions in '95.

Hanlon was roundly cheered, and the Citizens' Committee presented him and Von der Horst with a reproduction of the pennant in diamonds crossed by a bat of gold surmounted by a ball of pearl. Each player was greeted with deafening yells when they were called up one by one to receive generous checks. It was late into the night when everyone finally dispersed for their homes.[47]

The celebrations continued the next afternoon when the Orioles were given a special benefit performance at Ford's Theatre in Baltimore, where the renowned Broadway star Fanny Brice, much to the players' delight, performed a "clever impersonation" of Hanlon while singing "How We Won the Pennant." She presented Hanlon and each of the players with a gold pen and pin, gifts from theatre manager Charles Ford. Then the pennant-clinching game against Cleveland was replayed on Compton's Electric Game Impersonator, and the crowd applauded wildly for each player when his turn at bat was indicated by the board. The proceeds of the performance were divided among Miss Brice and the players.[48]

In the evening, the Orioles sat in stage boxes as guests of honor at the Harris Academy of Music, where the audience became hoarse from their constant cheering of the champions. The players watched a program which consisted of the balcony scene from *Romeo and Juliet*, a baseball parody of the opera *Ernani*, and a recitation of an ode to the Orioles, among other things. Hanlon and Von der Horst were called to the stage, where a committee of citizens presented them with magnificent diamond pins. The celebration concluded when the Orioles appeared on stage in their new gold and black uniforms, and amid repeated and enthusiastic applause, they staged living pictures of their famous plays.[49]

As the official celebrations ended, many of the players attended other smaller and more private celebratory events, where some of them forgot the temperance pledge they had previously made.[50]

* * *

From 1884–1890, a postseason series was played between the pennant winners of the National League and the American Association. That series ended when the American Association folded in 1891. To fill the postseason void, William Chase Temple, a past president and part-owner of the Pittsburgh Pirates, donated a silver cup set on an onyx base to serve as the prize for the winner of a postseason series between the first- and second-place teams in 1894. The National League gave its blessing, and thus began the Temple Cup Series.

Once it was determined that the Orioles and Giants would play for the Temple Cup, Hanlon and Ward met in late September to discuss some details, and the League began finalizing others. Temple may have provided the idea and the cup, but he had left most of the details, such as the number of games in the series, the dates, the locations, and the umpire selection, up to the participating teams and the League. However, he was absolutely resolute on one point: the winning players would divide 65 percent of the net profits, and the losing players would divide the remaining 35 percent.

The Orioles, however, were not happy with the plan for dividing the proceeds. When Hanlon and Ward met, they agreed to a 50-50 split, but Temple refused to agree to this because he believed it would remove the incentive to win and reduce the status of the series to merely an exhibition. A flurry of arguments, accusations, and ultimatums followed. Hanlon claimed that he was told that the pennant winner would get 65 percent, regardless of the outcome of the series. Ward accused the Orioles of being afraid to play the Giants, and he said they were agreeable to play under the original terms.[51]

Brooklyn President Charles Byrne, who was put in charge by the League to draw up the rules for the series, was so fed up with the haggling that he said he was perfectly willing to call it all off. League President Nick Young simply said that the series would be played according to the original terms, or not at all.[52]

Hanlon tried to work out a compromise with his players on the payout, but they made it clear they did not care to hear his views on the matter. Nevertheless, he met with John Ward at the Eutaw House on the morning of the first game of the series, and they both agreed to play the games under the original provisions set by the League.[53]

Although the players were still unsure if they would play the series, there was a festive atmosphere as thousands of fans made their way to Union Park for the first game. Various flags flew proudly at the ball park: the newly won pennant flag, the black and orange flag of the Orioles, and Old Glory. Vendors called out the sale of red lemonade and peanuts, and peddlers roamed through the crowd selling all manner of Orioles trinkets.[54]

Right before game time, Ward walked up to Robinson and asked him whether they would be playing a cup game or an exhibition. He said that if it was to be an exhibition, they would play for the benefit of the fans, but then would return to New York and claim the cup by forfeit. Robinson immediately consulted with his teammates.[55]

What many people in the stands at the time did not realize was that some Orioles had already cut private side deals with Giants to split the proceeds of the series 50-50

Amos Rusie and Joe Kelley struck such a bargain, as did "Dirty" Jack Doyle and Willie Keeler. The purpose of the meeting called by Robinson was to convince John McGraw, who was the last holdout, to play. McGraw relented and struck a deal with Giants third baseman George Davis, and the announcement was made to the crowd that the game was to be played for the Cup.[56]

The Orioles chose to bat first. Amos Rusie threw the first pitch, and the Temple Cup Series began. The Orioles played listlessly and were shut out through the first eight innings. They managed to scratch out a run in the ninth, but Rusie, who compiled a 36–13 record for the Giants that year, dominated the Orioles in a 4–1 victory.

McGraw petulantly announced after the game that he had changed his mind and would not play again in the series. His teammates were stunned as they were already short-handed because Frank Bonner was at the bedside of his sick wife and was unable to play.[57] Once again, uncertainty hovered over the series.

The *Baltimore Sun*, rarely critical of the Orioles during the season, called them to task for their reluctance to play the series and for their performance in the game. The reporter said that the Baltimore public had a right to "expect that the players would manfully assume the responsibility which had devolved upon them as pennant winners and not act like spoilt children."[58]

The next day, McGraw changed his mind and decided to play, but it would be of little consequence. For whatever reason, the Orioles played with an evident lack of enthusiasm and energy throughout the rest of the series, and they were swept in the best-of-seven series, which ended with an embarrassing 16–3 loss at the Polo Grounds. The first Temple Cup Series was mercifully over.

Once the receipts were sorted out, the shares came to $768 for each Giant and $360 for each Oriole; however, it appears that not all the Giants honored their agreement to split the shares 50-50. Amos Rusie kept his word and left Joe Kelley $200, but Giants first baseman Jack Doyle left town and never paid what he owed to Willie Keeler. This would cause a considerable amount of bad blood between Doyle and the Orioles in the future.[59]

There was much weeping and gnashing of teeth in Baltimore over the Temple Cup loss, and plenty of blame was thrown around. Although McGraw was harshly abused in most of the press and among the fans for his apathetic attitude, Albert Mott of the *Sporting News* defended him. He claimed that McGraw's reason for not wanting to play was because he knew many of his teammates had not honored their temperance pledge and were in no condition to compete.[60]

Certainly, the performance of the Orioles in the Temple Cup was a disappointment to the city and team, but when all was said and done, they were still the pennant winners, and Nick Young publicly reminded everyone that the Temple Cup had no bearing on which team was the League champion.

* * *

The team had much to be proud of in 1894 as they had finished the year with a regular season record of 89–39–1, and the winning and unselfish culture that Hanlon created was reflected in the fact that he had gone the entire season without having to fine a player.[61]

The Orioles hitters had an outstanding year. The team batting average was .343, and every starter in the lineup hit .335 or higher, except for Heinie Reitz, who hit a respectable .303. Joe Kelley led the team with a .393 average, and Wilbert Robinson had the highest average of his career (.353). The Orioles also drastically improved their defense. In 1893, they were seventh in the league in errors (384) and finished ninth in fielding percentage (.929). In 1894, they made the fewest errors (293) and had the highest fielding percentage in the league (.944). Hanlon's spring training work and morning practices had paid off.

In addition, the organization had a wildly successful year. Under Hanlon's leadership as President of the club, the steps they took in improving the ball park, stirring up fan interest, and being willing to spend the money to acquire players, resulted in the team drawing a total of 328,000 fans, third-best in the 12-team league. This translated into a financial bonanza, and the club confessed to having made a profit of $36,000 for the season.[62]

The success of the Orioles was attributed to the teamwork, pluck, and aggressiveness of the players. Praise also poured in from Hanlon's peers. Cleveland player-manager Patsy Tebeau declared that Hanlon's wise player moves strengthened every weakness as soon as it became apparent, and Cap Anson sent a telegram to Hanlon saying, "I take off my hat to you. May you hold the pennant until the [Chicago] Colts take it from you."[63]

Although the players' unselfish attitudes were given much credit, the majority of the praise for the team's remarkable ascendency went to Hanlon, and the overflowing adulation that Hanlon was getting started to rankle some of the Orioles, particularly John McGraw. Neither McGraw nor any other player ever took a direct shot openly in the press at Hanlon as the architect of the Orioles' success, but a belief had started to fester in some of the players that Hanlon was getting too much credit for it. This led to a jealousy which built in the coming years in confrontations that took place privately between Hanlon and some players. One of the first public signs of this jealousy was evident in a cryptic one-liner that appeared in the gossip column of *Sporting Life* after the season was over: "It is said that Manager Hanlon has become very unpopular with some of his players, especially young McGraw."[64]

Hanlon did, however, receive some criticism from detractors who claimed that he tended to leave ineffective pitchers in a game too long. Some thought that Hanlon was making his pitchers "take their medicine" for some offense they may have committed in order to teach them a lesson. Others believed that he could not bear to hurt their feelings by removing them in the presence of spectators. If he did have any sentimentality for his pitchers, however, it was dissipated by the concerns of the pennant race. Coming down the stretch, when a pitcher weakened, Hanlon did not wait for the crowd to yell at him to remove him, and "he [was] pulled off like a dishrag—limp and saturated—to swab off the bench."[65]

* * *

Despite all the success of the Orioles during the season, Baltimore fans worried because it was reported that Hanlon would not manage the Orioles in 1895 due to a serious falling-out with Von der Horst. The issue was a financial disagreement that originated when Hanlon had lent Von der Horst $7,000 at the end of 1893 and was given stock in the team as security for the loan. It was said that at that time, the transaction was understood by Hanlon to be a practical sale of the stock. However, when the season ended, and the stock was valued at $15,000 because of the phenomenal success of the team, Von der Horst demanded the return of the stock, took the profits for himself, and merely repaid Hanlon the original amount of the loan.[66]

When Hanlon's business acumen is considered, it is highly improbable that Hanlon could have misunderstood the agreement. Throughout his life, there can be no question that Hanlon had a firm grasp on business and personal finances. *Sporting Life* depicted Von der Horst as unscrupulous and commented that "Hanlon, who has done so much for the team, now draws a simple salary."[67]

The Baltimore players sympathized with Hanlon on the issue, and Joe Kelley spoke out publicly in support of Hanlon, attributing the successful season to his energy and ability. By mid–November, not a player on the Baltimore team had signed a contract for the next season. There was an attempt under way to form a new version of the American Association, and it was reported that if Hanlon did not get his due from Von der Horst, he would go to the new league and the players would join him.[68]

The players had another reason to be upset with Von der Horst. During the season, he had promised Wilbert Robinson a house and building lot if the team won the pennant. The other players were aware of it, and they had great fun shouting, "There goes a brick off Robbie's house" after every Orioles win.[69] The popular Robinson had clearly played a vital role in the team winning the pennant, so naturally the players were angered when Von der Horst reneged on the deal. Once again, it was reported that the players would jump to the new league if it got off the ground.[70]

Publicly, both Von der Horst and Hanlon declared that the rumor of a rift in their relationship was false, and the press was frustrated with its inability to glean details about the disagreement: "Von der Horst says there is nothing going on, Ned Hanlon says there is nothing going on....So there you are....Still, the players are reported to be talking about it and expressing sympathy for Mr. Hanlon, who would stop the whole clatter by a published denial over his own signature. Some wonder that he does not do that, if he truthfully could."[71]

The purported breach between them was said to be the sensation of the League meeting in November, where it was reported that Hanlon was demanding a $6,000 salary and one-twelfth of all profits for the coming season. It was also reported that he had been offered $10,000 to manage the Pittsburgh Pirates, and this gave him leverage in his negotiations with Von der Horst.[72] By December, Hanlon had worked out his differences with the Baltimore owner, and he signed again as manager of the Orioles. The Pirates, unable to entice Hanlon to come to Pittsburgh, hired Connie Mack as interim manager.[73]

Now that fences had been mended with Von der Horst, it was time for Hanlon to turn his attention to other matters: preparations for the 1895 baseball season and the defense of the National League pennant.

7

Band of Brothers (1895)

On the afternoon on January 14, Union Park groundskeeper Tom Murphy, who lived in a cottage in the northeast corner of the park, discovered a small fire near the clubhouse used by the Baltimore players, and he quickly put it out. He went to Hanlon's house at 2403 North Calvert Street, just two blocks from the ball park, to inform him of the situation. Hanlon was not home, so Murphy returned to the ball park and stayed alert for further trouble.

Shortly before midnight, Murphy saw flames shooting from the grandstand right behind home plate. He ran there and tried to put the fire out, but it grew so rapidly that he could not extinguish it. He ran out on Huntington Avenue, where he met a patrolman who sent out an alarm. When an engine company arrived, it was able to save the bleachers, but the grandstand and both clubhouses were destroyed.[1]

Hanlon and Wilbert Robinson had gone together to the theatre that evening, and they saw the fire as they returned home. Von der Horst estimated the damages at $12,000 and said they only had $7,500 in insurance on the park. Hanlon lamented, "We were about to put more insurance on."[2] After considering other locations for a brief time, Hanlon and Von der Horst decided to rebuild on the same site.

While business was conducted at the League meeting in March, Hanlon found an occasion to poke fun at his old Brotherhood cohort, Buck Ewing. The Cincinnati Reds manager boasted to Hanlon that his team would not finish in the second division in the coming season, and Hanlon responded by saying, "Where in thunder will you finish? There is no third division." *Sporting Life* reported that "the temperature fell to zero,"[3] but one can't help but feel that Ewing had to take it as a joke among old friends.

After the League meeting, Hanlon was busy making plans for the upcoming spring training trip to Macon, and he also had player issues that required his attention. By the first week, some of the team had signed contracts, including Duke Esper, who agreed to a special clause in his contract that provided for a reduction of salary if he drank beer, as it caused him to gain weight.[4] However, Bill Hawke, Brodie, McGraw, Kelley, Keeler, and Jennings were all holding out for pay increases.

Bill Hawke's holdout was not actually pay-related, but a ruse to disguise another reason for not reporting on time. A few weeks before, he had fallen off a horse and had broken his wrist. He attempted to cover up the injury by refusing to report, hoping it would give him time to recover; however, when Hanlon seemed to be willing to come to terms with him, he had to admit the injury. He anticipated a return later in the season, but the bone never sufficiently healed, and the brief career of Bill Hawke came to a premature close.[5]

But the holdouts of the Big Four and their fifth wheel, Brodie, were all about the money. Although the players vigorously denied it, it appeared to Hanlon and the press that their holdout was a planned "combine" created to strengthen their bargaining position. As they had done in previous years, McGraw and Jennings were working with the St. Bonaventure team in the off-season, and Hanlon cited as evidence of the combine a letter he had received from Jennings that "did not sound at all like bashful Hughie....It reads as McGraw talks."[6]

Hanlon sent letters to the players and publicly announced that he would not change his terms. He had offered them a raise of about $500 on top of the $1,500 they were paid in 1894,[7] and he considered that to be generous considering the $2,400 salary cap which was in existence at that time. Hanlon took a firm stance and said that if they did not accept his offers, they would endanger the financial security of their families and cause ill-feeling among the Baltimore fans. He also made it clear that if they did not report on time, the team would head for spring training without them, and if they decided to report at a later date, they would be offered lowered salaries at that time.[8] Hanlon went on record saying that he would let all five players watch the game from the grandstand at 50 cents per head before he would change his terms.[9]

When Kelley had earlier met with Hanlon to discuss contract matters, Kelley said Hanlon's offer was less than what the Pittsburgh outfielders received the previous year. Hanlon contacted Pirates manager Connie Mack to see if that was true, but Mack disputed Kelley's claim and said that Hanlon's offer was as much as his outfielders made. He added that it was probably as much as any other outfielder in the League made except for established stars such as Ed Delahanty, Hugh Duffy, and Billy Hamilton.[10]

In general, the local newspapers agreed with Hanson's stance and reminded the players that the recent profits were not even enough for the club to recoup their losses from previous years. The *Morning Herald* declared that "Baseball is a business, and must be carried on on business principles."[11]

By mid-March, McGraw and Jennings relented and came to terms. It is not clear who made the necessary concessions, but it most likely was not Hanlon, who was dealing from a position of strength. Shortly after, Keeler, Kelley, and Brodie did the same.[12] As Hanlon would say years later, "Players always hold out at this time of the year and try to get all they can. There isn't one case out of one hundred where players fail to report when the time comes."[13]

The disputes about contracts were not the only issues that kept Hanlon busy during the early part of the year. Dan Brouthers was not sure that he would play in 1895, so Hanlon searched for someone to play first if Brouthers decided to retire. He attempted to trade for Pirates first baseman Jake Beckley, but when that deal fell through, Hanlon drafted first baseman George "Scoops" Carey from the Milwaukee Brewers of the Western League.[14] Hanlon also was searching for pitchers because it was uncertain if Sadie McMahon would bounce back from the arm injury that had sidelined him at the end of the previous season, and they had lost Bill Hawke. To that end, he signed pitcher Bill Kissinger from the Virginia League.[15]

In November, Hanlon obtained a pitching prospect when he drafted the 23-year-old Bill Hoffer from Buffalo in the Eastern League. Hanlon's old Detroit manager, Jack Chapman, had strongly urged Hanlon to make the deal, saying that Hoffer had great speed and a good curve ball.[16] The signing of Hoffer would greatly benefit the Orioles for the next three seasons.

Most of the players left Baltimore together on March 11. Originally, the team was scheduled to leave on the 13th, but when it was suggested that Hanlon changed the date due to superstition, he said, "No, there isn't a superstitious bone in my body; but—well, it's just as convenient to leave on the 11th as the 13th." The time on the train was pleasantly consumed with players telling baseball tales and playing cards, and Hanlon was the big winner in the card game.[17] McGraw and Jennings arrived in Macon on March 16, saying they were ready to help the Orioles win another pennant and still claiming that there was never a combine. They insisted that they harbored no ill will regarding their contract negotiations, although later events would indicate that was not true.[18]

The team practiced in Macon from March 12--21; however, a great deal of rain and a series of nagging injuries hampered many of the scheduled practices. The weather problems even inspired Hanlon's children to playfully write to him and enclose a small sponge so he could wipe up the Macon grounds.[19]

Despite the poor weather, the team seemed to be in high spirits, and after missing a practice due to rain, the players gathered on the hotel steps and

Bill Hoffer led the league in shutouts and won 31 games for the Orioles in 1895. In his three full years with the Orioles, he compiled a record of 78–24. He was the losing pitcher in the first American League game ever played (Babe Ruth Birthplace & Museum).

sang "Push Dem Clouds Away" with great gusto. When the players could not practice, they stayed in the hotel, playing billiards and otherwise whiling away the time.[20] Kelley and Keeler, still denying any collusion in their holdouts, seemed particularly cheerful and treated the alleged conspiracy as a joke by composing a song called "Who Broke the Lock," which they sang to the amusement of their teammates. With a satisfied smile on his face, Hanlon joined in the chorus of the song.[21]

While in camp, the players vied with one another to see who could lose the most weight during training, and they crowded around the hotel scales every evening to check on their progress. Even the normally portly Robinson was caught up in the weight loss competition. One morning, he went out before breakfast and ran three miles, and dripping wet with sweat, he went to Hanlon's room to show him how hard he was exercising. Hanlon kidded him by responding, "Oh, you can't fool me; you've been in your room pouring water over your head."[22]

During their stay in Macon, the players were treated as heroes, and everywhere they went they were followed by young boys clamoring for their attention. Hanlon made sure that the pennant that they won was flown from a flagpole from their hotel, and it attracted a great deal of attention from the locals.[23] Hanlon also issued new uniforms to the players, and when he opened a crate of new bats for them to choose from, the *Baltimore Sun* playfully reported that "there was considerable scrapping over the possession of several desirable sticks, but no blood was shed."[24]

During an early intra-squad game in Macon before a crowd of 500 spectators, Kid Gleason served as the umpire and entertained his teammates by imposing $50 fines on them, and when McGraw argued with a decision, Gleason ordered him off the field. McGraw refused to leave, but Hanlon convinced Gleason to allow McGraw to finish the game.[25] It is unclear from the reports if McGraw's kicking was good-natured or because his fiery nature could not contain itself even in a friendly contest.

But the next day, things took a decidedly uglier turn. During a meaningless practice game designed merely to give his players exercise before leaving Macon the next day, Hanlon served as the umpire "to the utter dissatisfaction of both teams." McGraw went on one of his tirades and made insulting remarks to Hanlon. Joe Kelley did not go as far as McGraw in his insubordination, but he certainly contributed to an unruly situation. Because the players were not under contract until April 1, Hanlon could not fine them or suspend them, but he was greatly offended by their derogatory comments.

The *Baltimore Sun* attributed the situation to lingering hard feelings regarding the contract disputes:

> The attitude assumed by some of them toward Mr. Hanlon by no means exhibits the spirit which members of a championship club should show toward their leader, and unless it be nipped in the bud it is calculated to do damage to the club's work. The bumptiousness of some of the ex-kickers sets a bad example to the rest of the team, and especially to the new men, and it is far from pleasing to those who hear their sarcastic remarks.[26]

Harry Von der Horst also played a role in fomenting discontent among the players. Earlier in March, he had been highly critical of the holdout and said, "Ball players invariably affect an independence that is nauseating to those who know them best." He added that the discontented holdouts, after they swore they would not play if they had to agree to Hanlon's terms, turned out to be "like a lot of Hamelin rats [who] flocked to Baltimore when the adroit Hanlon, in the role of the pied piper, piped for the last time..."

He also ranted about the ingratitude of players who were paid salaries well above that of the average worker, and who while on road trips, were treated to the finest hotels, ate the finest food, and traveled in luxurious Pullman cars.[27]

Comparing the players to rats who marched to Hanlon's tune certainly had to infuriate this group of proud men, and it must have outraged even the players who did not hold out. Hanlon, who now bore the brunt of his players' ire, most certainly could not have been pleased with Von der Horst's indiscrete comments, and it fell fully on him to defuse this situation, restore harmony, and direct the focus of his team on a shared goal: to win the pennant once again.

Von der Horst, likely after a rebuke from Hanlon, attempted damage control by sending a letter to *Sporting Life* in which he categorically denied saying anything about the players. He insisted that public statements about club issues were entirely in the purview of Hanlon. He claimed that the remarks attributed to him were "manufactured news without my knowledge."[28] Evidently, the accusation of "fake news" did not originate with early twenty-first-century politics. In any case, no one bought Von der Horst's denial.

Von der Horst's unfortunate comments were not the only problem that Hanlon was forced to deal with in the spring. His fears about the condition of Sadie McMahon were realized, and it became clear that arm troubles would keep him from pitching for at least a few months.[29] In early April, Hanlon held a meeting with a small group of unidentified players with whom he was dissatisfied. He told them that they "seem to think they are taking a Southern trip for their health," and they were not meeting his expectations regarding work ethic and personal conduct. He ended by telling them that he did not intend to warn them about these issues again.[30]

From Macon, the team moved to New Orleans, where they worked out for a week. While there, a potentially deadly incident occurred as they headed to the hotel after practice. The train car in which Hanlon, Brouthers, Kissinger, and Hemming were riding was struck by lightning and lifted from the track. For a moment, there was great concern and confusion, and Hemming said he shut his eyes, thinking that he would die. Miraculously, no one was injured.[31]

After leaving New Orleans to head home, the team stopped along the way to play exhibition games in Montgomery, Atlanta, Raleigh, Danville, Roanoke, Lynchburg, Petersburg, Portsmouth, Norfolk, and Richmond.[32] In the meantime, Von der Horst was overseeing the plans that he and Hanlon had made for rebuilding Union Park. They had decided to replace the single-level grandstand with a double-decker with private boxes and a press box on the second tier, supported by seven iron girders weighing 7,000 pounds each. The use of iron pillars, instead of wooden ones, would lessen the viewing obstructions and make the structure less susceptible to fire. The new grandstands were ornamented and allowed seating for 4,000 people, and Hanlon arranged for opera-type seating in the reserved sections. The stands extended even further down the right field line than the previous one did.[33] Near the clubhouse, a bicycle barn was being erected and would come with attendants to check the wheels. In addition, spaces for carriages and horses were created.[34]

Wearing the orange-and-black-trimmed uniforms they first donned for the Temple Cup series, the Orioles opened the season against Philadelphia at Union Park before an overflow crowd estimated at 14,000.[35] They lost that game, 7–6, and it portended a rough start for the team. After winning only 10 of their first 21 games, they found themselves in eighth place, 6½ games behind the league-leading Pittsburgh Pirates.

The press attributed the poor play of the Orioles to several factors that caused a breakdown of the harmony that was so instrumental to the success of the 1894 team. One reason for discontent was that Hanlon, who had sensed that his old friend and teammate, Dan Brouthers, was losing his edge, sold him to Louisville.[36] This move upset the players, and it was said to have caused a clique to form against Brouthers' replacement, the slick-fielding George "Scoops" Carey.

There were also rumors of personal conflicts that were disruptive to team chemistry: supposedly Robinson and Hanlon were butting heads, Kelley hadn't spoken to Hanlon since the season opened, and McGraw was a "leading malcontent" because of lingering resentment over his salary.[37]

Sporting Life reported that the reason for the team's difficulties was that McGraw and Jennings now bristled at taking instruction from Hanlon because they believed they knew more about the game than he did.[38] The *Baltimore Sun* lamented that while the rest of the league was adopting the methods previously used by the Orioles and performing much better as a result, the Orioles had "forgotten the lessons which Manager Hanlon taught them last year."[39]

McGraw emphatically denied that there was dissension on the Baltimore team. He further insisted that Robinson and Hanlon were not at odds and that no clique against Carey existed.[40] Hanlon supported McGraw's assertions and declared that the players were on the best terms. He maintained that the team's poor results were the result of a lack of practice caused by games that had been rained out.[41]

Although the Orioles presented a united front publicly, it is likely that bad feelings still persisted among some Orioles regarding their contracts and other issues. This was particularly true of the enigmatic McGraw, who always seemed to have an axe to grind about something and felt he knew more about everything than anyone else. It was simply his nature.

Throughout their lives, many of the Orioles commented about the family atmosphere that existed on the team. As is the case with most families, the players would fight with one another on occasion, sometimes brutally. Nevertheless, no matter what was going on behind the scenes during the heyday of those great Orioles teams, they never aired their dirty laundry in public. This was true in 1895, and it would remain so as long as they lived.

To deal with the issues that were simmering within the Orioles team, Hanlon resorted to a time-tested strategy: he would unite the discontented elements of his squad against a common enemy. In this case, the enemy was the National League.

Hanlon began an all-out assault on the League and argued that there was a conspiracy between the teams and umpires to do whatever was necessary to dethrone Baltimore.[42] When Brooklyn owner Charles Byrne heard of Hanlon's charge, he was outraged: "That talk of Ned Hanlon about President Young being in a conspiracy to down Baltimore was the most childish charge I have ever read. Does Hanlon think that no one in the League has a license to beat the champions?...The man talks as if he was crazy!"[43]

Hanlon leveled his sights on the League umpires and claimed that the stricter rules against rowdyism were designed solely to strangle the competitive fire of his team. He proclaimed that he was strongly in favor of rules to prevent unnecessary and prolonged kicking, but he argued that the umpires were not using discretion and good sense in enforcing them:

> Ball players are not school children, nor are umpires schoolmasters. It is impossible to prevent explosions of impatience or actions indicating dissent with the umpire's decisions when a player in the heat of the game thinks he has been unjustly treated. The public...[likes] to see a little scrappiness in the game, and would be very much dissatisfied, I believe, to see the players slinking away like whipped schoolboys to their benches, afraid to turn their heads for fear of a heavy fine from some swelled umpire.[44]

Hanlon, not letting up his pressure on Nick Young, also contended that as the league champions, they were entitled to good umpires, but he argued that they were getting the worst ones in the league. He declared that he had made official protests against umpires he felt were incompetent, but Nick Young did not give him the courtesy of a reply.[45]

Baltimore players joined in on the fun by sending a sarcastic telegram to Young, asking him to send his worst umpire to Chicago. Young dismissed Hanlon's charges as being absurd, and he admonished the Orioles for blaming their defeats on umpires no other clubs had complained about.[46]

Along with his diatribe against an alleged league conspiracy, Hanlon gathered his players together in the mornings and worked them hard on tactics that emphasized winning teamwork over individual records, and he did not stop a drill until he was satisfied.[47]

Whether Hanlon's accusations of a League conspiracy united the Orioles in an "us against the world" mentality or not, it is interesting to note that as the press coverage of Hanlon's dissatisfaction grew, rumors of dissension within the Orioles vanished from the press. More importantly, when McGraw's denial of dissension on the team was published, the Orioles were just four games over .500. After its publication, the team went 71–31 for the rest of the year.

* * *

As the Orioles snapped out of their funk, renowned baseball writer Henry Chadwick attended a game and expressed admiration at how the team would take batting practice from live pitching instead of just fungo hitting, a practice he had long advocated. He was also impressed with the defensive skills displayed:

> I never before have witnessed such brilliant catches, pick-ups and such swift and accurate throwing to bases as they exhibited. Their infielding was especially brilliant, particularly that of McGraw at third base, and of Jennings at short stop, and every ball was attended to in the outfield...exhibitions of this kind are seen only at practice, the more serious work in the actual game often showing a falling off. But in this exceptional contest the brilliancy of their practice exhibition, was kept up throughout the game itself, the Baltimore work in pitching, fielding, batting and base-running being a great treat to me.[48]

Even as the Orioles began to play better, they faced a number of problems that left a second straight pennant in doubt. In mid–May, McGraw was ill with what was believed to be malaria, and Hanlon sent him home, where he could recover more quickly under the care of a physician. In all, McGraw would miss 36 games, and Wilbert Robinson was also dealing with a variety of injuries that kept him out of the lineup for 55 games.[49] The pre-season loss of McMahon and Hawke was a serious blow to the pitching staff, and it was only compounded when Kid Gleason, who had pitched so well for the Orioles in 1894, was plagued by arm troubles and was only able to make five starts.

Hanlon knew that if they were to contend, he would once again need to strengthen the pitching staff, so he engineered a trade that sent utility man Frank Bonner and little-used pitcher Bill Kissinger to St. Louis for pitcher Arthur "Dad" Clarkson. Clarkson was thrilled to leave the dysfunctional Browns and the team's eccentric owner, Chris Von der Ahe, and told the press that he knew that players who came to Baltimore often showed marked improvement. He said he hoped that would be the case for him and promised to work hard to be valuable to the club.[50] Clarkson did indeed provide instant pitching help to an Orioles team desperately in need of it, and he compiled a 12–3 record for the team.

* * *

During the season, it became clear that the new rules regarding kicking were being ignored by the Orioles. Robinson, the captain and the only player authorized to argue with an umpire, would often be unable to make a valid protest because a furious crowd of angry Orioles would immediately surround the arbiter. Many spectators were disgusted by the behavior of the players and believed the protests did the team more harm than good.[51]

After McGraw was thrown out of a game in July, Hanlon called a meeting to inform his players that the kicking must stop. He ordered that challenges to the umpire must be handled only by Robinson and explained that having their best players thrown out of games hurt their chances of winning. *Sporting Life* wryly observed that Hanlon was beginning to realize that it was up to the club, and not the umpires, to discipline their players.[52]

To compound the woes of the Orioles, in a game at New York on June 28, Heinie Reitz fell chasing a pop up and hurt his shoulder. Although Reitz said he would be all right in a day or two, he was in considerable pain, and Hanlon insisted that he be examined by a doctor. It was determined that he had broken his collarbone,[53] and Hanlon now needed a second baseman. Kid Gleason had hit .346 in 26 games for the Orioles the previous year, so Hanlon decided to try him at second. Gleason responded well, hitting .309 for the season, and Hanlon was so satisfied with his play that he kept him as the regular second baseman after Reitz recovered from his injury.

In July, fans in Baltimore became concerned when it was reported that Giants owner Andrew Freedman had met with Hanlon and offered him a large sum to manage the Giants the following season.[54] There was excitement in New York about the possibility, and it was said that fans would erect a statue of Freedman in gratitude if he could land Hanlon.[55] When asked if he would be going to New York, Hanlon said that he had no reason to leave Baltimore because he considered it his home, and he felt great personal pride in the Baltimore team he helped create.[56]

Hanlon and the Orioles finally received some good news at the end of July, when groundskeeper Tom Murphy met the team in Chicago and gave Hanlon glowing reports about how well Sadie McMahon was throwing at Union Park. Hanlon left the team after the Pittsburgh series and took newly signed catcher Frank Bowerman with him to give McMahon a tryout as the team went to Louisville without him.[57]

Throughout the season, Baltimore fans had incessantly speculated about the condition of McMahon's arm and when, or if, he would rejoin the Orioles. In May, McMahon told the *Baltimore Sun* that he had been undergoing treatment since the previous August and that, although doctors had given him permission to begin pitching again, he would not throw before he felt he was ready. "There has been no disagreement between Mr. Hanlon and me about my not pitching....All the kick has been made by the public,

Wilbert Robinson was the calm eye of the storm on Hanlon's rowdy Orioles (Babe Ruth Birthplace & Museum).

and they don't understand the case." He concluded by joking that he would let his beard grow out, and then he would make his debut "as an unknown phenomenon."[58]

When Hanlon arrived at Union Park with Bowerman, McMahon assured him that he was ready to pitch. After watching him throw for five minutes, Hanlon pronounced McMahon as good as ever. McMahon announced that he was anxious to rejoin the team because he had been given good treatment by the club, and he wanted to win the pennant for the Orioles.[59] Many years later, McMahon told a more colorful story about his return to the Orioles. He said that the following conversation took place when he ran into Hanlon on a street in Baltimore:

> "What's the matter, Ed, you look downhearted," said McMahon.
> "I am, Mac," said Hanlon. "I'm afraid they've got us licked."
> "Don't worry. I'm ready to go to work now and I'll win you that championship."
> "Mac, that's the best news I've heard," replied Hanlon.[60]

On August 2, the Orioles were three games behind the league-leading Cleveland Spiders. The next day, McMahon made his first start and beat the Senators, 1–0, the first of eight straight games he won. During that streak he had four shutouts, which tied for the league title with teammate Bill Hoffer. He ended the season 10–4 with a 2.94 ERA.

Hanlon would carefully pick his spots with McMahon for the remainder of the season.

Of his 15 starts, six came in the second game of a doubleheader. This would allow McMahon to take advantage of the fading light and benefit from the possibility of a game shortened due to darkness.[61] Indeed, that did occur in five of those six starts, and McMahon went 5–1 during those nightcaps.

As the Orioles began the last two months of the regular season, Hanlon had a formidable pitching staff in place with Bill Hoffer, George Hemming, Sadie McMahon, Duke Esper, and Dad Clarkson. McMahon's return revitalized the Orioles, and from the day of his first start until the end of the year, the Orioles won 42 of their last 53 games.

Hanlon had another reason to celebrate a few weeks before the season ended. While the team was in Boston, Hanlon was sent word that he was now the father of his first daughter, the third child of Hanlon and his wife, Ellen. They would name her Mary Edwina Hanlon. A rooter traveling with the team said, "I have never seen the quiet, unimpressionable man so hilarious. He is going around the hotel corridor in such a fever of joy that it is hard to believe it to be Ned Hanlon."[62] Later in Boston, friends of Hanlon called him to home plate before a game and presented him with a doll carriage filled with flowers and decorated with ribbons in the colors of the Baltimore club.[63]

The Orioles clinched their second straight pennant on September 28 when they defeated the Giants, 5–2, behind Bill Hoffer in New York. Hughie Jennings made a spectacular game-ending play when he leapt high to snare a liner and double George Van Haltren off second base. Orioles fans poured out of the stands and carried Jennings off on their shoulders. Hanlon, always looking ahead, announced: "I am gratified at the conscientious efforts of our boys, and I feel that we will be able to land the pennant still another year."[64]

As they rode to the hotel on the elevated train, the celebration continued and the players sang, "There's only one team in the world for me. / Only one team that I care to see, / For they are two-time winners, and them I do adore; / There's only one team, and that's in Baltimore." Cheers went up for Hanlon and the players, individually and collectively all the way to their hotel.[65]

Near the end of the season, a reporter from New York who was on a boat excursion with the team was surprised by what he referred to as the "Jekyll-and-Hyde"

7. Band of Brothers (1895)

The 1895 pennant-winning Orioles went 87–43, but they lost their second straight Temple Cup Series to the Cleveland Spiders. Top row, left to right: Arthur "Dad" Clarkson, Duke Esper, George "Scoops" Carey, William "Boileryard" Clarke. Middle row, left to right: Steve Brodie, Heinie Reitz, Sadie McMahon, George Hemming, Frank Bowerman, Arlie Pond. Seated left to right: Kid Gleason, Joe Kelley, Ned Hanlon, Wilbert Robinson, Bill Hoffer, Hughie Jennings. Front row: John McGraw, Harry Hopper (batboy), Willie Keeler (collection of Tom Delise).

Orioles. He was amazed that the group so often referred to as thugs and hoodlums were well-dressed, well-mannered, and unassuming off the field. He was astounded that McGraw was the quietest member of the team and "talks in the most interesting way about baseball as a science." He also described how the players clearly displayed the respect they had for Hanlon and said that they were on the whole a harmonious group.

He noted that Hanlon did not sneak around to keep his eye on his players, and he related how when some of them walked into the bar to have a glass of beer, Hanlon, who was already there, smiled and said to Von der Horst, "Give the boys a chance," and left the players on their own. The reporter related how the players did not abuse their manager's confidence in them and they had only one glass each, and then left to go to bed, "dreaming of the Temple Cup series to come."[66]

* * *

As the season was winding down, there was a great deal of discussion regarding the upcoming Temple Cup Series. There were bitter feelings on the part of the Orioles regarding the division of the receipts in the first series, and there was still concern that the Temple Cup overshadowed the importance of the pennant. Some of the magnates felt the series wasn't worth the trouble and suggested that it be discontinued. Nevertheless, President Byrne of Brooklyn and League President Young, who comprised the Temple Cup committee, decided that the series would continue.[67]

The 1895 Temple Cup series proved a wild and rowdy affair for players and fans alike. The Orioles faced the team which was to be their arch-nemesis during the 1895 and 1896 seasons, the Cleveland Spiders. It was a team that could equal, if not surpass, the ferocity of the Orioles. They were led by two future Hall of Famers, pitcher Cy Young and hard-hitting outfielder Jesse Burkett.

To avoid the distractions of the pennant celebration that took place prior to the Temple Cup in 1894, Hanlon took the team directly from New York to Cleveland, where the first three games of the series were scheduled at League Park. In the first game on October 2, rowdy Spiders fans bombarded the Orioles with fruit, cabbages, rotten eggs, and bottles. Starting pitchers Sadie McMahon and Cy Young both struggled, and in an exciting, back-and-forth game, the Orioles took a 4–3 lead in the top of the ninth, but lost in the bottom of the inning.

The crowd for the second game was even bigger and more boisterous, and the fans were so rowdy that it prompted Cleveland management to offer a $25 reward to policemen who arrested anyone who threw objects at the players.[68] A big first inning led the Spiders to a 7–2 win, and after another lopsided loss in the third game, the Series returned to Baltimore, where the Orioles hoped to avoid an embarrassing sweep.

As the Spiders left their hotel in a horse-drawn wagon on their way to Union Park for Game Four, Orioles fans got revenge for the treatment of their players in Cleveland, pelting the Spiders with rotten fruit, vegetables, and stones. Behind a masterful pitching performance by Duke Esper, the Orioles finally won a Temple Cup game, defeating the Spiders, 5–0. After the game, the Baltimore police tried to sneak the Spiders out of the ball park, but a mob of 1,500 was waiting for them and bombarded them with anything they could get their hands on.[69] The next day, the Orioles lost their second consecutive Temple Cup series when Cy Young beat them. Once again, the Spiders needed a police escort to get back to the hotel as fans bombarded the Temple Cup winners with stones.[70]

Despite another Temple Cup loss, the city once again celebrated their team's second consecutive pennant with a big parade attended by large crowds and a big celebratory ball held at the Harris Academy of Music. The players were individually congratulated by the mayor, and the championship pennant was formally presented to Hanlon and the players on the stage. The crowd shouted out for Hanlon to give a speech.

He stepped forward and accepted the pennant on behalf of the people of Baltimore, assuring them that it belonged to them, and asserted that the credit for winning it belonged to the players and not to him. He concluded by saying, "I am not going to tell you the methods by which we won the championship in 1894 and 1895, and how we expect to win it in 1896, because then you would know as much as I do, and some of you might be applying for my position. That would never do, as I am by no means ready to leave Baltimore."

The crowd roared its approval.[71]

* * *

The 1895 Orioles produced some impressive team and individual performances. The team led the league in ERA and fielding and had the second-highest batting average. George Hemming won 20 games, but Bill Hoffer was even better as he compiled a record

7. Band of Brothers (1895)

of 31–6. Hughie Jennings hit .386, and Willie Keeler hit over .370 for the second consecutive year. Keeler was now regarded as one of the brightest stars in baseball. Sportswriter O. P. Caylor thought he knew why:

> Thanks to Manager Hanlon's superior judgment, Keeler stands today the leader of the batsman of the country. Hanlon tested Willie in right field, but he "made a mess of it" and after a few games, choking with emotion, he went to Hanlon and begged for his release.
>
> He said to Hanlon, "I am out of my class in the Big League, and I want to get back to the class where I can hold up my end, and I want to go there before I ruin my chance even in that company by a bad record here."
>
> Hanlon jollied the boy along and refused to let him go.
>
> Keeler begged and pleaded to no purpose, and Hanlon finally said to him:
>
> "You might as well understand me, Billy. You are going to play that field right along every day even if you miss half the balls that come out your way. So the quicker you dismiss the idea that you can't play on this nine and get to work doing your best the better it will be for you and the club." Keeler went back to his work despondently, but from that day his fielding improved. Confidence had been his lacking ingredient.... Before the season was half over Keeler's fielding and batting were the talk of admiring thousands and his fame was established throughout the broad land. To Manager Hanlon he owes everything.[72]

* * *

Throughout the season, there had been concern over first baseman George Carey's lack of hitting prowess and skill in running the bases. It was acknowledged that his defensive skills saved many errors for his fellow infielders, but the question was which was more valuable: the glove or a more potent bat at the position.[73]

As a result, gossip filled the sports pages regarding Hanlon's supposed interest in various first basemen. Shortly after arriving at the League meeting in November, Giants owner Andrew Freedman and Hanlon were spotted talking together in the lobby of the Fifth Avenue Hotel. Within 20 minutes, they consummated a deal that make Dirty Jack Doyle an Oriole. Hanlon would have to pay a big price for Doyle: Kid Gleason and $3,500 in cash.[74] Hanlon expressed sorrow in losing Gleason, acknowledging that he was always willing to do what was asked of him, was popular among his teammates and the fans, and won many games for the team.[75]

On the last evening of the League meetings, Hanlon and Von der Horst, evidently in a celebratory mood because of their acquisition of Doyle, bought champagne for their fellow magnates and offered a toast to the "twice champions." The joyful mood of the Baltimore contingent was somewhat diminished when in response to their toast, someone yelled out, "Temple Cup."[76]

There could be no argument that Doyle was an excellent player. He had hit well over .300 for the past three years, including a monster year in 1894, when he hit .368 with 103 RBI. Moreover, he was an accomplished base runner who averaged 42 stolen bases during his past five seasons. With his fiery personality, he seemed to be a perfect fit for the Orioles.

But was he?

The trade caused great apprehension in Baltimore. Gleason was beloved by Orioles fans, and to lose him for Dirty Jack Doyle, a player Orioles fans loved to hate ever since he reneged on his Temple Cup deal with Keeler, was hard for them to accept. Doyle also had the reputation of being a man who could not get along with his teammates, and it was no secret that some Orioles detested Doyle. Adding him could create an incendiary environment that could destroy the renowned team harmony of the Orioles.

Nevertheless, many Baltimore fans and local pundits had confidence in Hanlon to handle any issues that might arise with Doyle. Moreover, it was hoped that the winning culture of the team could allow Doyle to thrive as a player and help make the Orioles a three-time pennant winner.

Hanlon was supremely confident about the trade and said that Doyle was one of the best players in the League. Moreover, he said Doyle told him he was eager to play for the Orioles. Hanlon said of Doyle, "He is not only fast when he plays, but he plays all the time, and his mind is in the game."[77]

Whatever opinion a person chose to take on the Doyle acquisition, one thing was certain: a seat to watch this drama unfold would certainly be worth the price of admission.

* * *

Near the end of the season, an article in the *Boston Globe* featured Hanlon's rise as one of baseball's best managers. The reporter elaborated on how Hanlon had taken a Baltimore club that was in a state of financial and organizational ruin and turned it into a top club that was one of the most valuable in baseball. When asked to describe the training methods he employed with his team, he said:

> We rehearse in baseball just the same as actors do on the stage. We go through plays on the diamond. As a result, two years ago after I put the club through such a course of sprouts in the south, the men began the championship season as if they had been playing together for years, and the effects of this system were commented upon and praised by everybody. When we are home the men go to the park at about 10 o'clock, and we practice together for an hour or an hour and a half. If there is a slip-up in a play that needs attention, we go through it. If the player offending is one not liable to err again we pay no attention to it. In the game as it is played today there can be no let up. You must progress all the time and you must have men on your ball club who feel they are on the best ball club in the country and will work to show it.

The article described the "frictionless" relationship he had

"Dirty" Jack Doyle was an exceptional hitter, baserunner, and first baseman. Although he managed to aggravate most of his teammates and managers during his career, he and Hanlon got along well. He was a key contributor for the Orioles in 1896, when they won their third straight pennant and their first Temple Cup Series (Babe Ruth Birthplace & Museum).

with his captains, Wilbert Robinson and Joe Kelley. Kelley was interviewed for the piece, and he had high praise for his manager. He said that although "the men all know that [Hanlon] is a practical baseball man and knows more about the game than anyone under him," he rarely said anything to his players during the game; instead, he left the execution of the game plan to his captain and the players, occasionally offering a comment or suggestion. Kelley said that Hanlon "never takes a man to task before another player, and when he has occasion to find fault, he does so in the quietest manner imaginable, so that no sore is left. It is only when pushed to extremities that he will fine a man. At a word, he is an ideal man for a player to play under."[78]

As the year came to a close and the players headed to pursue their various off-season pursuits, Orioles fans had great reason for optimism when they learned that the Big Four had agreed to contract terms for the 1896 season before they left town.[79] There would be no distracting salary issues in the coming year.

The Orioles and their manager all had three-peat on their minds.

8

Dirty Jack Comes to Town (1896)

After the deal to secure Jack Doyle was made, he and Hanlon went to Nick Engle's bar in New York, where Hanlon told Doyle he was happy to have him on the team. At that time, Doyle expressed concern that he would not be welcomed by the Orioles, but Hanlon assured him that the players wanted him on their team, and he would be welcomed with enthusiasm in the city. The men parted amiably. But shortly after arriving back home in Holyoke, Doyle began having serious doubts about going to Baltimore.

When the deal was made public, rumors in baseball circles quickly percolated that the Baltimore players did not want Doyle on their team. Hearing this, Doyle began to think about the contentious relationships that he had with some Orioles and about the taunts he had received from Baltimore fans about being a dirty player and a welsher. Doyle changed his mind, and he declared that he did not want to play in Baltimore because he did not believe the city or players would be congenial to him. He wrote to Hanlon and told him he could not be convinced to play for the Orioles, and he defended himself against charges that he was not a team player, saying that he always was more concerned with whether his team won the game, rather than the number of hits he had made.[1]

Hanlon, shocked at Doyle's about-face, asserted that Doyle begged him to bring him to Baltimore before he ever discussed a possible deal with Freedman.[2] Hanlon protested that he never would have taken the chance to disrupt the harmony of the team, so he had held a meeting with the Baltimore players to make sure they would be willing to accept Doyle if he made the trade.[3] Kelley supported Hanlon's claim and said that all the players agreed that the deal should be made because the addition of Doyle would strengthen the team.[4] Hanlon made a point to say that even Willie Keeler, who had been upset with Doyle for welshing on the Temple Cup deal, urged Hanlon to make the trade. Hanlon also asserted that he never would have misled Doyle regarding his players' attitudes toward him.[5]

McGraw supported Hanlon's version of the events, and although he admitted that he had "given [Doyle] the shoulder in the past," he was clear in stating that Doyle was the best first baseman in the league, and he was certain the Orioles would win the pennant with him. He said, "when he comes to Baltimore next season, he will find the heartiest kind of a welcome. That is the secret of our success. There is no internal dissensions in our club, no religious troubles, and no individual playing for records. Everyone wants to win for the glory of his club and for the honor of the town he represents."[6]

Hanlon, acting on a suggestion by McGraw, invited Doyle to come to Baltimore to assure him that he was wanted. Doyle accepted the offer, and on February 13 he met Hanlon at Camden Station, where Hanlon had been empowered by the mayor to present Doyle with the key to the city in a gold snuffbox. They went to Ganzhorn's Steakhouse, where Von der Horst, Kelley, Robinson, McGraw, and other Orioles were there to greet them. They made a great effort to make Doyle feel wanted, and after a banquet of delicacies particular to Maryland, they took Doyle to a show at Ford's Theatre.

The royal treatment worked. By the end of the evening, Doyle said, "Mr. Hanlon and myself will have no trouble in coming to an understanding. I think perhaps I have misunderstood somewhat the feeling in Baltimore, and this is why I have been backward about signing. Now I know I was mistaken." Doyle declared that he would now be glad to join the Orioles and give them his best effort.[7]

* * *

In addition to the Doyle situation, Hanlon had to deal with other issues in the off-season. At the beginning of the year, the Scranton club of the Eastern League offered Hughie Jennings one-third ownership in the team and $800 a month to serve as player and captain. Jennings was interested and said, "Everybody knows how kindly I feel toward Baltimore and our club, but this is not a matter of feeling; it is a matter of business." However, Jennings was skeptical that Hanlon would grant him his release, and when he met with him to discuss the offer, he was right. An irritated Hanlon called the offer "an absurd proposition" and said, "Jennings is under contract, and everybody knows what that means in base-ball."[8] Hughie Jennings would remain with the Orioles in 1896.

Hanlon stayed busy looking for players to supplement his roster. He had concerns about the lingering poor health of McGraw, so in February he signed the 30-year-old Jimmy Donnelly as insurance. Donnelly had played seven years in both the American Association and National League, and he had briefly been a teammate of Hanlon's on the 1885 Detroit Wolverines. Although Donnelly had never hit above .201 in a season where he played more than 100 games, Hanlon evidently saw something in him.

Hanlon expressed confidence in his pitching staff, but his concern about how Sadie McMahon's arm would hold up led him to sign Arlie Pond late in the previous season and Joe Corbett in December. Corbett, who was the younger brother of boxing champion Jim, had started three games for Washington the previous season.

A promising development for Hanlon was that all the Orioles had signed contracts early in the off-season. The Big Four were given large raises, and Hanlon was thrilled: "We start south this year with an entirely different state of feeling than we did last year. All is peace and harmony this season, and the men will pull together from the start."[9] Hanlon pronounced the Orioles stronger than ever, and he predicted they would win the pennant again in 1896.[10]

McGraw had decided not to go to college with Jennings in the off-season as he had done in prior years because he felt it would be too much strain on his health. He said, "Baseball is my business now and I am, though reluctantly, going to sacrifice study so that I can be just right when the umpire says, 'Play ball!'" To that end, he spent the off-season in Baltimore, taking long walks to build up his stamina.[11] Prior to their spring training in Macon, Hanlon sent McGraw ahead to serve as his advance agent to arrange for lodging and the use of playing fields for spring training.[12] Hanlon was demonstrating an increasing trust in McGraw's leadership abilities, and this experience helped groom McGraw as a future manager.

In the meantime, the players who lived in Baltimore prepared for spring training by working out at a gymnasium, and in Virginia, Steve Brodie was reportedly "digging for woodchucks, chasing hens, and wrestling a bear" to get in shape.[13]

Hanlon was able to squeeze in some fun in February when he, Von der Horst, and some of the players attended a performance of a play, *The Derby Winner*, at the Holliday Theatre. St. Louis Browns star pitcher Ted Breitenstein played the role of a starter in a horse race, and Baltimore's own Joe Kelley had a small role in the play. In honor of the Orioles guests, the box where they sat was decorated with bunting and the Baltimore championship flags.[14]

* * *

The Orioles left Camden Station in Baltimore the evening of March 14. Hanlon had arranged for the team to stay in Macon for two weeks instead of the one week they spent in 1895. He had taken along an extra couple of young pitchers to give the players plenty of batting practice, and the players spent the first week getting the kinks out of arms, limbering up muscles, and working out soreness and stiffness. Hanlon said that he had "some brand-new tricks evolved at the winter fireside," and promised that the Orioles would "surprise and perplex" their opponents in the coming season.[15]

On the second day, some of the players were sore from the early workouts, and Hanlon reminisced, "This is the worst day. The soreness will begin to wear off tomorrow, and by next week there will not be a sore muscle in the whole crowd. I know how it is myself; I used to get so sore I could hardly walk."[16]

The general practice routine was for the regulars to take their positions in the field while the others took turns hitting. The pitchers and fielders eventually exchanged places with the batters. Hanlon coordinated all the activities so that everyone had a fair share of batting and defense in both the infield and the outfield. He also drilled his players in teamwork and on the mental part of the game, which had been a feature in the club ever since he became manager. The two-hour practice sessions would conclude with a mile run around the track, and then the players would run back to the hotel for dinner and baths.[17]

Reporters traveling with the team were impressed at what they saw: "Hanlon was right with 'em and the way that manager gets his men to work is a caution to the uninitiated."[18] The *Baltimore Sun* reporter added, "It's good, hard, steady work day in and day out, and no excuses go with him. There was nothing but hard work, but not a murmur of complaint was heard."[19]

Throughout the spring, Doyle impressed his teammates with his hitting, base running, and how he went into practice with great energy and enthusiasm. On one occasion, he ran to second base on a double and made a beautiful head-first slide into the bag, causing one of his teammates to remark, "That is something Carey did not do all last season."[20] Doyle was impressed with his first Orioles camp as well and said he had never worked so hard before in practice. He told his new teammates, "No wonder you fellows are pennant winners."[21]

Another bright spot in the spring was Arlie "Doc" Pond. Pond had graduated from medical school and was taking post-graduate courses at the University of Maryland's College of Physicians and Surgeons and Johns Hopkins University when Hanlon signed him in July of 1895. He had only appeared in six games that season, but Hanlon was impressed by the intelligent way that he approached pitching.[22]

Hanlon was aware that McGraw's health was still questionable, so he took it easy on him in practice and excused him from the mile run in Macon. Hanlon hoped McGraw would overcome the illness in time for the beginning of the season, but he expressed confidence that Jimmy Donnelly could fill in well if McGraw was unable to play.[23]

One evening during the team's classroom session, Hanlon and the players engaged in a lively discussion on the subject of kicking. Joe Kelley strongly believed that if kicking was abolished, the players would become mere machines and lose all interest in the game. He argued that the public wanted the players to show some spirit, and Hanlon and McGraw agreed. The animated discussion motivated the normally quiet and non-demonstrative Willie Keeler to declare his intention to do some kicking in the coming year.[24]

Along with the hard work that was taking place on the field, a major source of amusement during spring training was Hanlon's new hobby: bicycle riding. He had received a handsome bicycle by express from Baltimore, and though not very familiar with it, he began trying to ride it immediately. The players took great delight in this, and a number of bets were offered to Hanlon by the players that any one of them could run the mile track faster than he could ride it on his bicycle. Hanlon refused the bets, saying that he "did not want to take the boys' money," although shortly after, he started out to pace the runners around the track, but was quickly passed by them.

Early one morning, Hanlon slipped away to practice his riding under the supervision of his teacher, Wilbert Robinson. After the session, Hanlon proudly declared he was becoming an expert, but Robinson was not a believer and claimed Hanlon could only ride 100 yards without falling if he got a good start. Robinson also gleefully reported that during a practice session, Hanlon took a slide that would have made even an expert slider like McGraw envious.[25]

While in Macon, Hanlon's bicycle riding drew a great deal of attention, and he had a hard time finding a time and place to practice where he would not be constantly surrounded by spectators. He tried getting up as early as seven in the morning, and when he found he was still drawing a crowd, he said he would try to slip out a side door of the hotel at six. When the players heard about this plan, they declared they would make sure they were there to "see the fun."[26]

In addition to the attention Hanlon garnered for his bicycle riding, he was something of a pop star in Macon, and he was constantly approached by people who tried to get his endorsement for all sorts of advertising schemes. He also received many letters and telegrams that poured in for the same reason.[27]

After a pleasant and productive stay in Macon, the Orioles left that city on March 28 and arrived later that day at Atlanta, the first stop on their journey home. The players were happy to leave the hard work of training camp and looked forward to playing games.[28]

By the time the Orioles arrived in Atlanta, however, a number of health issues plagued the team. After an intra-squad game, McGraw fell ill with a high fever, and typhoid was eventually diagnosed. He continued to get worse and worse, and for a time it was thought that it might prove fatal.[29] At the recommendation of Doc Pond, McGraw was left behind at an Atlanta hospital while the team continued northward. As it turned out, McGraw would only play in 23 games during the regular season. In addition to McGraw's illness, other players suffered a variety of injuries: Jennings hurt his finger and lost the nail, Clarke sprained an ankle, Pond had a knee problem, and McMahon injured his hand.

Hanlon left the team on a quick side-trip to spend Easter Sunday with his family in Baltimore. It was reported that he was found in his parlor with his chubby baby Edwina in one arm and his two stalwart little sons climbing over his knees.[30] He rejoined the team in Petersburg a few days later, just in time for a game against a local team that resulted in a riot.

For that game, no umpires showed up, so backup Orioles catcher Frank Bowerman and local resident June Quarles, the brother of the Petersburg pitcher, umpired. After two innings, the Orioles were frustrated with the calls of Quarles and demanded that he be replaced. Petersburg supplied a local man named Powers, but things did not get better. In the seventh inning, Jimmy Donnelly was called out on strikes on three pitches, each one worse than the previous one, and the Orioles erupted in fury.

When Jennings stepped towards Powers to protest, he was sucker-punched by a Petersburg player. At that point, a man named Hubbard led fans from the stands, and they pounded the Orioles from all sides. Doyle, who went to the aid of Jennings, was blindsided from behind, and a group was pummeling him until Major A. K. Fulton, a Union Civil War veteran who was a "champion rooter" and often traveled with the Orioles, waded into the fray, knocking bodies left and right. He rescued Doyle and Keeler, who was being held down and beaten. Finally, with the assistance of police and some responsible Petersburg players and fans, the Orioles were quickly escorted back to their hotel.

But things got worse there. Quarles and Hubbard led an angry group to the hotel, and while the mob milled around outside, Quarles went into the lobby and confronted Jennings, who walked away from him. Quarles then turned to Kelley and told him he had something to settle with him, and Kelley suggested they go upstairs. As they headed up, Quarles hit Kelley from behind, and Hubbard and a group of men joined the attack on Kelley. Steve Brodie came to Kelley's defense, punching Hubbard repeatedly in the face as Jennings ran to help Kelley fight off the others. More of the crowd poured into the hotel, and during the brawl Quarles was pushed through a glass door and started bleeding profusely. Reports varied as to who it was that sent Quarles through the door: Kelley, Brodie, and Doyle were all named. By this time, the hotel proprietor and his son, police, responsible citizens, and Petersburg players were able to move the angry crowd out into the street.

Earlier, as things began to look ugly, Hanlon had phoned to demand more police on the scene. When they finally arrived, he gathered the team together and, as a group, they marched to the station, accompanied by concerned citizens who were appalled by the melee. Of all the Orioles, it seemed that Doyle received the worst of the beatings, but he took great satisfaction in the fact that he was able to knock down the man who struck Jennings. The brawl had the benefit of earning Doyle some style points for the way that he conducted himself during the skirmish and came to the aid of his new teammates.[31]

The team proceeded to Norfolk to play a game the next day. The fans, thrilled to watch the kicking of the famous Orioles, saw them beat the locals badly. Doyle was a center of attention, as was Joe Kelley, who pleased the fans in the left field bleachers with his quick-witted comments to the spectators. However, Kelley was not so pleased when some of the fans mocked the Orioles' failure to win the Temple Cup, but he diplomatically took these remarks good-naturedly.[32]

Although the Orioles were not aware of it at the time, warrants had been issued for the arrest of Doyle, Kelley, and Brodie, but before the Petersburg authorities arrived in Norfolk, the team had left for Baltimore to prepare for Opening Day.

8. Dirty Jack Comes to Town (1896)

* * *

While the team was in spring training, improvements were made at Union Park. The bleachers were made larger, both the bleachers and the grandstand were made more comfortable, and Tom Murphy had the playing field better than ever.[33] As was his nature, Hanlon neglected no details concerning his ball club, and he had even overseen the creation of a new and improved scorecard which was larger and in book form and provided more space for scoring and interesting baseball information. The lithographed cardboard cover featured a round space in the middle that would be used for portraits of the Orioles; above that were two crossed bats and below it the picture of a ball-field. On the sides of the portrait was printed "Baltimore BB Club" and "Champions 1894–1895."[34]

Hanlon had also ordered new uniforms. The road uniforms were gray, the home uniforms were white, and both featured black caps, belts, and stockings. The sweaters were black with orange stripes at the collar and around the bottom, and it had a big orange "B" on the breast. The cap was much deeper, so it would not fly so easily off the head. The team proudly displayed a sample of the new uniform in a window on Baltimore Street to whet the appetite of passersby for the upcoming season.[35]

As Opening Day approached, Baltimore fans worried how McGraw's on-field production and leadership would be replaced. Although Orioles fans took great comfort in Hanlon's well-demonstrated ability to provide for all emergencies, there was concern that Jimmy Donnelly would not fill in effectively for McGraw.

Nevertheless, there were still reasons for Baltimore fans to be optimistic about the coming season, and chief among them was Jack Doyle. From all accounts, Doyle was fitting in quite nicely. He had been given enthusiastic encouragement from his teammates, and the fans greeted him affectionately with wild cheers when he appeared on the field in the exhibition games played at Union Park prior to Opening Day.[36] For Doyle, whose rough exterior hid a man who was by nature insecure and defensive, this approval was vital to his ability to play well and keep the Orioles a harmonious unit.

The season opened in Baltimore on April 16, and the Orioles got off to a rough start. On Opening Day, they lost to Brooklyn, 6–5, and by the time they left Boston after a series on May 2, they had lost seven of their first 12 games of the season. Hanlon arranged a one-day stopover in Baltimore before they went on a Western road trip which was to begin in Pittsburgh. While they were home, Hanlon invited the players to his house on Calvert Street, where "his boys" always knew they were welcome. The players were served a dinner beginning with soup and ending with pie and all manner of beverages. After the feast concluded and the coffee and cigars were served, Hanlon stood, unbuttoned his vest, and after jokingly assuring the bashful Jennings that he would not be called upon to speak, he said to his players:

> Gentlemen, you are about to visit the West. Reserve your fire and place it where it will do the most good. Gentlemen, in the expressive vernacular of our beloved sport, I have no kick coming [McMahon and Jennings interrupted with "Hear, Hear!"] and trust that no member of this team has, but I am fairly well acquainted with the strength of our club, both collectively and in detail, and I have not been entirely unobservant since the championship games began. I know that nature alone has endowed the club with more than the average skill, and that if nature is not abused or interfered with, nature will cause you to win. Boys—gentlemen, I mean—do not interfere with nature. Boys—gentlemen, I mean—give nature a chance. I feel quite convinced in my own mind that when addressing gentlemen of this assembled

intelligence there is no reason why I should be more explicit. If you will indulge me one moment longer, I feel it incumbent upon me to remind you that you have your own professional welfare in your own hands. You yourselves…are entirely responsible for the size of your salaries. You, yourselves, must provide me with the means of disbursing those of the present season to you, and you yourselves, will fix the size of future ones by…full or depleted stands….Gentlemen, you are all natural born winning ball players. If I have observed any tamperings with nature in the past I do not feel justified in going into detail or to become invidious. I will simply repeat, give nature a chance. And now, boys—gentlemen, I mean—thanking you for the almost rapt attention which you have apparently given me, and to the patience with which you have indulged me I will close by simply saying—you men, go West—get at 'em.[37]

The speech was rhetorically quite effective. After playing poorly, some of the players may have felt they were about to get a dressing down by Hanlon. However, he immediately put his players at ease by kidding Jennings, and then saying that he had no complaints with them, and he repeatedly referred to them affectionately as "boys." But each time he called them boys, he corrected himself by calling them "gentleman," thereby showing his respect for them and implying that they were men responsible for their own course. He reminded them of their great skill as ball players and challenged them to use their natural abilities. If they did so, they would win many games, the stands would be full, and Hanlon would be able to pay them higher salaries. He politely thanked them and ended the speech by appealing to their emotions with the famous Orioles rallying cry, "Get at 'em!" A key component of Hanlon's managerial style was quite evident in his remarks: he had great affection for his players, but he treated them like men.

The players responded well to Hanlon's pep talk. Starting in Pittsburgh, the team won 10 of 12 games, and from the time of Hanlon's speech until the end of the season, they compiled an 85–32 record for an outstanding .727 winning percentage.

* * *

McGraw, after recuperating from his bout with typhoid fever in Virginia for several weeks, arrived in Baltimore on June 27. He declared that he was feeling much better and wanted to go on the upcoming Western road trip with the team. Hanlon did not allow it, insisting that he get more rest until the team returned home in early August.[38] Although there was no obligation on the part of team owners to pay men who missed time because of illness or injury, when McGraw returned, he was very grateful when Hanlon gave him $1,200 in back pay.[39]

Without the presence of McGraw's fiery spirit, Hanlon took the opportunity to encourage the Orioles to cut down on their kicking. Moreover, Von der Horst announced in July that players were now expected to pay their own fines. He cited an instance where Joe Kelley was fined $25 and appealed to Hanlon, who refused to pay his fine. Von der Horst was quick to add, "Of course I never have anything to do with the players, but I know whereof I speak when I say that Mr. Hanlon's effort is always against useless or acrimonious kicking."[40]

While in Louisville on July 14, Wilbert Robinson had to have part of the pinky finger on his throwing hand amputated. He had hurt it a few weeks earlier, and it had become infected. The doctors felt blood poisoning would occur, so the finger below the first joint was removed. Robinson refused anesthesia and watched the procedure.[41] Hanlon said that the doctors felt that losing the tip of the finger would not be detrimental to

Robinson's throwing ability because the crooked finger was already getting in the way of throwing the ball.[42] Robinson saw the team off as they left by boat for Cincinnati and went to the hospital for the remainder of the week. Luckily for the Orioles, as much as they missed the play and personality of Robinson, they had an able replacement for him in Boileryard Clarke, who hit a respectable .297 while playing 67 games behind the plate and 14 at first base.

In the meantime, Hanlon continued to add strength to the team for its stretch run. In early July, in need of a utility infielder after the trade of Frank Bonner, he obtained Joe Quinn, the first Australian to play in the major leagues. Quinn was a solid 11-year veteran who had hit .314 in 135 games with the Browns in 1895. He had a well-deserved reputation for being a consummate teammate and had been voted America's most popular player in a *Sporting News* poll in 1893.[43] For the Orioles in 1896, Quinn would fill in admirably, hitting .329 in 24 games.

In early September, Hanlon purchased the contract of Jerry Nops from Wilmington in the Atlantic League to strengthen the pitching corps. Nops started only three games for the Orioles in 1896, but he was the winning pitcher when the team clinched the pennant on September 12 with a victory at home against Brooklyn.

Hanlon also proved true the old baseball adage that sometimes the trade you do not make is the best trade, when in August Washington Senators manager Gus Schmelz offered him $5,000 for John McGraw. Hanlon responded by saying, "When I let men like McGraw loose it will be when I am leaving the baseball business myself."[44]

After a season where they clearly demonstrated their dominance, the Orioles clinched the pennant in mid–September, and once more Baltimore had a championship to celebrate. A special benefit performance was held at Ford's Grand Opera House, consisting of vaudeville acts filled with baseball references. The show benefited $1,000 for the players, and when it concluded, Hanlon presented Von der Horst with a jeweled gold

Joe Quinn was the first Australian-born major league player and manager. He was known as an upright individual who was highly respected by all, and he was sometimes stunned by the behavior of his Orioles teammates (Babe Ruth Birthplace & Museum).

button upon the face of which were the championship flag, the words "The Champion Baltimores," and the dates "1894, 1895, 1896." In the first date was a ruby, in the second a sapphire, and in the third a diamond. The button was inscribed "E. Hanlon to H. R. Von der Horst."[45]

* * *

Now that the championship season was over, it was finally time for the team to exorcise the demons of the Temple Cup, and one thing was certain: the Orioles desperately wanted to win it. They were tired of being called "Fake Champions,"[46] and they were tired of the catcalls that rained down on them about it. Once again, their opponents would be the rough and rowdy Cleveland Spiders, who had dominated the Orioles by winning eight of 11 games that season.

When the series opened on October 2 at Union Park, the Spiders immediately faced a serious problem when McGraw, leading off the game, smashed a line drive that hit Cy Young on his pitching wrist. Young, who had won four of his five starts against the Orioles in 1896, was clearly hampered by the injury, and although he pitched a complete game, he gave up 13 hits and seven runs, while Orioles pitcher Bill Hoffer held Cleveland to just one run. After the game, it was said that "Ned Hanlon's smile has extended until it threatens to engulf his ears."[47]

Young's wrist became badly swollen, and he was unable to pitch again in the series. To make matters even worse for Cleveland, team captain and first baseman Patsy Tebeau wrenched his back with an awkward swing at one of Hoffer's curveballs and wound up in the hospital. It was his last game in the series.[48]

For Game Two, Hanlon made the surprising decision to start 20-year-old Joe Corbett. Corbett had only pitched 41 innings in eight games during the season, starting just three games and compiling a 3–0 record and a 2.20 ERA. Hanlon's hunch worked, as Corbett gave up just seven hits and the Orioles convincingly won, 7–2.

The Orioles took a commanding lead in the series when Bill Hoffer beat George Cuppy, 6–2, in Game Three, and the scene shifted to Cleveland for Game Four on October 8. On that day, the Orioles scored five runs as Corbett shut out the Spiders to complete the series sweep. In their third attempt, the Orioles were finally the winners of the Temple Cup Series.

After the game, the team celebrated at the Hollenden Hotel, and William Chase Temple joined the festivities. Harry Von der Horst filled the Temple Cup with champagne. Temple took the first drink, and he was followed by Von der Horst, Hanlon, and the players.[49] Back in Baltimore, the headline in the *Baltimore American* proudly declared, "Who Now Disputes the Orioles Are the Greatest Team in the World."[50]

The Orioles and Ned Hanlon were ecstatic to have finally removed the Temple Cup monkey from their back. Prior to leaving on the train for Baltimore, the players gave rounds of cheers for Cleveland's owner, Frank Robison, and Hanlon presented Temple with the last ball used in the game. Arriving in Baltimore, the team was greeted at Camden Station by a cheering crowd that packed the platform, and police led them in carriages to Ganzhorn's Hotel, where a banquet was waiting for them. Speeches were given praising the players, and when Hanlon was called upon to speak, he spoke affectionately about his players and attributed to them all the success of the season. He concluded by expressing his wish that they would meet again next year at the same time to celebrate another Temple Cup victory.[51]

Throughout the season, debate continued about the value of the Temple Cup series.

Many of the magnates called for its abandonment because all the profits were divided among the players. Hanlon criticized the owners who were not interested in anything unless they were able to turn a profit on it, and he argued that they should be willing to give the players a chance to earn some extra money. Moreover, he maintained that the series kept up interest in the baseball season because the battle for second place became much more important if a berth in the Temple Cup series was at stake.[52]

Hanlon suggested a substitute for the series. He proposed that each club in the League put in one percent of their receipts, which would then be divided among the three top finishers: 50 percent to the pennant winners, 30 percent to second place, and 20 percent to third place. "Now let us see," said Hanlon, "if these gentlemen, when their own pockets are touched, will be friends of the ball players."[53] The owners rejected Hanlon's proposal.

Most of the Orioles had outstanding seasons. Hughie Jennings hit .401 and was hit by pitches 51 times—a single-season record that still stands. Willie Keeler hit .386 and stole 67 bases, and Joe Kelley hit .364 with 87 stolen bases. Jack Doyle justified Hanlon's trade as he hit .339 and swiped 73 bases. And Jimmy Donnelly surprised most people by hitting .328 and playing good defense while filling in for McGraw.

The 1896 Orioles ran up a record of 90–39, won their third straight pennant, and defeated the Cleveland Spiders to win their first Temple Cup Series. Top row from left to right: Joe Quinn, Sadie McMahon, Duke Esper, George Hemming, Frank Bowerman, Bill Clarke, Jimmy Donnelly. Middle row left to right: Steve Brodie, Bill Hoffer, Joe Kelley, Ned Hanlon, Wilbert Robinson, Hughie Jennings, Heinie Reitz. Bottom row: Jack Doyle, John McGraw, Sam (mascot), Willie Keeler, Arlie Pond (collection of Tom Delise).

On the pitching side, Hoffer had another outstanding year as he compiled a 25–7 record with a 3.38 ERA. Arlie Pond also lived up to Hanlon's expectations by winning 16 games against eight losses, and George Hemming (15–6), Duke Esper (14–5) and Sadie McMahon (11–9) all made solid contributions to the team's success.

The Temple Cup series also provided a financial windfall for the Orioles players. When a meeting of the team was held at its headquarters to settle accounts, each player received almost $300 from the proceeds of the Temple Cup, exhibitions games played in preparation of the Temple Cup, and the Ford's Theater benefit. As was the custom for the past few years, groundskeeper Tom Murphy also received individual monetary gifts from the players which totaled between $125 and $150.[54]

Most importantly, throughout the entire season, everyone got along well with one another and with Hanlon. After the season, Jack Doyle said, "A great many people wonder how so many scrappy ball players manage to get along together. We do fight on the field and during the games, but that is due to the intense desire to win, but as soon as the game is over, we walk off arm in arm. Hanlon isn't slow as a peacemaker, and he can always be relied on to patch up any trouble."[55]

Although everyone in the Orioles' organization was pleased with one another, they did not feel they had received the acclaim outside Baltimore that was their due for winning three consecutive pennants. Hanlon said, "It has always been the custom since I have been in base ball for the presidents, managers and even the captains of the clubs in the League or Association to send a congratulatory telegram to the management of the club that has won the pennant. Not a single manager, president or captain has congratulated the Baltimore Club on its victory this year....I guess we can get along without it, but it is rather queer just the same."[56]

Von der Horst also lashed out, saying that other teams in the league were upset because "a little Association town" beat them three straight times. He said no one could claim that it was just luck any more, and predicted they would set a record by winning four straight pennants.[57] Boston sportswriter Tim Murnane stated that some of the hard feelings against the Orioles throughout the league could be attributed to the belief that their success had made them full of themselves:

> I noticed this last spring when the Boston and Baltimore Clubs met at Norfolk. While the Boston players went around the hotel in a quiet, modest way, several of the Baltimore boys sported loud jewelry and heavy canes, and were conspicuous in many ways that told plainly of inflated top pieces. Manager Hanlon, however, was a marked exception, as always he was the quiet, unassuming gentleman....Hughie Jennings has such an exalted opinion of Hughie Jennings that he cannot see exactly where any other ball player in the League comes in, and Joe Kelley is just as much infatuated with Joe Kelley....Reitz and Keeler are also enamored of themselves, and even Jack Doyle is said to be a victim of the elephantasis of the skyline.[58]

After the season, Hanlon and Von der Horst were greatly embarrassed when some of the Baltimore players lashed out at "the coldness of the Baltimore fans" and publicly declared that they would welcome a trade to another city. Indeed, attendance at Orioles games had steadily decreased from 328,000 when they won their first pennant in 1894 to 249,448 in 1896, and some players did not hesitate to take offense at the lack of support accorded to a three-time champion. The decrease in attendance had received much attention from the local press, who repeatedly warned fans that they could lose a great team and manager if they did not provide more support for them.[59]

8. Dirty Jack Comes to Town (1896)

When Hanlon caught wind of the players' comments, he was quick to implement damage control:

> There was never a ball club or a manager treated better or supported better than we have been in Baltimore....I shall never forget the kindness, hospitality, and royal treatment we have received in Baltimore. That great reception in 1894 was the proudest moment of my life, and I shall not forget it....I have belonged to championship teams before, and I know. In Detroit we got one little banquet at which there were one hundred people or so.
>
> My home is in Baltimore; I am a Baltimorean. I propose to stay there, and you couldn't drag me away from Baltimore with a derrick. I mean that. And the Baltimore Club as a whole appreciates how well they have been treated, even if a few of the men have made foolish remarks about not being appreciated and wanting to get away. It must be remembered that they are young, and if they don't appreciate it now, they will understand their treatment in Baltimore in the years to come and will speak of it with pride.[60]

As Hanlon prepared to leave for the League meeting in Chicago, he was asked about the rumors circulating that the Baltimore club would be transferred to another city because of poor public support. Hanlon said the reports were fiction, but he admitted that game receipts had gone down 30 percent from the previous year and that the team had taken in $12,000 more for its road games than it did at home.[61]

* * *

In November, Hanlon made another of his blockbuster deals when he traded the popular Steve Brodie and Jimmy Donnelly to Pittsburgh for star center fielder Jake Stenzel, who was at odds with the Pittsburgh management. Brodie had hit .297 in 1896 after compiling batting averages of .348 and .366 in the two previous years, and Hanlon had become concerned that Brodie's hitting and base running were not enough to help the team to a fourth consecutive pennant. Harry Von der Horst could not resist commenting on the trade and said that Brodie "was excitable and caused considerable friction on our team."[62] Although not as strong a defender as Brodie, statistically Stenzel was a clear offensive upgrade as he had hit .363 with 57 stolen bases with the Pirates the previous season.

Hanlon had been lavish in his praise of Donnelly throughout the season and described him as an intelligent ball player who could handle difficult situations.[63] Hanlon, however, had noticed how once McGraw returned, Donnelly played much better on the road than at home, where the Baltimore fans kept calling for McGraw to play. Considering McGraw's temperament, Hanlon was convinced that Donnelly and McGraw could not peacefully coexist, and since Hanlon was happy with Joe Quinn as the utility man, that made Donnelly expendable.[64]

Steve Brodie was greatly surprised by the trade, and he was not happy about it. Because he believed that he was on friendly terms with Von der Horst and Hanlon, he was offended that neither of them had informed him of the deal, which he learned about from reading a Baltimore newspaper. He was reluctant to leave a team that he had helped to win three successive pennants.[65] Nonetheless, in December Brodie signed his Pittsburgh contract and sent a letter to Pirates owner William Kerr saying that he was pleased to be playing in Pittsburgh and would do his best to please. But it was clear that he was shocked and confused by the circumstances. He said he "could not understand what Ned Hanlon had against him, as he had always given up his best efforts for the Baltimore Club."[66]

Hanlon, in the meantime, was furious with the reporter for the *Baltimore Herald* who first broke the story. Hanlon indignantly claimed that the reporter had assured him that he would not print the story until Hanlon had the opportunity to speak with Brodie to inform him of the trade.[67]

When Hanlon asked Jennings about what he thought of the Brodie for Stenzel deal, Jennings was enthusiastic about it and said he did not think the Orioles could be beat in 1897.[68] The move was widely thought to provide the Orioles with the strongest outfield in the League.[69] Hanlon was again hailed as "the shrewdest of all….They say that other managers when they see Hanlon coming tuck their hats under their arms and steal away. As soon as Harry Pulliam sees him coming, he throws up both hands and yells, 'Robber.'"[70]

* * *

Hanlon spent part of the off-season collecting various personal wagers, mainly for hats, that he had made on the Orioles. The most satisfying bet he won was with St. Louis Browns owner Chris Von der Ahe, who bet a $75 suit of clothes that Philadelphia would beat the Orioles in their season series. To Von der Ahe's chagrin, the Orioles swept all 12 games they played against the Phillies.

In a letter to Hanlon, Von der Ahe said, "My! my! but clothes come high in Baltimore, don't it?…When the wonderful magnate-manager gets on that suit all trimmed in yellow and black I would like a picture of him to hang in my grandstand." Hanlon sent a reply to Von der Ahe in which he assured him that he would send a picture of him in the suit because "it would be the only thing in the grandstand or grounds to draw a crowd or excite interest."[71]

In December, Hanlon enjoyed some free time with his family. He went on a rabbit-hunting expedition with some rooters just outside Baltimore, which was followed by a dinner with the host of the estate.[72] Later in the month, it was reported as that his mind was not on business because he was spending his time ornamenting Christmas trees, filling stockings, and engaging in other holiday festivities. When he was visited by a reporter after Christmas, Hanlon was found giving a magic lantern exhibition to his two boys.[73]

9

Chasing History (1897)

The National League meeting at the end of February 1897 was held in Baltimore, and Harry Von der Horst and Ned Hanlon proved to be excellent hosts. They reinstituted a practice that had not been seen since the days of the American Association when they provided the magnates, newspapermen, and special guests with an elaborate banquet in a private dining room in the posh Rennert Hotel. The room was filled with flower arrangements, and they lavishly treated their guests to Maryland delicacies such as duck, terrapin, and oysters, along with copious amounts of Rhine wine, sherry, and champagne to wash it all down.

The banquet helped to provide a degree of amiability that had been lacking at previous meetings as the magnates and newspaper men conversed, renewed old friendships, and patched up some old differences. At the banquet, there were toasts to Von der Horst and Hanlon, who was asked to reveal his strategies for winning pennants. He refused "to give the snap away" and said, "As you all know, I am no speaker. Speaking is out of my line, my occupation being principally winning pennants." He mentioned the assistance the press provided to all the clubs, and he had everyone rise as he offered a toast to the fourth estate which was enthusiastically joined by all present. Throughout the meeting, Hanlon was in a good mood and greatly enjoyed his role as co-host.[1]

During the off-season, Hanlon attended to a number of personal business matters. In April, he paid $7,500 in cash for a fashionable, large house for his ever-increasing family at 1401 Mt. Royal Avenue in the upscale Bolton Hill area of Baltimore.[2] This would be his home for the rest of his life. Later in the year, he purchased three other properties for nearly $12,000. In June, he bought a house on St. Paul Street near 27th Street for $4,727.27.[3] *Sporting Life* reported, "When Hanlon first came to Baltimore, it was estimated that he was worth about $10,000. Today he can show $50,000 in gilt-edge securities, and is getting richer every day, and all this has been made out of baseball."[4]

Unlike some previous years, Hanlon had little difficulty getting his players under contract for the upcoming season. Jack Doyle proclaimed that he was looking forward to playing with the champions again and described the previous season as one of the most pleasant he had spent in baseball. He made a point to say how well he liked the treatment he had been accorded by both the Baltimore management and the public.[5]

The off-season proved bittersweet as Hanlon attended John McGraw's marriage to a young Baltimore woman named Minnie Doyle in February, but shortly after the wedding, he made a sad trip to New York to attend the funeral of his friend, the popular ex-manager of Brooklyn, Dave Foutz, who died of an acute asthma attack at just 40 years old.[6] While there, he met with Brooklyn owners Charles Byrne and Ferdinand Abell, who were interested in obtaining an Orioles player to captain their team and provide a spark of aggressiveness. When Hanlon refused a trade, the frustrated Byrne remarked, "You Baltimore people hang on to every one of your good players like grim death. You seem to want to hold the pennant here in perpetuity."[7]

Although other teams would have liked to deal for Baltimore players, many baseball executives had become extremely leery of engaging in any kind of player transaction with Hanlon, who had gained the reputation of someone who could make opposing managers look foolish in a trade. When Hanlon offered to sell him one of his pitchers in the pre-season, Boston manager Frank Selee summed up the general attitude toward trading with Hanlon when he responded that he was not interested in buying anything Hanlon had to sell.[8]

As spring training approached, Hanlon irritated the venerable Henry Chadwick, who had sent members of the rules committee a rule book that was printed with large margins so members could write notes in them. Chadwick grumbled that he had received thanks from all members of the committee except Hanlon. He claimed that Hanlon had also ignored him when he sent him a list of suggested rule changes in 1894. Chadwick said he could not understand Hanlon's discourtesy, especially considering that he had given Hanlon repeated credit for the way he managed his pennant-winning teams.[9]

* * *

On March 16, most of the Orioles left Camden Station, stopping in Washington to board a special Pullman sleeper. Some players were given permission to meet the team in Macon, including Joe Quinn, who sent a telegram to Hanlon requesting to stay in St. Louis until March 25 to attend to business matters. Quinn amusedly reported to his teammates that Hanlon's response was brief and to the point: "Report March 25 or stay in St. Louis until October 16."[10]

After arriving in Macon, Hanlon kept the first day's practice short due to the wet and muddy fields; however, it was a rigorous session that surprised the players who had never experienced a Hanlon camp before and caused one of them to remark, "I never saw a team train like this."[11] Elmer Horton, a pitcher who was trying out for the team, remarked in wonder, "They play more with their heads than with their hands. It is like going through college to watch them work….It is…the unexpected all the time and it is a wonderful game."[12]

Spring training was plagued by cold, rain, and muddy conditions, and Hanlon was concerned that the water in Macon was suspect, so he arranged for mineral water to be imported for his players and said, "No chance of fever or malaria among the champions."[13] After completing their workouts in Macon, the team played exhibition games in Southern cities. When the team finally disembarked from a steamer on April 11 and set foot on Baltimore soil, Hanlon expressed satisfaction with the work of his team in the spring and optimism for the coming season.[14]

Shortly before Opening Day, Hanlon made two moves that startled Baltimore fans when he sold George Hemming to the Browns and gave Sadie McMahon his unconditional release. McMahon, contending that his pitching arm was sound and that he could still win games, immediately signed with the Brooklyn Bridegrooms.[15] The old Orioles warhorse did not have much success with Brooklyn, compiling an 0–6 record in nine games, and the Bridegrooms released him on July 21. McMahon would never again pitch in the major leagues. Hemming fared little better with the Browns in his last year in the majors. Hanlon had now released three pitchers who were instrumental in the three pennants won by the Orioles, and he rested his hopes for a fourth one on a staff that consisted of a number of younger, less proven pitchers.

* * *

The Orioles' quest for a fourth straight pennant opened on April 22 with a parade that began at the Eutaw House, where the Boston players were staying. The teams and their followers were escorted by the police and the Fifth Regiment band, and the parade circled Baltimore's Washington Monument and proceeded through large crowds until they reached Union Park. When they arrived, the grandstand was already filled with an enthusiastic crowd waving hats, flags, and handkerchiefs. Amid music and wild cheers, the Orioles, accompanied by the Beaneaters, marched onto the field in their new uniforms and displayed the Temple Cup along with their three pennants. The players marched in formations of four and wheeled through maneuvers like trained soldiers, ending in a circle in the outfield as the three pennants were raised on the flagstaffs, and the band played "The Star-Spangled Banner."[16]

Much to the delight of the home fans, the Orioles won, 10–5, as Bill Hoffer allowed only two earned runs and Jack Doyle was the offensive star, going five-for-five with two stolen bases. The day did not go so well for John McGraw, who sprained his ankle in the first inning. He would not return to the starting lineup until May 10.

Although no one recognized it at the time, history was made Opening Day when Willie Keeler began a 44-game hitting streak that remained a record until it was broken by Joe DiMaggio in 1941. Pete Rose tied this National League single-season record in 1978, but considering that Keeler had a hit in his last game of the 1896 season, he still currently holds the multi-season record with hits in 45 consecutive games.

The Orioles swept Boston in the opening series, a fast start that saw the team compile a 33–9 record by June 18. During the second series of the season against Brooklyn, Hanlon was asked why he had not yet started the young phenom, Jerry Nops, who had performed so well in spring training. Hanlon explained that he preferred to use his three most experienced pitchers against the Beaneaters and did not want to use the left-handed Nops against a Brooklyn team that was dominated by right-handed hitters.[17] He announced his intention to use Nops in the following series against the Giants, who featured six left-handed hitters in their regular lineup. Nops received his first start on April 29, and he responded by scattering nine hits, all singles, and allowing only one earned run in a 6–3 win over the Giants. Nops won nine of his next 10 starts. This strategic thinking regarding advantageous pitcher and hitter matchups was unusual, if not unique, for the time.

In late May, the team became embroiled in an umpire dispute. During a tumultuous loss in Cincinnati in which they were relentlessly pelted with debris by fans, the Orioles were further aggravated with the work of umpire Jack Sheridan. At the end of the game, Robinson furiously confronted Hanlon, saying, "Do you propose to play here tomorrow with this umpiring? If you do, I for one will not play, and none of the other men will play. He [Sheridan] roasted Pond all the way through and gave [Cincinnati pitcher] Rhines everything."[18]

Hanlon agreed with his captain's sentiments and immediately fired off a protest of the game to Nick Young, stating that Sheridan had intentionally robbed his team. He also sent affidavits from the players charging that Sheridan was incompetent. "It was the worst skinning I have had for a long time.... There could be no mistake about it and there was no excuse for it. I do not protest an umpire once a year, but I shall protest this one."[19]

The Orioles received little satisfaction when Nick Young responded that he could not get another man to Cincinnati in time to umpire the next day's game, but he promised to investigate the claim against Sheridan. Later in the month, Hanlon received a telegram from Young asking if he objected to Sheridan being assigned to an upcoming game, and Hanlon responded that he never wanted Sheridan to umpire in Baltimore again.[20]

Many of the umpires, however, had their own complaints to make about the Orioles. For years, certain Orioles had baited umpires to the point where Tom Lynch said in August that he would never work another game involving the Orioles, who were, in his opinion, "a vile lot of blackguards." Lynch claimed that the umpires had been called a variety of profane and disrespectful names that would "bring a response in the shape of a bullet if they were off the field."[21]

Sportswriters also complained about the rowdy behavior of the Orioles and other teams in the league:

> Manager Hanlon may look on his men as aggressive ball players. Captain Tebeau can drive respectable people from the game in Cleveland by the filthy language of his ill-bred aggregation, and New York may heap abuse on all umpires that refuse to rob the visiting teams.... Edward Hanlon should be held wholly responsible for the unwholesome actions of his players, just as much as Tebeau and the National League, though Mr. Young should give both a call for allowing their men to bring disgrace on the sport. Mr. Lynch and Sheridan can tell some interesting stories about these people who hoodwink the public by calling dirty ball aggressive ball.[22]

Starting with a June 19 loss to the Pirates, the Orioles lost 12 of their next 17 games. A series of injuries was likely a factor. In addition to McGraw's Opening Day sprain, Doyle was hit in the face with a batted ball and later was hit in the head and knocked unconscious.[23] Amos Rusie beaned Jennings, who missed five games with a fractured skull and later broke the index finger on his glove hand. Wilbert Robinson was spiked and suffered other injuries that limited him to only 48 games that season. His backup, Boileryard Clarke, split open his thumb and was lost for a month.[24]

Hanlon was frustrated with the poor play of the team, so he focused on teamwork drills in his morning practices. In addition, he ordered his players to stop the unnecessary kicking that he believed caused the team more harm than good. He told them to direct their energies instead to playing ball.[25]

These actions did not result in the improvement Hanlon had hoped for, so on the morning of July 9, he summoned the players to a meeting. He called upon Arlie Pond to read an extract from an article in the *Sun* which described the play of the Orioles in a loss to an inferior Reds team. The article attributed the poor play to the fact that they had forsaken their usual winning style of play, which was dependent on teamwork, using their brains, and doing the unexpected: "the Hanlon method of playing ball." The *Sun* charged that the players were too concerned with their individual stats and attempting to knock the ball over the fence, which caused them to lose to teams that were employing the usual techniques of the Orioles against them.[26]

When Pond finished reading, Hanlon tersely warned the players that they must immediately remedy the situation. He said he had confidence in them and that if they did not get discouraged, they could resume their winning ways if they played as they had in the past. He called special attention to the *Sun's* statement that individual work was being stressed at the expense of team play.[27]

The Orioles responded to Hanlon's talk that day and beat Louisville in a game that showed the spirit and sense of teamwork for which they had become renowned.[28] The victory began a period during which they won 15 of their next 20 games and crept to just two-and-a-half games behind the league-leading Beaneaters.

To this point in the season Corbett, Nops, and Pond had pitched well, but the press had become disenchanted with Bill Hoffer. He had a respectable won-lost record, but his high ERA was a cause for concern, and the Orioles' offense and excellent fielding had bailed Hoffer out many times during the season. The press, who usually supported, or at least quietly accepted, Hanlon's every move, was critical of him for sticking with Hoffer.[29]

It is easy to see why Hanlon was unwilling to give up on Hoffer. During the past two seasons, he had a combined 56–13 record, and it could be argued that he had been the best pitcher in baseball during that time. Hanlon stuck with Hoffer, who would pitch over 300 innings and win 22 games against 11 losses.

* * *

As the Orioles once again looked like a team that would sweep on to another pennant, commentators expressed dismay with Baltimore's perceived monopoly of the League. The Chicago correspondent for *Sporting Life* lamented, "I am not surprised to see Baltimore win. The Orioles are getting too strong. They will have to be legislated against, or they will exterminate all the weaker teams. Why should that man Hanlon have a monopoly on picking out star players? What X-Ray power does he possess that he can select men with the most unerring eye … ?"[30]

Frustration outside Baltimore with the repeated success of the Orioles resulted in a ground swell of anti–Baltimore hysteria. Charles Comiskey, Cap Anson, and John Montgomery Ward were just a few of many baseball people who openly expressed their hope that the Orioles would be denied a fourth pennant.[31] Prior to a five-game series against Chicago at Union Park in mid–September, it was reported that $500 was offered to every Chicago pitcher who beat the Orioles during the series. The offer was supposedly made by "a wealthy Western man who is anxious to see the 'gentlemanly' Bostons defeat the 'ruffianly' Baltimores for the good of the game."[32] The reward did little good as the Orioles won four of those games and tied the other.

* * *

When the day ended on August 10, Boston's record of 61-28-2 left them four games ahead of the third-place Orioles, who were 55-30-3. From that day until the end of the season, both teams played at a torrid pace: Boston went 32-11-1, and the Orioles were 35-10-3. The Orioles' success coming down the stretch was attributed to the morning practices Hanlon held: "Hanlon conducts a sort of school during these ante-meridian gatherings of the Oriole flock.... All managers do as Hanlon does, but as the results are different the other teams must either have poor manager-teachers or very stupid player-pupils."[33]

As the season neared its end, all eyes were turned to a crucial series between Baltimore and Boston scheduled for September 24, 25, and 27 at Union Park. Even though both teams had one more series to play after their matchup, the general opinion was that whoever won this series would win the pennant. Entering this crucial matchup, the standings stood as follows:

	Games	Wins	Losses	Ties	Pct.	Games Back
Baltimore	129	87	36	6	.707	0.5
Boston	129	89	37	3	.706	-

Boston took the first game, winning 6–4 as Kid Nichols beat Joe Corbett, but the following day, the Orioles rallied to win, 6–3, behind Bill Hoffer to move into first place by just one percentage point. After an off-day Sunday, it came down to the final game. Corbett started and pitched poorly, and in the seventh inning Boston clung to an 8–5 lead. With two Boston runners on base, a deep fly ball was hit over the head of Jake Stenzel in center. The overflow crowd that ringed the outfield parted to allow him to catch the ball, but Stenzel had hesitated briefly before pursuing it, and it was a devastating delay. The ball fell in safely, and both runners scored. More Boston runs followed, and the Beaneaters won, 19–10. After the game, groundskeeper Tom Murphy expressed the view of many when he said, "If Stenzel made the catch, we probably would have won."[34]

Hanlon, however, was perturbed about another player on his team. In the first inning, Joe Corbett was hit on the hand by a batted ball, and Corbett asked Hanlon to take him out of the game. Hanlon did so, but to an old-school baseball man like Hanlon, it made him question his pitcher's heart.[35]

As most had anticipated, the winner of that series did indeed win the pennant. The Orioles only

Jake Stenzel took over in center field when Steve Brodie was traded. Some blamed him for the loss of the pennant in 1897, when he misjudged a fly ball that led to a late-season loss to the rival Boston Beaneaters (Babe Ruth Birthplace & Museum).

9. Chasing History (1897)

Union Park during the key 19–10 loss to Boston on September 27, 1897. The home plate-shaped building to the right of the grandstand still stands, as do the row homes along Barclay Street behind the left-field bleachers (Babe Ruth Birthplace & Museum).

managed a split in their final four games with Washington, and Boston won two of three games in Brooklyn to clinch the pennant and end the three-year reign of the Baltimore Orioles.

Most of the Orioles were magnanimous in defeat, and Joe Kelley wired the Beaneaters congratulations on behalf of his teammates.[36] Hanlon also wired the Boston team: "Congratulations from the old champions to the new." Hanlon and Von der Horst also sent a congratulatory telegram to Frank Selee, and as was his nature, Selee was gracious in victory. He called the Orioles a great team and said that the rest of the league was "trying to build up the standard which Hanlon has established."[37]

Baltimore's fall was met with joy from the rest of the league. Both John Ward and Chicago president Jim Hart declared Boston's win as a victory for clean ball. Henry Chadwick also chimed in: "the Orioles had long ago forfeited the good will of every lover of ball playing."[38]

With the pennant now in the hands of the Boston Beaneaters, the Temple Cup series began on October 4 at the South End Grounds. In a wild game, Boston defeated the Orioles, 13–12, but the Orioles won the next two games in Boston and wrapped up the series with two straight wins at Union Park. Once again, the Temple Cup series was a lopsided affair. Not once in the four-year history of the series had the losing team won more than one game.

With each game played in the series, the attendance steadily dwindled. The first game saw a crowd of about 9,500, but by the time the final game was played, fewer than 1,000 fans showed up.[39] The amount taken in from the series barely paid the expenses of the umpires and other park personnel. At the Eutaw House after the final game, the celebration was not as enthusiastic as it had been the previous year at Cleveland, and the entire series had more of an anti-climactic aura around it than ever before.[40]

The repeated arguments over the division of the proceeds, the lack of competitiveness, and the general disinterest among the players, owners, and fans ultimately caused League leaders to determine that the series was more trouble than it was worth. When the League voted on the matter, Hanlon was the only one who voted to continue it, so the trophy was returned to Charles Temple.[41] It can still be seen in the National Baseball Hall of Fame.

* * *

In the postmortem analysis of the 1897 season, it was generally agreed that the deciding factor in the pennant race was the difference in the pitching staffs of the two teams. Although the potential of Baltimore's young pitchers was acknowledged, it was noted that none of them were able to handle the stress of a pennant race as well as proven pitchers such as Kid Nichols, Fred Klobedanz, and Ted Lewis of the Beaneaters.[42]

Others placed the blame on Hanlon and claimed he had encouraged a culture that was permeated with overinflated egos which he ultimately was unable to control. Indeed, the Orioles had made themselves very unpopular among other players in the league because of the assumed arrogance and superiority they allegedly displayed both on and off the field.

Although the Orioles may have antagonized their opponents, serious altercations took place within the team itself. Throughout the season, sports writers had increasingly reported on the personal differences and selfish play on the part of some members of the team.[43]

John McGraw was quick to direct blame for the lack of team harmony on Jack Doyle. Whatever his true feelings were about acquiring Doyle two years earlier, there is no doubt that he no longer wanted him on the team. After Doyle was traded, McGraw said that his "heart was not in the game when he was with us. He did not want to play in Baltimore." McGraw also claimed that after Doyle had taken a "cowardly" punch at him during the season, and said, "I got a bat and would have broken his jaw if Manager Hanlon had not stopped me."[44]

Yet to some, John McGraw was a major cause of the turmoil that festered in the team.

Although the Orioles nearly always publicly demonstrated a band of brothers attitude, they readily upbraided each other for mistakes on the field. McGraw always asserted that the Orioles would criticize one another when mistakes were made, and he seemed to regard it as a responsibility and a badge of honor. Nonetheless, it is clear that some players could handle the self-policing practices of the Orioles better than others. In addition, some of McGraw's teammates felt that he went too far with his "roasts." One of them later said, "He had a mean way of nagging a man that worked against the success of the team."[45]

As a newcomer on the Orioles in 1897, Jake Stenzel had been quickly introduced to the barbs of his teammates when he was chastised for dropping a routine fly ball. He described his experience:

> I got my Dutch up, but when I cooled down, I came to the conclusion that I was not the best outfielder in the world and should not object to taking a lesson occasionally. So after that, instead of kicking when my mistakes were pointed out I held my tongue and waited until someone else blundered, when I turned in with the rest and helped roast him. The boys jolly

just as often, and are never afraid of giving a man too much praise for a good play. It is either a roast or a jolly, and the constant talking keeps the team awake all the time.[46]

Others on the team did not accept the criticism as willingly as Stenzel did, and the constant roasting even grated on the nerves of one of the cherished members of the Big Four, Willie Keeler.

For some reason, McGraw seemed to enjoy picking on Keeler; it may be that Keeler was the only man on the team smaller than he was. After one defeat, McGraw cursed out Keeler for failing to throw home to prevent a run that started an opponent's winning rally. On his way to the shower, Keeler confronted McGraw: "What did you mean by cursing me like that today?" McGraw snapped back, "Play ball!" Keeler lost his temper and went after McGraw, and they ended up wrestling on the dressing-room floor. Doyle grabbed a bat and threatened to break the head of anyone who interfered and offered 5–4 odds that Keeler wouldn't be the first to give up. In fact, McGraw did.[47]

By this point, even Ned Hanlon was being treated disgracefully by McGraw. A player who was on the 1897 team reported a year later when he was with another team that McGraw said awful things to Hanlon and "made no bones of roasting Ed." He described one incident where McGraw shouted at Hanlon, "We made you what you are, and here you are putting on airs. It don't go with me. You were a stiff until we boosted you and your head is swelled by newspaper praise you don't deserve."[48]

The player who related this incident was shocked that Hanlon tolerated McGraw's disrespectful accusations: "How Hanlon took all he did from McGraw I don't see, but he made the sacrifice for the good of the club….I've seen hot old times at the Baltimore grounds, and I often wonder how McGraw got away with some of the plays he made on and off the field."[49]

It is puzzling to think that Hanlon would have tolerated such abuse. But in 1940, three years after Hanlon's death, an interesting story about another McGraw-Hanlon incident was published by columnist Malcolm Bingay, a longtime reporter and editor for both the *Detroit News* and *Detroit Free Press*. The account described an incident in a game against the Phillies when the Orioles had a runner on second and nobody out, and Steve Brodie attempted to bunt. The bunt was a poor one, and the runner was thrown out at third. To make matters worse, Brodie was also thrown out at first. Bingay picks up the story:

> "Who," screams John McGraw, "told that such and such of a so and so to bunt?"
> "I did," said Ned Hanlon.
> "Oh, you did, did you," yelled McGraw and Jennings and Kelley and the rest of them in chorus. "Haven't we got enough to do, trying to win this game, without you handicapping us by your presence? If you would get the hell out of here, mebbe we could win. We can't beat Philadelphia with ten men against us."
> And a lot more to the same effect.
> Ned Hanlon gets off the bench in his business suit which he always wears. He straightens his necktie very calmly and half smiles.
> "All right, boys," he ses. "I quit. Manage yourselves."
> He walks right off the field and out of the park.
> Well, sir, you could 'a knocked them lads over with a baseball bat, they are so stunned. They look at each other, frightened at what they had done, for they loved Ned Hanlon like he was a father. McGraw is the first one to speak.
> "We gotta win now," he says. "We gotta win for him. We hurt his feelings. And, besides, he can't make suckers out of us."

Well, my hearties, they tear and claw and fight and bite and kick and gouge to keep themselves in that game until the tenth inning, when as luck would have it, McGraw gets on, steals second, and comes home on Jennings' single with the winning run. They feel they had to win—alone and without the leadership of the man who had taught them all they knew.

Instead of being proud and happy they are a shame-faced bunch of kids when they get to the clubhouse and the old man isn't there. They go to his house to apologize. He isn't home. They search the town for him. He isn't to be found. They have a funny, hollow feeling all that night wondering what has happened to him.

That feeling isn't gone the next morning when they come out for practice. No Hanlon. They are dressed and ready to go take the field when he comes in, very quiet like.

"Good morning, boys," he says.

"Good morning, Mr. Hanlon," they answer, kind o' queer like.

"You won the game yesterday without me, I see," he says.

"We did," says McGraw. "We are sorry we said what we did, but—"

"That's all right," cut in Mr. Hanlon. "You insulted me and humiliated me and you got away with it. I walked out on you. Now I'll tell you why I quit. I was more interested in winning the game than I was in winning my argument. I knew if we started to argue we would be licked. I knew, too, that if I walked out, as I did, you would gang up together and break your necks, if necessary, to show me up. I didn't care how we won as long as we won. That is why I swallowed my pride and let a bunch of brats like you think you were making a sucker out of the old man. And now let me tell you something—"

Well, my lads, when he gets through bawling 'em out even the tough young Mugsy McGraw is crying. They promise never to be bad boys again and to always pay him the respect that was due him as their boss.[50]

At first glance, this seems to be a highly fanciful story, but a close reading provides sufficient evidence that components of the story have, at the very least, a ring of truth to them. First, although Hanlon would not hesitate to forcefully speak his mind to them, he was not the type of manager to discipline his players in front of an audience, as was reported often throughout the years by the players themselves. Hanlon also clearly demonstrated throughout his managerial career that winning games must always be placed above individual ego, so the fact that he took the abuse and walked away is believable. In addition, it cannot be denied that Hanlon was loved and respected by the vast majority of the men who played for him, and that some did indeed look at him as a father figure.

Finally, there is the interesting portrayal of McGraw that emerges from the story. McGraw clearly is the ringleader in the verbal assault on Hanlon, but the account also depicts him as being concerned about Hanlon's feelings. Yet he immediately covers up that sentiment with a remark about winning the game so they won't be made out to be "suckers." Also, when McGraw makes his apology to Hanlon, he immediately follows it up with a "but"—as if he is going to launch into an excuse for his actions. But the no-nonsense Hanlon would have none of it, and he immediately cuts off McGraw and follows up with a tongue-lashing of the team. The young McGraw seen in this anecdote is one who is quite consistent with the complex man that history would come to know. Now, whether McGraw broke down in tears, well....

In fairness to McGraw, there is evidence that the practice of the Orioles vigorously roasting one another over their play might very well be traced back to Hanlon. When Joe Kelley was player-manager for the Cincinnati Reds in 1902, he vigorously defended the practice. He claimed an organization had little chance for success when the players simply sugarcoated mistakes, and he maintained that it was a philosophy instilled in him by

Ned Hanlon. He said that Hanlon's quiet demeanor on the bench gave a false impression that he wanted that same behavior from his players. Kelley said:

> Hanlon realizes…that in order to keep a team on edge all the time it is necessary to give them something besides encouraging words. There's nothing that Hanlon hates so much as to see all his men sitting on a bench all satisfied with each other. Many a time during my career with him, when there was nothing doing on the bench, he would call me over to him and suggest that I start a wordy war of some kind among the players in order to wake them up. After a few hints of this kind I knew exactly what was wanted, and thereafter we had many a verbal scrap during every game. The result was that the players were keener to do good work, and we were more alert and anxious that they would have been if everything had been smooth sailing; and they won many more games in consequence.[51]

Kelley's account is not the only evidence that Hanlon saw nothing wrong with players criticizing one another on the field. If early on in his management of the Orioles he did indeed sow the seeds that either instituted the practice of "roasting" or simply encouraged it once it began, then it seems that he could hardly complain when it was directed at him.

In any case, whether it was a fair assessment or not, the individual who was generally blamed as the main instigator of team dissension was Jack Doyle. One specific incident in a game at Brooklyn on August 9 was frequently mentioned as a prime example of Doyle's negative influence on the team. In the third inning with the Orioles ahead, 6–0, Brooklyn had a lucky bloop hit which was followed by an infield single and errors by Quinn and McGraw. Pitcher Joe Corbett became noticeably agitated by the lack of support. Corbett's agitation grew when McGraw fell down attempting to field a ball on the next play, and when Doyle made an outstanding play and threw home and Boileryard Clarke dropped the ball.

Corbett erupted in fury, and one of two things happened, depending on the source. In one account, Doyle and Jennings tried to give him encouragement and calm him down and suggested that he change his pitching strategy.[52] In the other, Doyle went to the mound to suggest that Corbett should give another pitcher a chance, and Jennings joined the conference and roughly told Corbett, "Yes, get out. You are no better than any of the other pitchers."[53] In any case, Corbett exploded, angrily contending that he was pitching well but was being blamed for the poor play of his teammates. He threw the ball into the stands and stormed off the field. Hanlon now was in a bind because the only pitcher he had available was Jerry Nops, who would have to pitch on one day's rest. Nops did his best, but Brooklyn battered him and came away with a 16–9 victory.[54]

After the game, Hanlon indignantly called Corbett's meltdown foolish and said he could not understand or justify it. He admitted that comments by Doyle and Jennings may have contributed to the situation, but he said that Corbett should be used to it at this point because the players had been criticizing each other all season.[55] He refused to say if he would fine Corbett, but he did say that when Corbett realized what he had done, he would be remorseful enough to make a fine unnecessary.[56] The *Baltimore Sun* commented that Corbett was lucky to have an understanding manager such as Hanlon.[57]

"Just a few weeks after this game, it was reported that the only friend Jack Doyle had on the team was himself,"[58] and he was unable to get along with his teammates and was disputing Hanlon's authority.[59] Hanlon angrily denied these rumors, and he declared that Doyle's relations with his teammates were pleasant and that he fit into the team nicely. He further maintained that no player worked harder to win and that he was always willing to obey orders.⁶⁰ Hanlon's denials notwithstanding, Doyle assumed the role of the whipping boy for all Orioles dissent, and after the season ended, *Sporting Life* laid the entire blame for the loss of the pennant on Doyle's "despicable" treatment of Corbett in that August game.⁶¹

* * *

After the season was completed, several Orioles went on a barnstorming tour to California. While they were there, Jay Hughes, a pitcher on the Sacramento team, beat them and so impressed the Baltimore players that they told Jennings to contact Hanlon to encourage him to sign Hughes. Hanlon knew that Jennings was a good judge of talent and not easily impressed, so he wired him back to arrange terms for a contract with Hughes. Hanlon notified Nick Young of the deal, expressed his hope that Hughes would be as good a pitcher as Corbett was, and went off to the race track.⁶²

Later, Hanlon received a letter from Jennings which informed him that the California trip made money for all the promoters and the team; however, he reported that Joe Corbett had been assaulted by Doyle in Sacramento, and the men had to be separated before they did any serious harm to one another.⁶³

Things had reached a point where it was impossible for Jack Doyle to remain with the Orioles. The bad press he was receiving, his deteriorating relationship with some of his teammates, and his desire to captain or manage a team all contributed to Doyle's desire to leave Baltimore. Hanlon agreed to Doyle's wish for a trade because he did not want anyone on the team who did not care to stay, and he felt the harmony that was lacking might more easily be restored if Doyle was not around. As a result, Hanlon met Senators president Earl Wagner at the Eutaw House in Baltimore, and they quickly agreed to the terms of a big trade which sent Doyle, Doc Amole, and Heinie Reitz to Washington in return for pitcher Doc McJames, second baseman Gene DeMontreville, and first baseman Dan McGann.⁶⁴

McGraw had privately been clear that he would not play on the same team with Doyle again, but publicly he tried to play both sides of the issue. He said that he believed Baltimore was getting the short end of the deal on paper, but quickly added that restoring harmony was the most important thing, even if it resulted in a slight loss in playing strength.⁶⁵

"Others supported the trade. Although they acknowledged Doyle's skill as a first baseman and the fact that he played hard and with daring, they also felt that, along with the disharmony he caused, he was too reckless on the base paths. It was also claimed that he was not a team player and seldom tried to move baserunners over and never attempted to execute the hit and run."⁶⁶

Yet not everyone in Baltimore was happy about the deal. Some believed that Doyle's play and attitude had been misrepresented in the press, and this had forced Hanlon to make a trade that he would have preferred not to make. Wilbert Robinson had doubts about how beneficial the trade would be when he said, "I hope it will turn out all right. I believe McJames is all right, and, to a certain extent, so is DeMontreville, but I know two finer men in their positions never walked than Reitz and Doyle."⁶⁷

In Washington, there was great apprehension about the trade. People had heard the rumors about Doyle's inability to get along with teammates, but of more concern was Hanlon's Foxy Ned reputation. Washington fans "could not understand how any man could have had sufficient nerve and confidence in his own judgment to broach a deal to Hanlon; and then, having opened negotiations, to escape without being skinned alive."[68]

Baltimore fans also worried in the off-season that they might not only lose Doyle, but McGraw and Robinson as well. The fact that Robinson and McGraw's Diamond Café was doing so well stoked rumors that they were planning on devoting themselves solely to that business. Hanlon, with characteristic aplomb and probably recognizing it for a salary negotiation ploy, dismissed these rumors by saying that neither of the two men ever hinted to him that they would retire.[69]

In an interview with the *Baltimore Sun* after the season, Hanlon expressed an interest in obtaining two proven veteran pitchers because he felt the strain of a pennant race was overwhelming for young, inexperienced pitchers. With this statement, he was certainly thinking of Corbett, who on more than one occasion showed that the moment

Although Hanlon was reluctant to do so, he traded Jack Doyle because some of the Orioles, most notably John McGraw, did not want him on the team. Doyle also asked Hanlon to trade him (Babe Ruth Birthplace & Museum).

was too big for him. He wistfully said that if he had a pitcher like a sound McMahon or Kid Nichols, Baltimore would have won the pennant.

Hanlon proclaimed that his team did less kicking than in the past, but he said that players had a right to stand up to dispute unfair calls. He called upon the umpires to immediately fine or expel players if they crossed the line and engaged in "useless abuse."[70] Hanlon made a point to exonerate the umpires of any corruption and said that they were honest and simply made mistakes from time to time. Hanlon concluded by claiming that rowdy behavior had originated with the Cleveland Spiders, and that other players began to emulate them because they thought they had to do the same thing to win.[71]

* * *

Hanlon had long been amused by reports that other managers were afraid to make deals with him, and this prompted him to try a humorous experiment at the League meeting. He went around to various managers and proposed very one-sided trades that would have benefited them greatly, but which he had no intention of really making. He was turned down by them all.[72]

Throughout the season, Hanlon had once again been a hot managerial candidate. It was reported that Pittsburgh had made him a lucrative offer to manage the Pirates[73] and that the Phillies were trying to induce Hanlon to come to Philadelphia.[74] To all these reports, Hanlon responded that he had no intention of leaving Baltimore. He further stated that although he was making less than the offers he had received, he was making enough to satisfy him.[75]

In an interview on the tenth anniversary of Hanlon's Detroit team winning the pennant, he was asked to compare the old Detroit team to his current Orioles. Hanlon declared that the Wolverines were "the greatest team of hitters ever seen," but he said:

> You must remember that base ball as played by the Detroit champions and the Baltimores is not the same article. The game, like all things, has progressed, and it is to-day more scientific than 10 years ago. It requires more thought and head work. It is in some respects like checkers and chess, and must be played upon systematic plans.
>
> The game is more aggressive, too. There is more kicking, more ginger, faster base running, more bunting, systematic team play at the bat, which means the hit-and-run system, and the players are younger.

Hanlon said that if the current strategies used by his Orioles were used in his Detroit days, the crowds would have howled in protest if they saw sluggers like Sam Thompson and Dan Brouthers attempt to bunt.[76]

* * *

As the year came to a close, Hanlon was in his cozy home making plans for spring training and analyzing the strengths and weakness of his upcoming opponents. The *Sun* assured the Baltimore faithful that "Many a game has been won by the Orioles through strategy, the result of long hours, perhaps, of thought by Mr. Hanlon in the long winter evenings."[77]

Indeed, there was reason for optimism for the Orioles in 1898. Considering all the internal and external problems that the Orioles encountered in 1897, they finished the season with a .692 winning percentage. In the 15 seasons from 1887 through 1901, only three National League teams had a higher winning percentage than the Orioles did in 1897.[78] Many believed that if the team was kept intact and the star players were able to stay healthy, the Orioles could be pennant winners in the coming season because they "have forgotten more about the game than some base ball teams will ever learn."[79]

However, strong forces were tugging at the very structure of the National League that would not portend well for the Baltimore franchise. Syndication and league contraction were on the horizon.

10

Summer of Discontent (1898)

The New Year got off to an inauspicious start with the death on January 4 of popular and influential Brooklyn owner and co-founder Charles Byrne. Hanlon attended his funeral and was much affected by his death. In speaking of Byrne, he said, "Baseball never had a better friend than Charles H. Byrne. He loved the game and was an energetic and busy man.... He always seemed to know what was the wisest course for the League to pursue for the general good of base ball, and he had great influence in shaping legislation and making baseball history."[1]

As the February League meeting approached, Rules Committee Chairman James Hart proposed several rule changes. One was that instead of merely fining players, umpires should be given unlimited power to eject players from a game and then suspend them for as many games as they wished. If he wanted to, the umpire could blacklist a player, or even a whole team, forever. Hart argued that this would curb the rowdyism which he believed had permeated the game. He grandiosely stated that the umpire "has been a long-trodden-upon individual. Let's put a sword in his hand and make him a general."[2]

Hanlon publicly expressed his opposition to Hart's proposal. He believed the rule would allow umpires to use such broad powers unjustly or corruptly to punish a team; however, he asserted that it was more likely that most umpires would be afraid to take the responsibility of suspending a player, and this would therefore do nothing to curb rowdy behavior. He maintained that the League should keep the current rule, which required umpires to report bad language and inappropriate behavior to the league president, who would then decide on the punishment.[3]

Hanlon was quite aware that Hart's proposal was directed at his team, and he insisted that he was opposed to foul language and delays in the game caused by arguments with the umpire. He agreed to adhere to the league rule which prevented management from paying player fines, and he said that he would cooperate in any league legislation that drew a sharp line between aggressive play and rowdyism. However, he maintained that there was more to the proposal than simply curtailing improper behavior: "It is an old story, but nevertheless true, that the alleged rowdyism of the Baltimore players has had its root in the bitter enmity against the club—a three-time winner of the pennant."[4]

Hanlon also objected to another Hart proposal that called for the earned run rule to be abolished. Indeed, a number of the league scorers and writers had met and declared that the rule for calculating earned runs useless, and the rule as it stood was ludicrous. To be counted as an earned run, a batter had to reach base on a hit and then score on a hit. To illustrate the absurdity of the rule, the *Sun* provided the following scenario: if a pitcher filled the bases with three walks, allowed a triple, and then a sacrifice fly, four runs would score but not a single one would be earned.[5]

Rather than simply abolishing the rule, Hanlon wanted to revise it in such a way that it would accurately measure the pitcher's effectiveness. Hanlon felt the rule should make the pitcher responsible for bases on balls, hit batters, fielding errors by the pitcher, and wild pitches, in addition to base hits.[6]

Finally, Hanlon disagreed with Hart's ideas regarding how to credit a stolen base. On attempted steals, Hart did not want to give the runner credit for a stolen base if the catcher made a throwing error on the play or the infielder dropped the ball. As a renowned base stealer in his playing days, Hanlon wanted to give the runner the benefit of the doubt and give him credit for a stolen base if he attempted to steal and reached the base successfully, regardless of any poor defensive play by the catcher or infielder. He believed that Hart's rule would discourage base stealing.[7]

As it turned out, the league did not adopt any of Hanlon's suggestions, but his ideas for how to credit earned runs and stolen bases was close to what ultimately was adopted and applies today. It was not long into the season before Brooklyn magnate Gus Abell and others admitted that they should have accepted Hanlon's proposals.[8]

When the league met in St. Louis at the end of February, one of the main points of business was the Brush Rule, called by some the Brush "Purification" Rule. The 21-point plan was authored by Cincinnati Reds owner John T. Brush, and its main purpose was to eliminate rowdy behavior and vulgar language during games. It stated that any player who talked to an umpire or another player in a "villainously filthy manner" could be banned for life if found guilty by a board of discipline.[9] It further required that all players sign the resolution before the beginning of the season.

Hanlon, although he realized this rule was directly aimed at his team, rose during the discussion of the rule and spoke in favor of it, which elicited applause from all. The rule was unanimously adopted; however, some fans and reporters feared it would cause a "Sunday school-type game."[10] The Brush Rule would prove to be much ado about nothing, as it was largely ignored in the coming season.

At the meeting, the schedule for the 1898 season had been distributed, but Hanlon did not get a chance to examine it closely until he was back in Baltimore. When he did, he was upset at what he perceived to be a schedule that was unfair not only for its financial implications for his club, but also for how physically taxing it would be on his players.

He indignantly declared that whoever made out the schedule did so in a calculated attempt to defraud the Orioles and should be sued: "The more I study the thing the more I am convinced that the other clubs' dates were fixed as conveniently and profitably as possible for each, and that afterward Baltimore was stuck in to fill the undesirable dates." He claimed that virtually all the profitable holiday dates were scheduled with poor drawing teams and that Baltimore was assigned very few profitable Sunday dates. He summed up his diatribe saying, "No other club was ever treated to such a dose as this."[11]

Wilbert Robinson seconded Hanlon's comments about the schedule and said, "It seems to be a case of play ball, grab a sandwich and run for the train. I'm going to buy a jumper, a pair of overalls and a big sponge, and that will be all my baggage. We will not have time to change uniforms, so I will haul the jumper and overalls on over my uniform when not playing." He sarcastically suggested sending Nick Young a bouquet of flowers to thank him for their schedule.[12]

10. Summer of Discontent (1898)

President Young protested that the schedule was fair and said that Hanlon should have made his objections immediately in St. Louis, instead of waiting until he reached home and bringing the case to the public. He said, "I gave him his individual club schedule, and in five minutes he could have told me whether it suited him or not." The *Sun* firmly supported Hanlon and agreed that an adequate study and comparison of the schedule would take several days.[13]

Between Hart's suggested rules regarding the umpires, the Brush plan, and the allegedly unfair schedule, Hanlon had plenty of material to use to rally his players once again with an "us against the world" mentality as the season approached.

* * *

As Hanlon prepared for spring training and the upcoming season, the new players he had received in the Jack Doyle trade stated their pleasure in joining the organization. Dan McGann expressed his satisfaction with joining a team under such "able direction,"[14] and Gene DeMontreville wrote to Hanlon and declared his enthusiasm to play ball according to the "Hanlon idea."[15]

Not all the players, however, were as eager to report. Kelley, Jennings, Keeler, Corbett, Bowerman, and Clarke all refused to sign their contracts unless they received significant pay raises. Although Bowerman and Clarke did not hold out long, the other four were adamant that they would not sign unless their demands were met. Keeler said,

> Of course, we like to play the game…but our livelihood is as vital a question with us as with the majority of people. Now, it's this way: we can count on our fingers the number of years that we shall be able to play. At the end of that short period, our ability to earn money as base-ball players is ended. We maintain that the people come to see us: that we are the attractions; that we do as much to win the pennants, and that we are worth what we ask.[16]

The holdouts maintained that since the league was increasing the number of games from 132 to 154, they were entitled to a raise. Moreover, they were dismissive of going South for spring training and felt they could get in playing shape on their own. Kelley, who was working out at Union Park with Boileryard Clarke, said, "I do not see the justice of trying to make us go to Macon to work for nothing. I have been going South several years, and last year I contracted stomach trouble at Macon and have been paying doctors' bills ever since. McGraw also was taken sick there with a malady which almost put him out of the game."[17]

At first Hanlon downplayed the holdout, but as they became more entrenched in their positions, he became more and more infuriated. He was particularly angry with Kelley, who he considered the ringleader of the group. Hanlon claimed he offered Kelley $2,700, which was accepted, but then Kelley suddenly demanded $100 more, and when that request was denied, he backed out of the deal.[18] Finally, Hanlon reached the limit of his patience and began trying to arrange a trade for Kelley. For his part, Kelley was upset that he was being considered the leader of the strikers and said that Jennings and Keeler had their own personal reasons for holding out.[19]

Hanlon took the recalcitrant players to task in the press:

> The trouble is they have been treated too well.…I have always tried to treat my players fairly and with just as much consideration as possible, because I have been a player myself and know what it means to play for tyrants. But some of the Baltimore players have not appreciated it. They feel because I am lenient, I am easy to bulldoze into anything.…Last year, while the players were under contract to and being paid by the Baltimore Club, I divided money

from exhibition games with them. Did any club before ever pay its men for exhibition games during the playing season? Well, I guess not.

Hanlon also argued that he offered the players a cash bonus of $4,000 to be divided among them if the team won the championship, and $1,800 if they came in second. "We have the largest salary list in the league and the players certainly ought to give the club their best efforts anyhow, but we offered the bonus as an extra inducement and to show that we wanted to be as liberal as possible." Hanlon said there were plenty of good players in the country who could be called upon if needed.[20]

Although many did not side with the players because their salaries far exceeded that of the average working American, some had sympathy for the holdouts and generally agreed with Keeler's assessment that ball players had a limited window in which to earn their living playing baseball. Fans knew that once a player had outlived his usefulness to management, he would be released, and many believed that the players had more than earned their pay by bringing championships and pride to Baltimore.[21]

Most fans and reporters felt the players would sooner or later fall into line because, after all, they had no other option. Nevertheless, there was fear that the antagonism developed during the process would have a detrimental effect on the play of the players and could ultimately cost the team the pennant.[22]

* * *

As the Orioles left for spring training on March 12, Hanlon's patience, which was considered by most observers to be nearly inexhaustible, was running out. He withdrew offers to the holdouts and planned to sign substitutes at a considerable savings for the club.[23] Throughout spring training, he tried to deflect attention away from the no-shows and focus it on the players on the field. During practices, he drilled his team relentlessly on bunting and teamwork tactics, particularly the hit-and-run. He believed these strategies were poorly executed in 1897, and he was determined to improve them in the coming season.[24] There were some bright spots in the spring. Gene DeMontreville was thrilled to be part of the famous Orioles, and his hard work and enthusiasm pleased Hanlon. Another was Jerry Nops, who, coming off a 20-win season, looked like he was getting even better.[25]

When the team left Macon, they played a series of exhibition games as they made their way north. While in Savannah, Hanlon was not happy when he felt his team was outplayed in almost every area of a game there, and he let them know it. He was particularly dissatisfied with the effort of pitcher Jay Hughes, so he met with him that night to give him specific instructions in how to handle critical moments in a game. After the meeting, Hanlon came away believing that Hughes was intelligent and had good baseball sense, and he believed he would learn from the advice he was given.[26]

Arriving in Richmond, the Orioles had time to relax and spend a few days quietly, and on Sunday most of them attended church. They enjoyed the antics of Hanlon's seven-year-old son, Ed, who had been taken along on the trip, and they had a great deal of fun at Joe Quinn's expense when they found out that a con man had swindled him out of 75 cents. Hanlon joked that he was sure that any man who could get 75 cents from Quinn was sure to have fleeced other members of the club for much higher sums.[27]

Despite the occasional moments of levity, it was reported that throughout spring training, the absence of the holdouts cast a shadow that demoralized the team. With each passing day, Hanlon grew more irritated with the stubbornness of the strikers, and he made it clear that if they did not come to terms quickly, they would be disciplined severely.[28] Finally, about a week later, Hanlon met with Keeler and Kelley, and they signed. Hughie Jennings arrived the next day, and he signed as well. Corbett was the only remaining holdout, but Hanlon had confidence in his pitching staff as it stood, and he was not concerned about Corbett's absence.[29]

After the team arrived back in Baltimore, they continued to work out until the evening before Opening Day, when Hanlon met with his team to give them his final instructions. He drew their attention to the newly instituted Brush Rule and explained to them that there was to be no kicking because they did not want to fall into the trap the League had set for them. He encouraged them to use all their energies in ball playing and not in raising objections. He handed them the receipt forms that the League mandated be given to players that acknowledged they would adhere to the rules. Hanlon told them they could sign them, if they wished. They all declined.[30]

Hanlon reminded the players of his pledge to divide up $4,000 among them if they won the pennant, or $1,800 if they finished in second place. He made it clear that the money would be divided only among players who were deserving. If they all played to win and conducted themselves properly, they would all be given an equal share. But he warned them that if they played with indifference or were "loose in habits," they could receive either a smaller share or even nothing at all. He ended by expressing his confidence that they would not betray his trust in them and told them he thought they were the greatest team on earth. He expressed his sincere hope that they would earn the $4,000.[31]

As Opening Day approached, many wondered how the Orioles would fare under the new Brush Rule. Hanlon, of course, downplayed any concerns about that and addressed the reports that accused him of either encouraging rowdy play or not doing enough to suppress it. He said, "I have been before the public as both player and manager for a long time, and I think my reputation for fair play has been pretty well sustained. When I was captain of the Detroits, I never resorted to rowdyism."[32]

* * *

Prior to Opening Day, the club erected new bleachers along the left field line, and Hanlon made sure that the committee of the Building Trades of the local Federation of Labor was given the job.[33] Groundskeeper Tom Murphy had graded and leveled the field, and he declared that it was better than ever.[34] The Orioles were scheduled to open the season on the road in Washington on April 15, but inclement weather canceled the game, so they opened the next day against Washington at Union Park. As usual, a parade took place before the game, and the home crowd was treated to an 8–3 Orioles victory behind Doc McJames.

Best of all for Baltimore fans, the Orioles appeared committed to returning to the style of play that they had abandoned at crucial times in 1897. The *Sun* complimented the team for doing the unexpected, executing the hit-and-run to perfection, and playing "the kind of baseball that has been the admiration and despair of the other National League teams since 1894....It was the real genuine Hanlon scientific article. It was evident from the moment when McGraw stepped to the plate and beat out a bunt for a base hit."[35] After just one game, optimism was high in Baltimore. At least among the fans who bothered to show up.

Despite the efforts by Orioles management to improve the park and the roster, only 6,518 fans showed up for the first game, and this would be the largest crowd of the year.[36] For the entire season, the Orioles drew only 123,146, good for sixth in the 12-team league. This was a significant decrease from the 249,448 they drew in 1897 and a far cry from the 328,000 they drew in the first pennant year of 1894.[37]

As attendance continued to disappoint both players and management throughout the season, various reasons were suggested for why fans were not flocking to the games as before. Some speculated that Baltimore was bored by the consistent winning of the team. Some claimed that the city was simply not a major league baseball town. Some attributed it to disgusted patrons who had tired of what they perceived to be the greedy attitude of players who held out for unreasonable salaries. And some were said to be disgruntled over a style of play that seemed to be more concerned with individual accomplishments rather than the unselfish play that brought three championships to Baltimore.

The Orioles won their second game of the season the next day when Jay Hughes threw a two-hitter to shut out Washington, 9–0 in his first major league game. When Hughes triumphantly walked to the bench at the end of the game, "he threw his chest forward and laughingly remarked to Hanlon: 'I guess it's in order for me to get stuck on myself.'" This sense of humor made Hughes popular among his Orioles teammates.[38]

The Orioles got off to a fast start, winning nine of their first 11 games, and the pitching staff led by McJames and Hughes looked strong. Hanlon was complimented for his ability to handle pitchers and get results out of them that they would not produce if they were on other clubs.[39] He was also heralded for the moves he made to acquire DeMontreville, McGann, and Hughes, and was lauded as "not only a man of keen perception, remarkably good judgment, but [he is] also quiet, gentlemanly, and withal a fighter who cannot be bluffed. He is a credit to the national game."[40]

After the good start, however, the rest of the season proved a struggle for the Orioles, and Hanlon grew increasingly frustrated with a variety of issues. In early May, he dashed off a letter to Nick Young protesting that although his team was playing clean ball and did not need to intimidate umpires to win, the umpires were making no attempt to adhere to the Brush Rule and curtail the rowdiness of other teams. He argued that the league needed umpires who had the nerve necessary to enforce the rules.[41]

By the end of May, Hanlon reluctantly announced that poor attendance and its corresponding loss of revenue had forced him to start listening to offers for some of his players to pare down expenses, which he claimed were the highest in the league. Hanlon largely attributed these financial losses to the poor schedule the League had imposed on his team.[42]

By late May, Hanlon had also grown dissatisfied with the play of Jake Stenzel, so at the beginning of June, he traded him and Joe Quinn to St. Louis for outfielder Ducky Holmes and cash. Although Stenzel could be a good defender, there were times when he was not reliable in the field.[43] It is also possible that Hanlon had never forgiven him for his misplay in the final Temple Cup game.

After making this deal, Hanlon was accused of being more concerned with the finances of the club than with the team on the field, but he adamantly denied that he had weakened the club with his transactions. He pointed out that the Orioles were losing $400 a day, and although he was offered $10,000 each for two of his best players, he had refused. He said he would try Holmes in center field and felt that with proper coaching, he would hit well above .300. Hanlon said, "If he fails, I know where I can get other good

| McGraw | Keeler | Nops | DeMontreville | Hughes |
| Robinson | Kelley | Kitson | McGann | Jennings | Clarke |

BALTIMORE BASE BALL CLUB, 1898.

Hanlon's last team in Baltimore in 1898 went 96–53 after the league increased the number of games from 132 to 154 (collection of Tom Delise).

men, and I will. I have found good ball players before and can again. The team needs new blood in it, and that is just what I am getting."[44]

As the uneven play of the Orioles became a well-established pattern, fans were not the only ones dissatisfied with the play of the team. Hanlon was also frustrated with his players: "I have the strongest team individually I ever had, but some of the men know too much. The meetings we used to have to discuss team work don't go any more; they are considered useless by the wise ones, and do no good for that reason." He indicated that some radical measures might be necessary to shake up the club.[45]

Most of the press and fans in Baltimore placed the blame solely on players who were insubordinate and refused to play with a sense of teamwork. It was reported that some of Hanlon's old players thought they knew more about the game than Hanlon, and they did what they wished and not what was ordered. It was pointed out that the style of play that was once practiced by the Orioles was now being used to great success by the Boston Beaneaters.[46] Hanlon's discontent with the insubordination of some of his players once again increased speculation that he would be willing to leave Baltimore. This time it was rumored there was a deal in the works to make Hanlon the manager in Philadelphia.[47]

Many fans were surprised that Joe Corbett never returned to the Orioles. For this, he was generally considered ungrateful because Hanlon had coached him and paid him a fair salary for doing virtually nothing in the 1896 season, and he had given him a pay raise the following year. For 1898, Hanlon offered Corbett a raise to $2,400, but Corbett reportedly demanded a salary that was $1,000 higher than what Amos Rusie and Kid Nichols were getting.[48] Hanlon did not blame Corbett publicly for his refusal to come to terms, but he did correctly attribute the holdout to Joe's brother, Jim, who Hanlon believed had filled Joe's head with overblown expectations about salary. Jim claimed that Hanlon was "the cheapest magnate in baseball," and he would not allow his brother to sign for such "a measly salary."[49]

The Orioles' pitching staff, however, performed well without Corbett. McJames, Hughes, and Nops had outstanding years. The staff was reinforced by Al Maul, a tough 13-year veteran Hanlon had signed the previous season, but who had only appeared in one game. However, Hanlon would squeeze out another excellent performance from a player the rest of the league had considered washed up, and Maul went 20–7 for the Orioles. It proved the last good season for Maul, who after the 1898 season would only pitch in 12 major league games over a three-year period.

That season, the Orioles said goodbye to an old comrade and welcomed back another. In June, Hanlon gave Arlie Pond his release after he was unable to duplicate his solid 1896 and 1897 seasons. Pond was ready to leave baseball as he aspired to join the army as a surgeon. After a farewell dinner with Hanlon, he reported for duty; he served for many years in the Philippines and was regarded as a hero there for his work with the local population.[50]

Although the Orioles had lost the respected Pond, they celebrated the triumphant return of the popular Steve Brodie, who had been released by Pittsburgh. Brodie could not disguise his joy at being reunited with his old Orioles teammates, and the Baltimore press corps and fans were happy to have him back. Unfortunately, an injury curtailed his effectiveness, and he played only 23 games for the team in 1898.

In 50 of the first 72 games of the season, the Orioles were without the services of one or more of their regular players. In addition to Brodie's injury, Keeler, Kelley, and Robinson missed many games, and there was also great concern about the status of Jennings. His consistent arm troubles led to speculation that he had reached the end of the line as a valuable player, and there were calls for Hanlon to sign a new shortstop.[51]

* * *

When the Orioles faced the Giants at the Polo Grounds on July 25, an event occurred which had far-reaching consequences for the National League. As Giants owner Andrew Freedman sat in his box, Ducky Holmes, who played sparingly for the Giants in 1897, came to the plate and struck out. As he made his way to the bench, a friend of Freedman's shouted out, "Oh, Ducky, you're a lobster. That's why you don't play here any more." Holmes shot back, "Well, at least I don't have to play for a Sheeney no more."

When Holmes' remark was conveyed to Freedman, he was enraged and sent an emissary to the Baltimore bench to demand that Hanlon remove Holmes from the game. Hanlon refused and said that if there was a complaint, it should be taken up with umpire Tom Lynch. Freedman charged onto the field with a policeman and demanded that Lynch throw Holmes out of the game. Lynch refused to do so, claiming that he did not hear Holmes' remark. An irate Freedman then ordered Giants manager Bill Joyce to keep his players on the bench, and when the Giants refused to take the field, Lynch forfeited the game to the Orioles.

Freedman reimbursed the fans who attended the game and stopped payment on the check he had already given the Orioles for their share of the game receipts. He further demanded that the League take action under the Brush Rule to punish Holmes for remarks that were personally offensive to him and "an insult to the Jewish people and the Hebrew patrons of the game."[52]

Freedman ratcheted things up even more when he wired Hanlon that Ducky Holmes would not be allowed to enter the Polo Grounds in the future, and he informed Hanlon that it was wrong for him to allow such a man as Holmes to play on the team. Hanlon admitted that Holmes' remarks "were in bad taste," but he argued that because they were not, in his view, considered insulting, profane, or obscene, the remark did not fall under the auspices of the Brush Rule. He also defended Holmes and said it was natural that the player would make some retort after the provocation he received.[53]

When Hanlon was asked what he would do if Freedman tried to bar Holmes from the grounds, he said, "The thing is absurd, and I propose to play whom I please in New York as elsewhere. If Freedman can bar out any man who is distasteful to him, I have the same right, and then either of us could bar out an entire team, or all the good players on a team, upon any trumped-up charge of insulting somebody. The idea is preposterous."[54]

Hanlon further maintained that no matter what words Holmes used, Freedman had no right to force an umpire to eject a player or step onto the field and interrupt the game.[55] He also declared that Freedman needed to be taught a lesson because "he is consumed with a sense of his own importance." Hanlon said that because Freedman had connections to the corrupt Tammany Hall political machine, it made him think he could do anything he pleased.[56]

On August 15, the League's Board of Directors met in Philadelphia to settle the matter. After listening to the arguments made by both sides, the board made a decision that managed to infuriate everyone involved. They ruled that the forfeit awarded to the Orioles would stand and that the $1,000 fine for refusing to play the game would be awarded to the Orioles in lieu of the game receipts, provided that within ten days, Baltimore suspended Ducky Holmes for the remainder of the season. Hanlon and Von der Horst were angry because they felt they deserved the game receipts in addition to the fine amount, and they believed the loss of Holmes' services would hurt their pennant chances. Freedman was angry at how the racial remark made by Holmes was not taken seriously, and he felt he should not have been assessed the $1,000 fine.

The board's decision created a firestorm of outrage throughout the baseball world. Cincinnati owner John T. Brush immediately condemned the ruling, stating that the Board had exceeded its authority and acted illegally because Holmes was never proven guilty of an offense and was not given an opportunity to defend himself in front of the board.[57]

Virtually every League magnate who was not on the board that issued the decision joined Brush in publicly censuring its ruling. Furthermore, players on many teams organized petitions in support of Holmes, and most newspapers declared that the decision was an injustice to him. Holmes received a flood of supportive letters from fans across the country, and he became something of a culture hero in the minds of many. Holmes himself expressed no remorse for the incident, saying, "My remark was not addressed to [Freedman]. It was only intended for the man who insulted me. Freedman treated me like a dog when I was a member of his team, and I cannot say that I'm sorry he has made a monkey of himself."[58]

The Orioles found themselves in an undesirable position. If they disobeyed the League's mandate to suspend Holmes, the League might forfeit any game Holmes played in during the ordered suspension period. Moreover, they would not receive either the game receipts or the $1,000 fine assessed against Freedman. If they did suspend Holmes, they would lose the services of a valuable player and might seriously hurt any pennant chances they had. Furthermore, by suspending the now extremely popular Holmes, they would infuriate their own fan base for not having the backbone to stand up to the generally unpopular decision.[59]

Hanlon, Von der Horst, and Holmes handled the delicate situation brilliantly, if not with any degree of racial sensitivity. They met and decided on a plan to protect all parties from League action. First, they suspended Holmes for the remainder of the season in accordance with the League mandate. Then, with the blessing of the team, Holmes hired a lawyer who served the Baltimore Club with a writ of injunction restraining them from suspending him, pending a hearing in Court. The court date was set for September 3, and now the Orioles would have Holmes on the field and at the same time would not be subject to National League discipline.[60]

Public sentiment was still at a fever pitch, and the *Pittsburgh Leader* outrageously declared that even murderers were better treated than Holmes had been. It also increased the public clamor for better rights for players, who were believed to be suffering under the grasp of tyrannical owners. This encouraged outraged players to openly contemplate the formation of a new league that would better protect their rights. In a remarkable turn of events, the public outside Baltimore even sympathized with the hated Orioles, believing that Freedman and the Board put them in an untenable situation.[61] Overwhelmed by all the negative publicity, the board called another meeting to reconsider the issue. This time, they voted to lift the suspension of Holmes; however, they did not rescind the $1,000 fine against Freedman.[62]

President Young did some serious back-pedaling as well, maintaining that he was "grossly misrepresented" in the entire affair. According to Young, he told the Board at its first meeting that if they suspended Holmes, Holmes would have good grounds for legal action to gain reinstatement and be awarded damages because he had not been given an opportunity to appear before the board and defend himself. Young said the board did not heed his warning.[63]

Freedman was astonished that the magnates did not support him, and he saw this for what it was: anti–Semitism and a personal insult. He would never forgive them for it, and he was determined to get revenge. Unlike most of his fellow owners, Freedman had a vast personal fortune that could allow him to lose large amounts of money, so he decided he would not invest in his team, ensuring that they were losers. The result was that in the following year, the record of the Giants fell from 77–73 to 60–90, and attendance decreased by almost 145,000. Every owner would come to feel Freedman's pinch every time they played the Giants. By the end of 1899, the owners were so desperate to make peace with Freedman that they not only refunded his $1,000 with interest, but they also agreed to his insistence on contracting the league from 12 to eight teams.[64]

In early August, as the fiasco was still a topic in full bloom, a *Sporting Life* correspondent commented that "Umpire Lynch expressed the opinion of many fair-minded people when he later declared that Hanlon made a mistake in not taking Holmes out of the game, and thereby preventing the trouble that followed."[65] Hanlon surely deserves blame for exhibiting the anti–Semitism so prevalent at that time; however, there is plenty of blame to go around for the disgraceful situation that emerged from the comment of Ducky Holmes. The National League powers-to-be clearly demonstrated their racial bias, and the inherent anti–Semitism of the non–Jewish population of the country was displayed in full view. Regardless of whatever prejudice Nick Young may or may not have had, the entire fiasco also clearly illustrated his weak and ineffectual leadership.

10. Summer of Discontent (1898) 143

* * *

As the pennant race entered August, the Orioles were still in fourth place and 9½ games behind league-leading Cincinnati. But beginning August 11, the Orioles caught fire and went 16–2 for the remainder of the month and propelled themselves to just one game behind the Reds and Beaneaters, who were tied for first.

Boston, however, was not to be denied. From September 1 until the end of the season, the Orioles played well and won 28 of 41 games, but Boston went on a torrid pace and won 31 of 37 to finish six games ahead of the Orioles. The difference may very well have come down to two things: first, the Orioles went only 5–7 in head-to-head match-ups with Boston; second, in the last month-and-a-half of the season, the Orioles played a back-breaking 11 doubleheaders, while Boston played just three.

After the season, Hanlon gave three reasons why his team failed to win the pennant. First, he felt the team's poor start resulted because not all the players had reported to spring training. Second, he pointed out the number of injuries the team suffered throughout the season. Finally, he described what he felt was the most important reason for his team's downfall, despite their solid record, in 1898:

> Instead of the winning spirit which actuated the players in '94, there has been a spirit of indifference to the success and welfare of the team among some of the older players. This was bound to affect the younger men at times. The players have gone on the field and played as a matter of form. If they won they were pleased, but if not, they did not bother about it so long as their big salaries were ready for them on pay day.[66]

Hanlon praised the excellent work of his pitchers, but the only position player for whom he had a good word was McGraw, who had "worked earnestly and effectively for the team's success." When asked about his plans for the next season, he said he had not yet made definite plans.[67] For a man like Hanlon, that was a telling remark. Hanlon was never a man without a plan. There certainly were things brewing, but Silent Ned was not about to reveal them at that time.

Baltimore baseball fans and the press were united in their belief that the team would not win any more pennants unless the players committed themselves to eliminating the "selfish indifference" that they had demonstrated in the past year. The *Baltimore Sun* summed up a feeling that can resonate with baseball fans of any time in history: "The public can forgive much to a team that is honestly straining every nerve to win, regardless of individual records, but it has no patience with men who do not run out hits, or loaf on bases, or simply play ball to earn their salaries. Enthusiasm is contagious. The spirit shown by the Orioles of '94 set Baltimore wild. Their indifference of this season was reflected in empty seats and general lack of interest and enthusiasm."[68]

Sporting Life concurred with the assessment of the *Sun* and blamed the team's problems on players whose discontent over salary disputes carried over into the season. The reporter commented that by the time they had put their bad feelings behind them, it was too late to make up the ground that they had lost, and in the meantime, they lost the good will of the fans. "Under these circumstances Manager Hanlon did well to land his team second."[69]

Considering the reaction of Hanlon, the press, and the fans to the 1898 season, it is interesting to note an interview that took place with McGraw, Jennings, and Kelley near the end of the season. While at the Gibson House in Cincinnati, the three players spoke with a reporter for the *Cincinnati Enquirer* and discussed the methods that had made them successful. They all discounted the widely accepted notion that the Orioles did more sacrifice hitting than any team in the league, stating that they actually did it less. They expressed disdain for the practice, claiming that it was a one-run strategy and that "one run nowadays won't win." They agreed that they bunted often, but it was for the purpose of getting a hit and not to move along a runner. They admitted that they would use the sacrifice bunt, but only in the final inning of a game if they needed one run to win or tie.

McGraw attributed the Orioles' success to their hit-and-run strategy and their ability to do the unexpected at all times, and claimed it was the only way to win. Jennings supported McGraw's statement: "I have known Hanlon to offer to hit out when you would think we ought to sacrifice," and he described a time when he thought he should sacrifice, but Hanlon told him to swing away. Later the same inning, in another situation that normally called for a sacrifice, Hanlon ordered Kelley to hit away, and he hit a home run. Jennings believed that the use of the sacrifice in that inning may have led to two runs, but Hanlon's decision to have his players hit away led to a seven-run inning and an easy Orioles victory.[70]

It is hard to reconcile the statements of the players in this interview with what was said about them by fans and the press. These do not sound like men acting as if they know more about baseball than Hanlon; in fact, they express a strong belief in the philosophy and tactics he taught them, and they are continuing to implement them. They do not appear to be ignoring the orders of Hanlon. What can be said is that the complex personal and professional dynamics of this group of men who had been in a pressure cooker of competition for the past six years may not be easy to discern today. In later years, Hanlon was readily given credit by all his players for being the architect of the team's success during their glory years in Baltimore, but along the way there were certainly flashpoints of discontent.

Despite the allegations that some players were resistant and disdainful of Hanlon's attempts to make them play scientific baseball, other players rallied around Hanlon at the end of the year. Doc McJames described him as a manager who treated his players with common sense, saying, "On losing days he never wields his sledge at the expense of his pitcher, though when he does send a shot over the plate he has lovely control. There are no rules in the club about getting out of bed at a certain hour when the team is on the trip. He has confidence in every one of his players, and if that confidence is imposed on, he is the first to know it. He is a great manager."[71]

When Joe Kelley was asked to explain how the Orioles were able to win three consecutive championships, he said,

> Of course, we played great ball, but behind it all was a serious purpose, that spurred us on and made our good playing effective. Take the Clevelands…they will never win a pennant, because they are not thoroughly serious in their purpose. Captain Tebeau will make pennant claims, but he is not serious in it, and the men of his team know it. With Hanlon it was different. He talked to us in a way that convinced us of his confidence in our ability to do big things, and we used every effort to deserve that confidence. The result was three championships in Baltimore and the loss of another by a fluke.[72]

Although the Orioles did not win the pennant in 1897 and 1898, it should be noted that in both years they had been a very good team—they just were not better than Boston.[73] Was their fall-off attributable to altering their style of play and becoming dominated by a handful of egotistical star players? Maybe. But it is to be remembered that in the history of baseball, indeed in any sport, it has always been difficult for championship teams to repeat. After all, the Orioles had won three straight championships just like the acclaimed White Stockings and Beaneaters had before them, but none of them had been able to win four. That can hardly be considered disgraceful.

* * *

Hanlon continued to pursue investments outside baseball, particularly in real estate. That year, he and his wife sold a property on St. Paul Street for $4,852.[74] A few days later, he took out a building permit and spent $12,000 to erect a five-story apartment house on Wylie Avenue in Pittsburgh.[75]

As Christmas neared, Hanlon was with Von der Horst and a few other men in a restaurant when he reached into his pocket to settle his share of the bill and found it empty. He excused himself and quickly walked to the club's office. He was only gone a few minutes before he returned and said, "I have done it. My youngsters gave me their Christmas bank roll and I have lost it. There was about $150 in the roll." His friends either consoled him, saying that it would turn up, or kidded him that he had probably bought himself a box of $150 cigars and forgotten the purchase. Hanlon was noticeably upset, but later he reached into his vest pocket and found the money. As "his countenance beamed with an angelic smile, he...reached around the table and gathered in all of the checks and settled for them."[76]

In 1898, there was joy mixed with sorrow. On August 25, Ellen Hanlon gave birth to a fourth child, named Helen Celeste. In November, Hughie Jennings' wife, Elizabeth, died from complications in childbirth, leaving him a young daughter named Grace. Jennings telegraphed Hanlon about his wife's death, but Hanlon received it too late to attend the funeral, and he sent flowers and his regrets.[77]

On December 4, a big storm swept through the northern portion of Baltimore, and what was believed to be a slight earthquake shook the city. Hanlon's home shuddered, and a concerned Ellen came in from another room to ask him if he felt the shaking. She was quickly followed by a frightened household servant who came running down the stairs. Hanlon told a reporter that he had never known his house to shake before, either from wind or the trains that ran near his house.[78]

Considering all the changes that were about to take place with the Orioles, maybe the storm was a harbinger of the tumultuous times ahead.

11

Hanlon's Superbas (1899–1900)

Throughout 1898, there had been great speculation about the future of the League and Baltimore's role in it. Some said the League would contract to eight teams and the Orioles would be dropped. Others said that there was a plan in the works to pool the resources of both the Baltimore and Brooklyn franchises under one ownership group.[1] This model became known as syndication. When Hanlon was asked to address these rumors, he was generally non-committal, but he did admit that Brooklyn's part-owner, Ferdinand Abell, had some time ago made him a big offer to bring him and his team to Brooklyn. The *Baltimore Sun* predicted that the loss of Hanlon would be greatly felt, not only to those interested in baseball, but to Baltimore as a whole since he had gained great respect and admiration ever since he came to the city. It concluded, "he has revolutionized baseball and put it upon a higher plane, and besides has made a solid citizen."[2]

During the off-season, Hanlon tried to assuage fears in Baltimore and said, "There will be a twelve-club league this year and while most of the Baltimore players will change their Oriole uniforms for Brooklyn suits, Baltimore will have a strong club to represent it." He stated that although the team's attendance had fallen off in recent years, he felt it was a natural reaction after having won pennants, and he felt the city would rebound in its support of a team and show that it was a great baseball town. Hanlon affirmed that he would maintain his residence in Baltimore because he and his family liked the city.[3]

Syndication became a reality in the early months of 1899 as Hanlon and Harry Von der Horst struck a deal with the owners of the Brooklyn franchise, Ferdinand Abell and Charles Ebbets, to share stock and ownership. Henceforth, the two franchises would be run in tandem, with the primary purpose being to turn a profit for the syndicate. Von der Horst and Ebbets each owned 40 percent of the stock in both clubs, with Abell and Hanlon owning 10 percent in each. In addition, Hanlon would manage the Brooklyn team for a salary of $10,000 per year. Hanlon was promised total autonomy by Abell: "Mr. Hanlon will have the same authority over the team in Brooklyn that he had in Baltimore. He will be the 'Great I Am,' with none to say him nay."[4]

The National League meetings that winter, always a busy place as managers and owners swung deals and players tried to find new teams or negotiate salary increases, were even more chaotic because of syndication. Hanlon was the center of much of the attention as reporters, players, and other managers tried to find out more information about this new baseball syndicate.[5]

Once Hanlon was announced as the manager, the *Brooklyn Daily Eagle* speculated that Hanlon's team might turn out to be better than Cap Anson's 1880s Chicago team, and even better than the famous Oriole and Beaneater teams of the 1890s.[6] Yet in Baltimore, fans were in a state of trepidation about just what kind of a team they would have. The key question was which players would remain in Baltimore and which ones Hanlon would take to Brooklyn. Hanlon had originally planned on taking John McGraw and Wilbert Robinson, but when McGraw was asked if he would go to Brooklyn, he said he would not. "I have gotten all the glory I can out of baseball and am not looking after any more," he said. "I am more interested in getting money." McGraw claimed that he could not be paid enough by Hanlon or anyone else to compensate him for leaving his business interests in Baltimore.[7]

At one point it appeared that McGraw might become the part-owner of the Baltimore franchise, along with his Diamond Cafe business partner, Wilbert Robinson. Early in January, both men called upon Hanlon to talk about a possible purchase of the club, and they wanted to get an idea from Hanlon about the expenses they could expect to have, beyond the salary list. Hanlon shared the expenses for the previous year and gave them an estimate about what they could expect for the next. He also gave them a general idea of his intended Brooklyn roster.[8] Regarding the sale of the team, Hanlon would not commit to selling it, but he left the door open to a possible sale, saying, "Everything I have, except my family, is for sale at a price."[9]

When asked if he and Robinson were in a position to buy the Orioles, McGraw replied that they were if they could get it for the right price. McGraw knew that stars such as Kelley, Jennings, and Keeler would be heading north with Hanlon, but it was vitally important to him to be left with enough good players to have a competitive team.[10] Hanlon assured him that whoever ended up managing the team would have a better roster than he had when he first assumed control of the Orioles.[11]

When Hanlon went to manage Brooklyn in 1899, John McGraw (left) and Wilbert Robinson (right) refused to go because they wished to remain in Baltimore to run their Diamond Café. McGraw took over as manager of the Orioles, and Robinson was his catcher and right-hand man (Babe Ruth Birthplace & Museum).

Ultimately, Hanlon and

Von der Horst decided not to sell the team, but he asked McGraw if he would like to manage it. McGraw accepted the offer after obtaining Hanlon's assurance that he would not treat the Orioles as a farm team and would not transfer any players from Baltimore after the regular season started.

Hanlon's first step in assembling his team was to assign Baltimore stars Keeler, Jennings, Kelley, and McGann to Brooklyn, along with three pitchers who were 20-game winners the previous season: Jay Hughes, Doc McJames, and Al Maul. From the 1898 Brooklyn roster, Hanlon kept outfielder Fielder Jones, second baseman Tom Daly, and pitchers Jack Dunn and Brickyard Kennedy. In January, Hanlon finally obtained a player that he had been interested in for years when he traded Gene DeMontreville to Chicago for shortstop Bill Dahlen. McGraw's refusal to go to Brooklyn left a vacancy at third base, and Hanlon anticipated using Dahlen at that position.[12] Although by this time Dahlen had gained a reputation for having difficulty getting along with teammates and for being hard to manage,[13] many in the baseball world believed that Hanlon would be able to get the best out of him. Hanlon himself said he was confident that Dahlen would do "gilt edge work" for him.[14]

Although Willie Keeler was thrilled to be moving back to his beloved Brooklyn, both Jennings and Kelley had reservations. Jennings said, "I think the Baltimore fans have been treated shamefully. If there is any way in which I could remain here I would do so. If I am put in Brooklyn, I suppose I would be forced to go, but it would be with great regret."[15] Hanlon talked with both players and persuaded them to report to Brooklyn.[16]

Though he would be well-compensated for his efforts, Hanlon played down the financial part of his deal, saying that he wanted a winning team and nothing more. "I guess I am satisfied and I expect to have a pleasant time of it in Brooklyn during my stay," he said. "I have a fine lot of men under me and we will start right out after the pennant."[17]

Baltimore players remaining with the Orioles were Steve Brodie, Ducky Holmes, and pitchers Frank Kitson and Jerry Nops. To fortify the Baltimore club, Hanlon transferred a number of Brooklyn players there, including outfielder Jimmy Sheckard, shortstop George Magoon, first baseman Candy LaChance, and pitchers Harry Howell, Kit McKenna, and Ralph Miller.

In Baltimore, John McGraw was undaunted and expressed satisfaction with his roster: "By no means have I got a weak team. With my partner Robinson behind the bat during most of the games, and such pitchers as Nops, Kitson, Miller, Howell, and McKenna, the Orioles ought to be and will be very strong."[18] Moreover, McGraw knew that he had a hot pitching prospect in Joe McGinnity.

Hanlon agreed with McGraw, yet as a part-owner of both franchises, he would naturally build up the idea that both teams would be competitive. Nevertheless, in March, when Hanlon plucked pitcher Dan McFarlan from the Baltimore roster, he was criticized for using the Orioles as a farm team. The indignant Hanlon fired back:

> McGraw has so many good pitchers ready to go right in and pitch good ball that he hardly knows which to send in first....I don't think Baltimore ought to kick because I took just one, or even if I took two. I might just as well have taken Miller and McGinnity, too if I were as careless of Baltimore's interests as some people seem to believe. I might also have taken Brodie or Holmes and might have kept Magoon. I would very much like to have Magoon. He is a great ball player. But as McGraw wanted him, and needed him, I let Magoon come to Baltimore.[19]

11. Hanlon's Superbas (1899–1900)

During spring training in Augusta, the Orioles and Brooklyn played a series of exhibition games against each other. In one of them, the Orioles beat the Superbas, 5–1, behind a strong pitching performance by Joe McGinnity. After the game, McGraw flippantly asked Hanlon, "Ned, shall we play you tomorrow? We prefer to go to Savannah tomorrow afternoon, but if you really hanker after another contest against these dubs of ours, we are willing to play you a morning game, just for practice you know. I think your team needs practice."

Hanlon was not amused, and he snapped, "For goodness sake, get out of the town as soon as possible." He spouted out a stream of language that could not be repeated in a newspaper and announced that his team would spend all the time remaining in spring training working to perfect the tactics he had taught McGraw so well.[20]

* * *

An overflow crowd of over 20,000 witnessed Brooklyn open their season in Washington Park on April 15 against the Boston Beaneaters. Although Kid Nichols outdueled Brickyard Kennedy, 1–0, in an 11-inning contest, Hanlon called it "as fine a game as I ever saw." The Superbas' excellent play made it clear that they were a team to be reckoned with in the coming season, and Boston manager Frank Selee remarked that Brooklyn had a great team in what he believed would be a heated pennant race.[21]

Brooklyn began the year slowly, sitting at 7–6 and in fifth place at the end of April. Because Jennings was unable to play because of his sore arm, Hanlon realized he needed to strengthen his infield. He engineered a trade with Washington in late April to obtain catcher Duke Farrell and third baseman Jimmy Casey, and moved Jennings to first base and Bill Dahlen to shortstop. Beginning on May 1, Brooklyn won 15 of 18 games to take over first place on May 22. They would never relinquish the lead.

Brooklyn observers were impressed with the morning pre-game practices where Hanlon drilled the players endlessly in his tactics and preached to them about using their heads as well as their physical abilities. Watching the agility of the players reminded some of a famous

Bill Dahlen was a player that Hanlon long coveted, and he finally obtained him from Chicago before the 1899 season (Babe Ruth Birthplace & Museum).

troupe of acrobats who were called Hanlon's Superbas. The Hanlon who ran that troupe was no relation to Ned Hanlon, but reporters began referring to the ball team as the Superbas, and the name stuck for the rest of Hanlon's stay with the team.

Brooklyn fans and reporters noticed that Hanlon was skilled at handling the disparate personalities that comprised a ball club. He maintained friendly relationships with his players, but that did not prevent him from administering discipline when it was needed. When he had pouting ball players, he corrected them as if they were "spoiled children," but he also attempted to keep his players as satisfied as possible with their role on the team.[22] Off the field, he was known for a sort of watchful leniency and trusted them to act like men and exhibit proper conduct.[23]

One small example of how Hanlon brooked no interference with his authority came when the team disembarked from the train for an away game. As equipment was loaded onto wagons to be shipped to the field, a new player suggested to Hanlon that it would be better if the equipment was shipped by bus rather than wagon. Hanlon sharply told the player to worry about playing, and he would worry about everything else.[24]

During a game, it was clear to Brooklyn fans that Hanlon was directing the play: "Before going to the bat the players consult him…[and] he does not hesitate to shout his order at a critical point, and these orders are rarely disobeyed."[25]

Pitcher Doc McJames described Hanlon's coaching style: "[He] is one of the frankest men I ever met, and he isn't afraid to give his players a slice of his mind." He related a story about a time he pitched poorly in Brooklyn and Hanlon removed him from the game in the middle of an inning. "I said to him 'See heah, sah (sir), what do you mean by taking me out of the box and showing me up like this sah?' He came back with this middle-of-the-plate twister: 'Show you up, you big stiff? Wasn't you making a sucker out of me with that bum pitching?'"[26]

One surprise of the season was how well John McGraw's Orioles played. After an uneven start, they improved to 21–17 at the end of May, and for those who tired of seeing the pennant won by either Hanlon's or Frank Selee's teams, fans began rooting for the upstart new Orioles.[27] Hanlon, always acutely conscious of the bottom line, reflected on the unexpected performance of the Orioles and said, "To think that we were supposed to be anxious to sell, and at a ridiculously low price at that. Why, the club will finish the season a financial winner." He also complimented McGraw and Robinson's ability to work together to get the most out of their players: "Ginger and steadiness combined win games."[28] Baseball insiders certainly knew which of those players supplied the "ginger" and which supplied the "steadiness."

* * *

By the end of June, the injury to Jennings' arm was still a concern to Hanlon, and no matter how much he liked Jennings both personally and as a player, he never let sentiment stand in the way of improving his team. Despite the sore arm, Jennings still had much to offer potential trading partners. He could still hit, run, and field, and there was nothing wrong with his instincts and competitive fire.[29] Consequently, Hanlon put together a deal that would have significantly changed baseball history had it been consummated.

Hanlon arranged for Jennings to be dealt to the Louisville Colonels along with $2,500 for a young infielder named Honus Wagner, who was in his third year in the league. Hanlon planned on using Wagner at third base, and the deal was agreed to in principle by both clubs. However, just to be certain, and perhaps because of Hanlon's "Foxy Ned" reputation, Louisville President Harry Pulliam contacted Jennings to ask if he could still play effectively. Jennings sent back the following reply: "Do not make the deal. Arm is lame, am sick, and will not play again this season."[30]

There is no question that Jennings had a sore arm that limited him to only a handful of games, but it is uncertain if he felt he could not play again that season. Jennings likely was reluctant to go to Louisville because he felt that the city would be a casualty of the rumored contraction in the following season.[31] Because of concern over the physical condition of Jennings, Harry Pulliam called the deal off and notified the newspapers that Hanlon could not fool the Louisville Club with this proposed trade. When Hanlon heard about the telegram Jennings had sent, he called him into a

Hughie Jennings, pictured here, angered Hanlon when he informed Louisville that he was unable to play when Hanlon tried to trade him for a young Honus Wagner. It resulted in a tangled web of events that affected the franchises in Brooklyn, Louisville, and Baltimore. (Babe Ruth Birthplace & Museum).

meeting. There Jennings was dressed down by the Brooklyn officials, some of whom wanted to suspend him indefinitely.[32] Hanlon, however, was more deliberate in his actions, and he refused to do so until he considered the situation more carefully.

Ultimately, Hanlon decided to send Jennings to McGraw in exchange for George Magoon. McGraw expressed great interest in having Jennings, but he abashedly admitted that he had just traded Magoon to Chicago for Gene DeMontreville. As Hanlon was President of both the Brooklyn and Baltimore clubs, McGraw did not have the authority to make a trade without his approval. Hanlon was furious, and in a fit of pique, he sent Jennings to the Orioles and took DeMontreville and pitcher Jerry Nops from Baltimore.

Now it was McGraw's turn to be angry, and he reminded Hanlon that he had promised not to interfere with the Orioles once the season started. McGraw said, "Jennings will strengthen our team...but taking away Nops is a hard blow. When he is in shape, he is the best left-hander living."[33]

The fans and newspapers in both cities were in an uproar, and the whole situation was an embarrassment for all parties involved. After Jennings had played only two games for the Orioles, Hanlon gave in to public sentiment and reversed the trade, sending the players back to their original clubs. After the fiasco, Jennings played well at first base for Hanlon, and hard feelings over the situation seemed to dissipate.

It is interesting to speculate how the Jennings for Wagner trade would have changed the baseball landscape. Without Wagner, it is possible that Pittsburgh would not have had the success they enjoyed during the subsequent 15 years. With Wagner, Hanlon might have continued the dominance of the Superbas for many years.

* * *

During the season, Hanlon demonstrated how he mentally sized up his players. He knew he did not need to motivate players such as Jennings or Kelley, but laid-back outfielder Big John Anderson was not one of that type. At that point, Anderson's principal claim to fame was that he had tried to steal second base when the bases were full. Hanlon decided to subtly prod Anderson to a better effort, so during a game against Cincinnati as the Superbas were rallying with the bases loaded, Hanlon called Anderson over and told him he was going to pinch-hit. Before he went to the plate, Hanlon told him, "See what you can do, as these Cincinnati players before the game told me you were the worst busher in baseball." An insulted and angry Anderson responded by hitting a double to win the game for Brooklyn.[34]

Later in the season, Hanlon, however, lost his patience with Anderson. Joe Kelley recounted a time when the Superbas were trying hold off the surging Beaneaters, and they needed one run to win the game. Anderson had a chance to score from second base on a hit, but because he did not slide, he was tagged out. When he came to the bench, Hanlon asked him why he didn't slide. Big John lamely explained that he did not have any padding in his pants. "Well," replied Hanlon, "you won't need any from this time on unless you want to make the bench seem softer," and he benched Anderson for the rest of the season.[35]

As the season progressed, the Superbas easily pulled away from all competitors, and they ended up with a 101–47 record, eight games ahead of second-place Boston. It looked as if Hanlon was ready to begin another period of league domination. However, throughout the season, one team proved to be a surprise. John McGraw's plucky Orioles played far beyond the expectation others held for them, and under his inspired leadership, the Orioles hovered in or close to the first division throughout the season. It was not only his managerial skills that kept his team competitive; he also had one of his best seasons as a player. He hit .391 and led the league in walks (124), runs (140), and on-base-percentage (.547). He achieved all this despite playing just 117 games.

Yet in the midst of his professional success, personal tragedy struck John McGraw in late August. While in Louisville with his team, he received word that his wife, Minnie, whom he married in February of 1897, was seriously ill. He handed over the managerial reins to Robinson and immediately caught a train to Baltimore. While he was on his way home, surgeons decided Minnie was too sick to move to a hospital, and they performed an emergency appendectomy on her in the McGraw home at 2738 St. Paul Street. They cleaned out as much of the infection as they could, and in this time before antibiotics, they hoped she would be strong enough to fight off what remained. Unfortunately, she was unable to do so. Shortly after noon on August 31, 22-year-old Minnie McGraw died with her devastated husband and her family by her side.

The funeral was held on Sunday, September 3, at Saints Phillip and James Church, just a few blocks away from the McGraw home. A huge crowd of mourners turned out, and hundreds had to be turned away from the packed church, which was overflowing with floral tributes. The pallbearers had served as ushers at their wedding just two-and-a-half years earlier: Hugh Jennings, Joe Kelley, and Willie Keeler. Hanlon, Harry Von der Horst, Wilbert Robinson, and league president Nick Young all attended the funeral and accompanied the body to the cemetery. With John McGraw sobbing over her grave, poor young Minnie McGraw was laid to rest in Bonnie Brae Cemetery in Baltimore, which was later renamed New Cathedral Cemetery.[36]

When McGraw left Louisville to go to Minnie, the team was 64–42. A heartbroken McGraw rejoined the Orioles on September 11, but he did not put himself into the lineup until a week and a half later. From the time McGraw left the team, they went 22–20 for the remainder of the season, and the Orioles finished in fourth place. It was the first of many winning seasons in the managing career of John McGraw, but it was marked by grief.

* * *

After the Superbas won the pennant, a testimonial dinner was held at the Brooklyn Academy of Music on October 21. Thousands of tickets were sold, and a portion of the ticket proceeds, along with other contributions, was presented as gifts to the winning players. Club president Ebbets and Hanlon spoke in praise of the championship club, and Hanlon was sure to mention each player by name in his speech. The players were given a $2,500 check to share among themselves.[37]

It might be tempting to dismiss Hanlon's accomplishment in 1899 by believing that he had merely transferred the successful Orioles team from Baltimore to Brooklyn, but it wasn't quite that simple. In 1898, Brooklyn, managed by Charles Ebbets, went 54–91 and was an awful team. Moreover, Hanlon's Orioles teams had not won the pennant in 1897 or 1898. In Brooklyn he also did not have McGraw and Robinson, two of his most important players in the championship years. Hanlon was able to blend a combination of Baltimore and Brooklyn players and make key transactions to build a dominant, pennant-winning team. It must also be noted that Hanlon could have strengthened his team even more if he wished to take every good player from the Orioles. Instead, he had left McGraw with more than enough talent to compete in the League. Brooklyn fans were pleased with the product, and attendance increased from 122,514 to 269,641.[38]

A sharply dressed Hanlon is ready to celebrate a pennant-winning season for the Superbas in which they compiled an impressive 101–47 record (National Baseball Hall of Fame Museum, Cooperstown, New York).

There were several factors that helped Hanlon win his fourth pennant in six years. The most important was that as Abell had promised, he had total control of the franchise. He was able to make the baseball moves he believed were needed to improve the club without interference from the owners. Having Kelley, Keeler, and Jennings on the team certainly helped. Not only were they exceptional players who knew how to win, but they also served as surrogates who could convey the importance of adhering to Hanlon's style of play to the other players. They believed in the system, and they believed in Hanlon.

A midsummer incident illustrates this. The Superbas were in Louisville in July, and players from both teams gathered in the hotel lobby to engage in post-game conversation. The center fielder for Louisville, Charlie Dexter, was bragging that he could get to first base faster than any player in the game. The others in the group looked at Keeler, who was thought to be the fastest player in baseball, for his response.

Keeler said quietly, "The home plate is the place to get to."[39] In his unassuming way, Keeler had demonstrated why Hanlon's teams won. His players did not get caught up in individual accolades but put their energies into doing the small things that won games. Everything in the Hanlon system centered on that idea.

After the season, Jack Doyle, then with the Giants, was asked for his assessment of Hanlon's abilities compared to other managers in the game. Hanlon's former first baseman said, "Hanlon has them all in the 'also-ran' class when it comes to diplomacy. This man Hanlon would make the greatest hotel manager in the land, and I honestly believe that he could fill the position of Secretary of State and make a good showing....While Ewing may be a little ahead in actual knowledge of the game, Hanlon is the more diplomatic, and therefore, the more successful of the two as a handler of ballplayers."[40]

In September, with the Superbas clearly heading towards a pennant, John Foster, the Brooklyn beat writer for *Sporting Life*, heralded Hanlon's role in the team's success. He remarked that Hanlon's only ambition was to win pennants, and "There isn't a harder fighter for a game than this same manager, nor a harder loser....It has been generally held that Brooklyn could not hope to win the championship the first year, owing to the fact that it would be hard to get the players to exercise the perfect team work."[41]

* * *

After the 1899 season, the National League realized that syndication was ineffective and a public relations nightmare. The Baltimore-Brooklyn syndicate had functioned reasonably well, but another was a disaster. Frank Robison, the owner of the Cleveland Spiders, had purchased the St. Louis Browns from Chris Von der Ahe, renamed them the St. Louis Perfectos, and promptly transferred every player of value to the St. Louis club. This left the Spiders with a ragtag roster that managed to win only 20 games and lose 134, the worst record in baseball history. The team only drew 6,088 fans by August, and they were forced to play the remaining 35 games on the road. As a result, the National League decreed that an owner could no longer hold shares in more than one team.

The failure of syndication also heightened the concern that owners had long held that the weaker franchises in the league were draining profits from the stronger teams, and rumors began to spread that the League was planning to contract. Louisville owner Barney Dreyfuss, realizing that his franchise was destined to be a victim of contraction, made a deal to purchase a half-interest in the Pittsburgh Pirates, and he arranged to have the best players from his Louisville team traded to Pittsburgh. Later, Dreyfuss bought out his partners and operated as the sole owner of the club until his death in 1932.[42] At the December

1899 league meeting, a committee was assigned to suggest which cities would be dissolved, and it identified Baltimore, Louisville, Washington, and Cleveland as likely candidates.[43]

To add to the National League problems, a new eight-team American Association was formed to challenge them, and it drew great interest from players because it declared that it would eliminate the detested reserve clause. Players would be initially signed to only a one- or two-year contract, after which they would become free agents.

John McGraw and Wilbert Robinson, anticipating that the Orioles would be contracted, became key investors in the new Baltimore American Association franchise. If they could bring a team in this new league to Baltimore, they could continue their baseball careers in the city and would not be forced to spend significant time away from their lucrative Diamond Café while playing for another National League team.

At the end of January, McGraw, Robinson, and their partners made a bold and shocking move when they secured Union Park for their team. The owners of the grounds signed over the lease to them for the same $3,500 yearly rate they had charged the National League Orioles. The grounds became available when Hanlon let the lease lapse in early January, likely believing that the Orioles would not be playing again in the spring. Once he heard of the deal to secure Union Park, Hanlon quickly informed the trustees that they would have a check the next day for the yearly lease of the grounds. But it was too late. No one, however, felt that would be the end of the matter, and it was expected that Hanlon would challenge the agreement in court.[44]

During the next few weeks, the story of the formation of the American Association and possible contraction of the National League filled the sports pages. After meetings in New York and Cleveland, Hanlon arrived back in Baltimore on January 26 filled with anxiety about the illness of one of his children. A reporter showed up at his house and was allowed in. As they settled in the parlor, Hanlon testily said,

> "I have absolutely nothing to say about baseball," and to make this more impressive, he said: "We expect to play ball in Baltimore as usual and with a 10-club or a 12-club league, but I cannot say whether or not Cleveland or Louisville will be in it."
>
> He was asked when he became aware of the fact that McGraw, Robinson, and others had joined in the American Association ranks and secured Union Park. He said, "I shall not answer any questions about the baseball situation. They told me nothing about their intentions nor did I know what their intentions were until I read about the matter in the newspapers."
>
> The question next put to him was: "If, as you know, the American Association has secured Union Park, what will you do for grounds?"
>
> Mr. Hanlon replied: "I have told you twice that I would not answer any questions about baseball matters. Don't you know we have some valuable improvements at Union Park?"
>
> "What will you do about blacklisting players who go to the American Association?"
>
> "There you go again. I told you I would not answer such questions. Blacklisting is a nasty word. We do not resort to it."
>
> "Do you want me to state to the readers of the *Sun* that you will not say what the franchise, the players, and other possessions you have seemingly lost, are worth?"
>
> "I told you I would not talk. I cannot answer. I don't know."
>
> The interview was brought to a close. As the reporter emerged from the front door, he remarked to Mr. Hanlon: "It's a cold night," and the wind wafted to his collar-muffed ears, "I don't want to discuss baseball matters."[45]

The prospect of an American Association team in Baltimore caused great excitement, and McGraw and Robinson were inundated by callers who came to congratulate them. "Much champagne was opened and a regular jollification meeting was held." Many men pulled McGraw aside to see if there was stock left to buy and were willing to give him checks immediately. They were told that all the stock had been subscribed, but they were assured their requests would be mentioned at a meeting of the company at the Eutaw House the next day. At that meeting, Wilbert Robinson was so thrilled that it was reported he tried to do a lively dance, but his weight prevented it from being a graceful success. He received enthusiastic applause for his attempt, nevertheless.[46]

On February 3, in a rather absurd development, a group of men from McGraw's Baltimore American Association team attempted to enter Union Park but were repelled by a group of guards hired by Hanlon's National League Baltimore club. Eventually, however, McGraw's men gained entry and settled in along the third base line, while Hanlon's men occupied a space around first base. Two days later, the *Sun* reported, "All quiet along the fence." The standoff would remain for nearly a month, with a policeman stationed in between the two groups to make sure no mischief occurred.[47]

The American Association was officially born on February 14 in Chicago, but the dream ended the very next day when the Philadelphia club owners wired McGraw that they had been unable to secure grounds for a park. Deeming a seven-team league untenable, the new league folded.

Now that the American Association was dead, officials of both Hanlon's and McGraw's teams met on February 24 to settle the financial issues that remained between them. Hanlon's club agreed to reimburse McGraw's group for the January rent they paid for Union Park, and other concessions were made. The *Sun* was impressed by the fact that throughout the uncomfortable situation between the two groups, "it has been particularly noticeable that these two [McGraw and Hanlon] have at no time abused each other."[48]

When the agreement was reached, Hanlon was asked if he would hire McGraw as manager of the Orioles. He replied, "Do you know of a better man, or a man who would be more satisfactory to the press and the patrons of the game?"[49] Within two weeks, Hanlon met with McGraw and Robinson at the Diamond Café, and McGraw signed a contract to manage the team. Robinson was signed as captain. It was reported that "perfect good humor prevailed on all sides."[50] Unfortunately, it all came to naught less than a month later when the National League voted to contract to eight teams. As expected, Baltimore, Cleveland, Louisville, and Washington all fell under contraction's knife.

The four teams received cash payments from the league. Baltimore ownership received $30,000 and whatever it could get from the sale of its players.[51] Hanlon pragmatically said, "We got our price. The deal goes through." Von der Horst was more sentimental about the transaction: "When I put my signature to that agreement, I said, 'Good-bye old Baltimore.' I can tell you sincerely that I felt bad."[52]

* * *

When the Baltimore franchise was dropped from the National League, all Baltimore player contracts were transferred to Brooklyn. Hanlon sold the contracts of McGraw, Robinson, and Billy Keister to St. Louis for $15,000. McGraw and Robinson balked at leaving Baltimore, so Von der Horst and Hanlon visited them at the Diamond Café to attempt to convince them to report. Frank Robison came from St. Louis for the same reason, but McGraw and Robinson refused to go. McGraw said, "Business reasons alone is [sic] what keeps us. We have no objection to Robison or St. Louis…but we can't afford it."[53]

It has been suggested that McGraw was trying to leverage a scenario where he and Robinson would land with the New York Giants so they could remain near Baltimore. According to Hanlon, he gave Giants owner Andrew Freedman the first chance to purchase McGraw and Robinson, but Freedman declared he would not take them for free. McGraw and Robinson went to Freedman to ask him if he had a personal grudge against them, and Freedman claimed he didn't. He did say he wasn't interested in buying them, recommended that they go to St. Louis, and dismissed them from his presence.[54]

Weeks later, McGraw and Robinson did agree to go to St. Louis, but they had wrangled some advantageous conditions. McGraw was given a salary of $10,000, and Robinson was paid $5,000. In addition, they were able to include a detail in their contracts that no other player had been accorded at that time in baseball: Robison agreed to eliminate the reserve clause from their contracts, making them free agents at the end of the 1900 season.

* * *

If Ned Hanlon was going to win a second consecutive pennant with the Superbas, he would have to do it in a more competitive league. The good players from contracted teams strengthened the remaining teams in the league, and the difference between the best team and the worst shrank considerably. Moreover, unlike his Orioles teams, which were generally composed of young, hungry players trying to prove themselves in major league baseball, Hanlon's roster would include five starting position players and two starting pitchers who were 30 or older.

While in Augusta for spring training in 1900, Hanlon would shuck off his suit coat, roll up his sleeves, and personally demonstrate tactics. A reporter watched Hanlon work with his pitchers to cover first base on a ball hit to the right side. "If a twirler does not cover first base properly on a ball hit in that direction, Hanlon will sprint across the field in a practical illustration of how it should be done. Then, too, the fielding of bunts is another thing of which Mr. Hanlon makes a specialty with his pitching corps." That same attention to detail was extended to the hitters: "Every once in a while, the premier manager will find something to say about the way a batter stands at the plate, and he will leave his post to give the needful instruction."[55]

Hanlon had the advantage of fielding virtually the same lineup as he had in 1899, but in May, displeased with the production of Jimmy Casey, he bought third baseman Lave Cross from St. Louis for $3,000. Hanlon's pitching staff, however, took two hits when Doc McJames, who had received his medical degree, left the team in April to become a partner in his father's practice.[56] In addition, Jay Hughes had accepted an offer to play for the Sacramento Brewers in the California League because he was newly married with a pregnant wife and had family business interests in his home state.[57] Between them, McJames and Hughes had won 47 games for the Superbas in 1899. Early in the season, Hanlon also lost pitcher Jack Dunn, who had won 23 games for the team the previous year, to a sore arm.

By June 7, the Superbas found themselves 21–16, 2½ games behind the league leading Phillies, but starting with a victory over Pittsburgh in their next game, they reeled off 14 wins in the next 15 games and moved into the lead by 3½ games. They remained in first place for the remainder of the season.

In a September game in Philadelphia, an incident occurred that was a forerunner to more modern sign-stealing scandals. After the game, Hanlon confronted Phillies manager

Bill Shettsline and accused him of stationing his backup catcher, Morgan Murphy, in a hotel room located behind center field to steal signs. Hanlon claimed that two of his players said they could see Murphy using binoculars to see the Brooklyn catcher's signs and then signal the Philadelphia hitter with a rolled-up newspaper. Hanlon fumed: "The glasses he uses are so powerful that he can see a catcher blink at 250 yards. They cost $75."

Shettsline shot back indignantly: "They did not. It was only $60!"

By the next season, the Phillies were also accused of using an underground wire leading to the coaching box, where it was attached to a buzzer. The coach would stand on it, receive the signal, and alert the batter to what pitch was about to be thrown. "No wonder opposing pitchers were hammered all over the lot at Philadelphia," Hanlon complained. "While on the road the Philadelphias couldn't hit a balloon."[58] Maybe Hanlon was on to something. The Phillies were 45–23 at home and 30–40 on the road. A Philadelphia player later said, "Murphy earned every dollar of his salary this season. Had it not been for the signal service department we would have been in the second division, as every game we have won has been won with the bat."[59]

Pittsburgh, greatly improved by the influx of stars from Louisville, provided Brooklyn with their only challenge. As late as September 25, the Pirates trailed the Superbas by only one game, but from then on, Brooklyn pulled away to win the pennant by 4½ games. The addition of "Iron" Joe McGinnity, obtained from the dissolved Baltimore club, was a major factor in Brooklyn's success as he compiled a 28–8 record, and Brickyard Kennedy had his second consecutive 20-win season. Willie Keeler, Joe Kelley, Fielder Jones, and Tom Daly all provided excellent offensive contributions.

During the season, bad feelings simmered between Pittsburgh and the Superbas. The Pirates were convinced that they were the better club, likely fueled by being the only team to win the season series with Brooklyn, winning eight of their 11 matchups.

The rivalry had reached a fever pitch during a series that began in Pittsburgh on May 23, when Brooklyn players razzed the eccentric Pittsburgh pitcher, Rube Waddell, so relentlessly that he was forced to leave the game. Infuriated Pirates owner Barney Dreyfuss wired Nick Young about the rude treatment his pitcher had received, and he also complained that umpire Tim Hurst had taken no action to stop the alleged abuse. Dreyfuss demanded that Young never allow Hurst to umpire in Pittsburgh again. For their part, the Superbas maintained that they did not harass Waddell any more than they did any other pitcher. Young refused to take any action against the Superbas or Hurst.

Finding no redress for his complaints, Dreyfuss took matters in his own hands prior to the last game of the series. He arranged for the Brooklyn bench to be surrounded with police officers with instructions to arrest players who "did anything much beyond going on and off the field."[60] As the game was about to begin, Dreyfuss marched over to the Brooklyn bench and demanded that the players gather around to hear him speak. The players flatly refused, and an outraged Hanlon ordered Dreyfuss to leave his bench area. Hanlon retorted, "You have no more right to interfere with the running of this team than I have to go over to the Pittsburgh bench and force them to do my bidding, or one merchant has to try to run another's store."[61]

Opposite: With the 1900 Superbas' championship, Hanlon had now won pennants in five of his last seven seasons. It was his last (collection of Tom Delise).

Dreyfuss left the Brooklyn bench in a huff that day, but for the remainder of the season, he continued to make derogatory comments about the Superbas and Hanlon.[62] Referring to a game where the Pirates beat the Superbas on June 7 at Washington Park, Dreyfuss said, "I never saw a crowd of men quit sooner than that team. Why, the day that Phillippe pitched against them on their own grounds they let down in a way that actually made me mad. I hated to see such a display of weak-heartedness for the sake of the people who had paid their money to see men give a display of the national game."[63]

Dreyfuss added sarcastically, "Oh. Yes, it is a great team. Hanlon will tell you that without giving him a chance." Dreyfuss also took umbrage over Hanlon receiving credit for the excellent play of Bill Dahlen since he had come to Brooklyn. Dreyfuss said he did not see any improvement in Dahlen's play, and he additionally claimed that Hanlon was trying to trade Dahlen because they were at odds with one another. He concluded by saying, "You always hear of the efforts Hanlon makes to buy a player. He will give that to the papers, but I take notice that you do not hear of him giving out any stories of the Dahlen kind. He is too slick for that."[64]

* * *

After the regular season concluded, the *Pittsburgh Chronicle-Telegraph* invited Brooklyn to play a best-of-five series against the Pirates. All games were to be played in Pittsburgh, the winner of the series would receive a $500 silver cup, and the players of both teams would evenly split the gate receipts.[65] Perturbed by the harping of Dreyfuss, Hanlon was glad to play this series to prove once and for all that the Superbas were the better team.

The *Chronicle-Telegraph* Cup began on October 15, but Hanlon, evidently believing his Superbas did not need him there to win this series, went home to Baltimore, and Joe Kelley managed the team. Game One featured a matchup between Joe McGinnity and Rube Waddell. McGinnity pitched Brooklyn to a 5–2 victory, and the Superbas went on to win the Cup in four games. The series was plagued by poor weather and poor attendance, and it had to be a final slap in Dreyfuss' face that Tim Hurst was assigned to umpire the series.

Yet although the Superbas had won their second consecutive pennant and a post-season series, not all was well in Brooklyn. Attendance had decreased from 269,641 to 183,000. This drop-off was attributed to a variety of causes. One was the alleged indifference of Brooklynites to the imported Orioles. Others felt that the Superbas were so good for the past two years that it made fans lose interest in the games. Others said that this group of players did not inspire the loyalty that previous Brooklyn players had. *Sporting Life's* John Foster seemed to express what was commonly believed to be at the root of the problem when he said, "You can't buy your way to the championship of the National League by corralling the best players in sight and expect that by holding a monopoly of playing talent you are going to induce very many to become fevered over your team's performance."[66]

Hanlon believed that the length of games might be keeping fans away from the ball park. Not for the first time, he railed that the games dragged on too long, in some cases going well over two hours. Hanlon announced his intention to suggest a rule that would require a pitcher to deliver the ball to a batter within ten seconds after receiving it from the catcher.[67]

"The fans were not the only ones who were dissatisfied with the season. A number of Superba players had been offended when Hanlon was the only team official who took the opportunity to congratulate them after they won the pennant."[68]

Around baseball, accolades poured in for "Hanlon's scientists."[69] Wilbert Robinson said, "Ned Hanlon is the king of managers. He has them all skinned. Not only has he surrounded himself with good ballplayers, but he is a sly old fox himself. He has more nerve than any of them."[70] The *Brooklyn Daily Eagle* agreed with Robinson and said, "If credit can be given to one man for winning this year's pennant, the glory must go to Hanlon. How he succeeded in carrying off the championship this season with the material at his command is a mystery to those who do not know the man....Hanlon's methods are peculiarly his own."[71]

* * *

Yet there would be more pressing problems for the National League to deal with in the coming season than the length of games. Ban Johnson had declared that his American League was now a major league, and he was ready to go to war with the National League.

12

All They Thought of Was Pay Day (1901–1905)

Since 1882, the National League had withstood the challenges of baseball organizations that aspired to major league status, including the American Association, the Union Association, and the Players' League, just to name the ones that actually put players on the field for at least one season. In November 1893, Cincinnati sportswriter Ban Johnson was named the president, secretary, and treasurer of the Western League, a minor league that consisted of Midwest teams. Johnson had long been disgusted at the rowdy behavior in baseball, and he immediately set to work to eliminate it in his league. He increased umpire pay, backed up their rulings with significant fines, and took action against players and managers who treated them inappropriately. Under Johnson's firm leadership, attendance steadily improved, and the league grew increasingly profitable.[1]

By 1899, Johnson believed that the oft-fractious relationships of the National League magnates and the rowdy reputation of the games made the league vulnerable to the challenge of a new league. When the National League contracted to eight teams, he saw it as a perfect opportunity to make his move. Johnson relocated the St. Paul club run by Charles Comiskey to Chicago and the Columbus franchise to Cleveland, and he changed the league's name to the American League. The new league played out its 1900 schedule with the full expectation that they would declare their status as a major league the following season.[2]

The American League made it official when they declared themselves a major league on January 28, 1901. The original eight franchises were the Baltimore Orioles, Boston Americans, Chicago White Sox, Cleveland Blues, Detroit Tigers, Milwaukee Brewers, Philadelphia Athletics, and Washington Senators.

Promising better rights for players, including the elimination of a salary cap and other player-friendly initiatives, over the next two years the American League lured over 100 National League players into their ranks, including such stars as Cy Young, Napoleon Lajoie, Ed Delahanty, Jesse Burkett, and Jimmy Collins.[3]

Inexplicably, Johnson hired John McGraw to manage the Baltimore franchise. Considering Johnson's goal of producing a more family-friendly and refined baseball product, McGraw's long history of boorish behavior and umpire-baiting clearly indicated that he would not be a good fit for Johnson's league. As things turned out, he was not.

As the war with the upstart American League loomed in the winter of 1901, Hanlon was asked what he thought about the impending conflict. He replied that it would be the worst thing that could happen to the game. Referring to the Brotherhood war, he said, "I

12. All They Thought of Was Pay Day (1901–1905)

went through one; I don't want to go through another. I made a mistake. I knew it after I had been in the other war four weeks. I knew that all of us were mistaken, and that there were some things which sounded well in theory which would not work out in practice. I found out that the players as players were wholly an impossibility when it came to managing themselves."[4]

Hanlon's statements help clarify how he was able to transition from a driving force behind the movement for players' rights to a manager and executive who drew such a hard line on player salaries and holdouts. Hanlon's experience with the Players' League made him change his views radically on the practical considerations of running a professional baseball franchise. Part of Hanlon's logic, in this case, however, was flawed. The American League would not be run by a bunch of players looking out for their own interest, as was the Players' League. The American League would be run by the extremely competent and iron-willed Ban Johnson.

* * *

In January, Hanlon was optimistic about his team's ability to win a third straight pennant. "There will be no weak spots in our team when we are ready to play....We may not win the championship, but I do say that any club that does get it will have to beat Brooklyn out."[5] At that time, he believed he would have virtually his entire roster back, but that was not the case as three of his key players jumped to the American League. Fielder Jones signed with the White Sox, Joe McGinnity went to join McGraw and the Orioles, and Lave Cross went to Connie Mack's Philadelphia Athletics.

Hanlon felt particularly betrayed by the defection of Cross. He insisted that when he had purchased Cross from St. Louis, he had pointedly asked him if he would remain with Brooklyn if the new league offered him a contract. Cross assured Hanlon he would but broke his word without offering Hanlon a chance to make a counter-offer.[6]

It could have been worse for Hanlon, because before the season began there were rumors that other important members of the Superbas would jump to the American League. Joe Kelley was reported to be going to manage in Washington, it was said that Hughie Jennings would manage in Philadelphia, and Bill Dahlen, Willie Keeler, Brickyard Kennedy, Deacon McGuire, and Frank Kitson were all linked to American League teams.

Although Hanlon lost McGinnity, there was hope for the pitching staff when both Jay Hughes and Doc McJames returned to the Superbas. Hughes had some family business interests fail while in California, and Hanlon welcomed him back. McJames had missed playing baseball, and after a long talk with Hanlon, he signed a contract for $3,000.[7]

Throughout the spring and well into the season, Hanlon continued to tinker with his roster. Hughie Jennings had informed Hanlon that he would not be able to join the club until early June, after he completed his law studies at Cornell University. Hanlon did not want to wait that long, so he sold Jennings to the Phillies for $3,000. Hanlon also sold Gene DeMontreville to the Boston Beaneaters.

After Cross jumped to the American League, Hanlon signed Frank Gatins to play third base and predicted that he would be a great player; however, Gatins was nothing of the kind, and Hanlon released him in July. Because Jimmy Sheckard had a strong arm, Hanlon decided to try him at third base. After Sheckard missed seven balls in one game, four scored as errors, Sheckard asked his manager the next day whether he should take third.

"No sir, don't you stop at third," Hanlon replied. "You keep right on going until you reach the outfield."[8]

Hanlon then tried Joe Kelley at third, but when Kelley became ill, Hanlon was forced to ask for volunteers, and Willie Keeler spoke up: "I'll make a stab at it, Ned," he told his manager, "if you increase my salary." There was no mention of Hanlon paying extra to Keeler, but in his first game at third base, Keeler handled eight chances flawlessly. When someone attempted to compliment him after the game, he said, "Don't do it. I may explode tomorrow."[9]

Keeler played nine more games at third, until Hanlon signed Charlie Irwin, who had been released by Cincinnati, at the beginning of July. Irwin's defense was an improvement over Gatins, but he provided little help offensively, hitting only .215 for Brooklyn.

By late May, Brooklyn was already four games behind the league-leading Giants, and Hanlon was worried that his squad might not catch them. Captain Joe Kelley tried to console Hanlon by saying he shouldn't worry because the team would rally soon. "Well, if you don't strike it pretty soon, you'll be so far out of the hunt that you won't be able to catch the leaders with a search warrant," Hanlon retorted.[10]

By mid-season, Brooklyn's play improved, and the pennant race looked to be a battle between the Pirates, Phillies, and the Superbas that would not be resolved until the very end of the season. Brooklyn's offense began to hit its stride, and pitcher Bill Donovan had a breakout season, winning a league-high 25 games. However, Hanlon became increasingly frustrated with the work of pitchers Frank Kitson, Jay Hughes, and Doc McJames. He was upset that these men were begging out of pitching late in games, and Hanlon complained that "There's a limit to this kind of work and it has been reached right now. If we are going to lose games as we are at present, we may as well do it experimenting. I know where there are a few youngsters who are at least willing to work, and if these three high-priced men don't make an effort to earn their salaries, I'll go out and dig up a few new ones."[11]

In Hughes' case, it was rumored that drink was the culprit. With McJames, it was something else entirely, of which Hanlon was not aware. As early as 1898, McJames had displayed weak stamina, which was described in the press as rheumatism.[12] His stamina in 1901 had deteriorated significantly. He was likely suffering from tuberculosis when he collapsed on the mound during a game in July. Afterwards, it was clear that he would be unable to play, and Hanlon was forced to release him on July 16, 1901. Barely two months later, on September 23, Doc McJames was dead at just 27 years old.

To bolster his pitching staff, Hanlon attempted to raid the American League when he sent a letter to McGinnity, urging him to desert the Orioles. Hanlon offered him $3,500 for the remainder of the season and offered to pay the moving expenses for his family. McGinnity replied that he would stick with McGraw.[13]

In mid–July, Hanlon found pitching help when he signed free agent Eustace "Doc" Newton. Newton went 4–13 for the Reds when they released him, but Hanlon made an adjustment in Newton's delivery, and for the remainder of the season he went 6–5 with a 2.83 ERA.

In a game in Baltimore against Detroit on August 21, an argument over a close call at first base by umpire Tommy Connolly resulted in Orioles fans pouring out of the stands in an attempt to assault the umpire. During the riot, Joe McGinnity spit tobacco juice in the face of Connolly. Police restored order, Connolly forfeited the game to Detroit, and he was led away under police protection. Ban Johnson suspended McGinnity indefinitely.

After the incident, it was reported that McGinnity would return to Brooklyn and the National League. Although it was said that McGinnity never saw eye-to-eye with Hanlon on salary issues, "he is beginning to realize the fact that it is better to play in an organization where a player can expectorate in an umpire's 'phiz' and do generally as he cares.... Than it is to work where one must always be polite."[14] But now it was Hanlon's turn to spurn McGinnity, and he said, "These players who jumped their contracts cannot expect to come back of their own free will. We have something to say about that. McGinnity is a fine pitcher, but he made a mistake and may have to suffer."[15]

McGinnity and McGraw went to Ban Johnson's office, where McGinnity expressed remorse for the incident and admitted that he had been guilty of improper conduct. Johnson accepted his apology and agreed to reinstate McGinnity if he paid a fine and apologized to Connolly. McGinnity did so, and he resumed pitching for the Orioles on September 4.[16]

* * *

From June 19 until the end of the season, the Superbas had a winning percentage of .619. It would not be good enough, however, as during that same time, the Phillies had a winning percentage of .636, and the Pirates played at a blistering .667 pace. Philadelphia finished in second, and the Superbas finished in third place, 9½ games behind the pennant-winners.

Despite the Superbas' failure to win a third consecutive pennant, Ned Hanlon had put together one of the most impressive eight-year runs in baseball history. During that time, he won five pennants and finished second twice and third once, with an overall winning percentage of .657. Despite key personnel losses, his 1901 record of 79–57 was just three games behind the pennant-winning mark of 82–54 in 1900.

By the end of the season, Ned Hanlon was convinced that the American League was going to fail, saying, "Why, how can any league hold out, when the clubs are paying such salaries as $3,000 and $4,000, and even more, to a single player?"[17] Others strongly disagreed: "If he means that the American League is about to take to the cemetery looking for a burial plot, Neddie is smoking that No. 6 again."[18]

Hanlon underestimated the strength of the American League. Overall, it drew a respectable 1,683,584 compared to the 1,920,032 of the Nationals. In the three cities where the two leagues went head-to-head, the junior circuit nearly doubled the attendance of the Nationals in Chicago and Boston, while in Philadelphia the senior circuit outdrew the Americans by only 20,000.

The American League was here to stay.

* * *

In the off-season, Andrew Freedman decided he wanted Ned Hanlon to manage the New York Giants. He offered him a two-year, $25,000 contract, certain that Hanlon would not turn down such a lucrative offer. It was reported that Freedman had slapped a contract on the table in front of Hanlon with the curt order, "Here, sign this."[19] Hanlon refused.

Hanlon admitted that Freedman did make him an offer for that amount and acknowledged that it was a great deal of money he would like to have. Nevertheless, he declared that although he had no contract with Brooklyn and was free to leave at any time, he would not do so without the good will of the officials of the club. "Mr. Von der Horst and myself have been friends for a great many years," he said. "He has done a great many good turns for me, and I told him that so long as I was in baseball, I would stick by him."[20]

The Brooklyn owners were united in their refusal to allow Hanlon to leave. Club Treasurer Ferdinand Abell said, "I will do anything for the good of the league, but I am for Brooklyn first and my selfishness in that respect is such that I will not agree to Hanlon going." Charles Ebbets was equally adamant and declared that Hanlon was necessary for the success of the Brooklyn club. Finally, Harry Von der Horst said, "I have found him honorable and upright, and know that he will not quit us unless we consent. That consent I cannot give."[21]

Hanlon announced he would remain with Brooklyn, but the issue was hotly debated in the press for months as Freedman stubbornly insisted that he and Hanlon had made a verbal agreement. Hanlon refuted that and said that the previous summer, John Brush had approached him about the job while Freedman was in Europe. Hanlon said he could only negotiate with the Giants if Brooklyn gave him his release. Hanlon claimed Brush told him that he could take care of that and, declaring that he was acting as an attorney for the Giants, Brush mailed him a contract. Hanlon said he still had the unsigned contract in his possession.[22]

Freedman threatened a lawsuit, but with the press solidly behind Hanlon and no signed legal document as proof to his claims, Freedman finally dropped the issue.

* * *

Although Hanlon remained loyal to the Brooklyn club, that was not the case with some of his players in 1902. The American League continued to offer contracts for more than the $2,400 salary cap that was set by the National League. In October of 1901, Hanlon lost the first of three key players from his 1901 team when Joe Kelley jumped to McGraw's Orioles. Kelley, who had married a Baltimore woman, now considered Baltimore his home and was additionally enticed when he was offered partial ownership of the club. Hanlon also lost second baseman Tom Daly, who jumped to the Chicago White Sox, and catcher Deacon McGuire joined the Detroit Tigers. Hanlon would shift outfielder Tom McCreery to first base to replace Kelley, and Daly was replaced by rookie Tim Flood. McCreery and Flood would both have disappointing seasons.

For Hanlon, there was also the concern that Willie Keeler might jump leagues. Keeler had received offers from American League clubs, and Detroit was reportedly willing to pay him $5,000. Keeler stoked the rumors by declaring that he was "not wedded to Brooklyn," and his decision was merely a matter of business. Keeler declared he would sign with whoever offered him the most money but promised that Hanlon would have the opportunity to make a final offer.[23]

Hanlon did not seem concerned that Keeler would sign with any American League club except for one: John McGraw's Orioles. By the time Keeler arrived in Baltimore in early January to serve as an usher for McGraw's second wedding, Joe Kelley had already joined the Orioles. Newspapers reported the possibility that Hugh Jennings would leave the Phillies to join McGraw's club and that Keeler was offered stock in the Orioles if he signed with them. Baltimore was abuzz with excitement that a reunion of the Big Four could take place.

12. All They Thought of Was Pay Day (1901–1905)

But Hanlon's old friend, John Montgomery Ward, came to the rescue. He organized a campaign to raise $1,000 to sweeten the salary offer to Keeler, and Ward himself was one of the 50 individuals who contributed to raise that sum.[24] Ultimately, Keeler decided to stay in his hometown and play another year for a man with whom he had established a cordial and comfortable relationship.

* * *

When the Superbas arrived for spring training at the University of South Carolina on April 1, Hanlon and his players were shocked to find that at the last minute, Jimmy Sheckard had signed with the Orioles. Sheckard had personally given his word to Hanlon that he would be with them for the season, and Hanlon was furious: "I have been a ball player fifteen years, but this last move of Sheckard makes me ashamed of the profession....A more contemptible action cannot be surmised."[25]

Throughout the spring, Hanlon had a difficult time reconciling himself to Sheckard's betrayal and could not stop fuming about it[26]: "Sheckard apparently knows nothing about honor. He sees nothing but the dollars and cents. I have no use for a man who will break his contract for a few extra dollars."[27] Hanlon reminded everyone that he could have jumped to other teams for much more money when he had nothing but his word binding him to Brooklyn: "But I never broke my word in all my ball career and I wouldn't do it now, no, not for a million dollars."[28]

Soon after, the Supreme Court of Pennsylvania overturned a ruling that had allowed Nap Lajoie to jump from the Phillies to Connie Mack's Athletics. Hanlon said that Sheckard originally jumped to the Orioles because he was told that the three-year reserve clause was not valid. Now the Pennsylvania Supreme Court had determined that it was. After playing just four games with the Orioles, Sheckard returned to Brooklyn. "That decision in the Lajoie case stirred him up considerably, and his conscience is evidently beginning to worry him," said Hanlon.[29]

McGraw was not happy about Sheckard's defection and contemplated legal action. He claimed that Sheckard owed the Orioles their money back and sent him a registered letter requesting repayment. Hanlon was unsympathetic to McGraw's plight and took a shot at him and his sixth-place team: "It is about time McGraw stopped trying to seek sympathy with the public and got down to business. Considering the position of the Orioles it looks as if his team requires all of his attention."[30] It was a rather hypocritical statement from a man whose own team was in sixth place.

The entire Sheckard situation was an embarrassment to both leagues. White Sox owner Charles Comiskey declared that because Sheckard had broken so many contracts, the American League did not want him. Tom Daly, the president of the Ball Players Protective Association, also disapproved. Hanlon's ex-second baseman said, "I am glad he has gone back to Brooklyn, for while he is a great ball player and a nice fellow personally, we do not countenance violating a written contract as he has done. I suppose Hanlon scared him into jumping [back]."[31]

On April 29, in the Superbas' 12th game of the season, Jimmy Sheckard was back in the Superbas' lineup at Boston.

* * *

During the 1901 season, the Pirates had little competition for the pennant. In 1902 they had none. One of the reasons for the dominance of the Pirates during these two years was that they were the National League team least harmed by American League raids on its roster.

Some have suggested that Pittsburgh players did not jump to the new league because they had a high sense of loyalty to owner Barney Dreyfuss. Others subscribe to the idea that Ban Johnson had ordered American League owners not to raid the Pittsburgh roster.[32] In this way, he could create one team in that league so dominant that it would essentially stifle all competition and thereby hurt National League attendance. Whatever the reason, the lack of American League interference with Pittsburgh's excellent roster allowed them to dominate the National League during the first three years of the American League.

By May 12, Pittsburgh was 19–3 and already 6½ games ahead of the second-place Cubs. As the season progressed, they would only widen the lead. By the end of May, Brooklyn was in third place, 13 games behind the Pirates, who had won 30 of their first 36 games.

In Brooklyn, Hanlon received much mail from disgruntled fans, and he sympathized with their frustration: "I can appreciate the feelings of the fans back at home. I get a lot of these letters when the club is losing and enjoy those that are signed with the names of the writers because it shows they are the sincere baseball lovers who will speak their minds and are not afraid to disclose their identity. Their letters I read, the anonymous ones I tear up and throw away."[33]

Although he acknowledged that his team was enduring a bad spell, he had not given up hope of catching Pittsburgh, and he said, "Mind what I said some time ago, this team will finish away better than a whole lot of people think. At present, we are in a ruck, but we will never stay there."[34] Beginning in June, the Superbas did indeed play better, and from then until the end of the season they compiled a 58–44 record; however, the Pirates were even better, winning 71 of their last 101 games to finish 27 games ahead of the second-place Superbas.

At season's end, Hanlon was reportedly disgusted with the performance of some of the players. He lamented that he was powerless to improve players who seemed "too dense to grasp the intricacies of the national game as the old Baltimores used to play it."[35]

Meanwhile, as Pittsburgh was firmly in control in the National League, a situation that had been festering in the American League finally came to a head. After fining and suspending John McGraw repeatedly for various abuses, Ban Johnson suspended him indefinitely in July. McGraw, fed up with Johnson's discipline, jumped to the National League, where he became the player-manager of the New York Giants. Several Orioles went with McGraw, including Joe McGinnity, Roger Bresnahan, and Dan McGann, while Joe Kelley and Cy Seymour jumped to the Cincinnati Reds. Due to a lack of players, the Orioles had to forfeit their July 17 game, but Johnson stepped in to seize control of the franchise. He gathered together enough players from other teams to enable Baltimore to limp on to the end of the season. Johnson later announced his intention to move Baltimore to New York, and that team was called the Highlanders. Later, the name was changed to the New York Yankees.[36]

* * *

After the season, the National League sent messages to the American League that it was willing to talk peace, and Ban Johnson was willing to listen. Committees for each league met on January 9, 1903, and two days later they created the National Agreement, which ended their two-year war. Both sides promised to honor each other's contracts, and they settled the issue of dispersing players who were claimed by both leagues.[37] Moreover, a three-man National Commission, which consisted of the presidents of the two leagues and Cincinnati owner Garry Herrmann, was set up to govern the game. The minor leagues were also included in the National Agreement, and they received accommodations regarding the drafting and reserve rights for their players, along with territorial rights.[38]

Hanlon continued to advocate for expansion in the hope that the majors would return to Baltimore. "My home is here, all my interests are here," he said, "and it would be perfectly natural if I should wish to get back here to manage Baltimore's baseball club."[39] Expansion, however, was over 50 years away.

Hanlon began to talk about reviving the formula that he had used in Baltimore with such great success. "If I owned a club now, I'd go to work and make up a team of young players and develop them for a couple of years," he said. "By that time, I would have a crack-a-jack team … [and] I would have a low-salaried club while the others would be staggering under a heavy load."[40] Unfortunately for Hanlon, he did not own the Brooklyn club. Charles Ebbets did.

* * *

As soon as the 1902 season concluded, Hanlon attempted to sign as many of his players for the following season as possible before they headed home for the winter. Hanlon continued to complain about "the evils in baseball," and he grumbled about the betrayal of players he trusted who had broken promises to him.[41]

As was the case in the previous year, there was speculation that Willie Keeler would jump to the American League. Keeler had written to Hanlon about an offer he received from the New York Highlanders, and Hanlon wrote back asking him not to sign until he met with him. According to Hanlon, Keeler promised to do so. Nevertheless, while he was barnstorming in California, Keeler announced that he had signed with New York. He was

Wee Willie Keeler spent his last year with Hanlon during the 1902 season. In his five years in Baltimore, he had a .388 batting average, and in his five years in Brooklyn, he hit .352.

said to receive a two-year contract for $10,000 per year. Keeler defended his action, saying, "I've only a few years longer to play ball and the money they offered me was enough to induce me to leave Brooklyn. I signed only a one-year deal with Hanlon and I believed myself free to sign wherever I liked." When Keeler was asked if he considered the sentiments of the Brooklyn fans, he responded, "Sentiment don't go when the coin is to be considered....Who remembers a ballplayer after he gets through with the game?"[42]

* * *

After two seasons during which the Superbas remained within shouting distance of the pennant-winning Pirates, the next three seasons produced increasingly disappointing second-division finishes.

The 1903 season was frustrating for Hanlon as he struggled to put together a team capable of carrying out his style of baseball. He repeatedly worked them hard in morning practices to drill them in the tactics that had produced so much success for him in the past, but it had little effect.[43]

When they lost a game in Pittsburgh in late July because the winning run scored when one of his pitchers failed to cover first base on a ground ball, Hanlon was incensed. At a pitchers-only meeting after the incident, Hanlon admonished them: "That is a play that is not hard to work, if the pitcher keeps his head and moves his feet. It is being pulled off by other teams, and we can do it just as well as any other aggregation if we try hard. Never lose a moment in starting and keeping up your speed until you reach the base. Depend on the first baseman making the throw to you true. If he doesn't, then he will have to settle with me."[44]

Hanlon's only accomplished players that year were Jimmy Sheckard, Bill Dahlen, and his old Orioles first baseman, Jack Doyle, whom he signed in January. The rest of the squad were generally young players he thought had potential, or players on the downside of mediocre careers. Hanlon tried to instill his youngsters with the tactics of scientific baseball and squeeze out whatever productivity was left in the others.

As his team struggled, Hanlon's old friend, Cap Anson, asked him what was wrong with his team. Hanlon replied that it would take time to get a group of young players ready to play winning ball. He said bitterly,

> "They've taken away all I've had except Dahlen and Sheckard in the past couple of years, and they don't make the kind I've lost in a season."
> Anson then asked him, "But can't you put together another like that old bunch of two or three years ago?"
> Without hesitation, Hanlon replied, "Never again."
> "And you don't think you'll ever get together a bunch like the old Orioles?"
> More firmly and decisively this time, Hanlon told him, "Never again."[45]

Although his team was struggling, many observers admired the way that Hanlon strove to make winners of a flawed Brooklyn team: "One thing is certain; there is patience in the make-up of Ned Hanlon and indomitable courage. No matter what the task is that confronts him he goes at it as if he would annihilate everything that opposed him."[46] He was still regarded as a manager who always gave his team a chance to win, even if he did not have any great stars.[47]

Yet the season was clearly taking a toll on him. When a reporter waggishly asked umpire Tim Hurst if Hanlon would be gray-haired by the end of September, Hurst answered, "If he isn't, I'll be gray-headed for him. Never have I seen an outfit like this, where one minute you would think them all champions on some brilliant piece of work and the next dub them the surest lot of tail-enders that ever faced a curve."[48] John Foster, the Brooklyn correspondent for *Sporting Life*, best described the 1903 Brooklyn season when he concluded, "Even so successful and so bright a man as Ned Hanlon cannot make bricks from sponges."[49]

The Brooklyn Superbas ended the 1903 season in fifth place with a 70–66 record, 19 games behind the pennant-winning Pirates.

* * *

Hanlon's last two seasons with Brooklyn were a disaster.

In 1904, he traded any older players of value in an attempt to construct a younger team. The most noteworthy of these was the cantankerous "Bad" Bill Dahlen, who was 34 years old and butting heads with Hanlon. The new players did not produce, and Hanlon was befuddled by their inability to play with intelligence. He lamented, "[I] wonder if the fellow in *The Wizard of Oz* who puts brains into people could do anything for some of my players?"[50]

The team continued its descent down the league standings and finished the season in sixth place. They only won 56 games and ended 50 games behind McGraw's first-place Giants. When asked how he felt about his team's performance, Hanlon did not pull any punches:

> It has been the worst I have experienced since I have been a manager of a team. I never remember having a team that played in such a lifeless manner as the majority of the players I had under my management this season. All they thought of was pay day. Some of them were not entitled to half the salary they got. These players played minor league ball and never seemed to exert themselves. Next year I will remember them. I intend to cut their salaries. If they play minor league ball, they are entitled to nothing else but a minor league salary.[51]

A poem printed in the *Standard Union* poked fun at Hanlon and the dreadful performance of his team:

> **"Back, Back, Back to Baltimore"**
> **(with apologies)**
> I'm going back, back, back to Baltimore,
> This managing business certainly makes me sore,
> A bunch of rank players, they are no bark,
> For people think I am a mark,
> I never cared for home so much before,
> They said they'd win baseball games galore,
> But instead we lost just ninety-four,
> The next man who says I'm talented, I'll put a big dent in his head,
> And then go back to Baltimore.
>
> Yours Truly,
> Ned Hanlon[52]

* * *

Just days before Hanlon was scheduled to go south for spring training in 1905, Ebbets informed him that if he wished to manage Brooklyn that year, he would do it at a greatly reduced salary, cutting his pay from $12,500 to $6,000. According to one account, Hanlon resigned on the spot and returned home to Baltimore.[53]

"I don't want to act hastily in this matter, but I feel that I have not been treated with ordinary courtesy," Hanlon said. "Just as I am ready to head south with the team, I am notified all at once that I am not wanted—for that is what the radical cut in salary means. The first notice of this that was given me was Saturday when I was taking lunch with Ebbets and talking over new arrangements for the southern trip. This is hardly fair, for last fall I turned down offers from three clubs that would have been glad to take me at my present salary."[54] Ultimately, Ebbets traveled south, and the two men met on a train to work out a compromise.

Not everyone was sympathetic to Hanlon's outrage at his salary cut, and it was said that he was being compensated quite well to "sit on a bench, try and look wise and tell a batter when to bunt or not, while the men do the work out in the broiling sun."[55] The *Pittsburgh Press* agreed and remarked that Hanlon could not complain about his salary cut when he had slashed the pay of his own players.[56]

His salary cut was not the only source of irritation for Hanlon as he began the 1905 season. He was becoming increasingly frustrated with the baseball acumen of the players he had worked with in recent years. He made it clear that he would not have men on his team in the coming season who could not learn quickly, and he griped, "If you tell some of them that the ball is square, they will believe you. And there are others to whom you might say something who are liable to ask you what it was all about after you had finished with your lecture. We've got three or four that wouldn't know a play or any part of a play if it was diagrammed, and illustrated with primer pictures."[57]

When asked to explain the poor performance of the team, Hanlon blamed it on the fact that he did not have the right kind of material, and that he could not get it.[58] He particularly expressed his disgust with players who were more concerned with their individual accomplishments and who refused to play with a sense of teamwork. He specifically named Jimmy Sheckard as a prime offender, and he announced that Sheckard would get a $600 pay cut from the $3,000 he received in 1904. He concluded by saying, "if he doesn't like the cut, he knows what he can do."[59]

Hanlon had some discipline problems that needed his attention, as well. He quickly became disenchanted with the behavior of his new young shortstop, Phil Lewis:

> That boy makes me sick and tired. He is a ball player of the first water, and I have done all in my power to keep him right, but he is his own worst enemy, and is not amenable to discipline. He simply won't do right. When our team started west, we went to Atlantic City for a couple of exhibition games, Lewis was in such condition that he lay down on the third base line and went to sleep, and I had to have two players carry him to the bench. That is just a sample. I have handled some mighty hard customers, and controlled them, but Lewis is too fast for me.[60]

Hanlon benched Lewis, and the angry player returned to his home and declared he would not return until Hanlon apologized to him. The *Buffalo Enquirer* skewered Lewis: "Hanlon, who knows more about ball players and ball playing in a minute than Lewis will ever know, was compelled to call him down and put him where he belonged—on the bench for disobedience of orders, as well as many another player was disciplined before Lewis was born." The *Enquirer* proclaimed that if Hanlon could handle players like McGraw, it was certain that Lewis would end up apologizing to Hanlon.[61]

There were also allegations that it was not just Lewis who was showing up under the influence or hungover. After a game in Pittsburgh in which Brooklyn blew a big lead, a friend of Hanlon said, "Ned, if you take the whole bunch out beyond the clubhouse and beat them with a barrel stave there wouldn't be a jury in the city that would convict you of assault."

"Barrel stave?" retorted Hanlon. "By the way they played this afternoon, some of them know far too much about barrel staves."[62]

Brooklyn ended its dismal season in last place with a 48–104 record.

* * *

The Brooklyn club was in a state of chaos, and to bring order to it, the primary obstacle that Ned Hanlon would have to overcome was Charles Ebbets. Ebbets was notoriously tight-fisted, and it was said that when Hanlon had walked into Ebbets' office with a companion, they found the room deserted and a $2 note sitting on the desk. Hanlon's friend asked, "What's that doing there?" Hanlon replied, "Oh, Charlie is airing it out. It's been in his pocket so long he's afraid it might mildew."[63]

This is an amusing little story, but it underscores the fact that Ebbets' parsimony prevented Hanlon from spending what was necessary to assemble a winning ball club. Ebbets had also increasingly begun to interfere with Hanlon's attempts to impose discipline on the club. When Hanlon first assumed the managerial duties, he was promised that he would have total control over the team, but nearly a year after Hanlon left Brooklyn, John Foster in *Sporting Life* described the depth of Ebbets' interference:

> After Ebbets was in a position where he could dictate much in regard to the policy of the club, players told more than one that he seldom cooperated with Hanlon, and the manager has intimated that he made it as hard for him as possible. By and by the team was in such condition that Hanlon could do nothing with it, for the players would go over him to Ebbets, and of course, when a state of affairs like that existed there was bound to be no discipline. Ebbets, as president, did overrule what Hanlon as manager had ordered, for that is on record.[64]

Hanlon realized that to run the team successfully, he needed to become the principal stockholder. As he attempted to accumulate stock, he was dealt a severe blow when he learned in the press that Harry Von der Horst had sold all his stock to Ebbets. This was a tremendous personal betrayal to Hanlon because Von der Horst had promised him that he would be given the first chance to buy his stock when he decided to sell. John Foster verified Hanlon's claim in his *Sporting Life* column and wrote that Von der Horst repeatedly told Foster that he promised to sell his stock to Hanlon whenever he decided to leave baseball.[65]

Hanlon regarded this as an arrangement between Ebbets and Von der Horst to oust him.[66] He was thunderstruck by the betrayal because in the 13 years that he served as Von der Horst's manager, they had always renewed their working relationship with a friendly year-to-year handshake agreement. Von der Horst would say to Hanlon, "All right for another year, Ned?" Hanlon would respond, "It suits me."[67] Moreover, Hanlon had made a $1,000 a year payment to Von der Horst from his personal funds "in gratitude for his many acts of kindnesses in past years."[68]

As late as October of 1905, Hanlon was still trying to secure Brooklyn stock, and he claimed that he had been offered a nice contract by Ebbets for the next season. He said he would accept it and would meet with Ebbets the next day and arrange all the minor details.[69] The professed deal, however, fell through, and Hanlon did not manage Brooklyn in 1906. For years, it had been rumored that Hanlon would leave Brooklyn for another managerial position, and now, it finally happened.

Realizing that his inability to secure financial control would prevent him from building the team he envisioned, Hanlon accepted Garry Herrmann's offer to manage the Cincinnati Reds for a reported $15,000 per season.[70] Hanlon explained his decision: "I have been up against the tough proposition of trying to make the best of a club which had no money to back it up. In Cincinnati I will have unlimited capital to make a pennant winning team, and it will be up to me if I fail."[71]

Shortly after he left Brooklyn, Hanlon filed two lawsuits that dragged on until 1907. One claimed that Ebbets and secretary-treasurer Henry Medicus received greater salaries than the Brooklyn club's constitution allowed, and another that they had not filed the necessary paperwork in time that notified the secretary of state of their annual gathering. If upheld, it would have made Ebbets and Medicus ineligible to hold executive positions in the club, and this would allow Hanlon and Gus Abell to assume control of the Superbas. It was thought that Hanlon would then attempt to move the club to Baltimore. Hanlon's attempt to unseat Ebbets failed, and in the end, he had to settle for receiving only $10,000 for the stock he still held in the Superbas.[72] His association with the Brooklyn franchise was now completely severed.

Harry Von der Horst's betrayal of Hanlon prevented him from assuming control of the Brooklyn franchise and moving it to Baltimore (collection of Tom Delise).

After Hanlon left Brooklyn, the club endured nine straight years of second-division finishes under three different managers. Not until 1915 did Hanlon's old friend, Wilbert Robinson, lead the team to a winning record.

13

Porkopolis Purgatory
(1906–1907)

Along with being famous as the pork capital of the country, Cincinnati long had the reputation of being an unforgiving place to play, even for the home team. Along the left field line in Cincinnati's Palace of the Fans, there was a notorious section that was nicknamed "Roasters Row." The fans there were infamous for interactions with opposing players that "ranged from the comedic to the terrifying."[1] Owner Garry Herrmann was forced to beef up security in the ball park to curtail the personal and abusive language that regularly erupted from Cincinnati fans and to prevent them from engaging in brawls with the players during games.[2]

Outside the Queen City, the Cincinnati press was harshly criticized for stirring up unreasonable expectations in fans. Christy Mathewson went on record as saying that Cincinnati was deprived of pennants because the carping directed at their own team's players had driven many of them out of the city. Veteran New York sportswriter Joe Vila claimed that the best thing for baseball in the city would be for their newspapers to suspend publication. He said, "I've said all along that to be the manager of the Porkville team a man must be deaf, dumb, and blind, else the journalistic shafts from the overheated press box could not fail to drive one to the booby hut."[3]

Shortly after arriving in Cincinnati after leaving the Orioles in 1902, Joe Kelley was named the manager of the team. Kelley began the job with definite ideas of what constituted winning ball players and winning teams. Kelley was always eager for a confrontation on the field, and he wanted players who were the same way. He wanted players who were not afraid to protest umpires' calls, to "stick up for their rights." In his first spring training, Kelley's goal was to eliminate from his roster any player who was too slow, either mentally or physically. Kelley had little use for players who could hit but did not know and could not execute the intricacies of the game.[4] These were ideas that had been forged under the tutelage of Ned Hanlon.

During his three full years managing the Reds, Kelley led the team to three winning seasons and a combined record of 241-204, a marked improvement over the three previous years. However, Kelley's tenure as manager was tumultuous, and he was condemned in the press for his inability to discipline his players. He was plagued by incidents such as when drunken outfielder Cy Semour had to be removed during a game, and when outfielder "Turkey Mike" Donlin threatened Kelley and challenged him to a fight.[5] Kelley also had problems with some of his pitchers, who complained that they were being overworked.[6]

Finally, in December of 1905, Joe Kelley was relieved as manager of the Reds, and

Ned Hanlon was hired to replace him. As a condition of accepting the job, Hanlon insisted that Kelley be retained and named the captain. Kelley was glad to relinquish the managerial position and said he was tired of being criticized. He blamed his lack of success as manager on hard luck and lamented that he could not get the best out of the material that he had.[7]

Sporting Life reported that Kelley's first experience as a major league manager had taken a toll, and he had aged visibly in the past four years. Now, at 34 years old, he stepped aside gracefully and agreed to stay on as a player under his old boss. "I will work as hard for the Reds next season as any man on Mr. Herrmann's pay roll," Kelley promised. "I know that Hanlon will get results."[8]

* * *

When Hanlon's hiring as manager was announced, it "was greeted in Cincinnati with something approaching euphoria."[9] Joe Vila predicted that Hanlon would make the Reds better than they had ever been, and he looked forward to seeing what Hanlon could accomplish "with Garry's open purse at his command."[10] Ren Mulford hailed the hiring as "the best possible [move] Garry Herrmann could have made,"[11] but Mulford, who was the Cincinnati-based correspondent of *Sporting Life* and a life-long Cincinnatian, was quite familiar with the vitriolic nature of the local press and fan base. He added a warning to Hanlon "to invest in a coat of mail before he ventured into the Buckeye woods."[12]

With the encouragement of the Cincinnati press, fans were convinced that Hanlon would get more out of his players than Joe Kelley had. Many believed a championship flag would fly over the Queen City at the end of the 1906 season. Others, while generally applauding Herrmann's move, were more cautious, noting that the Reds had finished 26 games behind McGraw's Giants the year before. They warned that Hanlon had his work cut out for him, and he could not be reasonably expected to turn around the team's fortune's instantly: "It will take him more than next year to construct a team according to his own ideas and requirements."[13]

When potential detractors asked Hughie Jennings why Hanlon was not successful recently with Brooklyn, Jennings responded that after the war between the National and American Leagues, "Brooklyn made no attempt to strengthen. Hanlon had no material, and the best manager on earth cannot succeed without material." He said that if Cincinnati would be patient, Hanlon would give them a pennant winner in a few years.[14]

As Hanlon took the team to Marlin, Texas, for spring training, he promised that if he could not put "baseball brains into the players' heads, he would at least make sure they made use of what gray matter they had."[15] During a meeting with his players, Hanlon made his expectations clear, telling them, "Ginger is the first requisite of a successful ball player. By ginger I don't simply mean dancing around on the coaching lines and attracting the attention of the spectators. I mean that intense desire to win that gets there in spite of the obstacles…that tenacity that makes him never even think of giving up until the last man is out in the ninth inning."[16] "Reds business manager Frank Bancroft was immediately impressed with what he saw in Texas and said that the Cincinnati team was the best he had ever been around, and that it was all due to Hanlon's teaching."[17]

Despite the optimism generated by spring training, the Reds got off to a disappointing start. By the end of April, the team was 6–13 and some players were grumbling.

Hanlon warned that changes might be necessary to bring the Reds up to his standards: "No man who will not work conscientiously and earnestly is going to retain a place for any length of time on the Cincinnati team, so long as I am running things here....I am going to be boss....My orders are going to be observed or I will know the reason why."[18]

The Reds struggled throughout the season, and spells of good play were almost immediately followed by periods where all the lessons Hanlon tried to instill in them seemed forgotten. Some reporters thought they could see an improvement in play at times, even if it did not produce wins. Johnny Evers of the famous Tinker to Evers to Chance trio of the Chicago Cubs also saw an improvement: "The Reds certainly are a different team since Hanlon took hold. Last year and the year before we could always tell what a batsman was going to try to do.... this year every man that goes to bat has us guessing, and as soon as Hanlon gets a little better grip on them, they will be even more difficult to follow."[19]

Hanlon began to make moves, dealing away some players, benching others, and searching for a winning combination. Center fielder Cy Seymour had his best season in the majors in 1905, hitting .377, but he slumped badly in 1906. Hanlon considered him uncoachable, so he was sold to the Giants for $12,000 in July. Fans in Cincinnati were not sad to see the eccentric Seymour go, and when he was sold, "there was more rejoicing than regret."[20]

Although some players resisted Hanlon's methods, others were receptive to his approach. Infielder Hans Lobert recalled how in his first year with the Reds, Hanlon took a liking to him because of his speed and enthusiasm, but he had concerns about his batting technique. Hanlon told Lobert to follow him, and he led him to one end of the park. Hanlon told him, "You can be a great player if you will follow me. You will never be great unless you change your batting style....Then he grabbed the bat and showed me how to hold it and swing. I was deeply interested, for it was the first time in my life any man tried to teach me how to hit." "Lobert claimed that Hanlon's batting instructions were the reason he was able to establish a successful fourteen-year major league career."[21]

On June 1, the Reds were in sixth place, and the pitching staff was struggling mightily. Orval Overall, who went 18–23 for the Reds in his rookie season in 1905, got off to a slow start, and the press and fans were brutally roasting him and Hanlon, as well, for continuing to pitch him.[22] Herrmann and Hanlon decided it would be best for everyone to trade Overall. The Reds approached Chicago, offering Overall for Mordecai Brown, Carl Lundgren, or Ed Reulbach, but Cubs manager Frank Chance refused to trade any of those pitchers and offered Bob Wicker instead. On paper, the trade looked like a good one, as Wicker had compiled a three-year record of 50–24 with the Cubs.

Herrmann handled the negotiations with Chicago, and he ended up including $2,000 along with Overall for Wicker. Unfortunately for Hanlon and the Reds, the trade proved one of the worst in franchise history. Wicker went 6–11 for the Reds and was out of baseball after the season. Overall went 12–3 for Chicago the rest of the 1906 season and became a star. In six years with the Cubs, he compiled an 86–43 record with a 1.94 ERA and appeared in four World Series.

When some looked back on this trade, they believed it marked the beginning of the end for Hanlon in Cincinnati. Over the next year and a half, Hanlon and Herrmann increasingly blamed one another for the trade. Hanlon adamantly protested that he never agreed to spending $2,000, and Herrmann began to question Hanlon's judgment

There was great hope for the Cincinnati Reds franchise when Hanlon (left) was signed by owner Garry Herrmann (right). Their partnership soured quickly, and after a two-year stay with the Reds, Hanlon's managerial career was over (courtesy Michael Reeve).

in evaluating players.[23] This deal ultimately hindered Hanlon's ability to make trades and acquire players in the future.

The inconsistent play of the Reds continued throughout the season. July was the only month where the club had a record over .500, when they went 15–12. The Reds finished in sixth place with a 64–87 record, 51½ games behind the powerhouse Chicago Cubs. With a 116–36 mark, the Cubs set a major league record with a .763 winning percentage that stands to this day.

* * *

By the end of the season, it was clear to Hanlon that the situation in Cincinnati was not what he was led to believe it would be. In Baltimore, and in his early days in Brooklyn, Hanlon had total control of the team, an admiring press, and a devoted fan base. In Cincinnati, he had hoped to recreate the Orioles' magic of 1894; however, Garry Herrmann was not the supportive owner that Harry Von der Horst had been. In Baltimore, players could not go over Hanlon's head to the owner, but in Cincinnati, Garry Herrmann was often willing to lend a sympathetic ear to a disgruntled player. This caused increasing problems for Hanlon as he tried to discipline unruly players.

Moreover, the close-to-the-vest tactics that had earned Hanlon the moniker of Silent Ned were not as well tolerated among the Cincinnati press as by Baltimore's fourth estate. Cincinnati sportswriters constantly demanded that Hanlon clue them in on moves that he intended to make. When Hanlon declined to do so, the press resorted to reporting speculation as fact, a practice that caused Hanlon to resent their interference. To a man like Hanlon, used to controlling every aspect of his baseball team, it was a frustrating experience, and his relationship with reporters continued to deteriorate.

It did not take long for some writers to become disenchanted with Hanlon: "If he could get some of the men who once composed the championship team he managed under his wing again, he would once more achieve fame, but at making ordinary baseball players into stars, 'Foxy Ned' is no better than the next one."[24]

In addition, it was alleged that Hanlon displayed an observable lack of interest in his team and that he was quick to take numerous opportunities to go to Baltimore to enjoy the comforts of home. It was pointed out that when the Reds played in Philadelphia, Hanlon would leave immediately after the game each day and go to Baltimore, sometimes returning just in time to see part of the game the next day.[25] Ren Mulford harped on this string as well, referring to a time in spring training when Hanlon took an absence from the team for a time, supposedly because he was ill. Mulford reported that a close friend of Hanlon told him, "Hanlon was no sicker in Texas than I was, and did wrong to quit the team. Why, on the day of the morning he left he was smoking a big, fat, cigar that I couldn't have tackled."[26]

Before the season was over, rumors sprouted that Hanlon would not be back for the 1907 season, and it was reported that he "has wearied of trying to accomplish wonders without talented helpers. Each season strips Hanlon of some of the prestige he once had as a great developer of players."[27]

The poor results of the 1906 season reinforced some of the criticisms levied against Hanlon in his last few years in Brooklyn. He was now accused of having lost the magic touch that allowed him to make unhallowed players into stars and make one-sided trades that made him feared by other managers. Now, it was said, he could not do what was necessary to improve his players, and the trades he made were dismal failures.

Hanlon's defenders pointed out that during the past 15 years, only four managers had won National League pennants, and Hanlon had won five of them.[28] Ren Mulford wrote that he did not think that Cincinnati "in its present form" could ever win a pennant under Hanlon or anyone else.[29] He dismissed the idea that Hanlon didn't have the ability to run quality team and said, "Good joke. Look the field and you will see few better pilots than the old man."[30]

Hughie Jennings strongly defended his old manager when asked to comment on Hanlon's competence. "No ball player can ever sit and listen to Ned Hanlon without learning something," Jennings said. "Good players have admitted to me that they thought themselves novices after listening to his ideas of play. Hanlon instituted a style of play that won pennants for Baltimore. As fast as other clubs copied the Baltimore idea, he dug up something else....I owe to Hanlon all that I ever was in baseball, and his quiet talks made me more determined."[31]

When faced with criticism for hiring Hanlon, Gary Herrmann defended the choice. He said that Hanlon had virtually no input in selecting the team in his first year, and that he was "handicapped by having under him a lot of old players who could not be properly handled under existing circumstances."[32] Herrmann promised that the 1907 Reds team would be one of Hanlon's choosing.

* * *

It certainly was a disappointing year for Hanlon, but he immediately went to work making changes for the 1907 season. His plan was to return to what initially made him successful with the 1890s Orioles. The first order of business was to assemble a team of enthusiastic and spirited youngsters who were willing to learn "baseball as she is played." As a result, Hanlon and Herrmann jettisoned many of the high-salaried veterans, and by Opening Day, only catcher Admiral Schlei, infielders Miller Huggins and Hans Lobert, and pitchers Bob Ewing, Jake Weimar, and Andy Coakley remained of his regulars from 1906.

The next step was to teach the tactics that made the Orioles champions. Hanlon declared that he would teach his players to use the bunt as a weapon, just as his old Baltimore teams had done. "It was bunts that won three pennants in Baltimore when I managed the Orioles," he said, "and if the Reds can become successful bunters, they'll be in the pennant race."[33]

With his re-made roster, he believed he could improve the team by instilling the other old methods used by his successful Orioles and Superbas teams. He said, "Our team is young and inexperienced, but very fast, and the boys have developed a clever system of inside play. The club looks better to me right now than it has at any previous time this season," and he expressed confidence that the Reds would be better than they were in 1906.[34]

Not everyone shared Hanlon's optimism. Ren Mulford said that the Cincinnati pitching staff looked "like a bunch of Louisiana lottery tickets,"[35] and the newly acquired captain of the Reds, John Ganzel, told a reporter. "I am not highly elated over our prospects."[36] To Hanlon, this surely was a disappointing statement from a man who was acquired to help instill spirit into a group of generally untested players.

There were other factors that added to the sense of pessimism that seemed to pervade the team as the season approached. During the off-season, there had been contract disputes between Herrmann and two of the returning veteran pitchers, Bob Ewing and Jake Weimar. In addition, Herrmann and Hanlon had locked horns over Ewing. Hanlon had been displeased with Ewing in 1906 because of what he perceived to be a lack of intestinal fortitude and competitive fire. Hanlon let Ewing know his feelings, the 34-year-old veteran did not like it, and the result was a strained relationship between the two men. As a result, Hanlon wanted Ewing gone. Herrmann did not. Ewing stayed.[37]

One week before the 1907 season opened, an event took place that indicated the underswell of anti–Hanlon feeling in some quarters. Garry Herrmann threw a lavish banquet to honor the 1906 World Series victory of his old friend Charles Comiskey, owner of the Chicago White Sox. To that end, he rented out the ballroom of the Sinton Hotel in Cincinnati and had the room decorated to resemble a ball field, including ticket windows, turnstiles, and banquet tables shaped like a baseball diamond. As was usual with these types of affairs, important local businessmen made up a good portion of the audience, including some who were shareholders in the Reds. One of these was George "Boss" Cox. Cox had become powerful in Cincinnati as the head of the Republican Party machine, and Garry Herrmann was one of his chief lieutenants.[38]

At one point in the proceedings, Cox rose to speak. Perhaps buoyed by a few drinks, he shocked the crowd by saying, "Any man who manages a Cincinnati team in the future must make good or give way to someone who can." Although later Cox claimed his remarks were not meant to call out Hanlon, it was clear to everyone there that he was staring directly at the manager when he made them.[39]

13. Porkopolis Purgatory (1906–1907)

Hanlon, clearly offended, replied that he hoped to put together a team that would "satisfy Herrmann, Cox, and his other employers." Herrmann stood and awkwardly tried to diffuse the tension-filled moment with pacifying statements, but "hard feelings hung in the air."[40] A week later, Cox sold his interest in the Reds.[41]

* * *

The season for the Cincinnati Reds opened at the Palace of the Fans on April 11. The game was a close-fought contest, and the Reds came to bat in the ninth inning, trailing Pittsburgh, 3–2. Hanlon pinch-hit for Bob Ewing with Larry McLean, who slashed a double down the right-field line. Hanlon sent in a pinch-runner for McLean, and Miller Huggins bunted him to third. Hanlon pinch-hit for Lefty Davis with Ernie Tiemeyer, a right-handed batter facing a left-handed pitcher. Tiemeyer walked, and the crowd erupted into a roar. The next batter, third baseman John Kane, also walked to load the bases. Captain John Ganzel stepped to the plate and lofted a short fly ball just over the infield for a game-winning, two-run single. The players dashed to the clubhouse to escape the crowd that joyously ran onto the field.

In the final inning, Hanlon made three substitutions, ordered a sacrifice bunt, engineered a lefty-righty switch, and made a crucial pinch-running move for a pinch-hitter that allowed the winning run to score. The *Cincinnati Enquirer* called it "as grand and game a finish as ever was pulled on a ballfield" and was effusive in its praise of Hanlon's managerial genius: "Every move was made that could be thought of to give the team its slightest advantage, and the players did the rest."[42]

Although these moves are considered common practice in today's game, it is clear from the reaction of the Cincinnati press reports that they were considered unusual or revolutionary at the time.

Hanlon was complimentary of the way his young players had responded in a well-contested game. Possibly in an attempt to repair fences with Bob Ewing, he made a point to compliment Ewing for the strength of his performance.[43]

The Reds suffered through a tough April, winning only four of their first 14 games. But they rallied and played .500 ball during May and June.

During a series with the Phillies in May, a *Sporting Life* correspondent was sufficiently impressed with the Reds to comment that they were an improving team that "display better judgment and speed on the bases than any Cincinnati team of recent years." He said it would be hard to keep the team out of the first division, and it looked as if Hanlon was "building a future winner."[44]

However, in May the team was also in a state of near revolt because they were forced to play some exhibition games. As was the practice at the time, teams scheduled these exhibitions in between their regular season games as a way to bring in additional revenue. Players, however, intensely disliked these games, primarily because they were not paid for playing in them. The owners, on the other hand, felt that because they were played during the period of their six-month contract, no extra pay was necessary. To be fair, as manager of the Orioles, Hanlon had made a practice of paying players for exhibition games, but in Cincinnati, Herrmann controlled the purse strings. The players formally requested that they either be paid for playing in these games or that they no longer be scheduled. Herrmann refused.

The situation was exacerbated when the team was given substandard accommodations for an exhibition game in Yonkers, then played on a muddy field in front of an antagonistic crowd in New Jersey. The last straw occurred when rookie pitcher Cotton Minahan injured his shoulder in a collision on the base paths. He never played in the majors again, his brief career over after just two games.

The players were harshly criticized in the press for not being grateful for "their liberal treatment as to their salaries by the Princely Herrmann." Discontent with management simmered throughout the rest of the season.[45]

Then came the disastrous month of July, when the Reds lost 17 of 25 games and fell 28½ games behind the league leaders. The wrath of the fans and the Cincinnati press, which had sniped at Hanlon from almost the time he arrived, coalesced against him in full force. He was criticized for his frequent absences from the team, many supposedly on scouting trips that never produced anything. He was accused of trying to manage the team by telephone. A reporter suggested that the team played better when Hanlon wasn't around.[46]

It was reported that some of the young players weren't committed to Hanlon's approach to the game, some of the veterans were openly antagonistic, and players were refusing to put forth their best efforts for Hanlon.[47] The press also took shots at Hanlon over his salary, claiming that he was not worth it and that he was just a washed-up manager living on his reputation: "Hanlon has dreamed, and the fans helped him dream for many years, that he is the greatest living ball manager that ever handed a release to a bush league recruit, and all simply because he was manager of the famous old Baltimore team that copped several championships."[48]

Near the end of July, Hanlon made a decision regarding his future. He announced, "The events of the past few weeks have brought the fact home to me forcibly that I am doing myself an injustice by allowing myself to be made the subject of all sorts of rumors and attacks, when there is no financial necessity for my doing so." He was seriously considering giving up baseball at the end of the season to devote the rest of his life to his family and other business interests which would not take him away from his home and not subject him to "the abuse and vilification, such as one is made to suffer in baseball."[49]

Not everyone around the league felt the blame should be attributed to Hanlon. The *Boston Globe* felt that it would be Herrmann's loss if Hanlon retired or was fired at the end of the season, pointing out that he had put together a team which was beginning to show "the results of the care Hanlon has taken to build it."[50] John Foster, who had reported on Hanlon and his teams for years, defended Hanlon: "He knows more baseball today than half the major league tutors." "He claimed that the young and inexperienced Cincinnati team was playing as well as the team did last year when they had more purported stars."[51]

* * *

In August, the Reds produced better results on the field, and the team's improvement caused Hanlon to have second thoughts about leaving Cincinnati at the end of the season. In early October, a fan in Cincinnati proposed an idea to entice Hanlon back for one more season. He maintained that Hanlon should have absolute control, and his salary would be directly tied to the performance of the team. If the Reds finished last, Hanlon would be paid nothing. If they finished seventh, he would be paid $1,000, and there would be increasing raises for higher finishes in the standings, culminating in a $15,000 salary if the Reds won the pennant. Hanlon was intrigued by the suggestion:

> I have failed and been under fire. I have said before that I wanted to enjoy one more good year before I quit the active side of baseball, and nobody regrets as keenly as I do that this has not

been the year.... I have no idea that I will ever manage a ball club after this season, but if I did I would accept this fan's offer with any club. Money won't figure in any other attempt at success if I make one.[52]

Neither Garry Herrmann, nor anyone else, accepted Hanlon's offer. His 19-year managerial career had come to an end.

* * *

Numerous factors led to the lack of success that Ned Hanlon experienced in Cincinnati. If Hanlon's two years with the Reds are compared to his first two years in Baltimore, some interesting contrasts emerge. In Baltimore, Hanlon had the absolute power to construct his roster and an owner who would not overrule him. In Cincinnati, Garry Herrmann did not offer the same level of support; as a result, the players knew they could take advantage of Hanlon. Hanlon's friends claimed, "Players have been signed, released, forgiven their misdeeds, and allowed to run themselves by those higher in authority."[53]

Moreover, Ned Hanlon did not have instant success in Baltimore. It took him nearly two years to build a winner. The Cincinnati ownership, press, and fans were not as patient, and they demanded immediate results.

A close look at some performance statistics of the 1907 Reds might indicate that Hanlon was building a team headed for success. The team's batting average, hits, and total bases were all above the league average, as was the team ERA. The team committed the second-fewest errors and tied for the second-highest fielding percentage. Most telling, the team's Pythagorean Win-Loss percentage, a modern tool used to project the expected record of a team based on its run differential, indicates that the Reds should have finished the season with a 77–76 record.

The Reds in 1907 were the second-youngest team in the National League, and just like Hanlon's young Orioles, they needed time to learn to win. They lost 39 of 61 one-run games, and their home record was significantly better (43–36) than their road record (23–51).

Another problem with the Reds was that except for players like Miller Huggins and Hans Lobert, they did not embrace Hanlon's tactics in the way that Joe Kelley, Hughie Jennings, Willie Keeler, John McGraw, and the other old Orioles did. Because of the limitations on his authority, he could not weed out those who refused to buy in. The willingness to play as a team would make the old Orioles better than the sum of their parts, but the Cincinnati Reds in the Hanlon years did not place the same value on teamwork, and the team was not as good as it should have been.

Nevertheless, a close look at the Reds' roster in those two years clearly indicates that the Reds at best were just an average team. As the *Pittsburgh Press* commented about Hanlon's plight, "All the knowledge of the game in the world won't make a poor club win, for poor ball players cannot carry out instructions, and a manager to be successful must have a team which can play baseball."[54]

In the end, Hanlon knew that he was fighting a losing battle. The fact that the old baseball warrior announced during the middle of a season that he would not return was at odds with his competitive, never-say-die attitude. It was a clear indication that his heart was not in this battle. He said, "I have a family and want to be at home. Twenty years, and then some, on the road, is enough for a man."[55]

It was time for Ned Hanlon to go home.

14

Baseball in the Blood (1908–1937)

After the 1902 season, Ned Hanlon had become the principal owner of a group that purchased the Montreal Royals of the Eastern League for $5,000. The team was renamed the Orioles and transferred to Baltimore, and Wilbert Robinson, who was part of the ownership group, was named the player-manager. The team played in American League Park, which had been abandoned by that league's Orioles, and purchased by Hanlon for $3,000. That price was a steal, as it had been constructed just two years earlier at a cost of $12,000.[1] Hanlon announced that his goal was to "secure young and ambitious men who are in the business to make name and fame and who are capable ... to play at least the fast, snappy ball that is loved by the Baltimore public."[2]

Robinson did not serve as manager long, for when the team struggled, Hanlon named Hughie Jennings, who also invested $3,600 in the club, as manager in July.[3] The ever-loyal Robinson continued to fill in as a part-time catcher for the next few years.

When Hanlon returned home to Baltimore in 1907, he was content to be out of the hopeless situation in Cincinnati. When asked if he intended to leave the game, he said that he would not, and he looked forward to directing his attention more strongly to his Eastern League Orioles, from whom he expected to earn good profits.[4]

Hughie Jennings did a good job managing the Orioles, and during three

Jack Dunn bought the Eastern League Orioles from Hanlon in 1910. Competition with Hanlon's Federal League team forced Dunn to sell Babe Ruth's contract to the Red Sox in 1914 (Babe Ruth Birthplace & Museum).

full seasons he led the team to a 236–160 record, good for two second-place and one-third place finish.[5] Jennings' success attracted the attention of Detroit Tigers owner Frank Navin, who contacted Hanlon in 1906 to negotiate Hughie's release so he could manage the Tigers. Hanlon wanted $5,000 for Jennings and wouldn't budge on the price. Navin, however, was not to be denied. At this time, players in the minor leagues could be drafted by major league teams in the off-season, so Navin, realizing that Jennings had played 75 games with the Orioles in 1906, drafted him as a player for $1,000.[6] Foxy Ned, for once, was outfoxed.

After losing Jennings, Hanlon was in the Diamond Café one evening when he ran into his old Brooklyn Superbas player, Jack Dunn. Dunn had recently been released as manager of the Providence Clam Diggers of the Eastern League, and Hanlon quickly struck a deal with him to be the player-manager of the Orioles.[7]

A few years later, Hanlon sold the Orioles and the ballpark to Dunn, who always wanted to own his own franchise. Dunn financed the deal with the help of a loan from Connie Mack, and he named Wilbert Robinson as one of the directors. Ned Hanlon's foray into minor league baseball was over.

* * *

Hanlon, his wife Ellen, and their five children, along with an unnamed driver, are pictured in the family auto. In the front seat are the driver and Hanlon. Behind them, left to right, are son Edward, wife Ellen, son Joseph, and daughters Lillian, Helen, and Edwina. The expensive automobile indicates the level of prosperity that Hanlon had achieved (National Baseball Hall of Fame and Museum, Cooperstown, New York).

Now, without a direct connection to baseball, there was more time for the family that he loved so dearly. They took long trips in the expensive family automobile, to Maine in the summer of 1908 and to the White Mountains in New Hampshire in 1911.[8] Doubtless there were many more that did not receive public notice.

Although Hanlon was no longer a part of the professional game in an official capacity, his love for baseball never wavered. He remained an enthusiastic fan of the minor league Orioles, and he told a reporter, "I never miss the Toronto and Buffalo series. There is always a good diamond fight on them." He also maintained that he still felt that Baltimore was a big-league city and said, "Back in the old days the conditions were different. The Baltimore fans did not want to pay the price. I think conditions have entirely changed."[9]

As he continued to attend major and minor league games, he repeatedly moaned about the fact that games took more than two hours. He believed that a game of two hours was the absolute limit a game should reach, and he felt a one hour and 45-minute game would be appreciated by the fans. He said, "I have been catering to the baseball public for twenty-three years now, and come pretty near knowing what it wants. Dinners are waiting for many shortly after six o'clock, and if home is not reached by six thirty o'clock there are excuses to be made and trouble follows."[10]

He recounted an Eastern League Orioles game that lasted an "unconscionable" two hours and 25 minutes, and he said, "I nearly wore my trousers out in my nervousness to get away." At that same game, he was driven nearly to distraction by a myriad of delaying tactics between pitches that were used by pitchers and batters alike. "If a pitcher insists upon using up all afternoon in going through his gymnastic performances," Hanlon fumed, "let the umpire begin to call balls upon him, and he will pitch according to the laws laid down for him."[11] No doubt he would take some solace in the recently instituted pitch timer, but he would still be appalled at a two-and-a-half-hour game.

He frequently attended the World Series, especially when they featured one of "his boys" who had followed in his footsteps as a manager. In 1905, he led the Giants to their first World Series championship against Connie Mack's Philadelphia Athletics. Hanlon took a strong personal interest in this series because he wanted McGraw to "vindicate his style." He watched the third game in the press box and commented that Christy Mathewson was the best pitcher he had ever seen with men on base. After Mathewson led the Giants to a 9–0 victory, Hanlon left the press box and made his way to the Giants' bench. While there, he pulled aside a few players he thought lacked confidence, and in a "fatherly way" he gave them words of encouragement and "instilled in them new thoughts."[12]

He also stayed in touch with his old players through the reunions of the champions that were held every year. Most were held in Baltimore, and some were extremely lavish affairs that consisted of parades, banquets, and other diversions. As long as they were physically able, the old Orioles played against the minor league Orioles or teams made up of former foes such as Honus Wagner, Jimmy Collins, and Clark Griffith. When Willie Keeler got ill years later, the reunions were held in New York so he could attend.[13] During these meetings, the personal bonds that were originally forged on the playing fields of the 19th century grew only stronger each year as they ate and drank, and as they told and retold the tales of their old exploits. These stories were no doubt embellished with each retelling.

One such story was told in Wilbert Robinson's house, where Hanlon, Steve Brodie, and others gathered. Hanlon told about the time he grew tired of Brodie always swinging at the first pitch, so he ordered him to take the first one. Brodie did not like the idea, but he took the first pitch. It was a called a strike. Brodie looked over at Hanlon with disgust, and while he did so, the pitcher threw another one right over the plate. Strike two. Brodie, now totally frustrated, looked over at Hanlon as the pitcher sneaked the third strike by him. Brodie, now in a rage, stormed back to the bench and roared, "'Now manager, I hope you're satisfied."

As the men chuckled over the oft-told story, Brodie plucked at Hanlon's coat and pulled him to one side. "Boss," he said, "I never told you about it before, but I'm going to tell you now. I never meant to wait out any of them balls, but they just natch'ly fooled me."[14]

Years later, at another gathering at his house, Robinson related a story of the Orioles' glory days. Hanlon, Kelley, McGraw, Keeler, and Robinson had heard of an illegal boxing match which was to take place at a site far outside Baltimore. When they arrived at the isolated tavern, they found that the owner was concerned because a deputy sheriff had ridden by shortly before and given him a hard, suspicious look. Nevertheless, the owner decided to go ahead with the fight, and the players, a bit worried, began picking out the windows they could use to make their escape if the law showed up. The fight began, and Robinson picked up the story:

> They were just starting the second round when, bingo, the locked front door was broken down and in poured six coppers with drawn revolvers. I took one slant and headed for that window. I leaped through it headfirst and landed on my tummy. Every time I would try to get up one or t'other boys would land on me and flatten me out again. Finally, I got to my feet and when I heard shooting inside, I stepped on the gas and lammed it down the pike.
>
> I was wearing a long blue overcoat, as it was rather cool, for it was about dawn. Ahead of me and just hitting the high spots was another speed merchant. I set out after him. I never saw such running as that fellah did. I wanted to catch up with him, as I craved company on my marathon.
>
> Well, we went a mile and I never gained an inch on him. Finally the man ahead stopped, and yelled, "Is that you Robbie?"
>
> "Sure thing," I replied, panting.
>
> "Gosh, Robby; I thought you were a policeman chasing me all that time, because of your blue overcoat."
>
> "The runner was Ned Hanlon. Well, the outcome of the business was that all of us walked back to our homes, about twelve miles. That experience cured me of going to those unchaperoned fights."[15]

* * *

On December 1, 1911, Hughie Jennings was seriously injured in a car accident near Scranton when his car slid off an ice-slicked bridge. Baltimore papers reported that the injuries could prove fatal, and an emotionally distraught Hanlon rushed to see him. He arrived late in the evening by train and was met by reporters who heard he was coming. As soon as Hanlon saw them, he anxiously asked how Jennings was doing. Told that Jennings was recovering rapidly and would soon be released from the hospital, Hanlon smiled broadly with palpable relief, and he exclaimed, "I knew it. He'll be all right: sure as fate Hugh will get out of this." Hanlon peppered the reporters with all manner of questions regarding how the accident happened, the extent of Jennings' injuries, what the doctors had done, and what they would do for him.

His fears now alleviated, Hanlon's deep feelings for Jennings gushed out of him:

"Wonderful fellow: he always has been. I've known him as I know my own sons....Hugh Jennings is of the higher type of man. He's a wonderful character. No ball player has ever had the friends he has had...and this is because of his wonderful disposition. A disposition that has never changed with all the success that has come to him. Just as he is today, he was twenty years ago when I took him from Louisville."

A reporter who listened to Hanlon wrote, "Hanlon still follows the careers of his old players as interestedly and anxiously for their continued success as those same players were for his success in his palmiest days... .[He] evidently could talk the Baltimore team by the day and the hour without tiring."[16]

The next day, Hanlon sneaked into the hospital before visiting hours began, and he and Jennings spent hours jovially recalling baseball stories from their old days together. Hanlon told Jennings, "I knew you could not hurt that head, Amos Rusie failed to do it with an inshoot back in the old days.... I knew when I read that the head got the worst of it that there was nothing to it."[17]

* * *

In the summer of 1912, Hanlon and his old comrade, John Ward, sat in the most inconspicuous seats they could find in the grandstand of an unnamed National League ballpark. As they watched a runner get thrown out trying to steal second, Ward muttered that baserunning had become a lost art. They agreed that although the players of their time were slower and bulkier, they were better baserunners than the slimmer modern players. After they watched another runner get thrown out by ten feet when attempting to steal, Hanlon disgustedly moaned that the runner waited too long: "If he had been studying the man carefully, he would have stolen the base by almost the distance by which he was thrown out...yet the runner held back, waiting until he saw the ball go when he could have been underway almost at top speed."

The two aging baseball warriors reminisced about the state of the game they now watched, continually noting how what they saw fell short of the glorious strategies and tactics of the old game they loved so well. Far removed from the pitched battles they had waged for so many years on so many fields now gone, they wistfully expressed the desire to get ball clubs of their own again, so they could instruct them in proper base running.[18]

* * *

As the outside world moved ever closer to the war which would dwarf all previous wars, major league baseball prepared itself for a war of its own. In the ever-growing urban landscape that constituted 20th-century America, many cities were eager to have a major league team to call their own. These cities challenged Organized Baseball by creating a new major league called the Federal League.

On March 8, 1913, in Indianapolis, the Federal League was officially incorporated. The league operated as a minor league that year, and on October 14, 1913, the Federal League declared itself a major league that would actively recruit players from the National and American Leagues.[19] Less than a month later, the league added Baltimore and Buffalo. Baltimore, which had been pining for a return of major league baseball, was ecstatic to be a part of the new league.

The team in Baltimore was named the Terrapins, and Hanlon's good friend, Judge Harry Goldman, and 600 Baltimoreans raised $164,000 to capitalize the franchise. Goldman, knowing that Hanlon's involvement would give instant credibility to any baseball endeavor, recruited Hanlon to run it.[20] Hanlon owned property directly across the street from the ballpark of the International League Orioles, which had previously been the home of John McGraw's American League Orioles.[21] The Terrapins leased the land from Hanlon and built a quality concrete, steel, and wooden ball park for $82,649.[22]

On November 28, 1913, Federal League owners met to organize a strategy for recruiting major league players. During an important session on this topic, Ned Hanlon gave club presidents a "pep talk," and he assured them that every player on the St. Louis American League team and the St. Paul American Association team was ready to sign with the Federals. To help convince the owners, Hanlon had brought some of the players from those teams with him to the meeting to demonstrate that they were serious in their intentions to sign with their league. When news of the meeting reached Pirates owner Barney Dreyfuss, he wrote to Garry Herrmann and remarked that "Hanlon seems to be the Moses they are looking for to lead them out of the wilderness."[23]

Hanlon in his later years, about the time he was involved with the Federal League (National Baseball Hall of Fame and Museum, Cooperstown, New York).

Hanlon turned his attention to hiring a manager. He first approached Baltimore native Buck Herzog, McGraw's third baseman on the Giants. Herzog's salary demands, however, were much more than the Terrapins were willing to pay. Hanlon turned to his old comrade Wilbert Robinson, who had been a coach for McGraw, but recently had a falling out with him. Robinson showed interest in the job, but then he accepted the managerial job with Brooklyn. Hanlon finally hired Otto Knabe, the second baseman of the Philadelphia Phillies, as player-manager.[24]

When the wealthy Robert Ward committed to ownership in the league, Hanlon, still harboring hard feelings towards Charles Ebbets, convinced him to locate his franchise in Brooklyn. Hanlon hoped that if Ebbets had to compete with a Federal League team in his city, it would deal him a crippling financial blow.[25] That proved to be the case as attendance for Ebbets' team dropped drastically from 347,000 in 1913, when they had no competition, to 122,671 in 1914, when the Federals arrived.

In Baltimore, the establishment of a major league team literally right across the street from his ballpark had dire financial consequences for Jack Dunn's minor league

Orioles. Attendance at Orioles games fell precipitously, and in July, the team only managed to draw 29 paying fans for a Friday game, and only 20 the following day.[26]

In an address to a business luncheon in York, Pennsylvania, Connie Mack, a close friend of both Dunn and Hanlon, took Hanlon to task for situating the Terrapins' ball park right across the street from the Orioles: "Surely you men here who are in business would not stand for it for a minute if you bought out some person's business and good will to have the same person start up a rival business again just across the street from you. That is what Ned Hanlon has done."[27] Whether or not Mack had a valid point, it must be remembered that his loan to help Dunn purchase the Orioles had made him somewhat of a silent partner with Dunn.

Jack Dunn was furious, and he became even more outraged when he discovered that Terrapins representatives had waited outside of an Orioles game, took down the names and addresses of each spectator as they left the stadium, and sent them season passes to future Terrapins games. Dunn groused, "I don't see how that man sleeps at night. I couldn't, if I had done what he has done."[28]

During the season, rumors were published that Babe Ruth might jump to the Federal League Terrapins. When Ruth wrote his autobiography years later, he claimed that the Terrapins had offered him a $10,000 bonus and a $10,000 a year salary to sign with them. Ruth said he thought hard about it, but ultimately declined because Organized Baseball had warned players that if they jumped to the Federals, they would be banned for life. A Terrapins official denied they were trying to sign Ruth and claimed that they had an agreement with Dunn that they would not sign any of his players.[29]

Dunn took some satisfaction in the fact that the new league was struggling, and he claimed that the Terrapins had lost $18,000 in their first year. Although sources have claimed that Hanlon was a principal investor in the Terrapins, Dunn disputed that: "I don't believe that Hanlon at the present time owns a penny's worth of stocks. He's too wise to put his money into such a league."[30]

Dunn tried everything to keep the Orioles afloat, but nothing bore fruit. Finally, he had no choice but to sell some of his best players to raise cash. Within a two-week period, he sold eight of his best players, and one of them was Babe Ruth, who was sold to the Boston Red Sox. That transaction forever altered baseball history.[31]

By the end of the 1914 season, Hanlon had serious concerns about the ability of the Federal League to survive, and he was looking for a way out. It was reported that he had not been attending league meetings and was disgusted at the way the Federal League handled its business.[32] Anticipating that Dunn would have to sell the team because of his financial constraints, Hanlon secretly proposed a plan to International League President Ed Barrow. He proposed that the Federal League Terrapins would buy the Orioles and merge the Terrapins into it, which would stabilize the minor league Orioles.[33] That never happened, and the Orioles ended up moving to Richmond, Virginia, for the 1915 season.

In their inaugural year, the Baltimore Terrapins had a respectable 80–70 record, good for third place. The 1915 season, however, was an unmitigated disaster as the team fell to 47–107 and finished last.

The Federal League was ultimately unable to succeed for a variety of reasons. It was unable to attract many stars from the two established leagues, and the ones who jumped to the Federals were generally older, washed-up players who were looking for one last big payday. Moreover, the Federals were unable to prevail in an anti-trust lawsuit they initiated against the National and American Leagues. Finally, the owners lacked the financial commitment that would have provided the league with its only chance to survive.

When the league sued for peace, financial arrangements were made with all the clubs except the Baltimore Terrapins. Hanlon and the Terrapins ownership sued Organized Baseball for triple damages under the Sherman Antitrust Act. The case, "Federal Baseball Club of Baltimore Inc. *vs* National League of Professional Baseball Clubs *et al.*" wound its way over the years all the way to the Supreme Court. Finally, in 1922, the court ruled by a unanimous vote that baseball "is not interstate business in the sense of the Sherman Act." This decision had lasting implications for baseball for over 50 years as it provided the primary defense for major league baseball against challenges to the reserve clause.[34]

* * *

In September of 1916, Ned Hanlon was named to the Baltimore Parks Board by Baltimore Mayor James Preston. The *Evening Sun* strongly endorsed the move and noted his deep love for the city and his tireless efforts to bring professional baseball back to Baltimore. The *Sun* stated, "Mayor Preston might hunt a long time before finding a man who would devote more time, energy, and intelligence to the best interests of the parks and of Baltimore than Ned Hanlon would."[35] Hanlon served on the board for the rest of his life, and in 1931, he became its president.

After he was named to the board, one of the first things Hanlon did was to arrange the appointment of his old player, Steve Brodie, as custodian of the baseball diamonds in the city's parks. Together they worked tirelessly to increase the number and improve the quality of the baseball facilities throughout the park system.[36] Over the years, they regularly wandered the fields together, Brodie referring to Hanlon as "Manager" or "Boss," as they watched the young boys play.

On one trip to the ball fields, Hanlon commented, "the youngsters take to the game with all the seriousness of professionals, and if you want to see real earnestness, just watch one of the games in which the negro nines are engaged." He also expressed pride in the coaches who "took no foolishness off the baserunners" and told them not to "get married to that bag."[37] And, of course, many times he could not resist the urge to take off his coat and give some personal instruction to the youngsters. Just like in the old days.

In a comment that would have drawn a wry smile from his old opponents, Hanlon said, "We let the boys know we are there for them, but that rowdiness and rough play will not be tolerated. There are occasionally hot arguments, but that is all."[38]

"I was a kid once," said Hanlon, "and I know how these fellows feel about baseball. I want to do all I can for them, and so does the Park Board as a whole. When I was a kid, it wasn't so easy to play ball, but I loved it enough to walk several miles to another town to play a game once a week. And my mother scolded a lot because I was late for supper. But like all other mothers, she saw to it that I had enough to eat before I went to bed."[39]

* * *

Ned Hanlon's younger son, Joseph, was in New York City working at an engineering firm when the United States declared war on Germany in 1917. His work could have excused him from active duty, but he desired to obtain an officer's commission. His employers did not want him to go and threatened to stand in the way of the commission, but Joe insisted that if they tried to prevent it, he would quit and enlist as a private. They relented, Joe and his fiancée postponed their wedding, and he was commissioned as a Second Lieutenant and assigned to the First Battalion of Gas and Flame, nicknamed the "Hell Fire Battalion." While he was training at the American University Camp in Washington, D.C., Joe organized two baseball teams in the battalion. He wrote to his father and told him that Washington manager Clark Griffith was helping to fit out the teams, and he asked his father for baseball equipment. As part of his help, Ned sent two dozen baseballs to his son.[40]

Joe and his battalion were assigned to the 30th Engineers of the American Expeditionary Force and went to France. In early July of 1918, the Hanlon family was proud to receive a letter from Joe that informed them that he was awarded the Croix de Guerre, an award usually given to French allies who distinguished themselves by acts of heroism involving combat with the enemy.

On July 30, 1918, at Villers-sur-Fere during the Second Battle of the Marne, Joe and his platoon were moving forward with ammunition to support troops that were attacking the retreating Germans at the Marne River, when a large German shell exploded near him. The 25-year-old Hanlon was killed almost instantly.[41] Earlier, Joe had expressed a premonition about his death to his chaplain, and now he was the first officer of the Chemical Warfare Service to be killed in action.[42] He was so highly regarded by the French that just a month later, the Experimental Field of the Chemical Warfare Service outside Chaumont was renamed Hanlon Field.

In 1920, without his knowledge, Hanlon's fellow Park Board members secretly decided in a unanimous vote to name a 96-acre tract around Lake Ashburton "Hanlon Park," in honor of Joe. During a meeting of the Board, chairman J. Cookman Boyd rose and eloquently spoke of the character and bravery of Joe Hanlon, then informed Hanlon of the board's action. Ned Hanlon was greatly moved and expressed his thanks in an almost broken, almost inaudible voice.[43]

* * *

On New Year's Day in 1923, Hanlon and his old players received dreadful news: Willie Keeler was dead. He was just 50 years old. Hanlon and the old Orioles rushed to Brooklyn and gathered in the room where Keeler lay. John McGraw was overcome by emotion and had to be led from the room by Joe Kelley. On a chilly January 4, they gathered once again to lay Keeler to rest at Calvary Cemetery in Brooklyn. With tears pouring down his face, McGraw threw a spadeful of dirt on the coffin. Also crying heavily, Jennings prayed by the coffin. Hanlon, Gleason, Kelley, Robinson, McGraw, and Jennings served as pallbearers.[44]

In December 1924, there was a brush with death for another old Oriole. Hanlon, hearing that Wilbert Robinson was seriously ill with pleurisy, rushed to his home, where he found a priest and a solemn house. As Hanlon entered the sickroom, Robinson hailed him: "Hello, Ned. Come on in here. You are just in time as you were in the days when you taught me baseball. Just in time now, too. I want you to be my godfather. I am about to be baptized a Catholic." Hanlon's face lit up with joy, and overcome with emotion, he held the hand of his close friend throughout the ceremony.[45] Joe Kelley, who lived just two blocks away from Robinson, rushed over to his house to congratulate him when he heard the news.[46] Robinson, however, recovered from his illness and lived another ten years. After both Hanlon and Robinson were dead, they would be again linked when Hanlon's grandson, Joseph, married Robinson's granddaughter, Hannah, in 1941.

In 1925, Hanlon's children held a family dinner to celebrate the 35th wedding anniversary of Ned and Ellen Hanlon at the Maryland Country Club. In the center of the table, they arranged for a cake in the replica of a baseball diamond. Colored icings were used to reproduce the green of the grass, the base paths, and the white lines. In a tribute to the strong feelings Hanlon had for "his boys," nine small photographs of the men who played on the championship Orioles were distributed over the "diamond."[47]

* * *

In 1927, Wilbert Robinson caused a controversy among his old teammates and other baseball men when he declared that the powerful Yankees were possibly a better team than the old Orioles. The *Baltimore Sun* arranged for Hanlon to see the Yankees play the Senators in Washington "for the purpose of getting the real low-down on a situation that had become threatening to the peace, dignity, and digestion of the old timers' club." After the game, Hanlon said that he saw nothing that would change his belief that his Orioles championship teams were better than the present-day Yankees.

Hanlon called the Yankees a "great straight-away team," complimented Ruth as an excellent player, and predicted greatness for Gehrig. He also had kind words for his old Cincinnati Reds second baseman, Miller Huggins, saying he was a smart manager who deserved more credit than he was getting. When asked about how to hit the daunting Yankees' pitching, Hanlon said indignantly, "Do you think we would stand up there and swing like a barn door in a windstorm? Huh!"

As might be expected, he waxed nostalgic about his Orioles. He said that their use of the unexpected to keep opponents off-balance and the way they studied opposing pitchers and adjusted their strategies to take advantage of their weakness, made the Orioles a better club than the Yankees. He spoke with pride of how they perfected the hit-and-run play and once executed it 13 times in succession. He reminisced about taking his place behind the pitcher in morning practices to umpire balls and strikes and to see any weakness that might show up. He described how they repeated drills until they produced perfect results. And he spoke of the classroom sessions where he played the teacher, but insisted that they were "in the nature of an open forum where all new ideas were aired and criticisms made."

When pressed to respond to Robinson's comments regarding the superiority of the Yankees, Hanlon merely said, "Robbie was a mighty wise catcher in the old days. He is still in baseball. He is with the moderns now and he is still mighty wise."[48]

* * *

In his retirement, Hanlon spent a great deal of time at Pimlico and Laurel race tracks. He would also run up to the track at Havre de Grace with Joe Kelley, where they met up with Kid Gleason, who had traveled down from Philadelphia.[49] Knowing his love for racing, a friend once asked Hanlon why he didn't buy a race horse himself. In a response that defined him in all his endeavors, Hanlon said that if he was going to put that much money into anything, he would have to have complete control and also be the trainer and the jockey so "I could be right on top of my business all the time."[50]

But for Ned Hanlon, who was entering his seventh decade, among the celebrations and meetings with old friends, there was also the sorrow that comes with long life. Hanlon's old Brotherhood partner, John Montgomery Ward, died in 1925. Just a few years later, the beloved Hughie Jennings passed away on February 1, 1928. Eight months later,

Hanlon was at Laurel Park race track outside Baltimore when he was informed of the death of Jack Dunn, who died when he fell off a horse while hunting with his dogs. Hanlon was stunned and could not speak for a few moments. When he composed himself, he spoke of how he had known Dunn for more than 30 years and extolled him for helping him win two pennants at Brooklyn and two pennants as manager of the minor league Orioles.[51]

On December 5, 1932, Ned Hanlon lost his beloved wife, Ellen Jane Hanlon, who died at 74 of a heart condition. They had been married for 42 years and had five children. Although it is not known how long he knew Ellen before they married, considering they both grew up in the same neighborhood and attended the same church in Taftville, it is likely he knew her almost his whole life.

In August of the same year, Hanlon lost his old Wolverines teammate, Dan Brouthers, and five months later, Kid Gleason was also gone.

Less than two years later, on February 25, 1934, the seemingly indomitable John McGraw died. As Hanlon, Steve Brodie, Joe Kelley, and others waited at the train station for McGraw's arrival for burial in Baltimore's New Cathedral Cemetery, a *Baltimore Sun* photographer took a picture of Hanlon and others. The look on Hanlon's face clearly shows his deep sorrow.[52] It had been said many times during the years that Hanlon regarded his players as sons, and they regarded him as a father. Now his favorite baseball son had left him.

While they waited at the station that day, a friend remembered, Hanlon said to him: "John McGraw never grew up for me. I always saw him as he looked as a youngster, slim and clean-cut. None of the old boys have ever grown up for me. See Joe Kelley over there? As I look at him, I see him in uniform, swaggering about the field, the idol of the home rooters, and the villain in the other cities."[53]

Just six months later, on August 8, 1934, the beloved old Orioles captain, Wilbert Robinson, took his final breath in Atlanta, where he was president of the minor league Atlanta Crackers. He had fallen in the bathroom of his home and broken his arm. When a doctor came to administer treatment, Robinson protested: "This broken arm doesn't hurt me. I'm an old Oriole. Wrap it up and let me stay here."[54] Nevertheless, he was placed in an ambulance, and as they headed to the hospital, he had a stroke and died before the end of the day.

"A hushed and bowed group" met Robinson's body at the train station in Baltimore, and it was brought to New Cathedral Cemetery and laid to rest near the top of a pleasant green hillside, not far from his old friend, John McGraw. Hanlon was too ill to attend, but Kelley and Brodie were at the gravesite.[55]

Finally, on October 30, 1935, Walter Scott "Steve" Brodie passed away. Almost all of them were now gone: McGraw, Wee Willie, Hughie, Robbie, Brodie, Big Dan, Miller Huggins, the Kid, all gone. And so many, many more.

In 1936, the Brooklyn Dodgers held a reunion of old-time players to celebrate the 60th anniversary of the National League, and the Dodgers held a luncheon for the old players at Ebbets Field. Dodgers manager Casey Stengel, Zach Wheat, Dazzy Vance, and Bill Dahlen were among the attendees. Ned Hanlon, now 79 years old, was invited, and a newspaper published on the day of the gathering announced that he would be there and referred to him as "one of Brooklyn's immortals."[56] Hanlon, however, was too ill to attend. Physically, Ned Hanlon was not immortal, and he now had only 217 days to live.

14. Baseball in the Blood (1908–1937)

* * *

In 1935, Ned Hanlon was admitted to Union Memorial Hospital for a serious heart ailment. At first, all were barred from visiting him except for his immediate family. It was reported that his "fighting spirit" was the only thing that was keeping him alive, and that he lay in his bed, living with his memories.[57] He soon recovered enough to talk baseball, and he once again stated his long-held belief that the players of his time played harder than did the moderns. His memory stirred, he recalled John McGraw: "The game lost an aggressive figure, a great ball player and a great manager when McGraw died. He was a man who was always a hard worker. I found him that way from the beginning." When he was asked to name the greatest player he ever saw, he could not help but name the man with whom he likely had the strongest bond: "Well, I think the late John McGraw was a great ball-player—perhaps not the best, but a smart boy, and willing too."[58]

During the last few years of his life, Hanlon lived with his elder daughter Edwina at her home at 200 Longwood Road. For much of that time, he was quite ill and was unable to travel much. He was able to manage a few trips to Ocean City with his family, a usual vacation destination. After dinner every night, he would tap one of his granddaughters, Edwina, on the hand, give her a nickel, and ask her to go upstairs and bring him down a cigar.[59]

In January 1937, three months before his death, Hanlon mustered the strength to attend a banquet as the guest of honor at the Knights of Columbus Father and Son banquet. Hanlon brought Joe Kelley, the last of the Big Four, with him.[60]

On April 10, 1937, he suffered a severe heart attack and began to sink steadily. It was clear that the tough, wily old Fox could not prevail this time,

Last photograph of Ned Hanlon. It was taken in Ocean City, Maryland, near the end of his life (courtesy Michael Reeve).

and members of his family gathered around his bedside. At 11:40 p.m. on April 14, Foxy Ned was gone.[61]

The funeral for Edward Hugh "Ned" Hanlon was held two days later at Corpus Christi Church, just across the street from the Mt. Royal Avenue home where Hanlon had lived for nearly 40 years. Former mayors James Preston and William Broening and current mayor Harold Jackson attended. Connie Mack and Clark Griffith were honorary pallbearers, and members of the Park Board served as the pallbearers.

Corpus Christi Pastor Reverend James F. Nolan spoke. "On my visits to Mr. Hanlon, I found him a man of a deeply spiritual interior life….Every Sunday we saw him here in his pew, following humbly, and devoutly the Holy Sacrifice of the Mass. Every morning in Lent we saw him in his pew, before the mass began, ready to adore his God and Saviour. He who made Baltimore known all over the country was a humble, prayerful man."[62]

After the service, the sad journey to New Cathedral Cemetery was made. Ned Hanlon was buried next to his wife, just a fly ball away from the burial sites of John McGraw and Wilbert Robinson. Joe Kelley would join them there in 1943. No other cemetery in the country has provided the final resting place for so many Hall of Famers.

He left an estate of $128,000,[63] roughly equivalent to over $2.5 million in 2023.

* * *

Tributes to the remarkable life of Ned Hanlon poured in after his death. Hanlon's friend, Vincent de Paul Fitzgerald, managing editor of the *Baltimore Catholic Review*, described Hanlon's strong piety and the fact that he gave all his children a strong Catholic education from parochial school through college. He also described the strong relationships Hanlon had with his old players and the deep affection he held for them all. He concluded, "Much happiness came to Ned Hanlon in his life, but I can truly say that one of the happiest days was when he stood as godfather in the room of a home on St. Paul Street in Baltimore when dear old 'Robbie' was baptized."[64]

New York sportswriter Sid Mercer called Hanlon a great player and a great manager who had now become "almost a myth" to modern fans. He said, "Ned Hanlon has gone to rejoin John McGraw, Wilbert Robinson, Hughie Jennings, Willie Keeler, Steve Brodie, Kid Gleason, Dan Brouthers and other wraiths of the famous Baltimore Orioles with whom he collaborated in a brilliant chapter of baseball history. If there is a celestial clubhouse in the Valhalla of sports where the old-time warriors congregate to swap reminiscences, the old Orioles must be there staging a welcome for the man who built their nest."[65]

His hometown *Baltimore Sun* remembered Hanlon as someone who "was never happier than when mixing with the youngsters on the diamond." The paper referred to Hanlon as "the father of modern baseball," who helped to transform a monotonous game that was a "crude slugging match" into one where "a run gained by strategy counted as big as a run gained by slugging by creating an offensive technique that made baseball something of an art…with the passing of Mr. Hanlon, baseball loses a historic personage."[66]

Long-time Baltimore sportswriter Roger Pippen evoked a sweet vision that might give some comfort to all who admired and would miss Ned Hanlon: "McGraw, Jennings, Keeler, Robbie, Gleason, Brodie and other pupils…have been waiting for their teacher…. On a bench, in a warm sun, with a soft wind, [they] will tell Ned for the hundredth time that they owe their success in baseball to him."[67]

*   *   *

Eighteen months before Hanlon's death, Joe Kelley had jumped off a trolley to speak to his old teammate, Steve Brodie, who was standing on a street corner. Brodie died suddenly just a few days later.[68]

Now Kelley attended the funeral of the man who had built the team that brought him and all his comrades such fame. The man who took him out to Union Park in the mornings to teach him how to hit and how to play the outfield. Now there would be no more trips to the race track with Hanlon and the others. No more reunions. No more gatherings at Robbie's house to talk about the glory days. No more....

Since the end of his baseball days, Kelley had bounced around at a number of jobs, never seeming to find the right fit. As Burt Solomon said in his definitive book about those old Orioles, "Kel began to seem lonely, as if time had passed him by." Which it had. Nothing much had changed in baseball, but everything had. Asked what was different from his day, he replied, "The first and fifteenth of the month."[69] Now he sat in the rocking chair on the porch of his house at 2826 North Calvert Street, thinking of what once was, until he died in that very house on August 14, 1943.

*   *   *

Hanlon left a valuable legacy to his beloved Baltimore in 1922. Relying on a long baseball career spent in many different ball parks, he played a key role in developing the plans of the Park Board for a new stadium to be built in Venable Park.[70] Over the years, the stadium would go by different names, including Baltimore Stadium, Municipal Stadium, and for a brief period, Babe Ruth Stadium. Until the 1940s, it primarily housed high school and college football games. When old Terrapin Park, home of the International League Orioles, was destroyed by fire on July 4, 1944, the city offered the Orioles the use of the stadium, and it was reconfigured for baseball.[71]

In 1948, the name was changed to Memorial Stadium, and over the next few years, major alterations and expansions were made. By 1953, the newly-born Baltimore Colts of the National Football League began play in Memorial Stadium. Later that same year, the city of Baltimore reached agreement with the management of the St. Louis Browns to bring that team to Baltimore. In honor of their old major league predecessors, they were renamed the Baltimore Orioles,[72] and they played their first game in their new home on April 15, 1954.

The remaining living members of the old Orioles were invited to attend the opening ceremonies of the new team. Bill "Boileryard" Clarke and "Dirty" Jack Doyle attended, as did Connie Mack. Although he was still alive, Bill Hoffer, the great Orioles pitcher of 1895–1897, was forgotten and did not receive an invitation.

Ned Hanlon had long worked to bring major league baseball back to his beloved Baltimore, and as it turned out, his work with the Park Board to build Baltimore Stadium eventually provided the venue that enabled the new Baltimore Orioles of the American League to return to the city he had loved so dearly.

Although it was 17 years too late for Ned Hanlon to see it, major league baseball was back in Baltimore.

Epilogue

Ned Hanlon managed his last two games in the major leagues in a doubleheader on October 6, 1907, against the Pirates. The Reds lost the opener, 3–2, but they beat the Pirates, 13–1, in the second game, which was called after seven innings due to darkness. That day ended a managerial career during which he had won five pennants, and his .668 winning percentage between 1894 and 1900 remains the best seven-year stretch of any Hall of Fame manager. Next closest are Joe McCarthy with .653 and Casey Stengel with .638.

Eighty-nine years later, Hanlon was voted into the National Baseball Hall of Fame. At that time, Veterans Committee member Allen Lewis said, "he should have been elected long ago. He was very inventive. He was probably the first great manager."[1]

So what took so long?

One reason suggested by *Baltimore Sun* sportswriter John Steadman is that Hanlon was ostracized when the Baltimore Terrapins filed the lawsuit against Organized Baseball when the Federal League folded.[2] Moreover, it did not help his cause that his great managerial years occurred in the 19th century, and his teams after 1900 did not have much success. When the Hall of Fame began operations, Hanlon was overshadowed by more high-profile managers such as Connie Mack and John McGraw, who operated primarily in the 20th century. Both Mack and McGraw were elected in the second year of balloting, in 1937.

As early as 1918, a reporter conjectured that one day, Connie Mack might be forgotten much like Hanlon. He wrote, "Today half the fans who attend major league ball games would have to be told just who Ned Hanlon was, but there was a time twenty years ago when Hanlon's fame in the big show was the equal, if not the superior, to that achieved by Mack in Connie's palmy days."[3]

Even though he was not inducted for so long, it must be said that Ned Hanlon was the first manager to be enshrined whose career took place largely in the 19th century. Frank Selee, Hanlon's old Boston Beaneaters rival, is the only other, elected three years after Hanlon.

* * *

The delay in giving Hanlon his due by the Hall, however, might also be due to an opinion that had worked its way into baseball discussions of the old Orioles. This school of thought suggested that the team's success was due not to Hanlon's influence and teachings; instead, the players were responsible for the tactics which created Hanlon's reputation as a managerial wizard.

In 1966, a book was published that referred to that controversy once again.

Lawrence Ritter traveled the country for five years, interviewing old ball players to capture their memories before they would be lost. The result of that journey was the popular book, *The Glory of Their Times*, in which the old Detroit Tigers star Sam "Wahoo" Crawford told this story about Hanlon:

> Ned Hanlon used to manage that Baltimore club, but those old veterans didn't pay any attention to him. Heck, they all knew baseball inside out....Like I said, those old Baltimore Orioles didn't pay any more attention to Ned Hanlon, their manager, than they did to the batboy. When I came into the league, that whole bunch moved over to Brooklyn, and Hanlon was managing them there, too. He was a bench manager in civilian clothes. When things would get a little tough in games, Hanlon would sit there on the bench and wring his hands and start telling some of those old-timers what to do. They'd look at him and say, "For Christ's sake, just keep quiet and leave us alone. We'll win this ball game if you only shut up."[4]

To fans who had little or no knowledge of Hanlon, Crawford's remarks painted an extremely unflattering portrait of him as a dithering, useless figurehead of a manager, but it should be noted that Sam Crawford never played for Hanlon. In his last year with the Cincinnati Reds in 1902, he was managed by Joe Kelley for the last 60 games of the season, and he jumped to Detroit in the American League in 1903. There he was managed by Hughie Jennings for the last 11 years of his career. It is hard to conceive that either Kelley or Jennings could have portrayed Hanlon in such an unflattering matter.

Much evidence has already been presented that clearly shows Hanlon as the main force behind the utilization of the techniques and tactics of his Orioles teams. That is not to say that the players had no input and did not contribute to the revolutionary overall stratagem that made the Orioles teams so successful. It has been shown that Hanlon laid the foundation for the offensive and defensive systems for the team, but when a player offered a suggestion that seemed viable to him, it would be incorporated into the plan. If not, Hanlon would not hesitate to reject its implementation.

Joe Kelley had on numerous occasions gone on record as crediting Hanlon's with the success of the Orioles,[5] and he also testified that Hanlon worked with him individually on a daily basis when he first joined the team to improve his hitting technique.[6] Jennings also spoke highly of Hanlon. When discussing the great Orioles teams in 1907, a reporter asked Jennings who was responsible for their success: "Some say it was McGraw and others say it was you. A few say Hanlon had charge of it." Jennings was unequivocal in his response:

> Ned Hanlon was leader first, last, and all the time. His was always the master mind. He knew more baseball than any of the rest combined and we all knew that he did. His ability was so far above ours we had to recognize him as a leader then and because of that we worked for him. On that old Baltimore team if a player started to go wrong the rest of the team got after him, McGraw and Kelley and those boys, and just jerked him right back on his feet. It was Hanlon's influence that held them together. Today I don't think there is a manager in baseball who knows as much about the game as Ned Hanlon.[7]

Bill Reidy, who played on Hanlon's Brooklyn teams in 1899, 1903, and 1904, scoffed at the notion that Hanlon had been nothing more than a figurehead. "I have read some knocks on Hanlon's ability recently," he said, "but I think if you will ask any man who ever worked for Hanlon, he will tell you that 'Foxy Ned' is the best ever. Why, the talk he would give us in the spring would be worth more than all the stuff other managers keep dinning into their players."[8]

Hanlon's captain, Wilbert Robinson said, "all of us admired Hanlon's genius from the beginning of our connection with him, and the longer we knew him, the stronger grew our feelings until I believe that there was not a man on the championship team who would not have gone through fire and water for 'Ned' Hanlon."[9]

Finally, Willie Keeler likely gave the best description of the working relationship between Hanlon and his players that resulted in those great Orioles teams:

> Hanlon was mainly the cause for its success. He was out on the field for two hours every morning, working with us, and cooking up new tricks all the time. Some of us might miss a morning or two, but Hanlon never did. He used to lie awake nights thinking of new tricks to spring on the other fellows....I don't say that Hanlon discovered them all, and I don't say that we did it ourselves.[10]

It was not only the men who played for Hanlon who admired his knowledge of the game and thought highly of him as a strategist and as a leader of men. The large majority of sportswriters who covered Hanlon in his career firmly believed in Hanlon's skill as a manager. John B. Foster was a baseball writer for New York newspapers for 50 years, later served as club secretary for the New York Giants, and was a writer and editor for the *Spalding Official Baseball Guide*. Foster said that it was "rather amusing...to hear that stereotyped old repetition of the assertion that not Hanlon but the players made the Baltimore Club." He claimed it was Hanlon who found value in players other clubs had tossed away and made them stars. Moreover, he maintained that John McGraw's success with the Giants came from employing the techniques and tactics that he first learned under Hanlon.

Foster continued: "[Hanlon's] success [has] not been the success of luck or chance. As a player he was among the best of his day. As a manager he has taught other managers things about the game that they never knew before."[11]

In 1954, when the St. Louis Browns moved and became the Baltimore Orioles, the city was wild with celebrations. As part of the festivities, the few living men who once played for the 1890s Orioles were invited back to the city for Opening Day. Prior to leaving for Baltimore, 84-year-old "Dirty" Jack Doyle was interviewed, and he declared that Hanlon's contribution to the game had been overlooked with the passing years. He said, "One man who never got full credit for that great Oriole team of ours was our manager, Ned Hanlon. He was a great player with Detroit. When he managed the Orioles in 1896 and 1897 he never wore a uniform, but he put that team together. It was his brains and development that made it the great team it was. The players loved him."[12]

If the players and reporters who were eyewitnesses to Hanlon's work with the team definitively declared that he was the tactical and inspirational leader of the Orioles, then how did the idea of Hanlon as merely a figurehead who rode the coattails of his players weave its way stubbornly into baseball lore?

John McGraw.

* * *

The relationship between Hanlon and McGraw was a complex one. Long before John McGraw came to the major leagues, he had heard of Ned Hanlon. He was excited about the revolt of the Brotherhood and the larger salaries for players that it brought,[13] and he knew that Hanlon was a leader in that union. When he was playing in the minors for Olean, he ran into a man who had played for Hanlon's Pittsburgh team in the Players' League, and McGraw badgered him with questions about the majors. He asked what

Hanlon was like as a manager, and he was told, "Great manager, great outfielder, great fellow. Wonderful man to work for."[14]

When McGraw was about 15 years old, he read a description in the newspaper about Hanlon's great catch in Denver as Albert Spalding's group headed west on their World Tour. He cut out the clipping, and his wife Blanche later described how he kept it as it yellowed with age. She recalled how he would pull that clipping out and remark how Hanlon "was a great outfielder and could really go get 'em." He said to his wife in amazement, "And that was in an exhibition game, too. With bare hands."[15]

When Hanlon first arrived in Baltimore, he immediately had to deal with a dysfunctional team that had to remind McGraw of the unsettled family life he had endured as a child. McGraw initially had to be in awe of his famous manager, and he admired the manner in which Hanlon used a mixture of stern discipline and fatherly guidance to transform a team in a state of chaos into one that quickly reached the pinnacle of the baseball world. What's more, Hanlon built a team of like-minded young men that would become the family that McGraw never had. McGraw embraced Hanlon's teachings, but in time his intrinsically compulsive and ambitious nature simply could not allow Hanlon to be the holder of the baseball knowledge he wished to possess. At the risk of delving into psycho-babble, it could be claimed that McGraw had an Oedipal Complex wherein Hanlon was the father figure, and McGraw's desire was to replace him so he could acquire the thing he loved most: baseball.

Blanche McGraw knew how important baseball was for her husband: "life without baseball had little meaning for him. It was his meat, his drink, his dream, his blood and breath, his reason for existence."[16] Once McGraw became the manager of the New York Giants, his dominant personality would not allow anyone to question his knowledge of the game. "With my team I am an absolute czar," McGraw proclaimed. "My men know it. I order plays and they obey. If they don't, I fine them."[17] In short, McGraw came to believe that he was the originator of the Orioles' tactics.

McGraw's claim that he called every play on the field and his insistence on taking credit for every victory by the Giants infuriated some of his players. His Future Hall of Fame first baseman, Bill Terry, grouched that "McGraw will call every move and every pitch, till the count is three and two and the bases are loaded. Then all of a sudden, he leaves the pitcher to fend for himself." On one occasion when McGraw angrily blamed a player for a loss after a game, Terry could not control himself any longer and shouted at McGraw: "You've been blaming other people for the mistakes you've been making for 20 years."[18] This might have been a moment of karma for McGraw, and he may have recalled the time that he furiously told Hanlon that the players made him.

By 1905, Hanlon had grown aggravated with the controversy, and when a New York writer claimed that McGraw had created the hit-and-run play in 1894, Hanlon sternly denounced the claim:

> I don't mind giving credit where credit is due, but I want to say that the hit-and-run game was played by the Baltimore team before McGraw ever became a regular member of that organization. The play was first introduced by me in the Baltimore Club in 1893, and Wilbert Robinson, the catcher, and [Heinie] Reitz worked it successfully a number of times. In the early spring practice down South in 1894 we made a feature of this style of play....I want to say, however, that I am the originator of the play and I think I ought to be given the credit due me.[19]

It is important to note, however, that as the years went by, McGraw was willing to give more and more credit to Hanlon. In his autobiography published in 1923, he admitted, "Hanlon was a wise manager in ways that I did not appreciate."[20] In addition, he said:

> Ed Hanlon had a wonderful faculty of organization, a trait that he never had the chance to develop fully until he came to Baltimore. His policy was always one of construction. I find it a general impression that Hanlon was more particularly noted for his ability to develop inside baseball. It is true that he doted on that, but if I were to decide between the two, I would say he was a greater organizer and builder than a field general. Everybody realized his ability as a field general, but only a few gave him credit for his really masterful work in building up a team.[21]

Fred Lieb, in his history of the Orioles franchise, believed that this was a back-handed complement to Hanlon, and he wrote, "The inference must be that McGraw gave Hanlon full credit for gathering this remarkable caste together, but that his [McGraw's] nimble-witted hands...deserve large assists in the All-Time Baltimore box score for thinking up the plays which made the old Orioles immortal."[22]

There is no question that some family members of Hanlon, particularly his eldest daughter, Edwina, long resented McGraw and blamed him for grabbing the credit for the Orioles' success that prevented her father from being acknowledged by the Hall of Fame.[23]

Yet others testified that McGraw had given credit to Hanlon. Hans Lobert, a member of Hanlon's Reds, later played for McGraw, and he claimed that he "always gave Hanlon full credit for making a star out of him, as well as Hugh Jennings, Willie Keeler, Joe Kelley, and other famed Orioles."[24]

In December of 1914, in the midst of the war between the Federal League and the National and American Leagues, John McGraw and future Yankees owner Tillinghast Huston ran into Hanlon in New York, and they invited him to a dinner they were holding later that evening for some baseball men. Hanlon did not want to go because he knew the event would be attended by those who were now his "enemies," but McGraw and Huston finally persuaded the reluctant Hanlon to attend. McGraw rose during the dinner and spoke glowingly of Hanlon, and he also called up Hanlon's old Reds boss, Garry Herrmann, who paid Hanlon a "great compliment." Tim Murnane, who had known Hanlon before he ever played in the major leagues, spoke and "eulogized Hanlon as one of the greatest leaders of all time." Hanlon was visibly moved by the flattering testaments by his old colleagues.[25]

Whatever disagreements they had over the years, Hanlon and McGraw had a deep admiration and respect for one another that lasted as long as they lived. McGraw was Hanlon's favorite son, and Hanlon was the mentor and father-figure that McGraw secretly craved. McGraw's obsessive yearning to be the preeminent source of baseball knowledge may have indeed hindered Hanlon's election to the Hall.

But it was not purposeful. He could not help himself. He was simply built that way.

* * *

Thankfully, the controversy is now over. Ned Hanlon is in the Hall of Fame, where he rightfully belongs.

As a boy, he dreamed of an escape from the mills of Taftville, and as that dream came true, he became a living embodiment of someone who had achieved the American Dream. For many first-generation Irishmen, that dream was never realized, but Edward Hugh Hanlon was a man of remarkable drive and determination.

Ned Hanlon lived the life that he had imagined.

He was a baseball man through and through, and he made contributions to the game that go beyond a Hall of Fame managerial career. He inspired many of his players to follow in his footsteps and become managers, and as a result, he assembled what may be the most impressive coaching tree in the history of any sport. Connie Mack, John McGraw, Miller Huggins, Hughie Jennings, Wilbert Robinson, Kid Gleason, and Fielder Jones all went on to win pennants. In total, managers who played for Hanlon won 32 pennants and 12 World Series, and virtually every manager in the game today inhabits a branch of the Hanlon tree.

Moreover, many of Hanlon's players managed in the college ranks, but Princeton's Bill "Boileryard" Clarke was the most successful college coach of them all. When he was 90 years old, he told the story of how he first came to Princeton. He recalled how he broke his thumb in the 1897 season and was unable to play. Hanlon told him that Princeton University needed someone to help straighten out the infielders on the team. Clarke did not even know where Princeton was at the time, but he went there and came to love the school. He coached there for 36 years, compiled a 564–322 record, and his team made history when on May 17, 1939, they beat Columbia, 2–1, in the first televised baseball game. Clarke remains a Princeton icon to this day.[26]

During most of Hanlon's 19 years as a manager, he was part of the National League rules committee that made changes that help transform baseball into our modern game: the pitching rubber was moved from 50 feet to 60 feet, six inches, the infield fly rule was enacted, the height of the mound was limited to 15 inches above the basepaths, batters were awarded first base on interference, and the plate changed from a square to a five-sided figure.[27]

Hanlon was most proud that he was a main proponent for the rule change made in 1901 which decreed that the first two foul balls hit by a batter would count as strikes. He said, "The League never put a better rule on the books that the new definition of strikes....The rule ensures quick action and prevents the game from dragging over the two-hour limit."[28] The American League adopted this rule in 1903.

Not all of Hanlon's ideas regarding the rules were incorporated into the game during his time on the committee, but he pushed for rules that were ultimately adopted years later. He was a strong advocate for Sunday baseball, arguing that it was a "clean, honest, manly sport," and watching it was not a sin. Moreover, he maintained that playing ball on Sundays would make the game accessible for the average working man, who worked five-and-a-half or six days a week.[29] Hanlon also proposed a training school which umpires would be required to attend every spring. There they would be quizzed on the rules and coached in the practice of calling balls and strikes.[30]

Most importantly of all, perhaps, what made Ned Hanlon such an extraordinary baseball man was that he was a superb leader of men. His understanding of human nature was constantly referred to in the press coverage of his time. Tim Murnane said, "I know of just two men who could lead from the field or the bench. The first was Harry Wright and the other Edward Hanlon." Murnane also commented that one of Hanlon's greatest traits was his ability to make his players feel appreciated, and his concern for his players' feelings was the reason that he was never demeaned by the men who played for him.[31]

Through all the scrabbles he had with his players over salary and other issues, they were always able to emerge from the disputes with a strong bond of brotherhood that united them as fast friends until their deaths. Damon Runyon wrote, "It was said that

Late in his life in his Iowa home, pitcher Bill Hoffer is surrounded by memorabilia of his Orioles career (Babe Ruth Birthplace & Museum).

'The old Orioles, a fighting, swearing, swashbuckling crew, hold Hanlon in an esteem that approaches reverence.' Some of his pupils have gone beyond his highest fame and great success in baseball, yet as old men they still look up to the still older Hanlon."[32]

* * *

Connie Mack once said of Hanlon: "I think it's safe to say [he] knew more about baseball than any other man of his day. And he knew how to teach the game to young players. He talked it from morning until night, on the bench, on the field, in hotel lobbies, at meals, aboard trains. Players on his clubs heard nothing, ate nothing and dreamed nothing but baseball."[33]

From his youth to his dying day, Ned Hanlon loved baseball.

In 1996, with his election to the National Baseball Hall of Fame, baseball finally loved him back.

Appendix 1

Timeline of Hanlon's Life

Years	Hanlon and Baseball	Notable U.S. Events
1857–1879	1857 Ned Hanlon born 1869 Cincinnati Red Stockings tour country 1871 National Association of Professional Baseball Players formed 1876 National League formed; Ned Hanlon begins playing for pay for town teams	1860 Lincoln elected, seven states secede 1861 Fort Sumter fired upon, Civil War begins 1865 War ends, Lincoln assassinated 1871 Great Chicago Fire 1876 *Tom Sawyer* published 1876 Battle of Little Bighorn wipes out Custer's cavalry 1879 Edison develops first commercial light bulb
1880–1888	1880 Hanlon signs with National League (NL) Cleveland Blues. 1881 Hanlon signs with NL Detroit Wolverines 1887 Team captain Hanlon and Detroit Wolverines win NL pennant 1888–1889 Hanlon goes on Spalding World Tour	1880 U.S. population reaches 50 million 1881 Gunfight at OK Corral 1881 President Garfield assassinated 1883 Brooklyn Bridge opens 1886 American Federation of Labor (AFL) organized. 1886 Haymarket Riot in Chicago
1889–1892	1889 Hanlon signs with NL Pittsburgh Alleghenys 1890 Hanlon marries Ellen Jane Kelley Hanlon becomes player-manager of newly formed Players' League team in Pittsburgh 1891 After Players' League folds, Hanlon signs with NL Pittsburgh Pirates 1891 Edward, first child of Ned and Ellen Hanlon, born 1892 Hanlon signs as manager of Baltimore Orioles	1889 Oklahoma Land Rush 1889 South Dakota, North Dakota, Montana admitted to US 1889 Johnstown Flood in Pennsylvania 1890 Wyoming admitted to the US 1890 Idaho admitted to the United States 1890 Sherman Anti-Trust Act passed 1891 James Naismith invents basketball 1892 Nellie Bly begins 72-day around the world race
1893–1898	1893 Son Joseph born to Ned and Ellen 1894 Baltimore Orioles win first pennant 1895 Daughter Mary Edwina born to Ned and Ellen 1895 Orioles win second pennant 1896 Orioles win third straight pennant 1898 Daughter Helen born to Ned and Ellen	1893 Panic of 1893 1893 Grover Cleveland becomes President 1896 Utah admitted to the US 1896 Yukon Gold Rush in Alaska 1898 Greater New York formed *USS Maine* sunk, war with Spain

Appendix 1. Timeline of Hanlon's Life

1899–1909	1899 Hanlon wins first pennant in Brooklyn 1900 Hanlon wins second pennant with Brooklyn 1901 American League begins inaugural season 1903 Hanlon buys Eastern League Montreal team, moves them to Baltimore, and names them the Orioles 1905 Hanlon's last year with Brooklyn Superbas 1905 Hanlon hired to manage Cincinnati Reds 1907 Hanlon's last year with Cincinnati Reds	1901 President McKinley assassinated 1902 First Rose Bowl game 1903 Ford Motor companies founded; Wright Brothers successfully fly motor-powered plane 1904 Theodore Roosevelt elected president of the U.S. 1906 San Francisco earthquake 1907 Oklahoma admitted to the US 1909 Robert Peary arrives at the North Pole 1909 William Howard Taft becomes President
1910–1937	1910 Hanlon sells Eastern League Orioles to Jack Dunn 1914 Babe Ruth's rookie season with Boston Red Sox 1915 Hanlon helps establish Federal League 1916 Hanlon appointed to Baltimore Park Board 1918 Hanlon's son Joseph killed in France 1919 Black Sox Scandal—White Sox throw World Series 1920 Roy Chapman dies from being hit in the head by a pitch from Carl Mays 1927 Babe Ruth hits 60 home runs	1910 NAACP founded 1912 *Titanic* sinks; New Mexico, Arizona admitted to the U.S. 1915 U.S. population tops 100 million 1917 US enters World War I 1927 Lindbergh flies the Atlantic Ocean solo 1929 St. Valentine's Day Massacre 1929 Wall Street Crash 1931 *The Star-Spangled Banner* officially becomes national anthem 1932 Franklin Delano Roosevelt elected President

Appendix 2

Ned Hanlon Player and Manager Statistics

(See following page)

Appendix 2. Ned Hanlon Player and Manager Statistics

Player Stats

Year	Team	Lea.	G	PA	AB	R	H	2B	3B	HR	RBI	SB	BB	SO	BA	OBP	SLG	OPS
1880	CLV	NL	73	91	280	30	69	10	3	0	32		11	30	.246	.275	.304	.578
1881	DET	NL	76	327	305	63	85	14	8	2	28		22	11	.279	.327	.397	.724
1882	DET	NL	82	373	347	60	80	18	6	5	38		26	25	.231	.284	.360	.644
1883	DET	NL	100	447	413	65	100	13	2	1	40		34	44	.242	.300	.291	.590
1884	DET	NL	114	490	450	86	119	18	6	5	39		40	52	.264	.324	.364	.689
1885	DET	NL	105	471	424	93	128	18	8	1	29		47	18	.302	.372	.389	.761
1886	DET	NL	126	551	494	105	116	6	6	4	60	50	57	39	.235	.314	.296	.610
1887	DET	NL	118	503	471	79	129	13	7	4	69	69	30	24	.274	.320	.357	.677
1888	DET	NL	109	478	459	64	122	6	8	5	39	38	15	32	.266	.295	.346	.641
1889	PIT	NL	116	521	461	81	110	14	10	2	37	53	58	25	.239	.326	.325	.652
1890	PIT	PL	121	572	485	107	132	16	6	1	45	65	81	24	.272	.381	.336	.719
1891	PIT	NL	119	507	455	87	121	12	8	0	60	54	48	30	.266	.341	.327	.669
1892	BAL	NL	11	46	43	3	7	1	1	0	2	0	3	3	.163	.217	.233	.450
TOTAL	13 yr.		1270	5577	5087	931	1318	159	79	30	518	329	472	357	.259	.324	.339	.663

Ned Hanlon Player Stats
Compared To League Averages

Year	Team	LEA. BA	NED BA	LEA. OBP	NED OBP	LEA. OPS	NED OPS	NED OPS+
1880	Cleve	.245	**.246**	.267	**.275**	.587	.578	85
1881	Det	.260	**.279**	.290	**.327**	.628	**.724**	122
1882	Det	.251	.231	.279	**.284**	.622	**.644**	105
1883	Det	.262	.242	.290	**.300**	.650	.590	83
1884	Det	.247	**.264**	.287	**.324**	.626	**.689**	124
1885	Det	.241	**.302**	.284	**.372**	.606	**.761**	147
1886	Det	.257	.235	.300	**.314**	.641	.610	85
1887	Det	.269	**.274**	.326	.320	.707	.677	85
1888	Det	.239	**.266**	.285	**.295**	.609	**.641**	103
1889	Pitt	.266	.239	.335	.326	.696	.652	90
1890	Pitt	.254	**.272**	.329	**.383**	.671	**.719**	100
1891	Pitt	.252	**.266**	.325	**.341**	.667	**.669**	99

Ned Hanlon Managerial Statistics

Year	Team	Games	Wins	Losses	PCT.	Finish
1889	PIT	46	26	18	.555	5
1890	PIT (PL)	131	60	68	.458	6
1891	PIT	78	31	47	.397	8
1892	BAL	133	43	85	.323	10
1893	BAL	130	60	70	.462	8
1894	BAL	129	89	39	.690	1
1895	BAL	132	87	43	.659	1
1896	BAL	132	90	39	.682	1
1897	BAL	136	90	40	.662	2
1898	BAL	154	96	53	.623	2
1899	BRK	150	101	47	.673	1
1900	BRK	142	82	54	.577	1
1901	BRK	137	79	57	.577	3
1902	BRK	141	75	63	.532	2
1903	BRK	139	70	66	.504	5
1904	BRK	154	56	97	.364	6
1905	BRK	155	48	104	,310	8
1906	CIN	155	64	87	.413	6
1907	CIN	156	66	87	.423	6
TOTAL		2530	1313	1164	.519	

APPENDIX 3

Ned Hanlon Coaching Tree

Many other managers can be linked to Hanon's tree. These are just a few branches.

Ned Hanlon	John McGraw	Casey Stengel	Yogi Berra	Don Mattingly	
			Roger Craig	Bob Melvin	
				Bud Black	
			Ralph Houk	Bobby Cox	Cito Gaston
			Billy Martin	Lou Piniella	Kevin Cash
		Billy Southworth	Gene Mauch	Joe Maddon	
		Bill McKechnie	Charlie Grimm	Eddie Mathews	Dusty Baker
	Connie Mack	Paul Richards	Earl Weaver	Davey Johnson	Bob Brenly
				Frank Robinson	
				Johnny Oates	Buck Showalter
			Tony LaRussa	Jim Leyland	Craig Counsell
			Whitey Herzog		
			Dick Williams	Bruce Bochy	Dave Roberts
				Terry Francona	Gabe Kapler
	Miller Huggins	Leo Durocher	Eddie Stankey	Red Schoendienst	Joe Torre
			Bill Rigney	Buck Rodgers	
			Larry Dierker	Brad Ausmus	
			Alvin Dark	Felipe Alou	

This chart is adapted from ESPN writer Steve Wulf https://www.espn.in/mlb/story/_/id/13189997/the-mlb-manager-tree

APPENDIX 4

Major Baseball Rule Changes from Hanlon's Birth Through His Career

Adapted from baseball-almanac.com

1857	Instead of ending a game when a team scores 21 runs, the game now ends when after nine innings played.
1858	A batter is out on a batted ball, fair or foul, if caught on the fly or after one bounce. Called strikes are introduced.
1863	Pitcher's box is now 12 feet by 4 feet Called balls and bases on balls introduced The pitcher is no longer allowed to take a step during his delivery and he had to pitch with both feet on the ground at the same time.
1868	Pitcher allowed to lift feet when delivering the ball.
1870	The batter-runner may overrun first base
1871	The batter is officially given the privilege of calling for a low or high pitch (in practice since 1864).
1872	Ball size and weight are made smaller, to dimensions currently in use today.
1873	Batter's box introduced.
1877	The base runner was out if hit by a batted ball.
1878	The number of "called balls" became 9 and all balls were either strikes, balls or fouls.
1879	The pitcher had to face a batsman before pitching to him.
1880	Base on balls was reduced to 7 "called balls." Front of pitcher's box moved to 50 feet from the center of home plate.
1882	Pitchers now allowed to throw sidearm.
1883	Six "called balls" became a base on balls.
1884	All restrictions on the delivery of a pitcher were removed.
1885	One portion of the bat could be flat (one side). The pitcher's box was changed to 4 feet by 7 feet.
1886	Calling for high and low pitches was abolished. Five balls became a base on balls.
1887	The batter was awarded first base when hit by a pitch. Strike zone established between shoulders and knees.
1889	Four balls became a base on balls.

Appendix 4. Major Baseball Rule Changes During Hanlon's Career

Year	Rule Change
1893	The pitching box was eliminated and a rubber slab 12 inches by 4 inches was substituted. The slab was moved from 50 feet to 60 feet 6 inches from rear of home plate. The rule allowing a flat side to a bat was rescinded.
1894	Foul bunts were classified as strikes.
1895	Infield-fly rule was adopted.
1899	Batter awarded first on catcher's interference.
1900	Plate changed from square to five-sided figure.
1901	All foul balls not caught on fly counted as strikes until batter has two strikes. Catchers were compelled to remain continuously under the bat.
1903	Height of the mound was limited to 15 inches higher than the level of the baselines. Foul strike rule was adopted by the American League.

Chapter Notes

Introduction

1. Steve Wulf, "'Father of Modern Baseball' Ned Hanlon helped usher the game—and managing—into the 20th century," ESPN, July 2, 2015. https:// www.espn.com/mlb/story/_/id/ 13190522/father-modern-baseball-ned-hanlon-helped-usher-game-20th-century-greatest-contribution-was-mentor.

2. Fred Lieb letter from the personal files of Michael Reeve, grandson of Ned Hanlon.

Chapter 1

1. Burt Solomon, *Where They Ain't: The Fabled Life and Untimely Death of the Original Baltimore Orioles* (New York: The Free Press, 2000), 44.

2. Greg Rhodes, John Erardi, and Greg Gajus, *Baseball Revolutionaries: How the 1869 Red Stockings Rocked the Country and Made Baseball Famous* (Batavia, Ohio: Baseball Revolutionaries Press, 2019), 276.

3. *St. Louis Globe-Democrat*, January 21, 1906.

4. Sam Crane's story was printed in the *Norwich Bulletin* (Norwich, CT), August 8, 1910. Crane was a player in the National League and Union Association from 1880 through 1890, and he played in part of the 1885 and 1886 seasons with Hanlon in Detroit. He became one of the best-known sportswriters of his day, wrote for the *New York Evening Journal* for 25 years, and was known as "the dean of baseball writers."

5. *Sporting Life*, July 25, 1888.

6. Steve Wulf, "'Father of Modern Baseball' Ned Hanlon helped usher the game—and managing—into the 20th century," ESPN, July 2, 2015. https:// www.espn.com/mlb/story/_/id/ 13190522/father-modern-baseball-ned-hanlon-helped-usher-game-20th-century-greatest-contribution-was-mentor.

7. Harold and Dorothy Seymour, *Baseball: The Early Years* (Oxford: Oxford University Press, 1960), 108.

8. *Boston Globe*, May 2, 1880.

9. *Cincinnati Enquirer*, May 2, 1880. A foul ball caught on one bounce that year was an out.

10. *Boston Globe*, June 12, 1880.

11. Brian Martin, *The Detroit Wolverines: The Rise and Wreck of a National League Champion, 1881–1888* (Jefferson, NC: McFarland, 2018), 53.

12. *Detroit Free Press*, May 11, 1881.

13. Jack Smiles, *"EE-YAH": The Life and Times of Hughie Jennings, Baseball Hall of Famer* (Jefferson: NC, McFarland, 2005), 29.

14. *Detroit Free Press*, June 24, 1881.

15. Brian Martin, *The Detroit Wolverines*, 71.

16. *Detroit Free Press*, January 10, 1882.

17. Information about Jack Chapman from Brian Martin, *The Detroit Wolverines*, 80.

18. *Detroit Free Press*, April 8, 1883, cited in Brian Martin, *The Detroit Wolverines*, 83.

19. *Detroit Free Press*, July 2, 1883, cited in Brian Martin, *The Detroit Wolverines*, 86.

20. *Detroit Free Press*, August 11, 1883, cited in Brian Martin, *The Detroit Wolverines*, 87.

21. Brian Martin, *The Detroit Wolverines*, 88.

22. *Ibid.*, 91.

23. *Detroit Free Press*, May 16, 1884.

24. *Sporting Life*, June 4, 1884.

25. Brian Martin, *The Detroit Wolverines*, 95.

26. *Detroit Free Press*, October 15, 1884, cited in Brian Martin, *Detroit Wolverines*, 96. The typical working man at this time earned about $500 a year.

27. Brian Martin, *The Detroit Wolverines*, 99.

28. *Ibid.*, 98.

29. *Detroit Free Press*, June 6, 1885, cited in Brian Martin, *Detroit Wolverines*, 104.

30. Brian Martin, *The Detroit Wolverines*, 104–107.

31. *Detroit Free Press*, September 19, 1885. The salary list that was reported was quite steep: Brouthers made $4,000; Richardson, $4,000; White, $3,500; and Rowe, $3,500.

32. Brian Martin, *Detroit Wolverines*, 118–123.

33. *Morning Call* (Paterson, NJ), January 21, 1908.

34. *Sporting Life*, July 22, 1885.

35. *Sporting Life*, October 21, 1885.

36. *Sporting Life*, February 3, 1886.

37. *Sporting Life*, March 17, 1886.

38. *Ibid.*

39. *Sporting Life*, February 17, 1886. At this time, the captain of a team was more like a present-day manager during a game. He would call plays, make personnel decisions, and levy fines.

40. Brian Martin, *Detroit Wolverines*, 141–142.

41. *Philadelphia Times*, January 8, 1888.

42. Information about the game in Philadelphia and the players' tongue-lashing by the directors

and Hanlon's confrontation with Getzien paraphrased from Brian Martin, *Detroit Wolverines*, 144–145.

43. *Sporting Life*, September 15, 1886.
44. *Sporting Life*, September 29, 1886.
45. *Detroit Free Press*, January 17, 1887.
46. *Sporting Life*, February 16, 1887.
47. Brian Martin, *Detroit Wolverines*, 154.
48. *Sporting Life*, May 4, 1887.
49. *Sporting Life*, May 11, 1887.
50. Brian Martin, *Detroit Wolverines*, 159.
51. *Ibid.*, 160.
52. *Ibid.*, 162.
53. *Baltimore Sun*, October 21, 1887.
54. *Detroit Free Press*, November 10, 1887.
55. *Detroit Free Press*, December 5, 1887.
56. *Detroit Free Press*, December 31, 1887.
57. *Sporting Life*, January 11, 1888.
58. *Sporting Life*, April 11, 1888.
59. *Sporting Life*, January 25, 1888.
60. *Detroit Free Press*, March 20, 1888.
61. *Detroit Free Press*, March 8, 1888.
62. *Sporting Life*, April 11, 1888.
63. *Detroit Free Press*, April 9, 1888.
64. *Detroit Free Press*, April 11, 1888.
65. *Ibid.*
66. *Detroit Free Press*, April 28, 1888.
67. Account of the game in May paraphrased from *Detroit Free Press*, May 4, 1888.
68. Brian Martin, *The Detroit* Wolverines, 174.
69. *Ibid.*, 177.
70. *Sporting Life*, September 12, 1888.
71. *Detroit Free Press*, August 28, 1888.
72. Peter Morris, *A Game of Inches: The Story Behind the Innovations That Shaped Baseball* (Chicago: Ivan R. Dee, 2010), 187.
73. Steve Wulf, "'Father of Modern Baseball' Ned Hanlon helped usher the game—and managing—into the 20th century," ESPN, July 2, 2015, Accessed January 11, 2023, https://www.espn.com/mlb/story/_/id/13190522/father-modern-baseball-ned-hanlon-helped-usher-game-20th-century-greatest-contribution-was-mentor.
74. Fred Lieb. *The Baltimore Orioles: The History of a Colorful Team in Baltimore and St. Louis* (Carbondale: Southern Illinois University Press, 1955), 34.
75. *Henryetta Standard* (Henryetta, OK), June 13, 1912.
76. *Detroit Free Press*, October 10, 1888.

Chapter 2

1. Thomas W. Zeiler, *Ambassadors in Pinstripes: The Spalding World Baseball Tour and the Birth of the American Empire* (Lanham, MD: Rowman & Littlefield, 2006), 29.
2. John Thorn, "Above the Fruited Plain: A Timeline of Colorado Baseball (Mostly Denver)," *Our Game*, July 10, 2021, Accessed January 12, 2023, https://ourgame.mlblogs.com/above-the-fruited-plain-dee0850f6635.
3. Mark Lamster, *Spalding's World Tour: The Epic Adventure That Took Baseball Around the Globe—and Made it America's Game* (New York: Public Affairs, 2006), 169.
4. *Ibid.*, 171–172.
5. *Ibid.*, 183.
6. *Meriden Daily Republican* (Meriden, CT), February 3 and February 7, 1890.
7. All details and quotes about the players' night in Paris from Mark Lamster, *Spalding's World Tour*, 206–207.
8. All details and quotes in this paragraph from Mark Lamster, *Spalding's World Tour*, 223.
9. *Ibid.*, 223.
10. *Ibid.*, 235.
11. *St. Joseph Herald* (St. Joseph, MO), April 25, 1889.
12. Mark Lamster, *Spalding's World Tour*, 234–235.
13. *Ibid.*, 241.
14. Thomas W. Zeiler, *Ambassadors in Pinstripes*, 172–173.
15. Fred Lieb, *The Pittsburgh Pirates* (New York: G. P. Putnam's Sons, 1948), 15.
16. *Pittsburgh Dispatch*, August 18, 1889.
17. *Pittsburgh Press*, August 13, 1889, and salary amount from baseball-reference.com.
18. *Pittsburgh Dispatch*, October 16, 1889.
19. *Pittsburgh Dispatch*, October 31, 1889.
20. Robert B. Ross, *The Great Baseball Revolt: The Rise and Fall of the 1890 Players League* (Lincoln: University of Nebraska Press, 2016), 86.
21. Information about Players' League summarized from Robert B. Ross, *The Great Baseball Revolt*, 137, 140.
22. *Evening Star*, Washington (DC), January 1, 1906.
23. *Sporting Life*, November 1, 1890.
24. *Pittsburgh Dispatch*, October 30, 1889.
25. Robert B. Ross, *The Great Baseball Revolt*, 100.
26. *Pittsburgh Dispatch*, November 10, 1889.
27. Robert B. Ross, *The Great Baseball Revolt*, 101.
28. *Sporting Life*, November 6, 1889, cited in Robert B. Ross, *The Great Baseball Revolt*, 101.
29. *Sporting Life*, November 27, 1889.
30. Robert B. Ross, *The Great Baseball Revolt*, 102.
31. *Pittsburgh Dispatch*, December 21, 1899.
32. *Pittsburgh Dispatch* November 7, 1889.
33. Gordon J. Gattie, "The Legacy of the Players' League: 1890 Chicago Pirates." SABR. https://sabr.org/journal/article/the-legacy-of-the-players-league-1890-chicago-pirates/. Originally published as "The National Pastime: Baseball in Chicago," 2015.
34. Robert B. Ross, *The Great Baseball Revolt*, 155–157.
35. Gordon J. Gattie, "The Legacy of the Players' League."
36. *Pittsburgh Press*, August 17, 1890.
37. *Boston Globe*, July 25, 1890.
38. *Pittsburgh Press*, October 5, 1890.

39. Gordon J. Gattie, "The Legacy of the Players' League."
40. Ed Koszarek, *The Players League: History, Clubs, Ballplayers, and Statistics* (Jefferson, NC: McFarland, 2006), cited in Gattie, "The Legacy of the Players' League."
41. *Sporting Life*, November 22, 1890, cited in Robert B. Ross, *The Great Baseball Revolt*, 184. Boston's profit was $138.89. At least five of the eight clubs in the league were unable to pay salaries toward the end of the season. The National League lost about $234,000 in 1890.
42. *Sporting Life*, October 25, 1890.
43. John Thorn, *Baseball in the Garden of Eden: The Secret History of the Early Game* (New York: Simon & Schuster, 2011), 242.
44. *Sporting Life*, November 1, 1890.
45. *Ibid*.
46. *Ibid*.
47. Harold and Dorothy Seymour, *Baseball: The Early Years* (New York: Oxford University Press, 1960), 248, cited in John Thorn, *Baseball in the Garden of Eden*, 242.
48. *Sporting Life*, November 1, 1890.
49. *Sporting Life*, November 15, 1890.
50. Craig Britcher. "We are now Pirates: The 1890 Burghers and Alleghenys." *Western Pennsylvania History* (Spring 2014): 49.
51. *Sporting Life*, October 11, 1890.
52. *Sporting Life*, October 18, 1890.
53. *Pittsburgh Dispatch*, June 28, 1891.
54. *Pittsburgh Dispatch*, June 24, 1891.
55. *Ibid*.
56. *Pittsburgh Daily Post*, June 6, 1891.
57. *Ibid*.
58. *Pittsburgh Dispatch*, June 22, 1891.
59. *Pittsburgh Dispatch*, June 24, 1891.
60. *Ibid*.
61. *Ibid*.
62. *Pittsburgh Dispatch*, July 26, 1891.
63. *Ibid*.
64. *Pittsburgh Daily Post*, July 25, 1891.
65. *Pittsburgh Dispatch*, July 26, 1891.

Chapter 3

1. Ken Mars, *Baltimore Baseball: First Pitch to First Pennant, 1858–1894* (Parkville, MD: Old Frog Press, 2017), 140.
2. *Ibid*., 174.
3. *Ibid*., 178–179.
4. Burt Solomon, *Where They Ain't: The Fabled Life and Untimely Death of the Original Baltimore Orioles* (New York: The Free Press), 38–39.
5. Jack Kavanagh and Norman Macht, *Uncle Robbie* (Phoenix: Society for American Baseball Research, 2000), 11.
6. Burt Solomon, *Where They Ain't*, 40.
7. Ken Mars, *Baltimore Baseball*, 222.
8. *Ibid*., 229.
9. Burt Solomon, *Where They Ain't*, 47.
10. *Ibid*.
11. Alex Semchuck, "Wilbert Robinson," SABR Bio Project, https://sabr.org/bioproj/person/Wilbert-Robinson/.
12. *Ibid*.
13. John J. McGraw, *My Thirty Years in Baseball* (New York: Boni and Liveright, 1923), 76.
14. Burt Solomon, *Where They Ain't*, 48.
15. John J. McGraw, *My Thirty Years in Baseball*, 47–48.
16. Jack Smiles, "*EE-Yah!*": *The Life and Times of Hughie Jennings, Baseball Hall of Famer* (Jefferson, North Carolina: McFarland and Company, Inc., 2005), 41.
17. Burt Solomon, *Where They Ain't*, 48.
18. *Ibid*.
19. *Pittsburgh Dispatch*, May 1, 1892.
20. *Baltimore Sun*, May 26, 1891.
21. *Sporting Life*, July 21, 1900.
22. Bill Lamb, "George Van Haltren," SABR BioProject, Accessed December 1, 2022, https://www.baseball-reference.com/players/v/vanhage01.shtml.
23. Jack Smiles, "*EE-Yah!*" 29.
24. *Baltimore Sun*, May 6, 1892.
25. *Ibid*.
26. All information about the May 10 meeting from *Baltimore Sun*, May 10, 1892.
27. Charles C. Alexander, *John McGraw* (New York: Viking, 1988), 31.
28. *Baltimore Sun*, May 16, 1892.
29. *Baltimore Sun*, May 25, 1892.
30. Charles C. Alexander, *John McGraw*, 31.
31. John J. McGraw, *My Thirty Years in Baseball*, 57.
32. Fred Lieb, *The Baltimore Orioles: The History of a Colorful Team in Baltimore and St. Louis* (Carbondale: Southern Illinois University Press, 1955), 36.
33. Fred Lieb, *The Baltimore Orioles*, 36.
34. John J. McGraw, *My Thirty Years in Baseball*, 57.
35. *Baltimore Sun*, June 3, 1892.
36. *Baltimore Sun*, June 15, 1892.
37. *Baltimore Sun*, June 26, 1892.
38. *Baltimore Sun*, June 11, 1892.
39. *Baltimore Sun*, June 23, 1892.
40. *Baltimore Sun*, June 28, 1892.
41. *Baltimore Sun*, June 29, 1892.
42. *Baltimore Sun Magazine*, September 24, 1978.
43. *Evening Star* (Washington, DC), August 5, 1892.
44. *Baltimore Sun*, August 13, 1892.
45. *Baltimore Sun*, September 5, 1892.
46. *Baltimore Sun*, September 3, 1892.
47. *Ibid*.
48. *Baltimore Sun*, September 5, 1892.
49. *Baltimore Sun*, September 6, 1892.
50. *Pittsburgh Press*, September 18, 1892.
51. *Baltimore Sun*, September 19, 1892.
52. *Nebraska State Journal*, September 18, 1892.
53. *Pittsburgh Dispatch*, May 1, 1892.
54. *Sporting News*, September 24, 1892, cited in Charles C. Alexander, *John McGraw*, 29.

55. *Boston Globe*, September 22, 1892.
56. James H. Bready, *Baseball in Baltimore: The First Hundred Years* (Baltimore: The Johns Hopkins University Press, 1998), 16.
57. *Baltimore Sun*, September 30, 1892; Smiles, 33.
58. Burt Solomon, *Where They Ain't*, 49.
59. Jack Smiles, *"EE-Yah!"* 33.
60. Jimmy Keenan, "Joe Kelley," SABR Biography Project, Accessed August 20, 2022, https://sabr.org/ bioproj/person/Joe-Kelley/.
61. Burt Solomon, *Where They Ain't*, 50.
62. Fred Lieb, *The Baltimore* Orioles, 42.
63. Jack Smiles, *"EE-Yah!*, 33.

Chapter 4

1. Burt Solomon, *Where They Ain't: The Fabled Life and Untimely Death of the Original Baltimore Orioles* (New York: The Free Press), 52; Danny Long identified in Lyle Spatz, *Willie Keeler: From the Playgrounds of Brooklyn to the Hall of Fame* (New York: Rowman and Littlefield, 2015), 280.
2. *Boston Herald*, from unidentified date in Clarke file at National Baseball Hall of Fame library.
3. baseball-reference.com, BR Bullpen, "Heinie Reitz," Accessed January 17, 2023, https://www.baseball-reference.com/bullpen/Heinie_Reitz.
4. *Baltimore Sun*, February 4, 1893.
5. *Sporting Life*, March 25, 1893.
6. Ibid.
7. Ibid.
8. *Baltimore Sun*, May 1, 1893.
9. *Baltimore Sun*, February 12, 1893.
10. *Philadelphia Times*, March 19, 1893.
11. *Baltimore Sun*, March 15, 1893.
12. Mark Lamster, *Spalding's World Tour: The Epic Adventure That Took Baseball Around the Globe—and Made it America's Game* (New York: Public Affairs, 2006), 263–264.
13. Charles C. Alexander, *John McGraw* (New York: Viking, 1988), 34.
14. *Sporting Life*, March 18, 1893.
15. *Baltimore* Sun, March 22, 1893.
16. *Baltimore Sun*, March 18, 1893.
17. *Baltimore Sun*, April 19, 1893.
18. *Baltimore Sun*, April 18, 1893.
19. Burt Solomon, *Where They Ain't*, 50.
20. Ibid., 49.
21. *Sporting Life*, May 13, 1893.
22. Ibid.
23. *Baltimore Sun*, July 3, 1893.
24. Jimmy Keenan, "Bill Hawke," SABR Biography Project, February 17, 2022, https://sabr.org/bioproj/person/Bill-Hawke/
25. *Baltimore Sun*, May 17, 1893.
26. *Sporting Life*, May 27, 1893.
27. Fred Lieb. *The Baltimore Orioles: The History of a Colorful Team in Baltimore and St. Louis* (Carbondale: Southern Illinois University Press, 1955), 39.
28. *Baltimore Sun*, June 7, 1893.
29. Burt Solomon, *Where They Ain't*, 54.
30. *Baltimore Sun*, July 13, 1893.
31. At this time in baseball, players would man the coaching boxes and were called "coachers." Boileryard Clarke was a regular in the boxes for the 1890s Orioles.
32. *Sporting Life*, November 18, 1893.
33. *Sporting Life*, August 5, 1893.
34. *Sporting Life*, June 3, 1893.
35. *Sporting Life*, June 24, 1893.
36. In a 13-year career, Mullane compiled a record of 284–220.
37. *Sporting Life*, July 1, 1893.
38. *Baltimore Sun*, June 30, 1893.
39. Burt Solomon, *Where They Ain't*, 52.
40. *Sporting Life*, July 15, 1893.
41. *Baltimore Sun*, June 30, 1893.
42. *Baltimore Sun*, July 17, 1893.
43. *Sporting Life*, July 22, 1893.
44. *Baltimore Sun*, August 1, 1893.
45. *Baltimore Sun*, June 30, 1893.
46. *Baltimore Sun*, July 7, 1893.
47. Burt Solomon, *Where They Ain't*, 54.
48. *Sporting Life*, January 6, 1893.
49. Jack Kavanagh and Norman Macht, *Uncle Robbie* (Phoenix: Society for American Baseball Research, 2000), 25.
50. Burt Solomon, *Where They Ain't*, 54.
51. Jack Kavanagh and Norman Macht, *Uncle Robbie*, 25.
52. Fred Lieb, *The Baltimore Orioles*, 53.
53. John J. McGraw, *My Thirty Years in Baseball* (New York: Boni and Liveright, 1923), 25.
54. William Aiken, "Steve Brodie," SABR Biography Project. Accessed October 17, 2022, https://sabr.org/bioproj/person/Steve-Brodie/
55. *Sporting Life,* August.12, 1893.
56. *Sporting* Life, November 18, 1893.
57. *Sporting Life*, June 10, 1893.
58. Ibid.
59. *Sporting Life,* August 5, 1893.
60. Ibid.
61. *Sporting Life*, October 7, 1893.
62. *Sporting Life*, November 11, 1893.
63. *Sporting Life*, October 28, 1893.
64. *Sporting Life*, November 25, 1893.
65. *Sporting News*, December 30, 1893.
66. *Sporting Life*, January 6, 1894.
67. *Baltimore Sun*, December 30, 1893.
68. John J. McGraw, *My Thirty Years in Baseball*, 67.

Chapter 5

1. *Sporting Life*, March 31, 1894.
2. *Sporting Life*, January 13, 1894.
3. *Sporting Life*, February 3, 1894.
4. Ibid.
5. *Sporting Life*, February 10, 1894.
6. Ibid.
7. Ibid.
8. Ibid.
9. *Sporting Life*, February 17, 1894.

10. *Baltimore Sun,* March 13, 1894.
11. Charles C. Alexander, *John McGraw* (New York: Viking, 1988), 38.
12. *Baltimore Sun,* March 21, 1894.
13. Burt Solomon, *Where they Ain't: The Fabled Life and Untimely Death of the Original Baltimore Orioles, the Team That Gave Birth to Modern Baseball* (New York: The Free Press, 1999), 46.
14. *Sporting Life,* April 7, 1894.
15. *Sporting Life,* March 24, 1894.
16. Burt Solomon, *Where They Ain't,* 51–52.
17. *New York Morning Herald,* August 17, 1897, cited in Solomon, *Where They Ain't,* 56.
18. Burt Solomon, *Where They Ain't,* 55
19. Jack Smiles, *"EE-Yah!": The Life and Times of Hughie Jennings, Baseball Hall of Famer* (Jefferson, NC: McFarland, 2005), 49.
20. Charles Alexander, *John McGraw,* 40.
21. *Baltimore Evening Sun,* March 31, 1954.
22. *Sporting News,* April 6, 1968, cited in Peter Morris, *A Game of Inches: The Story Behind the Innovations That Shaped Baseball* (Chicago: Ivan R. Dee, 2010), 1.
23. Peter Morris, *A Game of Inches,* 2.
24. *Chicago Tribune,* July 6, 1870, cited in Peter Morris, *A Game of Inches,* 43.
25. Fred Lieb, *The Baltimore Orioles: The History of a Colorful Team in Baltimore and St. Louis* (Carbondale: Southern Illinois University Press, 1955), 46.
26. Fred Lieb, *The Baltimore Orioles,* 46.
27. James Bready, *The Home Team* (Baltimore: Baltimore Orioles, 1985), 25.
28. Charles Alexander, *John McGraw,* 40.
29. James Bready, *The Home Team,* 17. Hanlon's biography page at the National Baseball Hall of Fame website states that Hanlon was one of the first to use platooning.
30. *Baltimore Evening Sun,* March 31, 1954.
31. *Sporting Life,* October 14, 1893.
32. *Sporting Life,* October 28, 1893. The word "cranks" was a word for "fans" at that time.
33. Burt Solomon, *Where They Ain't,* 59.
34. *Baltimore Sun,* April 4, 1894, and Burt Solomon, *Where They Ain't,* 59.
35. Until 1901, a foul ball with less than two strikes was not counted as a strike. This allowed batters who were expert at fouling off balls, like John McGraw, to wear down a pitcher and wait for the right pitch to hit. In 1901, the National League began counting all fouls as strikes. The American League followed suit it 1903.
36. Fred Lieb, *The Baltimore Orioles,* 36–37, 46; Burt Solomon *Where They Ain't,* 59.
37. Bill Felber, *A Game of Brawl: The Orioles, the Beaneaters & the Battle for the 1897 Pennant* (Lincoln: University of Nebraska Press, 2007), 11.
38. Burt Solomon, *Where They Ain't,* 59.
39. *Ibid.*
40. *Sporting Life,* July 5, 1902.
41. *Baltimore Evening Sun,* March 31, 1954.
42. *Baltimore Sun,* April 7, 1894.
43. Charles C. Alexander, *John McGraw,* 38.
44. Jack Kavanagh and Norman Macht, *Uncle Robbie* (Phoenix: Society for American Baseball Research, 2000), 13–14.
45. Mike Klingaman, "A Team of Stars and Grit," *Baltimore Sun,* July 7, 1996.
46. *Sporting Life,* April 7, 1894, cited in Solomon, 60.
47. Mike Klingaman, "A Team of Stars and Grit."
48. *Washington Times,* August 14, 1904.
49. Charles C. Alexander, *John McGraw,* 38.
50. James Bready, *The Home Team,* 17.
51. John J. McGraw, *My Thirty Years in Baseball* (New York: Boni and Liveright, 1923), 69.
52. Jack Kavanagh and Norman Macht, *Uncle Robbie,* 60.
53. Burt Solomon, *Where They Ain't,* 60.
54. Charles C. Alexander, *John McGraw,* 39.
55. John J. McGraw, *My Thirty Years in Baseball,* 68.
56. *Ibid.,* 60–61.
57. Jack Kavanagh and Norman Macht, *Uncle Robbie,* 17–18.
58. Peter Morris, *A Game of Inches,* 391.
59. *Chicago Tribune,* August 5, 1906 cited in Peter Morris, *A Game of Inches,* 391.
60. Peter Morris, *A Game of Inches,* 391.
61. Fred Lieb, *The Baltimore Orioles,* 52.
62. *Boston Globe,* March 27, 1918.
63. *Baltimore Sun,* January 22, 1911.
64. Jack Kavanagh and Norman Macht, *Uncle Robbie,* 22.
65. Fred Lieb, *The Baltimore Orioles,* 51–52.
66. *Baltimore Sun,* July 11, 1948.
67. Mike Klingaman, "A Team of Stars and Grit."
68. Jack Kavanagh and Norman Macht, *Uncle Robbie,* 18.
69. *Sporting News* June 30, 1894.
70. Harold and Dorothy Seymour, *Baseball: The Early Years* (Oxford: Oxford University Press, 1960), 290.
71. *Cincinnati Enquirer,* May 30, 1897.
72. Jack Kavanagh and Norman Macht, *Uncle Robbie,* 25.
73. Harold and Dorothy Seymour, *Baseball: The Early Years,* 290.
74. *Chicago Tribune,* September 26, 1886, cited in Peter Morris, *A Game of Inches,* 35.
75. Bill James, *The New Bill James Historical Baseball Abstract* (New York: Free Press, 2001), 52, cited in Brian Flaspohler, "Patsy Tebeau," SABR Biography Project, Accessed January 22, 2023, https://sabr.org/bioproj/person/patsy-tebeau/.
76. *The Buffalo Times,* March 1895.
77. Mike Klingaman, "'Foxy' Hanlon Was Sly But Successful," *Baltimore Sun,* July 8, 1996.
78. John J. McGraw, *My Thirty Years in Baseball,* 68.

Chapter 6

1. *Baltimore Sun,* April 2, 1894.
2. *Baltimore Sun,* April 5, 1894.

3. Hughie Jennings, "Rounding Third," *Star-Gazette* (Elmira, NY), January 13, 1926, cited in Solomon, 58.
4. *Baltimore Sun*, April 14, 1894.
5. Solomon, *Where they Ain't*, 60.
6. *Sporting Life,* April 14, 1894.
7. Charles C. Alexander, *John McGraw* (New York: Viking, 1988), 39.
8. *Baltimore Sun*, April 5, 1894.
9. Burt Solomon, *Where They Ain't*, 61.
10. *Baltimore Sun*, April 4, 1894.
11. *Ibid.*
12. Blanche McGraw, edited by Arthur Mann, *The Real McGraw* (New York: David McKay, 1953), 11.
13. *Baltimore Sun*, April 4, 1894.
14. *Sunday Herald* (Baltimore), April 8, 1894, cited in Solomon, *Where They Ain't*, 62.
15. *Sporting Life*, March 17, 1894.
16. *Baltimore Sun*, April 14, 1894.
17. *Ibid.*
18. Solomon, *Where They Ain't*, 64.
19. Details of the Opening Day Parade, game, etc., can be found in numerous sources, including *Evening World* (New York), April 19, 1894, *Baltimore Sun*, April 20, 1894, and Solomon, 64–67.
20. *Baltimore Sun*, April 20, 1894.
21. Fred Lieb, *The Baltimore Orioles: The History of a Colorful Team in Baltimore and St. Louis* (Carbondale: Southern Illinois University Press, 1955), 48–49.
22. *Sporting Life*, April 28, 1894.
23. *Ibid.*
24. John J. McGraw, *My Thirty Years in Baseball* (New York: Boni and Liveright, 1923), 70–71.
25. Solomon, *Where They Ain't*, 70.
26. Jimmy Keenan, "Bill Hawke," SABR BioProject, Accessed January 19, 2023, https://sabr.org/bioproj/person/Bill-Hawke/
27. *Baltimore Sun,* May 16, 1894.
28. *Sporting Life*, July 28, 1894, and October 6, 1894.
29. *Sporting Life*, September 15, 1894. "Cranks" was a 19th-century word for "fans."
30. *Sporting Life*, September 22, 1894.
31. *Sporting Life*, June 16, 1894.
32. *Sporting Life,* July 7, 1894.
33. The game was played here while the South End Grounds were being rebuilt after a fire that destroyed it earlier during a May 15 game against the Orioles.
34. *Baltimore Sun*, June 19, 1894.
35. *Baltimore Sun*, June 26, 1894.
36. *Baltimore Sun*, June 29, 1894.
37. *Baltimore Sun*, July 3, 1894.
38. *Baltimore* Sun, July 11, 1894.
39. *Ibid.*
40. *Baltimore Sun*, July 4, 1894.
41. *Baltimore Sun*, July 16, 1894.
42. Burt Solomon, *Where They Ain't*, 78.
43. *Ibid.*, 80.
44. Jack Smiles, *"EE-Yah!": The Life and Times of Hughie Jennings, Baseball Hall of Famer* (Jefferson, NC: McFarland, 2005), 52
45. *Washington Post,* September 26, 1894.
46. Jack Smiles, *"EE-Yah!,* 52.
47. The description and quotes about the Orioles' journey home after winning the pennant, the parade, and the dinner at the Rennert Hotel can be found in Burt Solomon, *Where They Ain't* 81–83 and the *Baltimore Sun*, October 3, 1894. Some information is found in both sources.
48. *Baltimore* Sun, October 4, 1894.
49. *Sporting Life,* October 13, 1894.
50. Burt Solomon, *Where They Ain't*, 84.
51. *Sporting Life*, October 20, 1894.
52. *Sporting Life*, October 6, 1894.
53. Jerry Lansche, *Glory Fades Away: The Nineteenth-Century World Series Rediscovered* (Dallas: Taylor, 1991), 241.
54. *Baltimore Sun*, October 5, 1894.
55. *Ibid.*
56. Burt Solomon, *Where They Ain't*, 84–85.
57. *Baltimore* Sun, October 5, 1894.
58. *Ibid.*
59. Burt Solomon, *Where They Ain't*, 82–86.
60. *Sporting Life,* October 13, 1893.
61. *Sporting Life*, September 29, 1894.
62. *Sporting Life*, December 22, 1894.
63. *Sporting Life*, October 6, 1894.
64. *Sporting Life*, October 20, 1894.
65. *Sporting Life*, September 22, 1894.
66. *Ibid.*
67. *Ibid.*
68. *Sporting Life*, November 3, 1895, and *Sporting Life*, November 24, 1894.
69. *Sporting Life*, September 1, 1894.
70. *Sporting Life*, November 3, 1894.
71. *Sporting Life*, November 17, 1894.
72. *Sporting Life*, September 15, 1894.
73. *Baltimore Sun*, November 16, 1894.

Chapter 7

1. Description of fire from *Baltimore Sun*, January 15, 1895.
2. Burt Solomon, *Where they Ain't: The Fabled Life and Untimely Death of the Original Baltimore Orioles, the Team That Gave Birth to Modern Baseball* (New York: The Free Press, 1999), 87–88.
3. *Sporting Life*, March 9, 1895.
4. *Baltimore Sun,* March 2, 1895.
5. Jimmy Keenan, "Bill Hawke," SABR BioProject, Accessed November 12, 2022, https://sabr.org/bioproj/person/Bill-Hawke/
6. *Baltimore Sun*, March 2, 1895.
7. Burt Solomon, *Where They Ain't*, 89.
8. *Baltimore Sun*, March 6, 1895.
9. *Sporting Life*, March 9, 1895.
10. *Baltimore Sun*, March 6, 1895.
11. *Baltimore Morning Herald*, February 10, 1895, cited in Burt Solomon, *Where They Ain't*, 90.
12. *Baltimore Sun*, March 11, 1895.
13. Burt Solomon, *Where They Ain't*, 90.
14. *Baltimore Sun*, January 29, 1895.
15. *Baltimore Sun*, January 18, 1895.
16. *Baltimore Sun*, November 17, 1894.

17. *Baltimore Sun*, March 13, 1895.
18. *Baltimore Sun*, March 18, 1895.
19. *Baltimore Sun*, March 20, 1895.
20. *Baltimore Sun*, March 15, 1895.
21. *Ibid*.
22. *Baltimore Sun*, March 18, 1895.
23. *Baltimore Sun*, March 13, 1895.
24. *Baltimore Sun*, March 14, 1895.
25. *Baltimore Sun*, March 20, 1895.
26. Description of disrespectful treatment of Hanlon and quote identifying contract disputes as cause for it from *Baltimore Sun*, March 22, 1895.
27. *Sporting Life*, March 30, 1895.
28. *Sporting Life*, April 6, 1895.
29. *Baltimore Sun*, April 1, 1895.
30. *Baltimore Sun*, April 11, 1895.
31. *Pittsburgh Press*, April 1, 1895.
32. *Baltimore Sun*, March 11, 1895.
33. *Sporting Life*, March 16, 1895.
34. *Baltimore Sun*, March 28, 1895.
35. Charles C. Alexander, *John McGraw* (New York: Viking, 1988), 45.
36. *Ibid*.
37. *Sporting Life*, May 25, 1895.
38. *Sporting Life*, July 20, 1895.
39. *Baltimore Sun*, June 28, 1895.
40. *Sporting Life*, June 1, 1895.
41. *Baltimore Sun*, May 22, 1895.
42. *Baltimore Sun*, July 8, 1894.
43. *Sporting Life*, July 20, 1895.
44. *Sporting Life*, May 11, 1895.
45. *Baltimore Sun*, July 8, 1894.
46. *Baltimore Sun*, July 11, 1895.
47. *Sporting Life*, July 27, 1895.
48. *Sporting Life*, May 11, 1895.
49. Lyle Spatz, *Willie Keeler: From the Playgrounds of Brooklyn to the Hall of Fame* (New York: Rowman and Littlefield, 2015), 65.
50. *Baltimore Sun*, June 12, 1895.
51. *Baltimore Sun*, July 19, 1895.
52. *Sporting Life*, July 20, 1895.
53. *Chicago Tribune*, July 3, 1895.
54. *Baltimore Sun*, July 13, 1895.
55. *Sporting Life*, July 20, 1895.
56. *Baltimore Sun*, July 19, 1895, cited in Lyle Spatz, *Willie Keeler*, 65.
57. *Baltimore Sun*, July 26, 1895.
58. *Baltimore Sun*, May 11, 1895.
59. *Baltimore Sun*, July 27, 1895.
60. *Baltimore Sun*, July 11, 1948, cited in Burt Solomon, *Where They Ain't*, 97.
61. Jerry Lansche, *Glory Fades Away: The Nineteenth-Century World Series Rediscovered* (Dallas: Taylor, 1991), 257.
62. *Sporting Life*, September 21, 1895.
63. *Sporting Life*, September 28, 1895.
64. *Baltimore Sun*, September 30, 1895.
65. *Ibid*.
66. Reporter's account of the Orioles' group on the boat ride from *Sporting Life*, September 28, 1895.
67. *Sporting Life*, August 17, 1895.
68. Jerry Lansche, *Glory Fades Away*, 262.
69. *Ibid*., 267.
70. *Ibid*., 269.
71. Details from Academy of Music celebration from *Sporting Life*, October 12, 1895.
72. *The Gazette* (York, PA), July 8, 1895.
73. *Sporting Life*, August 3, 1895.
74. *Sporting Life*, November 23, 1895.
75. *Baltimore Sun*, November 18, 1895.
76. *Sporting Life*, November 23, 1895.
77. *Baltimore Sun*, November 18, 1895.
78. All interview material from the *Boston Globe* reprinted in *Record-Journal* (Meridian, CT), September 19, 1895.
79. *Sporting Life*, November 2, 1895.

Chapter 8

1. *Sporting Life*, February 1, 1896.
2. *Sporting Life*, January 18, 1896.
3. *Baltimore Sun*, January 22, 1896.
4. *Boston Globe*, January 26, 1896.
5. *Baltimore Sun*, January 22, 1896.
6. *Buffalo Enquirer*, November 30, 1895.
7. *Baltimore Sun*, February 8, 1896.
8. *Baltimore Sun*, January 4, 1896.
9. *Baltimore Morning Herald*, January 26, 1896, cited in Burt Solomon, *Where They Ain't: The Fabled Life and Untimely Death of the Original Baltimore Orioles, the Team That Gave Birth to Modern Baseball* (New York: The Free Press, 1999), 101.
10. *Baltimore Sun*, November 18, 1895.
11. *Baltimore Sun*, January 4, 1896.
12. Charles C. Alexander, *John McGraw* (New York: Viking, 1988), 48.
13. *Sporting Life*, February 15, 1896.
14. *Baltimore Sun*, February 11, 1896.
15. *Baltimore Sun*, March 21, 1896.
16. *Baltimore Sun*, March 19, 1896.
17. *Baltimore Sun*, March 18, 1896.
18. *Sporting Life*, March 28, 1896.
19. *Baltimore Sun*, March 21, 1896.
20. *Baltimore Sun*, March 18, 1896.
21. *Sporting Life*, March 28, 1896.
22. *Baltimore Sun*, March 30, 1896.
23. *Sporting Life*, April 18, 1896.
24. *Sporting Life*, March 28, 1896.
25. *Sporting Life*, April 4, 1896.
26. *Baltimore Sun*, March 21, 1896.
27. *Baltimore Sun*, March 26, 1896.
28. *Baltimore Sun*, February 10, 1896.
29. Burt Solomon, *Where They Ain't*, 101.
30. *Baltimore Sun*, April 6, 1896.
31. Details of the Petersburg incident from *Baltimore Sun*, April 9, 1896; *Baltimore Morning Herald*, April 10, 1896; Burt Solomon, *Where They Ain't*, 102.
32. *Sporting Life*, April 11, 1896.
33. *Baltimore Sun*, April 16, 1896.
34. *Baltimore Sun*, March 12, 1896.
35. *Baltimore Sun*, March 10, 1896.
36. *Sporting Life*, April 18, 1896.
37. *Sporting Life*, May 16, 1896.
38. *Baltimore Sun*, June 27, 1896.

39. Harold and Dorothy Seymour, *Baseball: The Early Years* (Oxford: Oxford University Press, 1960), 271. Also in Blanche McGraw, edited by Arthur Mann, *The Real McGraw* (New York: David McKay, 1953), 102.
40. *Sporting Life*, July 4, 1896.
41. *Baltimore Sun*, July 15, 1896.
42. Burt Solomon, *Where They Ain't*, 105–106.
43. Rochelle Nicholls, "Joe Quinn," SABR Biography Project, Accessed February 3, 2023, https://sabr.org/bioproj/person/Joe-Quinn/.
44. *Baltimore Sun*, August 6, 1896.
45. *Baltimore Sun*, October 1, 1896.
46. Burt Solomon, *Where They Ain't*, 108.
47. Jerry Lansche, *Glory Fades Away: The Nineteenth-Century World Series Rediscovered* (Dallas: Taylor, 1991), 278.
48. Ibid., 277.
49. Burt Solomon, *Where They Ain't*, 110.
50. Jerry Lansche, *Glory Fades Away*, 283.
51. *Baltimore Sun*, October 10, 1896.
52. *Sporting Life*, September 12, 1896.
53. Ibid.
54. *Baltimore Sun*, October 17, 1896.
55. Howard W. Rosenberg, *Cap Anson 3: Muggsy John McGraw and the Tricksters: Baseball's Fun Age of Rule Bending* (New York: Tile Books, 2005), 149.
56. *Sporting Life*, September 26, 1896.
57. Ibid.
58. *Sporting Life*, October 24, 1896.
59. *Sporting Life*, October 3, 1896.
60. *Baltimore Sun*, October 8, 1896.
61. *Baltimore Sun*, November 9, 1896.
62. Charles C. Alexander, *John McGraw*, 53.
63. *Sporting Life*, September 5, 1896.
64. *Baltimore Sun*, November 12, 1896.
65. *Sporting Life*, November 21, 1896.
66. *Sporting Life*, December 19, 1896.
67. *Sporting Life*, November 21, 1896.
68. *Baltimore Sun*, December 14, 1896.
69. *Sporting Life*, November 14, 1896.
70. *Sporting Life*, November 21, 1896.
71. *Baltimore Sun*, December 12, 1896.
72. *Baltimore Sun*, December 16, 1896.
73. *Baltimore Sun*, December 29, 1896.

Chapter 9

1. The description of the banquet can be found in *Baltimore Sun*, February 27, 1897, and *Sporting Life*, March 6, 1897.
2. *Baltimore Sun*, April 24, 1897.
3. *Baltimore Sun*, June 9, 1897; *Baltimore Sun*, September 21, 1897.
4. *Sporting Life*, April 3, 1897.
5. *Baltimore Sun*, January 26, 1897.
6. *Sporting Life*, March 13, 1897.
7. *Baltimore Sun*, March 8, 1897.
8. *Boston Globe*, April 24, 1897, cited in Bill Felber, *A Game of Brawl: The Orioles, the Beaneaters & the Battle for the 1897 Pennant* (Lincoln: University of Nebraska Press, 2007), 74–75.
9. *Sporting Life*, March 13, 1897.
10. *Sporting Life*, April 3, 1897.
11. *Baltimore Sun*, March 19, 1897.
12. Charles C. Alexander, *John McGraw* (New York: Viking, 1988), 53.
13. *Baltimore Sun*, March 19, 1897.
14. *Baltimore Sun*, April 12, 1897.
15. *Baltimore Sun*, April 19, 1897.
16. Description of the procession of the teams to Union Park from Bill Felber, *A Game of Brawl*, 73.
17. *Baltimore Sun*, April 29, 1897.
18. *Baltimore Sun*, May 22, 1897.
19. Ibid.
20. *Baltimore Sun*, May 26, 1897.
21. *Sporting News*, September 4, 1897, cited in Charles C. Alexander, *John McGraw*, 55.
22. *Sporting Life*, September 11, 1897.
23. *Baltimore Sun*, May 19, 1897.
24. *Baltimore Sun*, May 28, 1897.
25. *Sporting Life*, May 29, 1897.
26. *Baltimore Sun*, July 6, 1897.
27. The description of the team meeting was in *Baltimore Sun*, July 10, 1897.
28. Ibid.
29. *Sporting Life*, August 21, 1897.
30. *Sporting Life*, May 1, 1897.
31. *Sporting Life*, July 10, 1897; *Baltimore Sun*, September 13, 1897; *Sporting Life*, May 22, 1897; *Sporting Life*, July 10, 1897.
32. *Baltimore Sun*, September 13, 1897.
33. *Sporting Life*, September 4, 1897.
34. Burt Solomon, *Where they Ain't: The Fabled Life and Untimely Death of the Original Baltimore Orioles, the Team That Gave Birth to Modern Baseball* (New York: The Free Press, 1999), 123.
35. Hanlon questioning Corbett's heart from Burt Solomon, *Where They Ain't*, 122.
36. Bill Felber, *A Game of Brawl*, 245.
37. *Sporting Life*, November 20, 1897.
38. Charles C. Alexander, *John McGraw*, 55–56.
39. Jerry Lansche, *Glory Fades Away: The Nineteenth-Century World Series Rediscovered* (Dallas: Taylor, 1991), 304–306.
40. *Baltimore Sun*, October 12, 1897.
41. Alexander, *John McGraw*, 56.
42. Kid Nichols was in a class above the Orioles' pitchers, or any of the Boston pitchers for that matter. He was elected to the Hall of Fame with 361 wins in his career, seventh-highest of all pitchers, and 116.7 WAR, the fourth-highest.
43. Charles C. Alexander, *John McGraw*, 54.
44. Incident between McGraw and Doyle reported in numerous sources, including Charles C. Alexander, *John McGraw*, 54; Burt Solomon, *Where They Ain't*, 119; *Baltimore Sun*, July 8, 1897.
45. Charles C. Alexander, *John McGraw*, 54.
46. Burt Solomon, *Where They Ain't*, 119.
47. This incident between Keeler and McGraw can be found in numerous sources, including Burt Solomon, *Where They Ain't*, 119–120; Charles C. Alexander, *John McGraw*, 54; *Sporting News*, February 3, 1899. It is the belief of Burt Solomon that McGraw took a special pleasure in picking on Keeler.

48. *Sporting News*, February 3, 1899, cited in Charles C. Alexander, *John McGraw*, 54.
49. *Sporting News*, February 11, 1899.
50. *Detroit Free Press*, September 22, 1940.
51. *Sporting News*, November 22, 1902, cited in Mike Lackey, *Spitballing: The Baseball Days of Long Bob Ewing*. (Wilmington, OH: Orange Frazier Press, 2013), 77.
52. *Baltimore Sun*, August 10, 1897.
53. This was Doyle's account in an interview with the *Baltimore Morning Herald*, May 25, 1899, cited in Burt Solomon, *Where They Ain't*, 119.
54. *Baltimore Sun*, August 10, 1897.
55. Bill Felber, *A Game of Brawl*, 181.
56. *Sporting Life*, August 14, 1897.
57. *Baltimore Sun*, August 10, 1897.
58. *Sporting Life*, August 21, 1897, cited in Felber, *A Game of Brawl*, 179.
59. *Sporting Life*, September 4, 1897.
60. *Baltimore Sun*, September 8, 1897.
61. *Sporting Life*, October 16, 1897.
62. *Baltimore Sun*, December 1, 1897.
63. *Sporting Life*, December 18, 1897.
64. *Baltimore Sun*, December 9, 1897.
65. Ibid.
66. *Baltimore Sun*, December 11, 1897.
67. *Sporting Life*, December 25, 1897.
68. Ibid.
69. *Sporting Life*, November 27, 1897.
70. *Baltimore Sun*, October 19, 1897.
71. *Sporting Life*, August 21, 1897.
72. *Baltimore Sun*, November 12, 1897.
73. *Sporting Life*, October 9, 1897, reported that he was offered $12,000 and a one-quarter interest in the Pirates.
74. *Philadelphia Evening Item*, cited in Jerrold Casway, *Ed Delahanty in the Emerald Age of Baseball* (Notre Dame: University of Notre Dame, 2004), 139.
75. *Baltimore Sun*, August 24, 1897.
76. *Sporting Life*, September 11, 1897.
77. *Baltimore Sun*, December 27, 1897.
78. The Orioles in 1894 (.695), the Orioles in 1896 (.698), and the Beaneaters in 1897 (.705) were the three teams.
79. *Sporting Life*, October 9, 1897.

Chapter 10

1. *Sporting Life*, January 15, 1898.
2. *Sporting Life*, February 19, 1898.
3. *Baltimore Sun*, February 25, 1898.
4. *Sporting Life*, February 19, 1898.
5. *Baltimore Sun*, January 10, 1898.
6. Ibid.
7. *Sporting Life*, February 19, 1898.
8. *Sporting Life*, May 7, 1898.
9. *Baltimore Sun*, March 2, 1898, cited in Charles C. Alexander, *John McGraw* (New York: Viking, 1988), 58.
10. *Baltimore Sun*, March 2, 1898.
11. *Baltimore Sun*, March 7, 1898.
12. *Baltimore Sun*, March 11, 1898.
13. *Baltimore Sun*, March 14, 1898.
14. *Sporting Life*, January 22, 1898.
15. *Sporting Life*, February 5, 1898.
16. *Baltimore Sun*, April 4, 1898.
17. *Baltimore Sun*, March 17, 1898.
18. *Sporting Life*, March 26, 1898.
19. *Baltimore Sun*, March 17, 1898.
20. Description of Hanlon's angst with the holdouts, particularly Kelley, and his explanation regarding what he thought was exceptionally good treatment of the players by Orioles management is from *Baltimore Sun*, March 12, 1898.
21. *Sporting Life*, April 2, 1898.
22. *Sporting Life*, March 26, 1898.
23. *Baltimore Sun*, March 16, 1898.
24. *Baltimore Sun*, March 23, 1898.
25. *Sporting Life*, March 26, 1898.
26. *Baltimore Sun*, March 28, 1898.
27. *Baltimore Sun*, April 4, 1898.
28. *Chicago Tribune*, April 4, 1898.
29. Jack Smiles, *"EE-Yah!": The Life and Times of Hughie Jennings, Baseball Hall of Famer* (Jefferson, NC: McFarland, 2005), 85.
30. *Baltimore Sun*, May 7, 1898.
31. *Sporting Life*, April 23, 1898.
32. *Daily Oklahoman* (Oklahoma City), April 10, 1898.
33. *Sporting Life*, January 15, 1898. The *Baltimore Sun* (March 11, 1898) reported that the new bleachers would be "larger, stronger, more comfortable than the old," and that the lowest row, previously at ground level, would be eight or ten feet above the ground to allow for better viewing angles. The seating was also wider at 19 inches and provided foot rests. They would allow for 200 more seats, bringing the capacity of the bleachers close to 4,000.
34. *Baltimore Sun*, April 7, 1898.
35. *Baltimore Sun*, April 18, 1898.
36. Jack Smiles, *"EE-Yah!": The Life and Times of Hughie Jennings*, 86.
37. Attendance totals from baseball-reference.com.
38. *Baltimore Sun*, April 19, 1898.
39. *Sporting Life*, May 7, 1898.
40. *Baltimore Sun*, May 6, 1898.
41. *Baltimore Sun*, May 7, 1898.
42. *Baltimore Sun*, May 31, 1898.
43. *Sporting Life*, May 28, 1898.
44. *Baltimore Sun*, June 9, 1898.
45. *Baltimore Sun* May 16, 1898.
46. *Sporting Life*, June 18, 1898.
47. *Sporting Life*, June 25, 1898.
48. *Sporting Life*, May 21, 1898.
49. *Sporting Life*, August 20, 1898.
50. *Baltimore Sun*, July 8, 1898.
51. *Sporting Life*, July 23, 1898.
52. All quotes and details from the July 25 game against the Giants from William Lamb, "July 25, 1898: The Ducky Holmes Game," in *Inventing Baseball: The 100 Greatest Games of the Nineteenth Century*, ed. Bill Felber (Phoenix: Society for American Baseball Research, 2013), 268–269.

53. *Baltimore Sun*, July 28, 1898.
54. *Baltimore Sun*, July 27, 1898.
55. *Baltimore Sun*, August 1, 1898.
56. *Sporting Life*, August 6, 1898.
57. Details from August 15 board meeting and reaction to their decisions from *Sporting Life*, August 20, 1898.
58. *Sporting Life*, August 6, 1898.
59. *Ibid.*
60. *Sporting Life*, August 27, 1898.
61. *Ibid.*
62. *Sporting Life*, September 3, 1898.
63. *Ibid.*
64. Details about Andrew Freedman's plan for revenge against the other owners paraphrased from William Lamb, "July 25, 1898: The Ducky Holmes Game," 269.
65. *Sporting Life*, August 6, 1898.
66. *Baltimore Sun*, October 17, 1898
67. *Ibid.*
68. *Ibid.*
69. *Sporting Life*, October 22, 1898.
70. All information about the interview with the players at the Gibson Hotel is paraphrased from the *Cincinnati Enquirer*, August 25, 1898.
71. *Sporting Life*, November 5, 1898.
72. *Ibid.*
73. The Orioles had an impressive .692 winning percentage in 1897 and a winning percentage of .644 in 1898.
74. *Baltimore Sun*, June 16, 1898.
75. *Sporting Life,* June 18, 1898.
76. Story of the misplaced bankroll in *Sporting Life*, December 31, 1898.
77. *Baltimore Sun*, November 29, 1898.
78. *Baltimore Sun*, December 5, 1898.

Chapter 11

1. *Baltimore Sun*, October 20, 1898.
2. *Ibid.*
3. *Baltimore Sun*, December 19, 1898.
4. Burt Solomon, *Where they Ain't: The Fabled Life and Untimely Death of the Original Baltimore Orioles, the Team That Gave Birth to Modern Baseball* (New York: The Free Press, 1999), 149.
5. *Brooklyn Daily Eagle*, March 5, 1899.
6. *Brooklyn Daily Eagle*, cited in Mark Armour and Daniel R. Levitt, *Paths of Glory: How Great Baseball Teams Got That Way* (Washington, DC: Brassey's, 2003), 5.
7. *Baltimore Sun*, October 24, 1898.
8. *Baltimore Sun*, January 9, 1899.
9. Burt Solomon, *Where They Ain't*, ix.
10. *Sporting Life*, January 7, 1899.
11. Burt Solomon, *Where They Ain't*, 152.
12. Lyle Spatz, *Bad Bill Dahlen* (Jefferson, NC: McFarland, 2004), 63.
13. *Baltimore Sun*, January 26, 1899, cited in Lyle Spatz, *Bad Bill Dahlen*, 64.
14. *Chicago Tribune*, January 23, 1899, cited in Lyle Spatz, *Bad Bill Dahlen*, 64.
15. *Baltimore American*, December 20, 1898, cited in Jack Smiles, *"EE-Yah": The Life and Times of Hughie Jennings, Baseball Hall of Famer* (Jefferson, NC: McFarland, 2005), 88.
16. Mark L. Armour and Daniel R. Levitt, *Paths to Glory*, 12.
17. *Brooklyn Eagle*, February 28, 1899.
18. *Brooklyn Daily Eagle*, March 5, 1899.
19. *St. Louis Globe-Democrat*, April 14, 1899.
20. *Baltimore Sun*, April 7, 1899.
21. *Brooklyn Eagle*, April 16, 1899, cited in Lyle Spatz, *Bad Bill Dahlen*, 66.
22. Observations of Hanlon's training camp paraphrased from the *North Adams Transcript*, May 8, 1899.
23. *Brooklyn Daily Eagle*, July 2, 1899.
24. *Ibid.*
25. *Ibid.*
26. *Philadelphia Inquirer*, May 8, 1899.
27. *St. Louis Globe-Democrat*, May 14, 1899.
28. *Brooklyn Daily Eagle*, May 30, 1899.
29. *Total Baseball* rated Jennings as the best player in the league in 1895, 1896, and 1897.
30. *Times-Tribune* (Scranton, PA), July 20, 1899.
31. *Ibid.*
32. *Ibid.*
33. *Baltimore American*, August 4, 1899, cited in Smiles, 91.
34. *Philadelphia Inquirer*, April 18, 1937.
35. *Wilkes-Barre Times Leader* (Wilkes-Barre, PA), April 17, 1905.
36. Details of the death of Minnie McGraw from *Baltimore Sun*, September 4, 1899.
37. Lyle Spatz, *Willie Keeler: From the Playgrounds of Brooklyn to the Hall of Fame* (New York: Rowman and Littlefield, 2015), 129–130.
38. Armour and Levitt, *Paths to Glory*, 11.
39. *Brooklyn Daily Eagle*, July 2, 1899.
40. *Brooklyn Citizen* September 29, 1899.
41. *Sporting Life,* September 2, 1899.
42. Sam Bernstein, "Barney Dreyfuss." SABR BioProect, Accessed February 15, 2023, https://sabr.org/bioproj/person/Barney-Dreyfuss/. Some of the players transferred were Fred Clarke, Honus Wagner, Rube Waddell, and Deacon Phillippe.
43. Harold and Dorothy Seymour, *Baseball: The Early Years* (Oxford: Oxford University Press, 1960), 305.
44. *Baltimore Sun*, January 26, 1900.
45. *Baltimore Sun*, January 27, 1900.
46. Description and quotes relating to excitement caused by the prospect of a new team in Baltimore and Robinson's dance from *Baltimore Sun*, January 26, 1900.
47. *Baltimore Sun*, February 5, 1900.
48. *Baltimore Sun*, February 26, 1900.
49. *Baltimore Sun*, February 17, 1900.
50. *Baltimore Sun*, February 28, 1900.
51. Burt Solomon, *Where They Ain't*, 147.
52. Lyle Spatz, *Willie Keeler*, 131.
53. *Sporting News*, March 24, 1900, cited in Charles Alexander, *John McGraw* (New York: Viking, 1988), 70
54. Charles Alexander, *John McGraw*, 70.

55. *Brooklyn Daily Eagle,* March 4, 1900.
56. Jimmy Keenan, "Doc McJames," SABR Biography Project, Accessed January 12, 2023. https://sabr.org/bioproj/person/Doc-McJames/
57. Bill Lamb, "Jay Hughes," SABR Bio Project, Accessed January 12, 2023. https://sabr.org/bioproj/person/Jay-Hughes/
58. Details from the binoculars cheating incident paraphrased and quoted from the *Philadelphia Inquirer,* September 27, 1900.
59. *Washington Times,* September 12, 1899, cited in Daniel R. Levitt and Mark Armour, *Intentional Balk* (Seattle: Clyde Hill, 2022), 19.
60. Lyle Spatz, *Bad Bill Dahlen,* 84.
61. *Brooklyn Daily Eagle,* May 27, 1900.
62. Lyle Spatz, *Bad Bill Dahlen,* 81.
63. *Sporting Life,* June 30, 1900, cited in Spatz, *Bad Bill Dahlen,* 81.
64. *Sporting Life,* June 30, 1900.
65. Spatz, *Bad Bill Dahlen,* 81.
66. *Sporting Life,* October 13, 1900, cited in Spatz, *Bad Bill Dahlen,* 87.
67. *Brooklyn Citizen,* August 7, 1900.
68. Lyle Spatz, *Bad Bill Dahlen,* 88.
69. *Sporting News,* May 5, 1900.
70. *Pittsburgh Press,* June 20, 1899.
71. *The Brooklyn Daily Eagle,* October 14, 1900.

Chapter 12

1. Joe Santry and Cindy Thomson, "Ban Johnson," SABR Biography Project, Accessed May 20, 2022, https://sabr.org/bioproj/person/Ban-Johnson/.
2. Warren N. Wilbert, *The Arrival of the American League* (Jefferson, NC: McFarland, 2007), 17.
3. Joe Santry and Cindy Thomson, "Ban Johnson."
4. *Sporting Life,* February 16, 1901.
5. *Sporting Life,* January 19, 1901.
6. *Dayton Herald,* June 8, 1901.
7. Jimmy Keenan, "Doc McJames," SABR Biography Project, Accessed January 12, 2023, https://sabr.org/bioproj/person/Doc-McJames/.
8. *Dayton Daily News,* February 11, 1915.
9. *Brooklyn Daily Eagle,* June 7, 1901.
10. *Evening World,* May 24, 1901.
11. *Brooklyn Daily Eagle,* July 5, 1901.
12. Jimmy Keenan, "Doc McJames."
13. *Pittsburgh Press,* June 24, 1901.
14. *St. Louis Globe-Democrat,* September 1, 1901.
15. *Pittsburgh Press,* August 27, 1901.
16. Chad Osburne, "August 21, 1901: Joe McGinnity Gives Two Spits Over Umpire's Call," SABR Game Project, Accessed February 19, 2023, https://sabr.org/gamesproj/game/august-21-1901-joe-mcginnity-gives-two-spits-over-umpires-calls/.
17. *Brooklyn Daily Eagle,* December 1, 1901.
18. *Buffalo Enquirer,* September 27, 1901.
19. *Brooklyn Daily Eagle,* December 12, 1901.
20. *Brooklyn Daily Eagle,* December 12, 1901.
21. *Ibid.*
22. *Brooklyn Daily Eagle,* January 9, 1902.
23. *Sporting Life,* January 4, 1902.
24. Doug Skipper, "Willie Keeler," SABR *BioProject,* https://sabr.org/bioproj/person/Willie-Keeler/.
25. *Brooklyn Daily Eagle,* April 1, 1902, cited in Lyle Spatz, *Willie Keeler: From the Playgrounds of Brooklyn to the Hall of Fame* (New York: Rowman and Littlefield, 2015), 170.
26. *Brooklyn Daily Eagle,* April 6, 1902.
27. *Brooklyn Daily Eagle,* April 21, 1902.
28. *Ibid.*
29. *Baltimore Sun,* April 28, 1902.
30. *Brooklyn Daily Eagle,* May 16, 1902.
31. Lyle Spatz, *Willie Keeler,* 171–72.
32. Lyle Spatz, *Bad Bill Dahlen* (Jefferson, NC: McFarland, 2004), 101.
33. *Brooklyn Daily Eagle,* May 24, 1902.
34. *Brooklyn Citizen,* May 17, 1902.
35. *Brooklyn Times Union,* May 20, 1902.
36. Today, a number of influential baseball historian do not regard the New York Highlanders as a relocation of the Orioles. They believe that the Orioles folded, and then the New York team was formed. The current Yankees do not include the statistics of the 1901–1902 team in their team records.
37. Harold and Dorothy Seymour, *Baseball: The Early Years* (Oxford: Oxford University Press, 1960), 322.
38. *Ibid.,* 323.
39. *Philadelphia Enquirer,* August 26, 1902.
40. *Brooklyn Daily Eagle,* September 16, 1902.
41. Lyle Spatz, *Willie Keeler,* 178.
42. Burt Solomon, *Where they Ain't: The Fabled Life and Untimely Death of the Original Baltimore Orioles, the Team That Gave Birth to Modern Baseball* (New York: The Free Press, 1999), 235.
43. *Sporting Life,* May 9, 1903.
44. *Pittsburgh Press,* July 26, 1903.
45. *Brooklyn Daily Eagle,* June 5, 1903.
46. *Sporting Life,* June 6, 1903.
47. *Pittsburgh Press,* July 8, 1903.
48. *Sporting Life,* August 29, 1903.
49. *Sporting Life,* October 3, 1903.
50. *Buffalo Evening News,* July 26, 1904.
51. *Evening World* (New York), October 12, 1904.
52. *Standard Union* (Brooklyn), October 3, 1904.
53. *Boston Globe,* March 21, 1905.
54. *Ibid.*
55. *Buffalo Enquirer,* March 24, 1905.
56. *Pittsburgh Press,* March 26, 1905.
57. *Sporting Life,* December 17, 1904.
58. *Pittsburgh Press,* February 7, 1905.
59. *Evening World,* March 9, 1905.
60. *Buffalo Enquirer,* July 28, 1905.
61. *Buffalo Enquirer,* June 24, 1905.
62. *Sporting Life,* December 16, 1905.
63. *Pittsburgh Press,* June 13, 1906.
64. *Sporting Life,* December 1, 1906.
65. *Ibid.*

66. *Philadelphia Inquirer*, March 21, 1905.
67. *Sporting Life*, March 21, 1905.
68. *Brooklyn Daily Eagle*, March 21, 1905.
69. *Inter Ocean* (Chicago) October 27, 1905.
70. *Brooklyn Citizen*, December 15, 1905.
71. *Evening Star* (Washington, DC), March 21, 1905.
72. Zack Triscuit, "Ned Hanlon." SABR Biography Project, Accessed February 17, 2023, https://sabr.org/bioproj/person/Ned-Hanlon/

Chapter 13

1. Mike Lackey, *Spitballing: The Baseball Days of Long Bob Ewing* (Wilmington, OH: Orange Frazer Press, 2013), 82.
2. *Ibid.*, 81.
3. Comments about the Cincinnati press by Christy Mathewson and Joe Vila are from Mike Lackey, *Spitballing*, 81. Porkville and Porkopolis were common nicknames for Cincinnati because of its fame as a pork-packing city.
4. Mike Lackey, *Spitballing*, 77.
5. *Ibid.*, 103.
6. *Ibid.*, 77.
7. *Sporting Life*, December 31, 1905.
8. *The Sporting News*, January 6, 1906, cited in Mike Lackey, *Spitballing*, 146.
9. Mike Lackey, *Spitballing*, 147.
10. *The Sporting News*, December 9, 1905, cited in Mike Lackey, 148.
11. *Sporting Life*, December 30, 1905, cited in Mike Lackey, *Spitballing*, 148.
12. *Sporting Life*, January 6, 1906.
13. *Sporting Life*, January 13, 1906.
14. *Washington Post*, June 30, 1907.
15. *Sporting News*, March 31, 1906, cited in Mike Lackey, *Spitballing*, 149.
16. *Chattanooga Daily Times*, March 25, 1906.
17. *Sporting News*, April 14, 1906, cited in Mike Lackey, *Spitballing*, 150.
18. *Pittsburgh Press*, May 3, 1906.
19. *Coshocton Daily Age* [OH] May 5, 1906.
20. *Sporting News*, December, 8, 1906.
21. *Philadelphia Inquirer*, "The Old Sport's Musings," undated article in Lobert file in National Baseball Hall of Fame library.
22. *Buffalo Currier*, March 15, 1908.
23. Mike Lackey, *Spitballing*, 152.
24. *Pittsburgh Press*, May 6, 1906.
25. *Standard Union* (Brooklyn), June 21, 1906.
26. *Sporting Life*, July 14, 1906.
27. *Omaha Daily Bee*, August 12, 1906.
28. Frank Selee (5), Fred Clarke (3), and John McGraw (2) were the others.
29. *Sporting Life*, August 25, 1906.
30. *Sporting Life*, September 15, 1906.
31. *El Paso Herald*, January 5, 1907.
32. *Sporting Life*, September 22, 1906.
33. *Wilkes-Barre News*, October 12, 1906.
34. *Dayton Herald*, April 11, 1907.
35. *Sporting Life*, February 2, 1907.
36. *Sporting News*, March 9, 1907.
37. Mike Lackey, *Spitballing*, 171–172.
38. William A. Cook, *August Garry Hermann: A Baseball Biography* (Jefferson, NC: McFarland, 2008); Mike Lackey, *Spitballing*, 174.
39. Mike Lackey, *Spitballing*, 174.
40. *Ibid.*
41. *Sporting Life*, October 20, 1906.
42. Game description and quoted material from Mike Lackey, *Spitballing*, 177–178.
43. Mike Lackey, *Spitballing*, 179.
44. *Sporting Life*, May 25, 1907.
45. Description of the exhibition games and the discontent of players resulting from them can be found in Mike Lackey, *Spitballing*, 181–182.
46. *Sporting News*, July 18, 1907.
47. *Sporting News*, January 30, 1908; Mike Lackey, *Spitballing*, 184.
48. *Lima Times-Democrat* (Lima, OH), August 10, 1907.
49. *Philadelphia Inquirer*, July 28, 1907.
50. *The Boston Globe*, August 26, 1907.
51. *Sporting Life*, August 24, 1907.
52. *Sporting Life*, October 5, 1907.
53. *Brooklyn Citizen*, July 20, 1907.
54. *Pittsburgh Press*, July 23, 1907.
55. *Sporting Life*, September 21, 1907.

Chapter 14

1. Zack Triscuit, "Ned Hanlon," SABR Bio Project, Accessed January 3, 2022, https://sabr.org/bioproj/person/Ned-Hanlon/
2. *Baltimore Sun*, February 9, 1903.
3. Jack Smiles, *"EE-Yah": The Life and Times of Hughie Jennings, Baseball Hall of Famer* (Jefferson, NC: McFarland, 2005), 105.
4. *Sporting Life*, September 21, 1907.
5. Records of Eastern League Orioles from Stats Crew, statscrew.com, Accessed January 20, 2023.
6. Jack Smiles, *"EE-Yah,"* 109.
7. Jimmy Keenan, "Jack Dunn," SABR Bio Project, Assessed February 3, 2023, https://sabr.org/bioproj/person/jack-dunn/)
8. Hanlon's six-cylinder automobile cost about $2,200, the equivalent of approximately $65,000 in 2023.
9. *Baltimore Sun*, June 18, 1923.
10. *The Gazette* (Montreal, Quebec), April 16, 1904.
11. *Ibid.*
12. *Evening World* (New York), October 12, 1905.
13. Burt Solomon, *Where They Ain't: The Fabled Life and Untimely Death of the Original Baltimore Orioles, the Team That Gave Birth to Modern Baseball* (New York: The Free Press), 1999), 8.
14. *Montpelier Morning Journal News* (Montpelier, VT), January 7, 1913.
15. *Brooklyn Times Union*, July 22, 1926.
16. Details and quotes relating to Hanlon's visit to Jennings in the hospital from *The Tribune* (Scranton, PA), December 6, 1911.
17. *Evening Star* (Washington, DC), December 7, 1911.

18. Details of Hanlon and Ward watching the game from *News and Observer* (Raleigh, NC), April 6, 1913.
19. Daniel R. Levitt, *The Outlaw League and the Battle That Forged Modern Baseball* (Lanham: Taylor Trade Publishing, 2012), 37.
20. Daniel R. Levitt, *The Outlaw League*, 45-46.
21. Ibid., 46.
22. Ibid., 55.
23. Details of Hanlon's meeting with Federal League owners and Dreyfuss quote from Daniel R. Levitt, *The Outlaw League*, 50–51.
24. Details about Hanlon's attempts to hire a manager from Daniel R. Levitt, *The Outlaw League*, 59).
25. Daniel R. Levitt, *The Outlaw League*, 88–89.
26. Ibid., 137.
27. *York Dispatch* (York, PA), January 24, 1914.
28. *Pittsburgh Press*, February 9, 1915.
29. Robert W. Creamer, *Babe: The Legend Comes to Life* (New York: Simon & Schuster, 1974), 77.
30. *Pittsburgh Press*, February 9, 1915.
31. Robert W. Creamer, *Babe Ruth*, 82.
32. *Pittsburgh Press*, March 28, 1915.
33. Daniel R. Levitt, *The Outlaw League*, 137–138.
34. Robert W. Creamer, *Babe Ruth*, 83.
35. *Evening Sun* (Baltimore) September 25, 1916.
36. *Baltimore Sun*, July 2, 1922.
37. Ibid.
38. Ibid.
39. *Evening Sun* (Baltimore), April 17, 1925.
40. *Baltimore Sun*, November 9, 1917.
41. *Brooklyn Daily Eagle*, October 28, 1918.
42. Theo Emery, *Hellfire Boys: The Birth of the U.S. Chemical Warfare Service and the Race for the World's Deadliest Weapons* (New York: Little, Brown, 2017), 289.
43. *Norwich Bulletin* (Norwich, CT), January 14, 1920.
44. *St. Louis Star and Times*, January 5, 1923.
45. *Pittsburgh Daily Post*, December 13, 1924.
46. *The Tablet* (Brooklyn), August 28, 1943.
47. *Baltimore Sun*, February 7, 1925.
48. Hanlon's quotes regarding his trip to see the Yankees and details of that trip paraphrased from *Baltimore Sun*, August 14, 1927.
49. *Baltimore Sun*, September 30, 1924.
50. *Miami Herald* (Miami, Florida), June 14, 1961, cited in Edwin Pope, *Baseball's Greatest Managers* (New York: Doubleday), 1960.
51. *Baltimore Sun*, October 23, 1928.
52. Photo referred to was in *Baltimore Sun*, March 1, 1934.
53. *The Tablet* (Brooklyn), April 24, 1937.
54. Burt Solomon, *Where They Ain't*, 273.
55. *Brooklyn Eagle*, August 12, 1934.
56. *Times Union* (Brooklyn), September 10, 1936.
57. *Evening News* (Wilkes-Barre, PA) May 18, 1934.
58. *Courier-Post* (Camden, NJ), May 18, 1934.
59. Interview with Edwina T. Reeve, granddaughter of Ned Hanlon, March 3, 2023.
60. *Baltimore Sun*, January 14, 1937.
61. *Baltimore Sun*, April 15, 1937.
62. *The Tablet* (Brooklyn) April 24, 1937.
63. *Baltimore Sun*, May 14, 1937.
64. *The Tablet* (Brooklyn), April 24, 1937.
65. Sid Mercer tribute to Hanlon from unidentified clipping in Ned Hanlon file at the National Baseball Hall of Fame library.
66. *Evening Sun* (Baltimore), April 15, 1937.
67. Roger Pippen tribute to Hanlon from unidentified clipping in Ned Hanlon file at the National Baseball Hall of Fame library.
68. *The Tablet* (Brooklyn), August 28, 1943.
69. Burt Solomon, *Where They Ain't*, 269.
70. *Baltimore Sun*, April 18, 1922.
71. David Stinson, "Memorial Stadium," SABR, last accessed January 14, 2023, https://sabr.org/bioproj/park/memorial-stadium-baltimore/#_edn59
72. Ibid.

Epilogue

1. Dom Amore, "He Established Position in the Field," *Hartford Courant*. August 1, 1996.
2. *Baltimore Sun*, February 15, 1995.
3. *Dayton Daily News*, January 11, 1918.
4. Lawrence Ritter, *The Glory of Their Times* (New York: Harper Perennial Modern Classics, 1966), 52–53.
5. Burt Solomon, *Where They Ain't, The Fabled Life and Untimely Death of the Original Baltimore Orioles, the Team That Gave Birth to Modern Baseball* (New York: The Free Press, 1999), 252.
6. Bill Felber, *A Game of Brawl: The Orioles, the Beaneaters & the Battle for the 1897 Pennant* (Lincoln: University of Nebraska Press, 2007), 8–9.
7. *Buffalo Times*, February 13, 1907.
8. *St. Louis Dispatch*, January 14, 1906.
9. Robinson's comments from undated *Baseball Magazine* article in personal files of Ned Hanlon's grandson, Michael Reeve.
10. *Brooklyn Daily Eagle*, February 16, 1902.
11. *Sporting Life*, April 8, 1905.
12. *Baltimore Evening Sun*, March 31, 1954, 58.
13. Blanche McGraw, edited by Arthur Mann, *The Real McGraw* (New York: David McKay, 1953), 42.
14. Ibid., 47.
15. Ibid., 62–63.
16. Ibid., 190.
17. Douglass Wallop *Baseball: An Informal History* (New York: W. W. Norton, 1969.
18. https://www.thedeadballera.com/BadBoneMcGraw.html.
19. *Pittsburgh Press*, July 31, 1905.
20. John J. McGraw, *My Thirty Years in Baseball* (New York: Boni and Liveright, 1923), 57.
21. Ibid., 56.
22. Fred Lieb, *The Baltimore Orioles: The*

History of a Colorful Team in Baltimore and St. Louis (Carbondale: Southern Illinois University Press, 1955), 47.

23. Interview with Edwina T. Reeve, daughter of Hanlon's daughter, Edwina, and Michael Reeve, great-grandson of Hanlon's daughter, Edwina, on March 11, 2023.

24. "Old Sport's Musings," *Philadelphia Inquirer*, undated article in Hanlon Hall of Fame library file.

25. Damon Runyan's account reprinted in the *El Paso Herald*, December 14, 1914.

26. Matt Albertson, "Boileryard Clarke," SABR Bio Project, Accessed March 8, 2023, https://sabr.org/bioproj/person/boileryard-clarke/.

27. https://www.baseball-almanac.com/rulechng.shtml.

28. *Dayton Herald,* June 8, 1901.

29. *Baltimore Sun*, December 3, 1897.

30. *Detroit Free Press,* November 22, 1882.

31. *Buffalo Times,* June 26, 1904.

32. *Wilkes-BarreTimes Leader (*Wilkes-Barre, PA), October, 24, 1925.

33. Steve Wulf. "'Father of Baseball' Ned Hanlon Helped Usher Game—and Managing—Into the Twentieth Century," ESPN, https://www.espn.com/mlb/story/_/id/13190522/father-modern-baseball-ned-hanlon-helped-usher-game-20th-century-greatest-contribution-was-mentor.

Bibliography

Books

Alexander, Charles C. *John McGraw*. New York: Viking, 1988.

_____. *Turbulent Seasons: Baseball in 1890–1891*. Jefferson, NC: McFarland, 2011.

Armour, Mark, and Daniel R. Levitt. *Paths of Glory: How Great Baseball Teams Got That Way*. Washington, DC: Brassey's, 2003.

Bready, James H. *Baseball in Baltimore: The First Hundred Years*. Baltimore: The Johns Hopkins University Press, 1998.

_____. *The Home Team: Our Orioles 25th Anniversary Edition*. Self-published, 1979.

Casway, Jerrold. *Ed Delahanty in the Emerald Age of Baseball*. Notre Dame: University of Notre Dame, 2004.

Christopher, Andre and John Veneziano, eds. *The National Baseball Hall of Fame Almanac, 2020 Edition*. Lynn, Massachusetts: H.O. Zinman, 2022.

Cook, William A. *August Garry Hermann: A Baseball Biography*. Jefferson, NC: McFarland, 2008.

Creamer, Robert W. *Babe: The Legend Comes to Life*. New York: Simon & Shuster, 1974.

_____. *Stengel: His Life and Times*. Lincoln: University of Nebraska Press, 1984.

Deford, Frank. *The Old Ball Game: How John McGraw, Christy Mathewson, and the New York Giants Created Modern Baseball*. New York: Atlantic Monthly Press, 2005.

Di Salvatore, Bryan. *A Clever Baseballist: The Life and Times of John Montgomery Ward*. Baltimore: The Johns Hopkins University Press, 1999.

Emery, Theo. *Hellfire Boys: The Birth of the U.S. Chemical Warfare Service and the Race for The World's Deadliest Weapons*. New York: Little, Brown, 2017.

Felber, Bill. *A Game of Brawl: The Orioles, the Beaneaters & the Battle for the 1897 Pennant*. Lincoln: University of Nebraska Press, 2007.

_____. *Inventing Baseball: The 100 Greatest Games of the Nineteenth Century*. Phoenix: Society for American Baseball Research, 2013.

Fleitz, David L. *The Irish in Baseball: An Early History*. Jefferson, NC: McFarland, 2009.

Flynn, Tom. *Baseball in Baltimore*. Charleston, SC: Arcadia, 2008.

Frommer, Harvey. *Old Time Baseball: America's Pastime in the Gilded Age*. Guilford, CT: Lyons Press, 2017.

Hittner, Arthur. *Honus Wagner: The Life of Baseball's "Flying Dutchman"*. Jefferson, NC: McFarland, 1996.

James, Bill. *The Bill James Guide to Baseball Managers: From 1870 to Today*. New York: Scribner's, 1997.

_____. *The New Bill James Historical Baseball Abstract*. New York: Free Press, 2001.

Kavanagh, Jack, and Norman Macht. *Uncle Robbie*. Phoenix: Society for American Baseball Research, 2000.

Kelly, Jacques. *Bygone Baltimore: A Historical Portrait*. Norfolk, VA: Donning, 1982.

Koppett, Leonard. *The Man in The Dugout: Baseball's Top Managers and How They Got That Way*. New York: Crown, 1993.

Koszarek, Ed. *The Players League: History, Clubs, Ballplayers, and Statistics* (Jefferson, NC: McFarland, 2006.

Lackey, Mike. *Spitballing: The Baseball Days of Long Bob Ewing*. Wilmington, OH: Orange Frazer Press, 2013.

Lamb, William. "July 25, 1898: The Ducky Holmes Game" in *Inventing Baseball: The 100 Greatest Games of the Nineteenth Century*, ed. Bill Felber. Phoenix: Society for American Baseball Research, 2013.

Lamster, Mark. *Spalding's World Tour: The Epic Adventure That Took Baseball Around the Globe—and Made it America's Game*. New York: Public Affairs, 2006.

Lansche, Jerry. *Glory Fades Away: The Nineteenth-Century World Series Rediscovered*. Dallas: Taylor, 1991.

Leerhsen, Charles. *Ty Cobb: A Terrible Beauty*. New York: Simon & Schuster, 2015.

Levitt, Daniel R. *Ed Barrow: The Bulldog Who Built the Yankees' First Dynasty*. Lincoln: University of Nebraska Press, 2008.

_____. *The Outlaw League and the Battle That Forged Modern Baseball*. Lanham: Taylor Trade Publishing, 2012.

Levitt, Daniel R., and Mark Armour. *Intentional Balk: Baseball's Thin Line Between Innovation and Cheating*. Seattle: Clyde Hill, 2022.

Lieb, Fred. *The Baltimore Orioles: The History of a Colorful Team in Baltimore and St. Louis*. Carbondale: Southern Illinois University Press, 1955.

_____. *The Pittsburgh Pirates.* New York: G. P. Putnam's Sons, 1948.

Light, Jonathan Fraser. *The Cultural Encyclopedia of Baseball, Volume I.* Jefferson, NC: McFarland, 2005.

Lowry, Philip J. *Green Cathedrals: The Ultimate Celebration of All Major League and Negro League Ballparks, Fifth Edition.* Phoenix: Society for American Baseball Research, 2019.

Macht, Norman L. *Connie Mack and the Early Years of Baseball.* Lincoln: University of Nebraska Press, 2007.

Mars, Ken. *Baltimore Baseball: First Pitch to First Pennant, 1858–1894.* Parkville, MD: Old Frog Press, 2017.

Martin, Brian. *The Detroit Wolverines: The Rise and Wreck of a National League Champion, 1881–1888.* Jefferson, NC: McFarland, 2018.

McGraw, Blanche, edited by Arthur Mann. *The Real McGraw.* New York: David McKay, 1953.

McGraw, John J. *My Thirty Years in Baseball.* New York: Boni and Liveright, 1923.

Morris, Peter. *A Game of Inches: The Story Behind the Innovations That Shaped Baseball.* Chicago: Ivan R. Dee, 2010.

Nemec, David. *The Beer and Whiskey League: The Illustrated History of the American Association—Baseball's Renegade Major League.* New York: Lyons and Burford, 1994.

_____. *The Great 19th Century Encyclopedia of Major League Baseball.* New York: Donald I. Fine Books, 1997.

Nowlin, Bill, et al., eds. *Baseball in Baltimore.* Phoenix: Society for American Baseball Research, 2021.

Palmer, Pete, and Gary Gillette. *The 2005 ESPN Baseball Encyclopedia.* New York: Sterling, 2005.

Pope, Edwin. *Baseball's Greatest Managers.* New York: Doubleday, 1960.

Reisler, Jim. *Before They Were the Bombers: The New York Yankees Early Years, 1903–1915.* Jefferson, NC: McFarland, 2002.

Rhodes, Greg, et al. *Baseball Revolutionaries: How the 1869 Cincinnati Red Stockings Rocked the Country and Made Baseball Famous.* Batavia, OH: Baseball Revolutionaries Press, 2019.

Ritter, Lawrence. *The Glory of Their Times.* New York: Harper Perennial Modern Classics, 1966.

Rosenberg, Howard W. *Cap Anson 3: Muggsy John McGraw and the Tricksters: Baseball's Fun Age of Rule Bending.* New York: Tile Books, 2005.

Ross, Robert B. *The Great Baseball Revolt: The Rise and Fall of the 1890 Players League.* Lincoln: University of Nebraska Press, 2016.

Seymour, Harold, and Dorothy Z. Seymour. *Baseball: The Early Years.* Oxford: Oxford University Press, 1960.

_____. *Baseball: The Golden Age.* Oxford: Oxford University Press, 1971.

Smiles, Jack. *"EE-Yah": The Life and Times of Hughie Jennings, Baseball Hall of Famer.* Jefferson, NC: McFarland, 2005.

Solomon, Burt. *Where They Ain't: The Fabled Life and Untimely Death of the Original Baltimore Orioles, the Team That Gave Birth to Modern Baseball.* New York: The Free Press, 1999.

Spatz, Lyle. *Bad Bill Dahlen.* Jefferson, NC: McFarland, 2004.

_____. *Willie Keeler: From the Playgrounds of Brooklyn to the Hall of Fame.* Lanham, MD: Rowman and Littlefield, 2015.

Thorn, John. *Baseball in the Garden of Eden: The Secret History of the Early Game.* New York: Simon & Schuster Paperbacks, 2011.

Thorn, John, and Pete Palmer, eds. *Total Baseball.* New York: Warner Books, 1989.

Tiernan, Robert L., and Mark Rucker, eds. *Nineteenth Century Stars.* Phoenix: Society for American Baseball Research, 2012.

Wallop, Douglass. *Baseball: An Informal History.* New York: W. W. Norton, 1969.

Wilbert, Warren N. *The Arrival of the American League.* Jefferson, NC: McFarland, 2007.

Zeiler, Thomas W. *Ambassadors in Pinstripes: The Spalding World Baseball Tour and the Birth of the American Empire.* Lanham, MD: Rowman & Littlefield Publishers, Inc., 2006.

Articles

Aiken, William. "Steve Brodie." SABR Biography Project. Accessed October 17, 2022. https://sabr.org/bioproj/person/Steve-Brodie/.

Albertson, Matt. "Boileryard Clarke." SABR Biography Project, Accessed March 7, 2023. https://sabr.org/bioproj/person/boileryard-clarke/.

Amore, Dom. "He Established Position in the Field." *Hartford Courant.* August 1, 1996.

Bernstein, Sam. "Barney Dreyfuss." SABR Biography Project. Accessed February 15, 2023. https://sabr.org/bioproj/person/Barney-Dreyfuss/.

Gattie, Gordon J. "The Legacy of the Players' League: 1890 Chicago Pirates." SABR. https://sabr.org/journal/article/the-legacy-of-the-players-league-1890-chicago-pirates/. Originally published as "The National Pastime: Baseball in Chicago, 2015.

Keenan, Jimmy. "Bill Hawke." SABR Biography Project. Accessed March 5, 2023. https://sabr.org/bioproj/person/Bill-Hawke/.

_____. "Doc McJames," SABR Biography Project. Accessed January 12, 2023. https://sabr.org/bioproj/person/Doc-McJames/.

_____. "Jack Dunn." SABR Biography Project. Assessed February 3, 2023. https://sabr.org/bioproj/person/jack-dunn/).

_____. "Joe Kelley." SABR Biography Project. Accessed August 20, 2020. https://sabr.org/bioproj/person/Joe-Kelley/.

Klingaman, Mike. "After the ball was over, Orioles scattered widely." Baltimore Sun, July 9, 1996.

_____. "'Foxy' Hanlon was sly but successful." *Baltimore Sun.* July 8, 1996.

_____. "A Team of Stars and Grit." Baltimore Sun, July 7, 1996.

Lamb, Bill. "George Van Haltren." SABR Biography Project. Accessed December 1, 2022. https://sabr.org/bioproj/person/george-van-haltren/.

Nicholls. Rochelle. "Joe Quinn." SABR Biography Project. Assessed February 3, 2023, https://sabr.org/bioproj/person/Joe-Quinn/.

Santry, Joe, and Cindy Thomson. "Ban Johnson." SABR Biography Project. Accessed May 20, 2022. https://sabr.org/bioproj/person/Ban-Johnson/.

Semchuck, Alex. "Wilbert Robinson." SABR Biography Project. Accessed November, 10, 2022, https://sabr.org/bioproj/person/Wilbert-Robinson/.

Skipper, Doug, "Willie Keeler." SABR Biography Project. Accessed November 12, 2022. https://sabr.org/bioproj/person/Willie-Keeler/

Steadman, John. "Shortchanged Hanlon Brought Baseball Riches." *Baltimore Sun*, February 15, 1995.

Stinson, David. "Memorial Stadium." SABR. Last accessed January 14, 2023. https://sabr.org/bioproj/park/memorial-stadium-baltimore/#_edn59.

Thorn, John. "Above the Fruited Plain: A Timeline of Colorado Baseball (Mostly Denver)," *Our Game*, July 10, 2021. https://ourgame.mlblogs.com/above-the-fruited-plain-dee0850f6635.

———. "Mister Muggsy: The Paradoxical John McGraw." *Our Game*, April 19, 2021. https://ourgame.mlblogs.com/mister-muggsy-ad2e44fef958.

Triscuit, Zack. "Ned Hanlon." SABR Biography Project. Accessed January 3, 2022, https://sabr.org/bioproj/person/Ned-Hanlon/.

Wulf, Steve. "'Father of Baseball' Ned Hanlon Helped Usher Game—and Managing—Into the Twentieth Century." ESPN. Accessed March 1, 2023. https://www.espn.com/mlb/story/_/id/13190522/father-modern-baseball-ned-hanlon-helped-usher-game-20th-century-greatest-contribution-was-mentor.

———. "Hanlon Coaching Tree." ESPN, July 2, 2015. Accessed March 1, 2023. https://www.espn.com/mlb/story/_/id/13189997/the-mlb-manager-tree

On the Web

Baseball-Almanac.com
Baseball-Reference.com
Baseballguru.com
Baseballhall.org
LA84.org
Newspapers.com
Retrosheet.org
SABR.org
Seamheads.com
StatsCrew.com
TheDeadballEra.com
ThreadsofOurGame.com

Newspapers

Many newspapers were consulted in researching this book; the following were the most heavily used:
Baltimore Sun
Boston Globe
Brooklyn Citizen
Brooklyn Daily Eagle
Brooklyn Times Union
Cincinnati Enquirer
Detroit Free Press
Evening Sun (Baltimore)
New York Evening Sun
Philadelphia Inquirer
Pittsburgh Dispatch
Pittsburgh Press
St. Louis Globe-Democrat
Sporting Life
The Sporting News
Wilkes-Barre News

Interviews

Edwina T. Reeve. Granddaughter of Ned Hanlon. March 3 and March 11, 2023.
Michael Reeve. Great-grandson of Ned Hanlon. March 3 and March 11, 2023.
Robert Saunders, great-grandson of Ned Hanlon
Burt Solomon. December 9, 2021.

Index

Numbers in ***bold italics*** indicate pages with illustrations

Abell, Gus 119–120, 134, 146, 153, 166
Allen, Lee 65, 66
Alou, Felipe 210
American Association ("Beer and Whiskey League") 12, 13, 23, 25, 26, 27, 32, 33, 35, 38, 86, 89, 119, 154, 162
American Federation of Labor 19, 205
American League 1, 12, 93, 161, 162, 163, 164, 165, 168, 169, 188, 190, 202, 206
American League Park (AL Baltimore Orioles) 184, 189
Amole, Morris "Doc" 130
Anderson, John 152, ***158***
Anson, Adrian "Cap" 2, 4, 20, 40, 66, 73, 88, 123, 146, 170
Atlanta, GA 109
Atlanta Crackers (minor league) 194
Atlantic Association (minor league) 33
Augusta GA 147, 157
Ausmus, Brad 210

Baker, Kirtley 49
Baker, Johnnie "Dusty" 210
Baldwin, Charles "Lady" 11, 12, 15
Baldwin, Mark 28
Baltimore American 114
Baltimore Catholic Review 196
Baltimore Colts 197
Baltimore Herald 118
Baltimore Municipal Stadium, (Venable Park, Babe Ruth Stadium) 197
Baltimore Orioles (AL 1901–1902) 162, 163, 164, 165, 166, 167, 168, 174, 184
Baltimore Orioles (AL, modern) 197, 200
Baltimore Orioles (American Association) 13, 32, 33
Baltimore Orioles (Eastern League/International League) 1, 184, 185, 186, 189, 190, 194, 197, 206
Baltimore Orioles (NL) 1, 34, 37, 38, 39, 40, 41, 45, 46, 47, 48, 51, 52, 55, 56, 58, 59, 65, 66, 67, 68, 69, 70, 71, 72, 73, 74, 76, 77, 78, 79, 81, 82, 83, 84, 85, 86, 87, 88, 89, 93, 94, 95, 96, 97, 98, 100, 101, 102, 104, 106, 107, 108, 109, 110, 111, 112, 113, 114, 115, 116, 117, 120, 121, 122, 123, 124, 125, 126, 127, 131, 132, 136, 137, 138, 139, 140, 141, 142, 143, 144, 146, 147, 148, 149, 150, 151, 152, 153, 155, 156, 168, 170, 178, 180, 181, 182, 183, 187, 188, 193, 194, 197, 198, 199, 200, 201, 202, 204 205
Baltimore Park Board 191, 196, 197, 206
Baltimore Sun 13, 39, 40, 42, 43, 53, 81, 87, 94, 96, 98, 108, 122–23, 129, 131, 133, 135, 137, 143, 146, 156, 191, 193, 194, 196, 198
Baltimore Terrapins (Federal League) 1, 188, 189, 190, 198
Bancroft, Frank 5–6, 63, 176
Barclay Street (Baltimore) ***125***
Barnie, William, "Bald Billy" 32, 33, 34, 38, 40, 53–54
Barrow, Ed 190
Baseball Writers Association of America 2
Battle of the Little Bighorn 205
Beckley, Jake 25, 28–29, 92
Bennett, Charlie 5, 10
Berra, Yogi 210
Bierbauer, Lou 28
Big Four (Baltimore) ***80***, 105, 107, 166, 195
Big Four (Detroit) 9, 10
Bingay, Malcolm 127
Black, Ella 27–28, 31
Black, Harry "Bud" 210
Black Sox *see* Chicago White Sox (AL)
Bly, Nellie 205
Bochy, Bruce 210
Bolton Hill (Baltimore) 119
Bonner, Frank 60, 76, ***83***, 87, 97–98, 113
Boston Beaneaters (NL) 23, 26, 31, 58, 121, 123, 124, 125, 137, 139, 143, 145, 147, 149, 163
Boston Globe 4, 104, 182, 198
Boston Red Stockings 3
Boston Red Sox, Americans (AL) 162, 184, 190, 206
Boston Reds (Players' League) 26, 27
Boundary Field (Washington, DC) 52
Bowerman, Frank 98, 99, ***101***, 110, ***115***, 135
Boyd, J. Cookman 192
Breitenstein, Ted 108
Brenly, Bob 210
Bresnahan, Roger 168
Brice, Fanny 86
Briody, Charles "Fatty" 12
Brodie, Walter, "Steve" ***57***–58, 59, 63, 67, 70, 71, 75, 78, 79, ***83***, 91–92, ***101***, 108, 110, ***115***, 117, 127, 139, 140, 148, 186–187, 191, 194, 196, 197
Broening, William 196
Brooklyn Academy of Music 153
Brooklyn Atlantics 6
Brooklyn Bridegrooms (NL) 38, 56, 82, 111, 120, 121, 125, 129
Brooklyn Bridge 57, 205
Brooklyn Daily Eagle 146, 161
Brooklyn Gladiators (American Association) 33
Brooklyn Superbas (NL, managed by Ned Hanlon) 1, 69, 146, 148, 149, 150, 151, 152, 153, 154, 156, 157, 158, 159, 160, 163, 164, 165, 166, 167, 168, 169, 170, 171, 172, 173, 174, 176, 178, 179, 180, 185, 189, 194, 199, 206
Brotherhood of Professional Baseball Players 1, 4, 13, 19, 24, 27
Brouthers, Dennis "Dan" 1, 9–10, 12, 25, 60, 61, ***62***, 66, 76, 78, 79–80, ***83***, 92, 95, 96, 132, 194, 196
Brown, Bill 54
Brown, Mordecai 177
Browning, Pete 29, 72
Brush, John T. 20, 134, 141, 166
Brush Classification Plan 20–21, 23–24
Brush "Purification" Rule 134, 135, 137, 138, 140, 141
Buffalo Bisons (NL) 4, 6, 9, 10
Buffalo Enquirer 172
Burkett, Jesse 102, 162
Burnham, George 72
Byrne, Charles 86–87, 96, 102, 119–120, 133

231

232 Index

California League (minor league) 157
Calvary Cemetery (Brooklyn) 192
Camden Station (Baltimore) 84, 107, 108, 114, 120
Carey, George "Scoops" 92, 96, *101*, 103, 108
Carnegie, Andrew 19
Carroll, Fred 28
Caruthers, Bob 13
Casey, Jimmy 149, 157, *158*
Cash, Kevin 210
Caylor, O.P. 103
Cedar Rapids Canaries (minor league) 35
Chadwick, Henry 2, 62, 97, 120, 125
Chance, Frank 178
Chapman, Jack 6–7, 9, 41, 92
Chapman, Ray 206
Charleston, SC 50–51
Chicago Cubs (NL) 168 177, 178
Chicago Fire (1871) 205
Chicago Tribune 65, 69
Chicago White Sox (AL) 81, 82, 162, 166 180, 206
Chicago White Stockings (NL) 4, 10, 11, 19, 20, 73, 145, 162
Chronicle-Telegraph Cup 160
Cincinnati Enquirer 143, 181
Cincinnati Red Stockings 3, 6, 205
Cincinnati Reds (NL) 5, 30, 32, 54, 121, 122, 128, 152, 164, 168, 174, 175, 176, 177, 178, 179, 180, 181, 182, 183, 184, 199, 202, 206
Civil War 205
Clarke, Fred 72, 179
Clarke, William "Boileryard" 48–49, 53, 65, 72, 76, 81, *83*, *101*, 109, 113, *115*, 122, 135, *139*, 197, 203, 216n30
Clarkson, Arthur "Dad" 98, 100, *101*
Clarkson, John 82
Cleveland, Grover 15, 205
Cleveland Blues (AL) 162
Cleveland Blues (NL) 4, 6, 162, 205
Cleveland Infants (Players' League) 24, 25
Cleveland Spiders (NL) 73–74, 81, 82, 83, 100, 102, 114, 131, 144, 154, 155, 156
Coakley, Andy 180
Cobb, George 44, 45
Cobb, Ty 17, 72
Collins, Jimmy 162, 186
Comiskey, Charles 2, 25, 65, 73, 123, 162, 167, 180
Compton's Electric Game Impersonator 84, 86
Connelly, Tommy 164–165
Conner, Roger 25
Cooperstown, NY 22
Corbett, Jim 61–62, 139
Corbett, Joe 107, 114, 123, 124, 129–130, 131, 135, 139

Cornell University (New York) 163
Corpus Christi Church (Baltimore) 196, 198
Counsell, Craig 210
Cox, Bobby 1, 210
Cox, George "Boss" 180–181
Craig, Frank ("Harlem Coffee Cooler") 63
Craig, Roger 210
Crane, Sam 3, 17, 213n4
Crawford, Sam "Wahoo" 199
Critchley, Morrie 3
Cross, Lave 157, 163
Cumberland, MD 84
Cuppy, George 114
Custer, Gen. George Armstrong 205

Dahlen, Bill 148, *149*, *158*, 160, 163, 170, 171, 194
Daly, Tom 148, *158*, 159, 166, 167
Dark, Alvin 210
Dauvray, Helen 13
Dauvray Cup 13
Davis, Alfonzo "Lefty" 181
Davis, George 65, 87
Delahanty, Ed 25, 92, 162
Delmonico's (restaurant New York City) 22
DeMontreville, Gene 130, 135, 136, 138, *139*, 148, 151, 163
Derby, George 6
The Derby Winner (play) 108
Detroit Free Press 5, 7, 8, 9, 10, 127
Detroit News 127
Detroit Tigers (AL) 162, 164, 166, 185, 199
Detroit Wolverines (NL) 5–15, 17–18, 132, 200, 205
Dexter, Charlie 154
Diamond Café (Baltimore) 131, 147, 154, 156, 185
Dierker, Larry 210
DiMaggio, Joe 121
Donley, "Turkey" Mike 175
Donnelly, Jimmy 9, 107, 109, 110, 111, *115*, 117
Doubleday, Abner 22
Dowd, Tommy 70
Doyle, John "Dirty Jack" 65, 66, 67, 71, 72, 87, 103, *104*, 106–107, 108, 110, 111, *115*, 116, 119, 121, 122, 126, 127, 129–130, *131*, 154, 170, 197, 200
Drauby, Jake 60
Dreyfuss, Barney 154, 157, 159, 160, 168, 189
Duffy, Hugh 92
Dunlap, Fred 11, 14, 23, 25
Dunn, Jack 148, 157, *158*, *184*, 185, 189–190, 194, 206
Durocher, Leo 1, 210

Eagle Brewery (Baltimore) 33
Eastern League 184
Ebbets, Charles 2, 146, 153, *158*, 166, 169, 171–172, 173, 174, 189

Ebbets Field (Brooklyn) 194
Edison, Thomas 205
Edward VII (Prince of Wales) 21
Esper, Charles "Duke" 82, *83*, 91, 100, 102, *101*, *115*, 116
Eutaw House (Baltimore) 87, 121, 125, 130, 156
Evers, Johnny 71, 177
Ewing, Bob 180, 181
Ewing, William "Buck" 10, 25, 69, 91, 154
Exposition Park (Pittsburgh) 25, 26, 30, 81

Falls River League (minor league) 4
Farrell, Charles "Duke" 78, 149, *158*
Federal Baseball Club of Baltimore v. National League of Professional Baseball Clubs et al. 191
Federal League 1, 188–189, 190, 191, 198, 202, 206
Ferguson, Bob 5
Fifth Avenue Hotel (New York) 63, 103
Fifth Regiment Armory (Baltimore) 84
Fitzgerald, Vincent de Paul 196
Flood, Tim 166
Ford, Charles 86
Ford Motor Company 206
Ford's Opera House (Baltimore) 79, 84, 86, 113–114
Fort Sumpter 205
Foster, John B. 154, 160, 171, 173, 182, 200
Foutz, Dave 13, 119
Francona, Terry 210
Freedman, Andrew 98, 103, 106, 140–142, 142, 157
Fullerton, Hugh 69
Fulton, Major A.K. 110

Galvin, James "Pud" 23, 25, 28, 57
Gantzel, John 180, 181
Ganzhorn's Steakhouse (Baltimore) 107, 114
Garfield, James 205
Gaston, Cito 210
Gatins, Frank 163
Gehrig, Lou 193
Getzien, Charles "Pretzels" 10–12, 214–215n42
Gibson House (Cincinnati) 143
Gilded Age 19
Gillette, William 51
Gleason, William "Kid" 81–*82*, *83*, 94, 97, 98, *101*, 103, 192, 193, 194, 196, 203
The Glory of Their Times 199
Goldman, Harry 188
Grafton, WV 84
Griffith, Clark 2, 186, 192, 196
Grimm, Charlie 210
Guilded Age 19
Gunfight at OK Corral 205

Index

Halligan, William "Jocko" 42
Hamilton, Billy 92
Hanlon, Edward Hugh Hanlon "Ned" ("Foxy Ned"; "Silent Ned"): Baltimore Park Board 191, 197; betrayed by Von der Horst 193; business outside baseball 11, 119, 145; coaching skill 52, 76, 97, 104, 105, 108, 140, 157, 177, 191, 197, 199; coaching tree 1, 203, 210; conflict with Ebbets 173; death 1, 196; defense of rowdy tactics 74, 96–97, 98, 131, 133, 137, 138; development of Scientific (Inside) Baseball 64–68; disparaged by Sam Crawford 199; Ducky Holmes game controversy 140–142; Eastern League Orioles 1, 184, 185, 186; election to Hall of Fame 202, 204; Federal League 1, 186, 188–189, 190, 191; first meeting with Orioles players 39; forgotten by baseball 2, 198; "Foxy Ned" reputation 46, 53–54, 57, 60, 81–82, 98, 103, 107, 111–112, 120, 123, 130–131, 132, 138, 151, 185; friendship with John Montgomery Ward 24, 77, 188; Hanlon's baserunning skill 10, 17, 66, 188; Hanlon's humor 22, 91, 94, 118–119, 132, 136, 152, 163–64, 171, 172–173, 186, 187, 188; hired to manage Orioles 39; holdout with Detroit 13–14; Jennings car accident 187–188; leadership ability 6, 8, 10, 11, 14, 15, 17–18, 41–42, 43, 44, 45, 49, 50, 51, 54, 55–56, 59, 60, 67, 68, 69, 74, 75, 77, 80–81, 95, 96–97, 101, 103, 105, 111–112, 122–123, 127–128, 129, 135, 144, 150, 152, 154, 161, 199, 203; life before baseball 3–4; love for Baltimore 117, 169, 197; manager of Cincinnati Reds (NL) 176–182; player/manager of Pittsburgh Alleghenys/Pirates (NL) 23, 28–31; player/manager of Pittsburgh Burghers (PL) 26; player with Cleveland Blues (NL) 4–5; player with Detroit Wolverines (NL) 5–17; relationship with McGraw 40–41, 63, 67, 76, 88, 94, 96, 112, 127–128, 153, 156, 186, 194–195, 200–202; reputation as defensive player 4, 5, 10, 14, 17, 20, 21–22, 57–58, 201; respect for his players 68, 101, 105, 111–112, 114, 127–128, 135, 137, 153; role in Players' League 1, 4, 13, 23–28, 162–163; rules committee 2, 63, 120, 133–134, 203, 211–212; "Silent Ned" 59, 76; Spalding World Tour 1, 20–22, 51, 205; statistics as player and manager 10, 17, 208–209; stock dispute with Von der Horst 89–90; tactics employed 1, 12, 40, 51, 56, 64–69, 72, 74, 76, 97, 100, 104, 108, 120, 132, 137, 143–144, 170, 179, 180, 181, 196, 200, 204; Wilbert Robinson baptism 192; World's Series with St. Louis Browns 12–13
Hanlon, Edward Kelley (son) 60, 136, *185*, 205
Hanlon, Ellen Jane (*nee* Kelley; wife) 1, 21, 60, 100, 145, *185*, 193, 194, 205
Hanlon, Helen Celeste (daughter) 145, *185*, 205
Hanlon, Joseph Thomas (son) 1, *185*, 191–192, 205, 206
Hanlon, Lillian (daughter) *185*
Hanlon, Mary Edwina (daughter) 100, 110, *185*, 195, 202, 205
Hanlon Field (France) 192
Hanlon Park (Baltimore) 192
Hanlon's Superbas (acrobatic troupe) 150
Harris Academy of Music 86, 102
Harrison, Benjamin 22
Hart, Jim 125, 133, 134
Hawke, Bill 53, 55, 56, 58, 63, 79, *83*, 91, 92, 97
Haymarket Riot 19, 205
Hellfire Battalion (First Battalion of Gas and Flame) 192
Hemming, George 82, *83*, 95, 100, *101*, 102, *115*, 116, 120
Herrmann, Gary 169, 174, 175, 176, 177, *178*, 179, 180, 181, 182, 183, 189, 202
Herzog, Charles "Buck" 190
Herzog, Whitey 210
Heydler, John 2, 73
Hoffer, Bill 92, *93*, 100, *101*, 102–103, 114, *115*, 116, 121, 123, 124, 197, *204*
Hollenden Hotel (Cleveland) 114
Holliday Theatre (Baltimore) 108
Holmes, John "Ducky" 138, 140–142, 143, 148
Holway, John 69
Homestead Strike 19
Hopper, Harry *101*
Horton, Elmer 120
Houck, Alfred T. 32
Houk, Ralph 210
Howe, Irwin 17, 20
Howell, Harry 148, 170,-171
Huggins, Miller 1, 180, 181, 183, 193, 194, 203, 210
Hughes, Jay 130, 136, 138, *139*, 140, 148, 157, *158*, 163, 164
Hurst, Tim 157, 159, 160, 170
Huston, Tillinghast 202

Indianapolis Hoosiers (NL) 12, 15, 20
Indianapolis Hoosiers (Western Association) 9
Inks, Bert 75, 78–79, 81, 82

International Association (minor league) 4
Irwin, Charlie 164

Jackson, Harold 196
James, Bill 12, 73
Jennings, Hugh 53–54, 55, 58, 60, 66, 68, *70*, 71, 72, 75, 76, 79, *80*, *83*, 84, *holdout* 91–92, 93, 100, *101*, 103, 107, 110, 111, 112, *115*, 116, 118, 122, 127, 130, 135, 137, *139*, 140, 143–144, 145, 146, 147, 148, 149, 150, *151*, 152, 153, 154, *158*, 163, 166, 179, 183, 184–185, 187–188, 192, 193, 194, 196, 199, 202, 203
Johns Hopkins University (Baltimore) 51, 108
Johnson, Al 23–24, 25, 27
Johnson, Byron Bancroft "Ban" 161, 162, 163, 165, 168, 169
Johnson, Davy 210
Johnstown Flood 205
Jones, Fielder 148, 157, *158*, 159, 163, 203
Joyce, Bill 140

Kalakua, King of Hawaii 20
Kane, John 181
Kapler, Gabe 210
Keeler, William "Wee Willie" 60, 61, *64*, 65, 68, *70*, 71, 75, 76, 78, 79, *80*, *83*, 87, 91–92, 94, *101*, 103, 106, 109, 110, *115*, 116, 121, 127, 135, 137, *139*, 140, 143–144, 146, 147, 148, 153, 154, 157, *158*, 159, 163, 164, 166, 168, *169*, 170, 183, 186, 192, 194, 196, 200, 202
Keister, Billy 156
Kelley, Joe 1, *45*–46, 52–53, 55, 59, 63, 67, *70*, 72, 75, 76, 78, *80*, 82, *83*, 87, 88, 89, 91–92, 94, 96, *101*, 105, 106, 107, 108, 109, 110, 112, *115*, 116, 125, 127, 128, 129, 135, 137, *139*, 140, 143–144, 146, 147, 148, 152, 153, 154, 157, *158*, 159, 160, 163, 164, 166, 168, 175–176, 183, 187, 192, 194, 195, 197, 199, 200
Kelley, Mike "King" 25, 38
Kennedy, William "Brickyard" 148, 149, 157, *158*, 159, 163
Kerr, William W. 25, 27, 66, 117
Kissinger, Bill 92, 95, 97–98
Kitson, Frank *139*, 148, 163, 164
Klobedanz, Fred 126
Knabe, Otto 190
Koszarek, Ed 26–27

LaChance, George "Candy" 148
Lajoie, Napolean 162, 167
Lamster, Mark 22
LaRussa, Tony 1, 210
Latham, Artie 72–73
Latrobe, Ferdinand 85
Laurel Race Track (Maryland) 193–194
Leadley, Robert 17

Index

Lewis, Allen 198
Lewis, Phil 172
Lewis, Ted 126
Leyland, Jim 210
Lieb, Fred 2, 17, 40, 70, 202
Lili'uokalani (Queen of Hawaii) 63
Lincoln, Abraham 205
Lindbergh, Charles 206
Lobert, John "Hans" 177, 180, 183, 202
Long, Danny 48, 216ch4n1
Long, Jim 49
Louisville Colonels (NL) 6, 33, 53, 72, 82, 123, 150, 151, 154, 155, 156, 188
Lundgren, Carl 177
Lynch, Tom 122, 140, 142

Mack, Corneilus "Connie" 1, 2, 28, 90, 92, 163, 167, 185, 186, 190, 196 197, 198, 203, 204, 210
Macon, GA 63, 93, 94, 95, 108–109, 120, 135
Maddon, Joe 210
Magoon, George 148, 151
USS *Maine* 205
Martin, Billy 1, 210
Maryland Country Club (Baltimore) 193
Mathews, Eddie 210
Mathewson, Christy 175, 186
Mattingly, Don 210
Mauch, Gene 210
Maul, Al 25, 28, 140, 148
Mays, Carl 206
McCallum, William 25
McCarthy, Joe 198
McCreery, Tom 166
McFarlan, Dan 148
McGann, Dan 130, 135, 138, *139*, 144, 148, 168
McGinnity, Joe, "Iron Joe" 148, 149, 159, 160, 163, 164, 165, 168
McGraw, Blanche nee Sindall 76, 201
McGraw, John 1, 34–*37*, 40–41, 48, 49, 50, 53, 55, 58, 59, 60, 63; 67, 68, 69, *70*, 71–72, 73, 74, 75, 76, 78, 79, *80*, *83*, 87–88, 91–92, 93, 94, 96, 97, 98, *101*, 106, 107, 109, 111, 112, 113, 114, *115*, 117, 119, 121, 122, 126, 127, 128, 130, 131, *139*, 143–144, 146, *147*, 148, 149, 150, 151, 152, 153, 155–156, 157, 162, 165, 166, 167, 176, 179, 183, 186, 187, 192, 194, 195, 196, 198, 199, 200–202, 203, 210, 217n
McGraw, Minnie (*nee* Doyle) 119, 152–153
McGuire, James "Deacon" 9, *158*, 163, 166
McGunnigle, William 30–31
McJames, James "Doc" 130, 137, 138, 140, 144, 148, 150, 157, *158*, 163, 164
McKechnie, Bill 210
McKenna, Kristian "Kit" 148

McKinley, William 206
McKnight, Denny 32
McLean, Larry 180
McMahon, John T. "Sadie" 33–*35*, 43–44, 45, 48, 50–51, 52, 54, 55, 56, 59, 63, 72, 75, 78, 79, 81, 82, *83*, 92, 95, 98–100, *101*, 102, 107, 111, *115*, 116, 120, 131
McNabb, Edward 49
Medicus, Henry 174
Melvin, Bob 210
Memorial Stadium *see* Municipal Stadium
Mercer, Sid 196
Miller, Ralph 148
Milligan John "Jocko" 54
Mills, Abraham 22
Mills Commission 22
Milwaukee Brewers (AL) 92, 162
Minahan, Edmund "Cotton" 182
Mobile (AL) 40
Moneyball 12
Montreal Royals (Eastern League) 184, 206
Montville, CT 1–3
Montville Historical Society 2
Morning Herald (Baltimore) 92
Morse, Jake 76
Morton, Charlie 9
Mott, Albert 80, 88
Mulford, Ren 27–28, 176, 179, 180
Mullane, Tony 54, 56, 76, 78, 81–82, 216n
Murnane, Tim 4, 72, 76, 91, 116, 202, 203
Murphy, Morgan 159
Murphy, Tom 69, *70*, 71, 77, 91, 98, 111, 116, 124, 137
Myers, Henry 32

Naismith, James 205
National Agreement 169
National Association (minor league) 4
National Association for the Advancement of Colored People (NAACP) 206
National Association of Professional Baseball Players 3, 205
National Baseball Hall of Fame 2, 52, 66, 126, 198, 202, 204
National Commission 169
National Football League 27, 197
National League 1, 3, 4, 12, 20, 23, 26, 27, 28, 32, 33, 41, 83, 86, 96, 103, 119, 132, 134, 140–141, 142, 161, 162, 165, 166, 169, 188, 190, 202, 205
Navin, Frank 185
New Cathedral Cemetery (Bonnie Brae Cemetery) 153, 194, 196
New England League (minor league) 4
New Orleans LA 95
New York Giants (NL) 7, 13, 15, 17, 19, 37, 58, 77–79, 86–87, 100,
121, 140, 142, 157, 165, 168, 171, 176, 177, 186, 189
New York Highlanders (AL) *see* New York Yankees
New York Mutuals (NL) 32
New York Yankees (AL) 168, 169, 193, 202, 223n36
Newton, Eustace "Doc" 164
Nichols, Charles "Kid" 2, 124, 126, 131, 139, 149, 220ch9n42
Nimick, William 23, 25
Ninety Days (play) 51
Nolan, James F., (Pastor Corpus Christi Church, Baltimore) 196
Nops, Jerry 113, 121, 123, 129, 136, 138, *139*, 140, 148, 151

Oates, Johnny 210
Ocean City MD 195
Oklahoma Land Rush 205
O'Neil, J. Palmer 28–31
O'Neill, James "Tip" 13
Oriole Park (American Association Orioles) 13
O'Rourke, Tim 49, 53–54
Overall, Orval 177
Oxford House Hotel (Baltimore) 79

Palace of the Fans (Cincinnati) 175, 181
Palmer, Harry 21
Panic of 1893 205
Pearce, Dickey 65
Peary, Robert 206
Petersburg, VA 110–111
Philadelphia Athletics (AA) 28, 34
Philadelphia Athletics (AL) 162, 167, 186
Philadelphia Athletics (NL) 32
Philadelphia Phillies, Quakers (NL) 7, 11, 12, 40, 73, 81, 95, 132, 139, 157, 159, 163, 164, 165181, 189
Phillips, Horace B. 22–23
Pimlico Race Track (Baltimore) 193
Piniella, Lou 210
Pinkertons 19
Pippin, Roger 196
Pittsburgh Alleghenys, Pirates (NL) 14, 15, 22, 23, 26, 27, 28, 29, 30, 31, 38, 39, 43–44, 81, 90, 95, 122, 132, 154, 157, 159, 160, 164, 165, 167–168, 170, 171, 172, 181, 198, 205
Pittsburgh Burghers (Players' League) 25–26, 200, 205
Pittsburgh Chronicle-Telegraph 60
Pittsburgh Chronicle-Telegraph Cup 160
Pittsburgh Daily Post 29, 30
Pittsburgh Dispatch 28, 30, 31
Pittsburgh Leader 142
Pittsburgh Press 26, 172, 183
Players' League 4, 21, 23–27, 28, 33, 162–163, 205
Polo Grounds (New York) 69, 140

Index

Pond, Arlie "Doc" **101**, 107, 108, **115**, 116, 121, 122, 123, 138, 140
Ponemah Mills (Connecticut) 3
Presque Isle Peninsula (New York) 28
Preston, James 191, 196
Price, Jim 17
Prince Albert 21
Prince, William 34
Princeton University 203
Providence Clam Diggers (Eastern League) 185
Providence Grays (NL) 6, 7, 24
Pulliam, Henry 118, 151

Quarles, June 110
Queen City Hotel (Cumberland, Maryland) 84
Quinn, Joe 70, **113**, **115**, 120, 136, 138, 146, 150, 199–200,

Radbourn, Charles "Old Hoss" 25
Raymond, Arthur "Bugs" 58
Recreation Park (Detroit) 5
Reidy, Bill 199
Reitz, Henry "Heinie" **48**–49, 53, 55, 68, 71, 76, **83**, 88, 98, **101**, **115**, 116, 130, 201
Rennert Hotel (Baltimore) 85, 119, 218n
reserve clause 4, 19
Reulbach, Ed 177
Rhines, Billy 121
Rice, Jim (sportswriter) 70, 71
Richards, Paul 210
Richardson, Hardy 9
Richmond, Lee 4
Richmond, VA 7
Rigney, Bill 210
Ritter, Lawrence 199
Roberts, Dave 210
Robinson, Frank 210
Robinson, Wilbert 33–34, **36**, 41, 48, 51, 53, 56, 58–59, 63, 66, 67, 68, 72, 73, 75, 81, 82, **83**, 85, 87, 88, 89, 91, 94, 96, 97, 98, **99**, **101**, 105, 107, 109, 112–113, **115**, 121, 122, 130, 131, 134, **139**, 140, **147**, 150, 153, 154, 155–156, 157, 161, 174, 184, 185, 186, 187, 189, 192, 193, 194, 196, 197, 199–200, 201, 203
Robison, Frank 114, 154, 156
Rochester, NY 4, 23
Rodgers, Buck 210
Rogers, John 73
Roosevelt, Franklin Delano 206
Roosevelt, Theodore 22, 206
Rose, Pete 121
Rose Bowl 206
Rowe, Jack 9
rules 2, 4, 6, 63–64, 134, 211–212
Runyon, Damon 203–204
Rusie, Amos 2, 63, 78, 87, 122, 139, 188
Ruth, George Herman "Babe" 58, 98, 184, 190, 193, 206
Ryan, Jimmy 40

Sacramento Brewers 157
St. Bonaventure University 63, 92
St. Louis Browns (AL) 197, 200
St. Louis Browns (American Association) 73
St. Louis Browns (NL, aka Perfectos) 12, 33, 57, 70, 73, 81, 98, 120, 154, 197
St. Louis Maroons (Union Association) 11
St. Phillips and James Church (Baltimore) 152
St. Valentine Day Massacre 206
San Francisco Earthquake 206
Sauerwalds Band (Baltimore) 78
Schlei, Admiral 180
Schmelz, Gus 113
Schmit, Frederick "Crazy" 49, 52–53
Schoendienst, Red 210
Scientific Baseball (aka *Inside Baseball*) 64–69
Selee, Frank 120, 125, 149, 150, 179, 198
Seymour, Cy 168, 175, 177
Sheckard, Jimmy 148, 163–164, 167, 170, 172
Sheridan, Jack 121–122
Sheridan, John B. 65
Sherman Anti-Trust Act 191, 205
Shettsline, Bill 159
Shindle, Billy 48, 50, 59, 60
Showalter, Buck 1, 210
Sinton Hotel (Cincinnati) 180
Soden, Arthur 62
Solomon, Burt 197, 220ch9n47
South End Grounds (Boston) 26, 125
Southworth, Billy 210
Spaulding, Albert Goodwill 2, 3, 20–21; *Mills Commission* 22, 201
Spalding Official Baseball Guide 12, 200
Spalding World Tour 1, 20–22, 25, 51, 205
Speaker, Tris 17
Sporting Life 7, 10, 11, 14, 25, 27, 28, 38, 49, 51, 59, 73, 80, 88, 89, 91, 95, 96, 98, 123, 130, 142, 143, 154, 160, 171, 173, 176, 181, 186, 189
Sporting News 2, 73, 113
Sportsman Park (St. Louis) 13
Springfield, MA 3
Standard Union (Brooklyn) 171
Stankey, Eddie 210
Star Spangled Banner 121, 206
Steadman, John 128, 198
Stearns, Frederick Kimball 9, 13–14
Steinbrenner, George 31
Stengel, Casey 1, 194, 198, 210
Stennett, Rennie 11
Stenzel, Jake 117, **124**, 126–127, 138
Stovey, Harry 44, 49, 52, 53, 56
Stricker, Cub 42
Sullivan, Ted 17

Sunday, Billy 23
Supreme Court of Pennsylvania 167
Swampdoodle Grounds (Washington, DC) 13
Syndication 132, 146, 154, 155

Taft, William Howard 206
Taftville, CT 1, 3, 194, 202
Talcott, Edward 63
Tammany Hall 141
Taylor, Harry 53–54, 60
Tebeau, Oliver "Patsy" 88, 114, 122, 144
Temple, William Chase 86, 114, 126
Temple Cup Series 83, 86–88, 101–103, 106, 110, 114–116, 125–126
Tenney, Fred 71
Terrapin Park (Baltimore) 190, 197
Terry, Bill 201
Thompson, Sam 9–10, 15, 17, 132
Thompson, William 9
Thorn, John 69
Tiemeyer, Ernie 181
Titanic 206
Toldeo Blue Stockings (American Association) 9
Tom Sawyer 205
Torre, Joe 210
Treadway, George 49, 60
Truxton, NY 34
Twain, Mark 22

Union Association 11, 162
Union Memorial Hospital (Baltimore) 195
Union Park (Baltimore) 40, 41, 43, 51, 52, 69, 76, **77**, 78, 79, 81, 82, 91, 95, 99, 111, 114, 123, **125**, 135, 137, 155–156, 197, 221n
University of Maryland College of Physicians and Surgeons, 108

Vance, Dazzy 194
Van Haltren, George 38, 39, 40, 42–43, 44, 45–46, 100
Vickery, Tom 44, 45
Vila, Joe 76, 79, 175, 176
Von der Ahe, Chris 53, 57, 62, 98, 118, 154
Von der Horst, Harry 33, 37, 38, 39, 41, 43, 46, 47, 49, 60, 78, 84, 85, 86, 89, 90, 91, 94–95, 101, 103, 107, 112, 113–114, 116, 117, 119, 125, 142, 145, 146, 148, 153, 156, 166, 173, **174**, 178
Von der Horst, John 33
Von der Horst and Son Brewery 33

Waddell, George "Rube" 58, 157, 159, 160
Wadsworth, Jack 49, 52
Wagner, Earl 130

Index

Wagner, Johannes "Honus" 2, 71–72, 150, 152, 186
Wall Street Crash 206
Waltz, John 38, 39
Ward, Frank "Piggy" 54
Ward, John Montgomery 2, 13, 17–18, 19, 21, 22, 23, 24, 25, 26, 27, 28, 63, 66, 69, 77, 78, 79, 86, 87, 123, 125, 167, 188, 193
Ward, Robert 189
Washington Senators (AL) 162, 193
Washington Senators (NL) 15, 33, 52, 82, 100, 125, 137, 138, 155, 156
Watkins, Bill 9–12, 14–15, 17, 56–57
Weaver, Earl 1, 210
Weidman, George "Stump" 12
Weimar, Jake 180
Welch, Curt 42
West Side Park (Chicago) 20
Western Association (minor league) 9
Western League (minor league) 92, 162
Wheat, Zach 194
White, James "Deacon" 9
Wicker, Bob 177
Williams, Dick 210
Wizard of Oz (book) 171
Wood, George 10
Worcester Ruby Legs (NL) 4, 5, 6
World Series (1887) 12–13
World War I 206
Wright, George 3
Wright, Harry 2–3, 203
Wright, Orville 206
Wright, Wilbur 206
Wulf, Steve 2

Yeager, Joe *158*
Young, Denton "Cy" 2, 63, 83, 102, 114, 162
Young, Nick 9, 79, 87, 88, 96, 97, 102, 121–122, 130, 134–135, 138, 140, 142, 153, 157, 159
Yukon Gold Rush 205